THE GULF COOPERATION COUNCIL STATES

The Gulf Cooperation Council States

Hereditary Succession, Oil and Foreign Powers

Dr Yousef Khalifa Al-Yousef

SAQI

Published 2017 by Saqi Books

Copyright © Yousef Khalifa Al-Yousef 2017

Published by arrangement with the Centre for Arab Unity Studies, Lebanon

Yousef Khalifa Al-Yousef has asserted his right under the Copyright, Designs and Patents Act, 1988, to be identified as the author of this work.

ISBN: 978-0-86356-147-4
eISBN: 978-0-86356-152-8

A full CIP record for this book is available from the British Library.

Printed in Lebanon

Saqi Books
26 Westbourne Grove
London W2 5RH
www.saqibooks.com

To Gaza, symbol of dignity and honour,
bastion of steadfastness and resistance,
I dedicate this humble endeavour,
with my fervent prayers for courage and victory.

Contents

Executive Summary

This book is an attempt to understand the reasons behind the failure of the Gulf Cooperation Council (GCC) states to achieve development and security over more than four decades. This failure may be summarised by the fact that the region is currently in the grip of a vicious triangle formed by the hereditary political systems that own large oil-based fortunes, are free of any public account-ability and depend on foreign powers for their protection. Therefore, to break this vicious triangle, these countries should begin by adjusting their course and replacing all three sides of this triangle. They should replace the current hereditary succession systems with free, participatory and accountable systems, abandon their over-reliance on oil by training and preparing productive human beings and replace their reliance on foreign powers with efforts towards regional inte-gration and reconciliation within the wider Islamic and Arab milieu. The book utilises the descriptive-analytical method and comprises five parts, distributed between nineteen chapters.

Part I: The Harvest of Autocracy

This part comprises four chapters that reveal the nature of the GCC's heredi-tary succession systems and the ensuing marginalisation of certain civil society elements on whose growth and interaction the region's social renaissance and stability depend. The chapters cover the following subjects:

Chapter One shows how the GCC's political systems that concentrate power and wealth into the hands of a single family are based on heredity rather than hard work and competence. This means that these countries do not maintain a single citizenship formula that guarantees equality among all social classes, but a hierarchy of classes according to which descendants of ruling families are first-class citizens, and the rest second-class citizens. This two-tier citizenship, or "deficient citizenship", is encoded in the articles of these countries' constitutions, which openly state that governance is the exclusive domain of specific families, and grant them financial privileges that other social classes do not have access to (although, as we shall see later, the Kuwaiti constitution did impose certain restrictions on its ruling family's prerogatives). The book shows how this type of political system has nothing whatsoever to do with the Islamic principle of consultation (*shura*) which has its own control mechanisms. Nor could one call it a tribal system since it lacks the equilibrium, advocacy and equity typical of tribal systems. Furthermore, hereditary succession was never a popular choice in the region. People have expressed their opposition to it in numerous ways, including writing, demonstrations and, sometimes, more violent means such as coup attempts. This shows that, in order for peaceful change to take place, these countries have to abolish their hereditary systems and replace them in the next few years with agreed-upon alternatives.

Chapter Two addresses a different component of this renaissance, one that has long been the object of ignorance by some and distortion by others, namely the cultural component. In the Arab region, regardless of where they came from, all renaissance leaders have highlighted the importance of culture given its inherent values, history and tenets, and its role in bringing prosperity and stability to the world's nations. The chapter tries, therefore, to treat Arab-Islamic culture as the basic delineator of the GCC states' renaissance by making a clear distinction between the pure origins of Arab-Islamic culture, the prime mover behind this culture's establishment, expansion and dominance, and the cultural accumulations that have distorted it over years of autocratic rule such that people have begun to confuse the two. The chapter clarifies the important role of culture in bringing about progress and stability to different nations and then looks at the condition of Arab and Muslim culture today, a phenomenon we could call "the culture of autocracy". We then cite the opinions of several contemporary intellectuals to explain the role of authentic Arab-Islamic culture in today's world and clarify one of its major components, namely the principle of stability and flexibility that allows it to renew itself and keep up with human development through time and space, without stagnation or rigidity.

Chapter Three looks at elites in the Gulf and tries to pinpoint the conditions that led to the weakness throughout civil society in the region, making these countries' political systems seem more like one-party systems than modern states. Had they been the latter, the GCC governments would have been a reflection of their societies and left ample space for the commercial, professional, cultural and other elites to play their rightful role, avail themselves of the country's resources, express their fears and aspirations, interact with other groups in society and contribute to building a vital, free and creative society. To this end, we begin by taking a quick look at the relationship between rulers and social elites in the Gulf, prior to the discovery of oil, a relationship characterised by a certain equilibrium since the rulers' revenue came mostly from pearls, dates, trade and other activities in which the locals were engaged. We then monitor the changes in this relationship as the rulers' revenues from oil increased and the way they used this newfound wealth to marginalise other social groups through methods differing from one Gulf country to another. We end the chapter by addressing some of these elites' weaknesses as well.

In Chapter Four, we analyse different state institutions since they are the main elements of renaissance in any society. We start by describing their respective responsibilities which include the mobilisation of individual efforts, the provision of necessary information to ensure wise decision-making, and the execution of contracts between individuals. In the context of introducing these duties, we try to shed light on four major groups of institutions in the GCC, namely the executive, legislative, media and legal institutions, to gauge their performance. This survey makes it clear that appointments and promotions in the GCC's executive branch do not depend on competency and experience as much as they do on loyalty and patronage. They also show that the legislative branch has hardly any prerogatives, that the media are tools of propaganda and material gain and that the GCC's legal institutions are mere extensions of the executive authority; in other words, they are not independent except in rare cases where governance is not an issue.

Part II: Oil Policies

Given the strategic importance of oil to the economies of the GCC states as well as the wider Arab world, it is necessary to look at the way these countries have so far managed their relationships with the international oil companies and, by extension, the governments of consumer countries, before examining the way oil revenues have been spent on development. The aim is to gauge the independence of oil-related decisions with regard to pricing, production and the integration of different stages of this vital industry in the national economy.

Chapter Five sheds light on the imbalance of power in the oil sector, since the discovery of oil in the early 1930s, between industry-savvy companies that possess knowledge, skills and technology and enjoy the backing of strong colonial powers, and oil-producing governments that lack accountability, institutional competence and openness towards society. We look at how this imbalance has empowered the oil companies and their governments and kept vital industries under their control, thanks to contracts skewed against the oil-producing countries. These companies rejected all efforts to indigenise this industry which actually has meant prolonging the producing countries' dependence on them for the management of different stages of this vital industry, a situation that is still ongoing today. This is taking place despite the efforts of some national leaders who appeared on the oil scene during that period, like Abdullah al-Tariki of Saudi Arabia and Juan Alfonso of Venezuela, who tried to rectify the imbalance between the companies and oil-producing countries.

In Chapter Six, we try to show how oil pricing and production policies were always at the receiving end of this unequal relationship between the oil-producing countries and international oil companies. This means that these policies have served the interests of the oil-consuming countries and international oil companies better than those of the oil-producing countries and their Arab milieu. In our opinion, this is undoubtedly due to the autocratic nature of governance in the oil-producing countries which made them more susceptible to foreign pressure and less able to forge a unified position within the Organization of the Petroleum Exporting Countries (OPEC). This will become clear when we look at oil price fluctuations and the quantities produced between the 1970s and beginning of the twenty-first century.

Part III: Development Policies

After addressing in Part II the factors that helped determine the amount of oil revenues that the oil-producing countries have managed to secure, in Part III we evaluate the way these countries have spent their oil revenues. We will assess their successes and failures in achieving their development objectives in terms of diversification of economic structures, human resource development, private sector promotion, foreign investments and aid, and all the corruption and waste that have dogged these countries' development efforts.

Chapter Seven considers a number of indicators that measure development levels in the different GCC states. The most important are the indicators used in this chapter to gauge the level of economic diversification in the GCC's economies, over the past thirty years, including the nature of economic growth, the importance of the oil sector to the overall economy, the role of manufacturing and volume of interstate commerce between the GCC states. The results clearly show that the GCC's economies are still oil driven; in other words, they are highly dependent on oil as the main engine of economic growth. If this source were to suddenly cease to exist, these countries' standards of living would drop to the level of many poorer nations.

Chapter Eight considers another important dimension of development, if not the most important, namely human resource development in the GCC states. Its importance lies in the fact that at the core of these countries' development is their ability to use their finite oil resources to build productive GCC citizens able to enjoy good living standards after the depletion of oil by using their skill and knowledge to produce goods and services vital for local and international markets. The reader will come to realise that these countries suffer from a real human resource crisis and that it is first, and foremost, a political crisis. The colonial countries have succeed in convincing the region's governments that raising the people's awareness, giving them the sense that they are the rulers' partners in the community and allowing them to maintain links with their Arab and Islamic milieu, is inadvisable because it is a threat to their own interests and those of the colonial powers. This way of looking at the people still prevails among the region's governments, albeit less intensely after independence, rendering all attempts at human development rather cautious. For this reason, we have examined the topic before and after independence and tried to support our claims with testimonies from inside and outside the region.

Chapter Nine focuses on the role of the private sector in these countries' economies, showing how the oil boom and the concomitant overexpansion of the public sector's role have eroded the position of the commercial class, once the backbone of the pre-oil economy. In the post oil economy, this commercial class was supplanted by a marginalised private sector whose ties to the corruption and cronyism of the state have robbed it of the ability to play any significant role in these countries' development. In recent years, however, the regions' governments have begun to realise that the public sector can no longer either absorb the large numbers of university graduates or maintain the welfare state of the 1970s. This has made them pay a little more attention to the private sector and try to develop it in a manner that allows it to absorb the ever-growing number of graduates so as to avoid any negative fallout. This is not a matter of wishful thinking, however, since the governments first have to tackle a series of obstacles. If the experience of the industrialised nations is anything to go by, the private sector's future in these countries is contingent upon the public sector taking the initiative to launch a genuine development process, including private sector development. We highlight some of these countries' experiences to warn against the quick-fix solutions proposed by some international organisations, most of which are designed to tighten the industrialised countries' control on the developing world.

Chapter Ten addresses the GCC states' foreign investment policies and the aid they have granted to a number of developing countries, starting in the 1970s. Foreign investments once represented a source of income diversification for countries with ample oil surpluses and a limited absorptive capacity. However, although this kind of source diversification is beyond reproach in principle, its implementation on the ground raises a number of reservations and objections, especially regarding their location and the mode of investment, as this chapter makes clear. Just as the GCC states tried to diversity their sources of income, for various reasons, they have also granted generous amounts of aid to other countries since the beginning of the oil boom, despite the negative aspects associated with this, a phenomenon that merits due consideration.

Chapter Eleven addresses the relationship of oil to corruption and the waste of resources, the most important example of which is the unchecked expansion of the public sector at the expense of the private sector. This is particularly noteworthy since this expansion was not the result of the public sector playing a pioneering role in launching a number of strategic industries, a development that can only happen in the shadow of an integrated vision involving joint Gulf and Arab projects. It was because the public sector acted like a cancerous growth intent on absorbing and controlling all elements of civil society. Other aspects of waste include the special allocations and privileges granted to ruling family members which today constitute a heavy burden on these countries' budgets, and are one of the reasons why efforts to safeguard public funds and fight corruption have so far failed. Finally, these countries' military expenditures which account for the major part of their budgets are of no economic or security benefit to the country. They symbolise both the acquiescence to foreign pressure and protection of powerful interests that thrive on bribery in countries where there is no public accountability and where the private intersects with the public.

Part IV: Security Policies

After looking at the GCC's development policies in Part III, Part IV examines their security policies to find out what happened in the region, and the wider Arab milieu, as a result of these governments' internal, regional and international policies. We cover these subjects over three different chapters.

Chapter Twelve focuses on the fact that the notion of security that has prevailed in the region since the discovery of oil has nothing to do with ensuring security and stability for the majority of the region's population. Instead, the term has come to mean preserving the current balance of power to ensure uninterrupted oil supplies to the West and safeguard its other interests. These interests include the Western weapons industry, the flow of oil funds to Western markets, and ensuring that no competent Arab regional order ever exists, as well as protecting Israel and other regional governments allied to the West. Except for a few rare cases, most events that have occurred in the region recently were designed to maintain security in the latter sense of the term, a fact that will become clear from our analysis in Chapter Thirteen.

Chapter Thirteen assesses the geo-political developments in the region over the past thirty years, a period characterised by revolutions, coups, wars, foreign presence and various manifestations of violence. This state of affairs has caused much destruction and the squandering of human and material resources. More ominously, it has led to the dislocation of the Arab regional order which today is on the verge of collapse and incapable of influencing the course of events in the region. Perhaps the most significant aspect of this collapse is the occupation and attempted dismemberment of Iraq and the negative impact all this has had on the Gulf countries' position vis-à-vis Iran and on the Palestinian people's position regarding Israel.

We devote Chapter Fourteen to the issue of Iran's nuclear programme given its significance to this country's future role not only in the Gulf region, but in the Arab and Islamic region as well. We address the level of progress the programme has so far achieved, the motives behind it and different ways of dealing with it in the next few years, as well as recent developments in this area.

Part V: Towards a Better Future

While the previous chapters of this book evaluate the past and the present, Part V takes a hopeful look at the future. It focuses on the subject of the desired reform by analysing the repercussions of the Arab Spring reforms that are required to correct the course of the GCC states and the wider Arab region. These are dealt with over five different chapters.

Chapter Fifteen analyses the repercussions of the Arab Spring which has lasted for more than four years so far. It focuses on its effects on both the hereditary systems and the Arab republics, and likewise the probable consequences of the Arab Spring on the regional and global balance of powers, particularly in the Gulf region and the Arab world.

Chapter Sixteen looks at the reforms needed in each Gulf country and their associated complexities, such as convincing various stakeholders of the inevitability of reform and defining the nature and issues involved in these reforms. These include the relationship between Islam and democracy, the impact of local and foreign stakeholders, the priorities of reform and significance of adopting a gradual approach, the impact of foreign workers on the course of reform and other issues aimed at redressing the relationship between the governments and their people.

Chapter Seventeen highlights the fact that Gulf unity is an objective of the much-needed cooperation in the region, since it is a prerequisite to achieving prosperity and stability. Experience shows beyond the shadow of a doubt that for economic, human, political and security reasons, the present national entities are no longer capable of achieving any significant progress in the domains of development and security. The chapter starts by evaluating previous efforts towards integration in the Gulf, suggesting a number of mechanisms to strengthen and expand it in the next few years, and highlights the expected economic and security benefits from an eventual successful integration.

Chapter Eighteen demonstrates clearly that although Gulf unity is a step in the right direction, it is not enough on its own, for both human and economic reasons, to ensure that the required development and security reforms do indeed happen. This makes adherence to the Arab regional order a necessity for survival and a condition for sustainable development. There is no conflict between these two paths because the Arab world is like an incubator to which the Gulf countries turn when they feel their development projects are restricted by population shortages, when their soil is not fertile enough, or when their resources other than oil prove insufficient, at which point the Arab world becomes the ideal solution. When foreign labour threatens the Arab identity of the Gulf, Arab workers become the safety valve, which is how the region will gradually gravitate towards more integration into its larger Arab milieu, thus achieving sustainable development, preserving its Arab identity and marking its presence in a stable environment, free from constant danger and war.

The final chapter, Chapter Nineteen, considers a third option that the GCC states, aided and supported by the wider Arab world, can resort to in the future to increase opportunities for further development and security. It is the significant presence they could potentially have within those international organisations which play a growing role and presence in a globalised world moving constantly towards closer integration and interaction. The chapter shows how this international presence requires that Gulf countries, in cooperation with the other Arab and Muslim countries, secure a foothold in these institutions' administrations and, by doing that, leave their mark on their policies by rendering them more sensitive to Arab and Islamic causes.

Introduction

In a book entitled *Dreams and Shadows: The Future of the Middle East*, American journalist and author Robin Wright justifies her choice of topic and omission of the GCC states by saying, "Some countries, like Saudi Arabia, I left out because the system has prevailed and the voices of change are not yet noisy enough."[1]

The above quote is eloquent enough in describing the absence of alternative voices in the GCC states, even though it has been more than four years since the start of the Arab Spring. However, what is more important than knowing this fact is realising its impact in terms of lost opportunities and the failure to achieve much-needed security in this region. The main idea of this book is that the absence of political participation and its significance in terms of accountability, transparency and scrutiny of government policies, as well as wise decision-making, have rendered the region's development unsteady and unsuccessful. This has gone hand in hand with official security policies that have resulted in even less security, and weakened the Arab regional order, the safety valve of the region's security and prosperity. We should also not forget all the blatant foreign interventions in the region's affairs and the imbalance of power in favour of Israel in the context of the Arab regional order, and in favour of Iran in the Arab Gulf region.

The ruling families' insistence on monopolising the decision-making process and confining their nations' wealth to a small circle of people, considering it their personal "booty", has had a negative impact on these governments' behaviour, both internally and externally in matters related to development and security.[2] Internally, they sidelined the elites and curtailed their role, distorted culture to suit the rulers' autocratic needs and incapacitated institutions, putting them in the hands of a few select individuals. Externally, autocracy forced these countries' rulers to compensate for their absent legitimacy at home by doing their best to please foreign powers, which resulted in behaviour mostly subservient to the West since it does not rest on authentic development and security visions based on the local population's interest, and that of the wider Arab and Islamic nation. The resulting chasm between these governments' autocratic vision and the requirements of genuine development and security meant that the region's oil wealth continues to be squandered, and its security policies remain akin to temporary alliances with the big powers. This has only led to further instability in the region, coupled with wasting these countries' finite resources without ensuring even the minimum level of development.

In this book, we elaborate further on this theory using a descriptive-analytical methodology, relying on available data regarding the region and supporting our theory with a number of relevant studies on the region. The book addresses the GCC states' political economies since the discovery of oil in the early 1930s, though the main analysis centres around the major events that have unfolded since the early 1970s, a period that witnessed fundamental changes at all levels, to the repercussions of the Arab Spring since 2010. Part I addresses the current condition of elements of development in the GCC states, elements which autocracy, using the national oil wealth and backed by foreign powers, has succeeded in turning into weak building-blocs incapable of sustaining genuine development or security policies. Part II, which is an extension of Part I, shows how those weak elements of developments have, in turn, weakened these countries' negotiating positions, making them incapable of pursuing policies that protect the region's resources from the abusive practices of the international oil companies and their governments, practices still ongoing today, albeit to a lesser extent. Part III highlights these countries' failed development policies resulting from the lack of a shared development vision between the governments and the people. This has led to much waste and limited the success of efforts to diversify economic infrastructures and produce competent individuals with the requisite skills to ensure continued revenues to the country once oil dries up. Just as Part III documents the failure of the GCC's development policies, Part IV underlines these countries' failure to achieve security and stability by reconciling the Gulf with its wider Arab milieus and reducing the foreign presence in the region. Part V is a call to correct the present course on three main levels: the introduction of domestic reforms, including Gulf integration, deepening inter-Arab cooperation at all levels, especially in the economic and security domains, and reconciling with the wider Islamic milieu, including an active and competent presence in international decision-making circles. This means that adjusting the course involves replacing the triangle of hereditary succession, oil and foreign powers with another, the essentials of which are freedom, productive human beings and integration in the wider Arab and Islamic milieus and the world at large.

PART I

The Harvest of Autocracy

In any society, development and security depend on the interaction between a number of cultural, political, economic and other elements. The stronger these elements are, the closer this society comes to achieving its objectives, and the more benefit it reaps from its contacts with the outside world. Despite the fact that any human society needs the minimum amount of knowledge and human and material resources in order to grow, examples of development from all over the world, both successful and unsuccessful, show that successful development process depends above all on a clear vision shared by all elements in society. The success of any development process depends also on the level of expertise in the management of the country's resources, whether in motivating the people and increasing their ability to produce and give, or exploiting various other resources. However, the correct exploitation of resources to achieve the desired development goals requires, in turn, the presence of institutions that act as a liaison between members of society to ensure the transfer of resources, proper exploitation of skills, resolution of conflicts and the unification of efforts. When we have clear development objectives, highly efficient resource management and competent institutions, the ensuing policies are usually correct and their outcome leads to increased prosperity and stability. This is why we decided to begin the section on development and stability in the GCC states by reviewing and assessing the elements of development in these countries, starting with the hereditary succession systems. We will also discuss Arab and Islamic culture and these countries' elites and institutions to show how the triangle of hereditary succession, oil and foreign powers has played a major role in weakening these elements, preventing them from interacting in a manner to ensure proper development and stability.

CHAPTER ONE

The Hereditary Succession System

All the GCC states[1] maintain "hereditary succession systems"[2] that vest power exclusively in a single family with the final say in important decisions and on all matters related the country's national assets. It would have been less dangerous had these families simply behaved against the spirit of their countries' constitutions and laws. In reality, however, and with the exception of Kuwait, the constitution legitimises their behaviour since it codifies their discrimination against the rest of the countries' citizens. In Kuwait, the constitution imposes a number of restrictions on the ruling family, stating in Article 6, Part One, that, "The System of government in Kuwait shall be democratic, under which sovereignty resides in the people, the source of all powers. Sovereignty shall be exercised in the manner specified in this Constitution."[3]

The other Gulf constitutions are very similar to the Saudi Basic Law, which states in Article 5, Chapter Two, that, "(a) The system of government in the Kingdom of Saudi Arabia is that of a monarchy" and "(b) Rule passes to the sons of the founding King, Abdul-Aziz bin Abdul-Rahman al-Faisal alSa'ud, and to their children's children." It totally sidelines the rest of Saudi society from the political scene and bars them from exercising one of their basic human rights. Therefore, any future attempt at reform in these countries should start with the articles of the region's constitutions to devise a common formula for a single citizenship. Consequently, despite some progress in the domain of public participation since the early 1970s, this participation is still nominal and subject to various restrictions by the ruling families. This forces the majority of the population to live with a deficient citizenship that increases or decreases depending on their closeness or distance from the ruling family's agenda. The autocratic nature of these governments makes them non-consultative, in the strict sense of not undertaking consultation (*shura*), and non-tribal, in terms of parity, justice and mutual support among the tribes. Finally, these governments were never entirely welcomed by the people who rejected them and tried to change them, though this rejection varied in intensity from one country to the other.

First: Is it a consultative system?

The GCC's hereditary systems have given rise to two different visions of development in the region. The ruling families believe that their presence in power, the freedom to use the nation's wealth at will, and having a free hand in making important decisions constitute their main objective, and all other objectives ensue from there. The people believe, on the other hand, that the ruling families' monopoly over power and wealth detracts from their fundamental rights as partners in the state. They see this not only as conflicting with the tenets of their religion and the requirements of modernity, but also as contrary to the tribal spirit that prevailed prior to the discovery of oil and advent of foreigners to the region. They also believe that this system has squandered the nation's resources and scattered its potential, a potential that should go in only one direction, serving all segments of society under a single standard of citizenship, with no distinction between them except based on ability and trust. These two principles are the cornerstones of any renaissance, whether it takes place under religious or non-religious auspices, based on the words of the Qur'an: "One of them said: O my father! Employ him; surely the best of those that you can employ is the strong man, the trustworthy one."[4]

No doubt this duality in citizenship and the presence of families with special privileges that set them apart from other members of society without a say in how their country is managed or the spending of their nation's wealth is, in this researcher's and other people's opinion, one of the main impediments to genuine development in the region. We believe, moreover, that this is a key issue as far as development and security in the GCC states are concerned, and is likely to remain so. This is why we can claim that unless this imbalance in relations between the ruling families and region's people is redressed, the next few years will witness more development failures and retreats in security, regardless of how hard these governments try to pretend otherwise. There is no escaping this fact even if the region's governments falsify facts, use security scare tactics, buy the loyalties of weak and short-sighted individuals, hide the truth, try to silence the voices of opposition to the status quo, or brandish the support of foreign powers that helped pilfer these countries' wealth through their oil companies, weapons and consultations. The latter have even infiltrated the region's education systems to make them more "moderate", in other words, void them of their Arab and Islamic values and belief systems so that future generations will have no loyalty to their Arab heritage or to Islam. Thus the region will remain in the grips of colonialism, backwardness and division. The events of the Arab Spring have confirmed that the peoples of the Arab world, including the population of the Gulf region, are longing for freedom, justice and unity because small states in the world today are usually on the margin of events and not at their centre.

Therefore, our objection to the current succession systems in the GCC states is based on principle, because heredity is incompatible with Islamic values. It is also practical because these regimes have continuously failed to achieve development and bring security to the region. This will become clear when we examine development and security policies later on in the book. This objection in principle rests on the fact that heredity conflicts with the clear text of the Qur'an, with the Prophet's personal conduct, with the course chosen by the first four "rightly guided" caliphs and with international law. In other words, this system is in clear contradiction of Islam's tenets and all legal and international rights, even if it has been enforced for a long time. The Prophet underlines the principle of consultation (*shura*) in the Qur'anic verses "And take counsel with them in the affair"[5] and "And those who respond to their Lord and keep up prayer, and their rule is to take counsel among themselves, and who spend out of what We have given them."[6] The Prophet consulted the Muslims during the battles of Badr, al-Khandaq, Uhud and others, although as the infallible Prophet he could have chosen not to do so. He wanted to highlight and entrench the importance of this principle among his followers. The medieval scholar al-Qurtubi writes that Umar bin al-Khattab made the office of caliph – one of the loftiest positions in the state – a matter of *shura*.[7] Moreover, when Abu Bakr was elected as caliph by the Prophet's companions, this became an example of direct nomination and election long before these terms came to us from the West, and the same could be said about the election of 'Umar. Although Abu Bakr chose Umar as his successor, instead of imposing him on the people, he left the oath of allegiance to the caliph (*bay'ah*) up to the people. The succession of Uthman bin 'Affan followed yet another form of *shura*. Umar chose six faithful and capable men and asked them to choose one of them as candidate, then submit his candidacy to the people for their oath. His son, Abdullah, who was the seventh member, was allowed to give counsel but not to nominate or vote.[8] Those are the caliphs whose example (*sunnah*) the Prophet instructed Muslims to follow after his own when he said, "I enjoin you to fear God, and to hear and obey even if it be an Abyssinian slave for those of you who live after me will see great disagreement.

You must then follow my *sunnah* and that of the rightly guided caliphs. Hold to it and stick fast to it. Avoid novelties, for every novelty is an innovation, and every innovation is an error."[9] The *shura* we are talking about here is "binding", that is, one that all the rulers should abide by unless there is a text to indicate otherwise; in other words, if the nation's representatives take a collective decision, the ruler has to abide by it or else, we believe, *shura* would have no value at all. The classical scholar Ibn Kathir relates that when the Prophet was asked about the significance of the word "decide" in the Qur'anic verse, "so when you have decided, then place your trust in God"[10] the Prophet replied, "Seek the counsel of wise men and follow it."[11] Therefore, the real *shura* at the core of Islam is the binding *shura*, not the one that is "in the manner of advice", because it is more logical, especially in today's world where misguided rulers and complex state management are the rule. Any deviation from this core, even if it endures, will never become "right", but will remain a deviation. Caliph Umar bin Abdul-Aziz confirms this fact when he was named the fifth caliph after having inherited the caliphate but rejecting it as there had been no oath from the Muslims, saying, " 'O people, I was burdened with this matter without my opinion, without my asking for it and without consultation with the Muslims. I relieve you of the allegiance to me that has been forced on you. Choose for yourselves another leader.' Upon which the people shouted, 'We choose you, O Commander of the Faithful, and want you, so accept it with felicity and blessings.' "[12] Is it, therefore, not religiously right, reasonable or fitting to call for correcting the deviation in the course of governance, based on Islam's core values and the example of Umar bin Abdul-Aziz, instead of seeking guidance from those who deviated from this nation's tenets and core values? This is all the more relevant given all that autocracy has brought in its wake in terms of backwardness, corruption, dependency, division and marginalisation in the international balance of power. More ominous still is that our silence with regard to this autocracy is an indirect confirmation of the claim, propagated by Islam's enemies through the years, that Islam is an autocratic religion. It is a claim that reveals a clear confusion between Islam's tenets that reject all forms of autocracy and this religion's history where, unfortunately, autocracy abounds. It abounds because of the profit it brings and the shortcomings in the leaders' performance compared with the lofty purpose God intended for them, a purpose that their ancestors had succeeded in achieving.

Bernard Lewis, the well-known Orientalist, says that the core of governance in Islam is epitomised by the word "justice" and adds that, based on the tenets of Islam, the just ruler should fulfil two conditions: "he must have acquired power rightfully, and he must exercise it rightfully. In other words, he must be neither a usurper nor a tyrant."[13] This is despite the fact, as Lewis points out, that this has often been the case during considerable periods of Islam's history, and we agree with that. On the subject of governance in Islam, Lewis confirms that: "Equality among believers was a basic principle of Islam from its foundation in the seventh century, in marked contrast to both the caste system of India to the east and the privileged aristocracies of the Christian world to the west."[14] Lewis believes the facts illustrate the point that Islam highlights the importance of equality and has been very successful in achieving it. He goes on to say that even the discrimination against women, slaves and non-believers in certain aspects of life with which Islam is often identified cannot be compared to the long-held discriminatory belief in the United States that "white male Protestants" alone were born free and equal only to their peers. As Lewis observes: "The record would seem to indicate that as late as the nineteenth or even the early twentieth century, a poor man of humble origins had a better chance of rising to the top in the Muslim Middle East than anywhere in Christendom, including post-revolutionary France and the United States."[15] Moreover, Lewis denies the claim by some in the West that Arabs are autocratic by nature and will remain so because of their religion. He says that the most noteworthy finding by analysts of the rich tradition of Islamic political thought is that governance in Islam has three main principles which are somewhat similar to democracy. They are the oath of allegiance (*bay'ah*) that grants legitimacy to the ruler,[16] the consensus of society (*ijma'a*) which makes participation in decision-making obligatory and restrictions (*quyud*) on the ruler's powers based on the tenets of Islamic law (*shar'ia*).

The Moroccan intellectual Muhammad Abed al-Jabri observes in the same context that the oath in early Islam was always conditional and the outcome of a consultative process, starting with the oath in the time of the Prophet and ending with those made to the four rightly guided caliphs Abu Bakr, Umar, Uthman and Ali. Al-Jabri seems to say that obedience at that time was conditional upon consultation, especially when there was no text to support it, just like Western democracies are today conditional upon the consent of the governed. As to the obedience to the rulers that has prevailed since the end of the rightly guided caliphate to the present day, in al-Jabri's opinion it is akin to the one that prevailed in ancient Persia, a type of obedience that the Arabs knew neither prior to Islam nor under the rightly guided caliphate.[17] The best testament to al-Jabri's words concerning this Persian-style obedience, or blind obedience as we like to call it, is that which prevailed when the Arab Muslim leader Mughirah bin Shu'bah wanted to sit on the throne of Persia near the king prior to the famous Battle of Qadisiya; Rustum's servants prevented him from doing so, and when Mughirah asked why, the answer was that this throne belonged only "to the king of Persia". This prompted Mughirah to utter his famous words, "I now know for certain that your king will soon disappear, and that you, Persians, enslave one another, while we, the Muslim Arabs are God's slaves, God's and no one else's. A king that rules through enslavement and autocracy will not last long."[18]

One wonders how did the Arab nation, a nation of over three hundred million people in the midst of over one billion Muslims, find ourselves in the early twenty-first century ruled by governments more Persian than those of Persia itself, even if some of them have fallen since the emergence of the Arab Spring and others are expected to?

Second: Is it a tribal system?

We should stop here and reflect on the claim, often touted by the ruling families and some of those who support them, that the Gulf societies are tribal in nature and that the current regimes are but a reflection of these societies. Our answer to these claims is that despite the dearth of documented information regarding the policies of the tribal systems that once prevailed in the region, the little that does exist refutes these claims because these simple systems were closer in nature to present-day democratic systems. They were closer to them in terms of advocacy, accountability and the protection of the rights of individuals who always played a role in their society. Tribe members played an active role in the affairs of their tribe and the tribe was active within the tribal association. Through this hierarchy, no one prevailed over anyone else, even despite the imbalance of power between the tribes; everyone had a voice and everyone had rights that merited protection. On the other hand, the regimes currently in power reduced this tribal system to single-family systems, the same families that once depended financially and in matters of security on other families and tribes for the establishment of their respective emirates. However, when they no longer needed these local tribes and families, thanks to the discovery of oil and advent of foreigners to the region, these ruling families managed to monopolise the region's wealth and decision-making processes, and made governance in the region akin to the caste system in India, a situation that still prevails today. Ali Khalifa al-Kawari, a Gulf researcher and activist, confirms this imbalance of power between the region's people and ruling families: "In general, these changes gradually transformed the region's governance systems from traditional tribal alliances, where the alliance is key and the Shaikh is first among equals, into royal family-led governments. Although they rule through overwhelming power, they left in place some of the trappings of the old tribal system, with its familial relationships and social decorum. What enabled this transformation to take place were the agreements that Britain concluded with the region's rulers and the financial resources that became available to these governments, first from customs duties and, later on, from oil. This transformation, which weakened the position of the tribes and families and strengthened power at the centre, led to the retreat of political participation, in general."[19]

Another researcher on the region says that Kuwait's governance experience began when the pearl and fish merchants appointed as emir a man they trusted, named Abdullah al-Sabah. This appointment was tantamount to a distribution of roles between commercial and administrative affairs, and by no means implied that the emir should enjoy privileges that set him apart from the rest of the people, or that his family would occupy a position above all other families. This researcher believes, therefore, that the emir's appointment was merely the act of entrusting an individual with the task of protecting society's interests, rather than a licence to seek his own, meaning that the other families were neither his nor his family's subjects. Moreover, politics at the time was not deemed more important than the economy; it was on an equal footing with it, if not dependent on it, given the merchant class's important role in financing and ensuring the survival of both the emir and his emirate. Furthermore, the emir did not resort to the use of force to ensure his and his emirate's survival; he relied instead on consultations and consensus among members of his society. This made his position rather similar to that of a chairman of the board charged with a specific task, which he neither can perform on his own, nor can he impose any decision that board members do not agree with.[20] This description of the Kuwaiti ruling family's relationship with the people is typical of the situation in all other GCC states prior to the discovery of oil, the exponential increase in the big powers' role, and the impact of all this on the relationship between ruler and subjects in the region.

Third: Is it widely accepted?

This is why the ruling families' gradual marginalisation of various sectors of Gulf societies has elicited so many objections and rejections, and why the people launched various counter movements in the twentieth century, particularly in the 1920s and 1930s.[21] Calls for political rights came in various forms, from making peaceful demands, forming labour unions and launching national liberation movements, to attempting coups. There is no doubt that all this pressure and advocacy helped, among other things, to introduce some form of participation at the municipal and consultative council levels, though most did not last long due to regional and international circumstances, except in Kuwait. Below are a number of examples of how the region's people showed their displeasure with hereditary systems before the Arab Spring, the repercussions of which will be discussed in Chapter Fifteen.

1.   Kuwait

The Kuwaiti experiment is the best and most effective in the region in terms of seeking to establish a balance between the ruling family and the people, to provide an environment of accountability and open healthy channels of public expression. Although this experiment began in the 1920s, it became active in 1938, a year that witnessed a series of events culminating in the constitution of 1962. The discovery of oil in the country that same year caused a shift in the balance of power between the ruling family and the people represented by the commercial class and other elites. No sooner had oil revenues started pouring into the country's coffers, than the al-Sabah family began asking for an increase in their allocations, at a time when the country's notables and merchants realised the need for public oversight of the management and distribution of this national resource. Emir Ahmad al-Sabah's response was to increase the ruling family's allocations and impose additional customs duties on the merchants.[22] This drove a large number of them, and some notables, to convene a secret meeting to draft a list of demands. Among these was a call for Ahmad al-Sabah's resignation in favour of Abdullah al-Salem, who was close to the opposition at the time, as well as demands for reforming the education and health systems and containing the spread of corruption.[23] However, despite the government's response with a number of arrests and other negative measures, a group among the opposition held its ground and insisted on its demands. They saw their efforts rewarded with the establishment of a Legislative Council with its own basic law. The law extended the Council's oversight prerogative on a large number of public institutions, among which were the treasury, judiciary, security services and service-oriented institutions. Emir Ahmad al-Sabah had no choice but to sign the Council's basic law which, despite lasting only six months, managed to score a number of successes, including placing limitations on the emir's prerogatives, reducing financial waste and establishing a number of important social institutions.[24] However, although the British government had earlier encouraged some form of partnership between the emir and his people, the Council's achievements, especially those related to oil, prompted it to take a middle-of-the-road position in recognition of the Council's power. Subsequent events that pointed towards the imminent dissolution of the Council revealed the true opportunistic face of British policy. When Emir Ahmad consulted Gerald de Gaury, the British Political Agent in Kuwait, regarding his intention to dissolve the Council, he agreed but cautioned against the risk of failure, as if encouraging the emir to deal a fatal blow to the Council. After the Council's dissolution, the Political Resident (the most senior British representative in the Gulf) wrote to his government, saying: "the balance of power as between Shaikh and Council has been readjusted in favour of the former which suits us."[25]

Britain's above position, compounded by its policies in other parts of the Arab world, mainly in Palestine, encouraged the alignment of various elements of Kuwait's opposition with the Arab Nationalist Movement against Britain. One of the outcomes of this shift was the formation of committees to gather donations in support of the Palestinian cause.[26] The 1938 uprising, or *intifada*, and the concomitant increase in oil revenues, prompted the emir of Kuwait to change his alliances in a manner that allowed him to reduce his reliance on the merchant class and establish a one-family, rather than a one-man, system. With this shift, as several sources indicate, came a 40 per cent to 50 per cent increase in the al-Sabah family's allocation and, in some cases, as much as 200 per cent. Family members hastened to acquire public lands, either to sell them off or to distribute them among their followers, and soon set their sights on the country's public positions.[27] These newfound privileges fostered among these family members, intentionally or unintentionally, the sense that they were a privileged class superior to all others in rights and responsibilities.[28] As a result, they no longer saw their family as being equal to others, or one among many, as was the case earlier under the tribal system. This feeling, nourished by newfound privileges, is common among all other ruling families in the region, albeit with some differences in the size of the gap between them and the people. In 1950, when Abdullah Salem al-Sabah took over power, he moved to organise and unite the ruling family, while using the increasing oil wealth to reduce the power of the merchant class and the opposition, in general. He did this either through the establishment of the Council for Development and Reconstruction, or the replacement of elected municipal council members with appointed ones, mostly ruling family members. He established the High Executive Committee, mainly staffed by family members and their supporters, and refused the merchants' request to be part of these institutions. Even the British Resident saw these steps as a clear retreat in the Kuwaiti people's attempt to manage the affairs of their own country.[29]

The 1950s witnessed the spread of nationalist sentiments, especially Nasserism. Like others in the region, the Kuwaiti government was anxious to avoid or, at least, contain its impact on the opposition as a whole. However, the winds of Arab nationalism continued to sweep the region unabated, compelling large segments of the Kuwaiti society to turn their cultural clubs into platforms for anti-British and French sentiments. In August 1956, around 4000 demonstrators gathered at the National Cultural Club to hear a speech in support of Nasser, and Abdullah Salem al-Sabah used various means to show his opposition to this nationalist fervour. At first, he tolerated peaceful popular manifestations, like the distribution of pamphlets and holding of speech rallies, and tried to distance the local population from the Arab immigrants to mitigate their impact, though he finally resorted to more forceful means like surveillance, bans and detentions.[30] However, as we shall see later, this attempt to prevent the citizens of the Gulf from opening up to the changes sweeping the rest of the Arab world was an entrenched British policy aimed at maintaining the colonial powers' domination of the region. The policy also aimed at keeping in place the region's incumbent family-led regimes and discouraging local attempts to take part in political decision-making. We already mentioned how the British Political Agent in Kuwait had not objected to but rather encouraged Shaikh Ahmad's dissolution of the Council, established in 1938, when he felt that it was interfering in matters related to oil and the oil companies' privileges. Thus, the fortunes of the Kuwaiti opposition, which involve numerous factors, have continued to ebb and flow to the present day. However, we could summarise the experience by saying that it is a political experiment born from a mixture of internal and external motives and challenges. It continues to function within parameters imposed by a lack of conviction on the part of some ruling family members about the validity of the entire process. Many emirs have found themselves, as a result, between those who oppose the process as a whole and popular opposition. Sometimes, the winds of change blowing across the region and the world blew in the direction of a ruling family trying hard to maintain its control on the affairs of states, using its political power and oil wealth together. At other times, it blew in the direction of an opposition trying in vain to raise the ceiling of its demands because this opposition has so far failed to act based on the common denominators among its different components. Instead, it allowed itself to sometimes get involved in tangential issues or self-interested pursuits.[31] The last episode in this ongoing struggle was the dissolution of the National Assembly in February 2008, though it was a constitutional solution, and the new elections that allowed Kuwaiti women to secure a foothold in the National Assembly for the first time ever. It is worth mentioning that one of the most important developments in the post oil period in the Kuwaiti political scene was the merchant class' retreat from political decision-making. They shifted from pearl fishing, related trade activities and political influence, prior to the discovery of oil, to contracting, commerce, services and agencies, coupled with a drop in their political influence. This shift in the balance of power between the ruling family and the merchant class was due to several factors, the most important being, of course, the accumulation of oil revenues in the government's coffers and expansion of the related administration and services sectors under the ruling family's control. Other factors include the rise of new social groups with their own cultural, confessional, regional and even ethnic dimensions, which helped the ruling family maintain and strengthen its control over power. The merchant class abandoned its political role in return for many privileges, including a free hand in running the country's private sector.[32]

2. Dubai

Another group to call for reform in the region was the Council that a number of notables and merchants from Dubai established in 1938. Among these were members of the Emirate's merchant class, like members of the al-Ghurair, Bin Dalmuk, Bin Thani and al-Huraiz families, and the group enjoyed the support of certain members of the al-Maktoum family, including Mani bin Rashid al-Maktoum.[33] Their demands were reform oriented, rather than revolutionary; in other words, they wanted to ensure a wise administrative decision-making process, a share of the Emirate's revenues, an independent judiciary, and to reduce British influence on the then ruler, Shaikh Said bin Maktoum. The reformists asked the ruler to allow public oversight of 85 per cent of the Emirate's revenues, and spend it on socio-development projects. The Political Resident (Britain's most senior representative in the Gulf) described these demands as "a democratic wave that aimed at putting more power in the hands, of the people", therefore it is not surprising that he deemed it more dangerous than transferring power from one ruler to another, at least from his own country's perspective.[34]

Nevertheless, though the Council that made these demands was short-lived, some believe that it managed to introduce a wide range of reforms, including establishing a municipal council and social security system for the elderly, electing customs officials accountable to the Emirate rather than the ruling family, and establishing a department of education.[35] When Shaikh Rashid assumed power in 1958, he personally adopted a number of the reformists' demands, including the municipal council whose decisions and financing he placed in the ruler's hands, despite the reformists' request that it be both elected and independent.[36] However, the period that followed the discovery of oil was again witness to a decline in the merchant class' political role, in return for privileges and influence in the economic sphere. Some say that many merchant families still own the same commercial agencies since the 1960s as a reward for staying away from politics.[37]

3. Qatar

The Qataris similarly showed their displeasure at the expanding power of the ruling family, at the expense of other sectors of society, in a variety of ways. In April 1963, while a demonstration in support of the proposed union between Egypt, Syria and Iraq was passing through one of Doha's streets, it was intercepted by a member of the ruling family who fired on the demonstrators and killed one of them. The incident was the spark that led to the formation of an opposition movement called the United National Front which promptly organised a strike that lasted an entire week. The Front's demands included curbing the ruling family's privileges, increasing social services, reducing the number of foreign employees in government departments and the oil sector, instituting a special budget for national revenues, establishing an elected municipal council and officially recognising labour unions.[38] The Front's membership included workers, a number of breakaway members of the ruling family and a few notables, led by Abdullah bin Misnad and Hamid al-Atiyyah. Shaikh Ahmad al-Thani, the ruler at the time, responded in two ways; on the one hand, he detained, exiled or imprisoned some demonstrators and, on the other, he introduced a number of reforms including reducing his and his family's allocations and making members of his family subject to the laws of the land like everybody else.[39]

4. Saudi Arabia

In Saudi Arabia, opposition to the regime took several forms, both in terms of the people's demands and the means used to make themselves heard. Faisal al-Duwaish, leader of the Muslim Brotherhood which formed the backbone of the effort to establish the Saudi Kingdom, rebelled against the Saudi government in 1927. He accused the royal family of subservience to the West, cooperating with the British, deviating from the true course of Islam and, consequently, of not being eligible to rule over Muslims. Ibn Saud cooperated with the British to quell the Muslim Brotherhood and al-Duwaish's rebellion, and the latter later died in prison.[40] On November 20, 1979, Juhaiman al-Utaibi and his followers occupied the Holy Sanctuary at Mecca during the annual pilgrimage and accused the Saudi government of allying itself with the United States, of relying on them to ensure the Kingdom's security and of being corrupt and dissolute. The Saudi government used French troops to put down Juhaiman's movement, and beheaded the man.[41] A Western observer described the objections behind the events in Mecca: "What the Mecca rebels rejected were the levels of corruption within the Royal Family and the inevitable acquiescence of the *ulama* [religious scholars] to such behaviour. Clearly, what is implied in the accusations made by the attackers is that the *ulama* have reconciled themselves to exercising their religious authority in tandem if not in the shadow of the political authorities."[42]

Another Western researcher confirms that the events that have taken place since the early 1990s show that a large segment of Saudi society sympathised with Juhaiman's demands, even if they choose other means of expressing them.[43] After the occupation of Kuwait, and the ensuing foreign presence in the region and apparent vulnerability of the Saudi regime, other mostly peaceful forms of opposition emerged in the Kingdom, calling for reform. In 1991, over 400 Saudi personalities signed a letter calling for reform of the Saudi system, most of whom were members of the Islamic "awakening" movement (*al-Sahwa*). A year later, in September 1992, around 107 Saudi religious scholars signed what became known as the "memorandum of advice", the response to which was detention, dismissal or containment.[44] In one observer's opinion, the Saudi government's response proves that although the Saudi royal family clothes itself in Islamic garb, its interests and influence take precedence over these religious scholars' opinions.[45] This unfortunate and rigid official attitude was the main reason behind the rise of an Al-Qaida offshoot in Saudi Arabia, and the instability it brought in its wake.[46] Like other opposition movements that came before, that of Osama Bin Laden was against Saudi Arabia's policy of seeking America's military assistance and allying itself with it.[47]

5. Bahrain

Bahrain was not an exception to the other GCC states as it too saw movements calling for the reform of the hereditary political system and voicing their opposition to several domestic and foreign policy decisions. In Bahrain, several factors motivated the calls for reform, some of which had to do with the education system and its impact on the people's level of awareness of issues in general, compared with other states in the region. Other factors ensued from the government's limited resources that reduced its ability to contain or weaken the opposition, while others had sectarian connotations. This explains the period of instability and demonstrations Bahrain went through in the 1950s during which people expressed their desire for political reform and rejected the British protectorate over their country, manifested in the British fleet's presence in Bahraini waters. They also protested against British troops taking part in quelling the demonstrations, against the Baghdad Pact and the tripartite attack on Egypt in 1956.[48] The Committee of National Union led the opposition that comprised both Sunni and Shi'a members, many of whom were either detained or deported. Later on, there were other reasons for continuing the protests, some of which involved teachers, oil workers and others and arose in reaction to events unfolding in the wider Arab region.[49] In the wake of the Iranian Revolution in 1979, the main character of the opposition to the Bahraini government shifted from nationalist to Islamist, particularly among the Shi'a who got involved in violent and bloody confrontations with the regime, though the Sunni opposition did not disappear from the scene either.[50]

6. Oman

In Oman, the largest expression of popular discontent with the political status quo was the Dhofar Rebellion that started in the mid 1960s and went on to assume wide regional implications. The military intervention by the Shah of Iran in 1973 succeeded in ending the rebellion by summer, 1975.[51] The Shah justified the move to help the Omani government quell the rebellion in Dhofar, saying: "Take the Dhofar rebellion in Oman. If it ever succeeded, just try to imagine what we would be faced with in Muscat, the capital, right in front of the Strait of Hormuz. At first a few a few rifles and then naval guns and missiles. It's a familiar pattern. I cannot tolerate subversive activities – and by that I mean anything that is imposed from the outside ... They [Oman] asked for our help and we sent it."[52]

No doubt, Sultan Qaboos' removal of his father, Said bin Taimur, from power with British approval shows that the former regime was incompatible even with the most basic hopes and aspirations of the Omani people. There was a need, therefore, to pre-empt the downfall and introduce enough reforms to absorb the people's ire, without significant changes. Moreover, some say that in 1994 the Omani regime learned that an opposition group, believed to be Sunni, was planning a coup involving a number of top commanders with foreign links, and although thirty-one of them were tried and condemned to death, a year later the Sultan pardoned them all.[53]

Fourth: The need to abolish the hereditary succession system

Although in the post independence period most of these countries drafted their own constitutions, ensuring popular participation and citizenship rights, they only served to strengthen the ruling families' power even further. They remain on paper until today, with the region's dictatorial regimes having obliterated anything positive in them by staging decorative exercises that fail to achieve the minimum level of participation by the region's people in determining their own affairs, with the relative exception of Kuwait.[54] We will come back to these experiences when we address the institutional environment underlying these states. Therefore, just as the election of Abu Bakr, the earliest example of Islamic consultation, is no longer workable given the complexities of this day and age, the old tribal formula, prior to reducing it to the one-family system that it is today, is incapable of keeping up with the necessities of modern life. Gulf researcher Said Harib agrees and says, "It is no longer possible to govern modern states and societies according to the systems and practices of a bygone era. It conflicts with democratic behaviour patterns founded on principles, criteria and tools that are missing from the tribal systems, which today are no more than a social reference framework, especially in light of the weakening ties between tribal members."[55]

Therefore, the fundamental tenets of Islam conflict with the region's hereditary systems. The behaviour of the first generation, namely the rightly guided caliphs, was based on consultation and choice. The real emirs could have once inherited leadership but their strong religious beliefs and deep knowledge of this religion made them turn it down, like Umar bin Abdul Aziz. Even the Orientalists attest to the fact that the fundamentals of Islam are founded on justice and consultation. Today's governments do not even portray the spirit of the old tribal system that once prevailed in the region and today we live in an age where democracy in its different shapes and forms prevails because the human mind realises that freedom is the cornerstone of social renaissance and stability. Since all the above is absolutely true, why do the ruling families in the Gulf expect their people to live outside their cultural heritage and human consensus, only to allow them to keep their autocratic rule in place, continue to squander the country's resources and turn their societies into a wilderness where the strong eat the weak? Can renaissance or stability take root in countries where the majority of the population has been turned into second-class citizens while members of the ruling family enjoy first-class citizenship, not because they are pious and capable, like God wants them to be, as is the case in all advanced societies, but only because they belong to the ruling family? We do not think so; what we do think, however, is that this view and this path, which started when Caliph Mu'awiyah assumed power after the rightly guided caliphs, has marked the beginning of a period without accountability, and signalled the Arabs' decline at all levels. This means that the notion and the path behind this form of government, which for a long time have been the reasons behind the backwardness and stagnation of the Arab-Islamic world, should be adjusted in line with the concept behind Mughirah bin Shu'bah's words. It is the notion of equality in the belief in God, and the need to seek inspiration in His words: "Surely God enjoins justice and good conduct and the giving to the kindred.

He forbids indecency and bad conduct and oppression. He admonishes you that you may be mindful."[56]

If we look at the Western nations' experience with hereditary systems, especially European countries like Britain and Denmark, we will realise that they would not have stabilised or developed over time had they not first abolished their hereditary systems, like in France, or turned them into "constitutional monarchies" where the monarch retains a ceremonial role, like in Britain. In these countries, political parties representing the will of the people compete for votes, and the party that wins the majority of seats in Parliament forms the government. The monarch does not interfere in the ruling party's affairs because the people have chosen it, and only they can hold it accountable based on the programme that brought it into office. This is the principle that underlies the exercise of power and accountability at all levels, and the safety valve on which contemporary Western societies rely; it is also the best of what the human brain has been able to conceive in this day and age. It is the closest to the spirit of the wise caliphate because, as noted by Abdul Rahman al-Kawakibi, one of the pioneers of Arab reformist thought, this modern system, and those who stand behind it, have benefitted from Islam more than the Muslims themselves did. He says in this context, "This lofty style of leadership is one and the same as Prophet Muhammad's, and no one has really followed him on that path save for Abu Bakr and Umar. It then began to decline and, from Uthman's time until today, the nation has continued to mourn it and ask for its reinstatement. They will continue to mourn it until the end of time if they are not wise enough to replace it with a political consultative (*shura*) system, the same system that some Western nations have adopted. We could say of these nations that they actually benefitted from Islam more than the Muslims themselves did."[57]

Chapter Two

Arab-Islamic Culture

Amidst all the stagnation, defeats and various manifestations of backwardness the Arabs are wallowing in today, there are voices calling for them to give up all of their long-standing values and traditions, heritage and history, even language. This is based on the belief that replicating the Western nations' experience, both positive and negative, is the Arab nation's only way out of its backwardness and misery. We believe that this view deserves some consideration in order to refute it and gauge its validity as far as Arab-Islamic heritage is concerned, with the hope that this exercise will serve as warning and a reminder that neither everything new is a sign of progress, nor is everything old a sign of backwardness. Given the present critical conditions the Arab nation is experiencing and their impact on the interaction between its different religious, sectarian and ethnic components, the use of the term "Arab-Islamic heritage" is our attempt to draw the attention of the new generation, whether Muslim or Christian, to the fact that the culture we are talking about here is the outcome of efforts by Arab Muslim alongside those of their Arab Christian brethren. This means that the future renaissance will only take place if the Arab world's constituent elements work together in harmony to solve various issues, especially controversial ones, in an atmosphere of honesty, freedom, mutual respect and diversity which avoids the majority's domination of the minority.[1]

First: The importance of culture in the Arab renaissance

Every society has its own reservoir of culture that defines its identity and forms a bridge linking it to its past and future. This reservoir also acts as a motivator because it provides society with the value system that unites its members, helps them formulate their vision of the universe they live in and allows them to prosper and achieve happiness and stability. It teaches them how to manage their relationships with other human beings and with the rest of God's creation, like animals, plants and the environment. This is why we believe Samuel Huntington, the father of the "clash of civilisations" concept, highlighted the importance of protecting the cultural components that make up Western society, or what he sometimes calls its "identity", the very reason behind its progress and stability. As Huntington sees it, among the most important components of the American culture, or identity, are language, religious values, especially Protestantism, the political and social values that determine the good from the bad and the institutions that reflect and express these values.[2] However, Francis Fukuyama believes that society's prosperity and renaissance depend on the social customs, values and morality prevailing in society, and these are "attributes that can be shaped only indirectly through conscious political action and must otherwise be nourished through an increased awareness and respect for culture".[3]

Natan Sharansky underlines the fact that the imagined struggle between freedom and identity among an increasing number of Western intellectuals is entirely unfounded. He believes that it is even wrong to believe in it since democracy cannot, on its own, fight against autocracy and terrorism. He adds that although democracy is well able to mobilise its human and material resources, "The enemy's will is strong because his identity is strong. And we must match his strength of purpose with strong identities of our own."[4] While addressing identity and its importance, Sharansky argues that when the spiritual leader of Al-Qaida, Osama Bin Laden, says, "We are going to win, because they love life and we love death," he is actually drawing attention to the power of identity. Sharansky writes: "This evil man is correct about one thing, identity is such a powerful force because it opens a world of meaning larger than physical and material life. It asserts that all of life is not merely immediate and that there are things for which life itself is worth sacrificing. By repudiating his words, the free world underestimates the power of its message at great peril."[5]

However, regardless whether we agree with Sharansky or not, what he is doing here is highlighting the fact that man's identity, with both its religious and secular dimensions, is a spiritual source and a self-renewing force in his effort to build the world and forge links with others, whether their outcome is positive or negative.

Second: The state of Arab-Islamic culture

There is no doubt that the cultures of societies, and whether they help them to advance or keep them back, is one of the most important subjects of current debate among research institutions and other international forums aimed at better understanding the factors of progress and backwardness. In recent years, an international project was launched in the United States of America, with the cooperation with experts from all over the world, aimed at better understanding the role of culture in the development of societies. This assessment of culture's role in development is based on a set of factors, the most important of which is finding out whether a given culture deepens society's ethical values that promote prosperity and stability. These values include: diligence, industriousness, discipline, desire to win, acquisition of knowledge, honesty, courage, education, productivity, love of competition, creativity, obedience to the law, fight against corruption, protection of rights, promotion of family ties and social harmony. When these factors were applied to 117 different countries, the results showed that Protestant values promoted modernity more that Catholic values did, and that Confucian values of China and other South-East Asian countries promoted growth and development more than Muslim values did. They also showed that the current condition of the world's Muslims puts them at the bottom of the list, in all categories, compared with Western and Confucian religions and values, although the researchers admit that the values currently prevailing among Muslims are not the same as those of the golden age of Islam.[6] We appreciate this outcome and largely agree with it, though we disagree with some of its details. Although it confirms the importance of culture as a determinant of development, it does indicate that the Muslim's current culture is an obstacle to development. For our part, although we do not deny the backward condition of the Muslim world today, we believe that the above statement is too general. It needs further discussion and clarity to avoid falling into the trap of judging Islam based on the Muslims' experience and current behaviour, which might or might not be in line with their true values. If these findings claim that the problem lies in Islam's original values, then we cannot agree with them because it means that we should abandon our values and adopt a different culture, something that no intelligent person would consider. On the other hand, if it means that the problem lies in the Muslim's behaviour and deviation from their true religious values, then it is incumbent on us to rediscover and reclaim these values. We should build our modern societies on this basis and, at the same time, benefit from the reservoir of knowledge and creativity gained by other cultures, provided it does not conflict with the spirit of our own values and without any embarrassment or shame, because this is what we have been ordered to do. Indeed, we have exported to the West much of the knowledge on which their contemporary civilisation was founded, as we will clarify later.

Third: Culture between theory and practice

To admit that the current culture of Arabs and Muslims is an obstacle to their renaissance and that it is not the same culture on which their golden age was built, as the above study shows, makes it imperative that we distinguish between the sources underpinning this genuine culture and those that underpin the culture of despotism by highlighting the following:

1. We should distinguish between the genuine Arab-Islamic culture, whose tenets are drawn from the Qur'an and the practice (*sunnah*) of the Prophet, and Arab-Islamic history which is rife with alternating periods of relative closeness and distance from this genuine source. Thus, while no one denies that the Arab and Muslim nation today is in a state of stagnation, if not backwardness, on more than one level, it is also true that at different historical periods this nation has reigned supreme as a pioneer and world leader, a fact many Westerners willingly admit. On the subject of culture as the delineator of development and renaissance, it might be useful to quote from Bernard Lewis' book *What Went Wrong?*. We should point out that by "wrong" Lewis refers to the deviation of Arab Muslim culture from its true path, i.e., the multi-faceted retreat it is witnessing today in the early twenty-first century. Lewis says that many wonder whether Islam is actually an impediment to the Muslims' progress and asks, "if Islam is an obstacle to freedom, to science, to economic development, how is it that Muslim society in the past was a pioneer in all three, and this when Muslims were much closer in time to the sources and inspiration of their faith than they are now?"[7] He says that the right question to ask here is not what has Islam done to the Muslims today, but rather what did the Muslims do to Islam to get them where they are today? Indeed, these words are those of an Orientalist whose sympathies are not necessarily with either Arabs or Muslims, a man who is aware of his reputation as a historian. Consequently, though we disagree with some of his interpretations and other positions, even with his intentions, the fact remains that he confirms what others have already said, that the genuine Islam was a pioneer among other world cultures. Historian Will Durant writes that while Europe was in a deep slumber in the Middle Ages, Arab-Islamic culture was living its golden age and contributing to humanity in a variety of fields, like the natural sciences, medicine and philosophy. For example, "Avicenna was the greatest writer on medicine,

al-Razi the greatest physician, al-Biruni the greatest geographer, al-Haitham the greatest optician, Jabir probably the greatest chemist, of the Middle Ages" and Ibn Rushd (Averroes) was the most renowned philosopher. Durant goes on to say that the Arabs were instrumental in the development of scientific research methods, and that Roger Bacon was under the influence of the Muslim Arabs of Spain when he carried these methods to Europe. In fact, the European scientists of the Renaissance stood on the shoulders of Arab giants while building the foundations of their modern culture.[8] Contemporary economic historian David Landes says that in the period between 750-1100 AD, the Arabs surpassed the Europeans in science and technology. He underlines the fact that Europe attained these sciences from its contacts with the Arab Muslims of Spain and that, during that same period, Islam was Europe's teacher.[9] Landes also states that when the Crusaders occupied Jerusalem in 1099, they wreaked destruction, raped and killed, but when Saladin restored it to Muslim hands in 1187, he took care of it and did not do what the Crusaders had done.[10]

What other culture, we wonder, can claim the same level of grandeur and development as that of the Arabs and Muslims when their culture was based on authentic religious sources rather than the dictates of autocracy in its various shapes and forms? Yes, the Muslim world is indeed backward today; however, we are certain that this backwardness is not due to our commitment to our faith and the desire to base our lives on its tenets, but to the fact that we have strayed from its authentic sources and the values of Arab Islamic culture. It is this Arab-Islamic culture that distinguishes us from other cultures, just like Landes' above example on the difference between Saladin and the Crusaders' behaviour in Jerusalem. Indeed, we might be equal to other cultures in terms of material and scientific achievements, and some cultures might do better than we are at certain times, yet we will always be ahead of all the others in terms of values and morality. History attests to that fact, especially when we are at the apex of our success, because humility is a virtue learned from our true leader and inspiration, Prophet Muhammad. Though he entered Mecca as a conqueror, he remained humble and merciful, telling the people of Mecca, "Go your way, for you are free", a civilised stance the likes of which has not been witnessed among either new or old cultures. Events in Iraq, Afghanistan, Gaza and Guantanamo Bay stand as at stark condemnations of today's occupation forces, or of the "great powers", and add a new dimension to what human beings are capable of when their behaviour does not conform to strict moral codes. The best testament to what we are saying here can be found in a speech by Prince Charles in 1996, in which he underlined the importance of culture in people's lives and the pioneering role that Arab-Islamic culture could play in humanity's renaissance. He said in this context, "There is much we can learn from that Islamic world view in this respect. There are many ways in which mutual understanding and appreciation can be built. Perhaps, for instance, we could begin by having more Muslim teachers in British schools, or by encouraging exchanges of teachers. Everywhere in the world people want to learn English. But in the West, in turn, we need to be taught by Islamic teachers how to learn with our hearts, as well as our heads."[11]

2. We would like to draw attention to the fact that neither the retreat of Arab-Islamic culture, nor the current crisis that Middle Eastern and Islamic countries, including the GCC, are going through, should prevent us from appreciating the depth of either Arab-Islamic culture or the value system that this religion has entrenched, despite all the backwardness and crises. Today, despite their undeniable shortcomings, some Islamist movements have achieved a number of successes to date, successes considered the cornerstone of our future renaissance. These include preserving the nation's identity, liberating occupied lands, uncovering the governments' efforts to use religion to advance their narrow personal agendas and safeguarding the nation's assets. Several objective researchers, who owe these movements no particular debt, attest to the validity of these preliminary achievements. Arab researcher Abdelilah Belkeziz states, in the context of assessing these movements and after warning them against monopolising religion like certain regimes do, "This critical remark does not change our belief, whether intellectual and moral, that the major role played by contemporary Islamic movements should be recognised. We should also recognise the numerous sacrifices they made in the social, political and cultural struggle against injustice, marginalisation and repression to safeguard the nation's identity from disintegration and liberate lands from occupation, contributions that brought them considerable political power in the past twenty years, and raised their profile and credibility among the public."[12]

3. Should we be content with this sense of pride in our past, and just stand there with our arms folded while security and development in the Arab and Islamic worlds decline at all levels? Of, course not. We want to be as precise as possible in diagnosing its present crisis, instead of allowing others to diagnose it and impose their findings on us, regardless whether their motives are good or bad. In light of the above situation, the logical question we need to ask ourselves here is not what did Islam do to us, as if all our ills could be blamed on our religion, but rather: in what manner did Arabs understand and apply this religion to end up bringing the rear of the human caravan? The short answer to this important question is that the root of the problem lies at the feet of our autocrats, and this

state of affairs that permeates every aspect of our lives has been going on since the end of the rightly guided caliphate. The autocrats began with politics and turned it into a hereditary system. They then shifted to the economy and made it a den of looting and theft, to education and made it a hub of ignorance, numbness and stagnation, and to the media and turned them into tools of publicity and distortion. Autocracy then dug its claws deep into the public administration and turned it into a deadly routine and a centre of endemic corruption. It assailed the family and turned it into a nucleus devoid of creativity, thought or distinction. One way or another, despotism permeated and destroyed every corner of this Arab nation, and became like a virus that attacks the body's defence system, allowing various diseases to attack the nation's heart and limbs, causing it to decline and its influence to wane. In doing this, they allowed its enemies to attack and incapacitate it, to better pillage, divide and destroy it later on. Here we are today, witness to an Arab world that does not enjoy the freedoms that others do, does not abide by the same rules, has neither the same awareness level nor the same living standards as others, and pays less attention to cleanliness, although it performs ablution before prayer five times a day. It is a world that has no appreciation for the value of time and could easily be up to one hour late for a personal appointment, despite knowing that prayer is a time-punctuated endeavour. It is a world that talks about responsibility towards one's country, family, institutions and religion, but its behaviour says otherwise. It talks much about trustworthiness, honesty and doing one's best but leaves room for deception, profiteering, abuse of power and a lack of diligence in the workplace. Here is the Arab world today, with over 350 million Arabs, yet a marginal European country like Spain manages a higher economic output in one year than the Arab countries combined. If we deduct the oil revenues from the gross domestic product, the Arabs' output would be half that of Spain's. In the same vein, although the population rate in the Arab world as a whole is close to that of the United States of America, our economic activity is less than 10 per cent of theirs. Serious personal ambition and distinction are the stuff of dreams, trustworthiness is a wasted asset gifted from the rulers to workers, and constructive criticism is lost between cowardice and subservience, on the one hand, and silliness and stupidity on the other, and the same can be said about all the lofty values that our religion has taught us. These are the values on which our forefathers have built their culture, and thanks to which many modern countries' achievements were made possible. They include respect for specialisation, diligence at work, respect for the rights of others and for the rule of law, flexibility in dealing with others and benefitting from their experience.[13] Of course, although these are the dominant patterns of behaviour in the Arab world, including the Gulf region, it does not mean that this region is devoid of individuals whose behaviour is a model for others to emulate; unfortunately, however, they have very little influence on society. The fact that we are taking the time to reflect on these tangential issues is proof of our belief that such behaviour is an indication of how ready Arab society is for a renaissance. We also want to show the extent of the disaster wrought by centuries of autocratic rule and subjugation, a system that led the people to where they are at today.

Fourth: Culture between stability and flexibility

If we understand that the problem is within us, rather than our religion, and if it becomes obvious that autocracy and the ensuing distortion and disfigurement of our culture was this nation's first deviation, not to mention the destruction of successive generations, the first step on our long journey towards a renaissance should be a return to our authentic cultural sources. We should re-examine all aspects of this culture, whether political, economic, literary, poetic, historical, or local and international relations, even those related to jurisprudence, and purify them from centuries of autocracy to serve as the solid basis of our future renaissance. We are certain that, just as it did in the past, this examination, or re-examination, and the ensuing purification of our accumulated traditions coupled with a return to the authentic sources of our religion, will form the basis of our future renaissance. If this actually happens, we will realise that much of what the autocratic culture has caused, in terms of division and disagreements in society, will no longer be there, and that the chasm between us and several manmade elements of the modern renaissance is actually the logical basis for them. We will realise as well that the legal tenets and basic principles we hold onto, and of which we constantly reminded, were and still are the safety valve against intellectual extremism, or forced extremism, as is clear from our current culture's shortcomings and increasing failures at all levels. These tenets are akin to the lines on a football field meant to prevent the players from straying from the main objective of scoring goals; since overstepping these lines becomes a costly endeavour, the player can use his mental and physical faculties to stay within them and secure victory for his team. We could say the same about the legal religious tenets whose role is to prevent people from overstepping their boundaries, whether on a whim, out of short-sightedness, for lack of experience or for any other momentary reason. Within the boundaries of these tenets, people could use their mind and abilities to understand this universe and its laws, use them for their benefit as they create and build as God has ordered: "He brought you into being from the earth, and made you dwell in it."[14]

Many daily life experiences emphasise the importance of these tenets. In the domain of governance, for example, we believe that Islam does not specify a particular system of government, or prescribe a particular way of electing the ruler. What it does do, however, is draw a set of general principles, centring round justice, equality and consultation, and leaves the manner of their implementation to man's judgement based on his circumstances, environment and the challenges he faces.[15] This is where the miraculous genius of this religion lies; it establishes a set of flexible tenets that do lend themselves to rigidity, yet leaves a wide enough space for creativity, invention and keeping up with the modern ways of life, while providing, at the same time, protection against extremes and extremism, of all kinds. What further confirms this fact are the numerous ways in which the Muslims elected the four rightly guided caliphs. Abu Bakr was nominated by Umar and then elected by the Muslims. On his deathbed, Umar nominated six companions of the Prophet with his son Abdullah as the seventh to break any eventual tie, yet prevented him from being a candidate. The group of companions chose Uthman and the Muslims approved their choice. After Uthman's death, a group of them nominated Ali who then won the allegiance of the majority of Muslims.[16] All the above election methods have national consensus at their core, without the slightest hint of heredity or specifying a particular formula to elect the caliph. The Muslims could well decide one day that one of the man-made formulas is more appropriate for this day and age, and adopt it; this does not mean that they deviated from the spirit of their religion, since the rightly guided caliphs would remain their main example as far as their firm and constant morality, beliefs, faith and practices are concerned. Other modes of behaviour imposed on the Muslims by a particular set of circumstances and their simple way of life, are no longer binding on subsequent generations. They might even conflict with the spirit of their religion because Muslim societies could remain stuck at the level of old simple formulas that were meant for an entirely differ- ent set of circumstances. If the first rightly guided caliph was elected in a small gathering place (known as the Saqifah Bani Sa'idah) because the Muslims were few in number, it does not mean that the nation should hesitate to choose a more modern method better suited for the large numbers that go to the polls today.

Flexibility within the context of constancy is not limited to governance in Islam, but applies to life's other aspects, as well. For example, there are constants in the economy like almsgiving and prohibiting usury, gambling, the production of harmful goods and services, and immoral practices including monopolies, cheating, injustice and other practices prohibited on account of their negative impact on the exploitation and fair distribution of resources. Once it abides by these constant tenets, a Muslim society could then work at developing its modern financial and administrative institutions in a manner that best serves its needs and interests. It could do this without being required to reproduce any of the old Muslim financial and administrative institutions, unless they are still of benefit today. What applies to politics and the economy applies to all other domains; there are constants and flexibilities relative to the family, the penal code, international relations and the treatment of minorities, among others. They are designed to keep Muslim society in a state of perpetual forward movement and constant change and creativity, and allow it to keep up with novelties without falling by the wayside or pursuing a path that could eventually lead to its decline, dislocation and weakness. The circle of constants is very limited, just as the lines of a football field are limited compared to the size of the overall field. In short, what should be emphasised here is that nothing in Islam will conflict with modern democracy, as long as we see it as an instrument for managing governance that fosters an environment of accountability and oversight, guarantees the freedom of the press, protects the judiciary's independence and ensures freedom of expression and a method of exercising power. However, as many contemporary religious scholars indicate, none of these principles should in any way conflict with the text and spirit of the Qur'an or the *sunnah*, or detract from the general intent of the *shar'ia*.[17] It is apt to highlight here the opinion of Gulf researcher Ali Khalifa al-Kawari expressed in the course of a debate on Islam's compatibility with democracy. Al Kawari said, "What is being said about the conflict between Islam and democracy emanates, in my opinion, neither from the core of Islam, nor democracy. It emanates either from an exclusive liberal view that sees democracy as a mechanism particular to the liberal doctrine and consistent with its values and references. Or it emanates from an extremist religious interpretation that confuses elements integral to Islam, namely the revelations and Islamic jurisprudence, with practices that reflect human thought and should be understood in their proper context, historical period and level of human knowledge at that particular time."[18]

The insistence on the lack of conflict between Islam and democracy, as a governance system, not only encourages a rapprochement between different reformist currents in the Gulf, it refutes the power pundits' theory that democracy is incompatible with *shar'ia*.[19] As for judging different patterns of behaviour based on their compatibility or incompatibility with Islam's legal tenets, we should be careful to avoid going to extremes or extremism. We should instead rely on clear legal and credible mechanisms to prevent the issue from becoming a cause for dissent and division, at a time when these societies badly need more national unity and solidarity. We should remember, in this context, that what we are talking about here is an Islamic society, rather than a theocracy governed by religious leaders, like Iran or the Vatican.

This is why we are certain that when the level of freedom allows the establishment of schools, universities, banks, media outlets and other modern institutions, within the framework of Islamic moral and doctrinal codes, the world will then judge for itself these institutions' worthiness and their ability to achieve progress, harmony and stability in a modern society. We are not speaking here about past experience but the present day. Despite all the obstacles, many Islamic economic institutions have proved more efficient, fair, stable, and more able to contribute to economic development than those that rely on usury and betting. It is the same with academic institutions, as evidenced by a number of schools in Britain whose academic achievement levels are superior to others with different underlying beliefs. Even at the government level, we have the example of Turkey's Justice and Development Party whose success, especially in the economic field, surpasses the achievements of all other parties combined since independence. We should not forget present efforts by many Islamic charitable societies that have come to the aid of the poor all over the world, and managed to become a partner in development and solidarity, so much so that they became targets in recent years. Let us also not forget the spirit of resistance born of this religion that was able to score a number of successes that took the enemy by surprise in Palestine, Lebanon, Iraq and Afghanistan. In short, the period of slumber that autocracy has imposed on us, and the concomitant obliteration of this Godly path, has lasted far too long; it is hard to believe that our culture today is the same Islamic culture whose glorious past, and few contemporary bright spots, we depict in this book. Is it time, therefore, to remove the residue that autocracy has heaped on our authentic Islamic culture in order to build our current lives on solid bases, or should we continue to submit to the waves of Westernisation, and fight everything related to our cultural fundamentals like our autocratic governments have recently done under foreign pressure, even if at varying degrees? We hope that the Arab Spring, which the Arab people have been living through since 2011, will be a turning point that corrects the track of these governments for the better.

CHAPTER THREE

The Elites

Just as autocracy has obliterated and distorted Arab Islamic culture, it has marginalised the social elite including, among others, the religious scholars, business people, intellectuals, managers and various professionals. In order to grasp the nature of this marginalisation and the reasons behind it, it is necessary to compare the relationship between the rulers and people in the Gulf, before and after the discovery of oil. This will help us to shed light on the circumstances that led to the marginalisation of different social elements in the Gulf.

First: Before the discovery of oil

Prior to the discovery of oil, the social composition of Gulf societies included social, economic and professional elements akin to what we know today as civil society, but much simpler in nature. Alongside the ruler, the merchant class and the religious scholars (*ulama*) enjoyed a level of influence in society, whereby the ruler depended on various social sectors in economic and security matters. This was at a time when the main sources of revenue were pearl fishing and its related activities like shipbuilding, and trade in agricultural products, such as dates and livestock in desert areas.[1] The pearl merchant class, or what we know today as the business class, was independent of the ruler to such an extent that some of these merchants had their own tribunals for conflicts associated with pearl fishing.[2] The pearl trade actually refers to an entire industry that included the ships' captains, divers, ship crews, and the buyers of these pearls who sold them to Indian or other merchants in return for foreign currency, which they then used to buy products from abroad.[3] Pearl fishing also contributed to the shipbuilding industry, whose products like ropes and sails were imported from Africa.[4] British historian John Lorimer estimates that in 1980 the income of the ruler of Abu Dhabi, Zayid bin Khalifah, also known as Zayid I, was around £6711 from various sources. The pearl trade accounted for 82 per cent of it, while the rest came from taxes on dates from the Liwa and Burimi oases, and from taxes the Sultan of Muscat paid Zayid I in return for preventing tribes from the al-Dhahira region from attacking his borders.[5] The income of Dubai's ruler was estimated at £4569, and those of Sharjah and Umm al-Quwain's rulers at £2227 and £1285, respectively. The size of their incomes was linked directly to the number of commercial diving ships owned by each emirate, with the largest part of this income going to cover the expenses of the rulers' family and guards. The rulers maintained neither administrative or judicial institutions nor an army, and did not have security and intelligence services to spy on their people, meaning that their responsibilities were very limited.[6] Jill Crystal, a researcher on Gulf affairs, says that the situation in other Gulf countries was no different from the coastal emirates. In Kuwait and Qatar, political life was subject to the alliance between the merchants and the emirs because the former were the link between the ruler and the funds he needed and, prior to the discovery of oil, this money came from the sea, i.e., from the pearl trade. The merchant class got the money from the divers and gave it to the rulers in the form of customs duties, taxes on diving ships or personal loans, and held sway in society thanks to marriages with members of the ruling families.[7] According to Saudi researcher Madawi al-Rasheed, Ibn Saud's income prior to the discovery of oil was made up of grants from the British government, income from the annual pilgrimage (*hajj*), alms (*zakat*) money collected by various regional princes and shaikhs, and the taxes imposed on the Hijaz. Ibn Saud used to force his country's merchant class to cover many of his expenses, including the war against the Saudi Muslim Brotherhood in 1927, and some of these merchants even represented the Saudi Kingdom abroad.[8] Likewise, most of the Bahraini ruling family's income came from pearls, trade and dates.[9] The economic power of the merchants prior to the discovery of oil was used often for political ends and, as described in the chapter on hereditary systems, the merchant class joined the call for political reform. After the discovery of oil, the relative equilibrium between the governments and the merchant class prevailing in the region prior to the discovery of oil turned into attempts by the governments to contain the merchants' power, though the level of this containment differed from one country to the other.

In the case of the *ulama*, the fact that these were Islamic societies gave them an influential position in the country, although the importance of the role they played or the level of their religious acumen and ethnic backgrounds differed from one country to another. Islam was a way of life for the region's people rather than just a matter of civil status. Hence, they rejected usury, and even the system based on which the pearl divers divided the cost of preparing the ships and distributing the profits relied on agreed-upon percentages and was meant to avoid usury. Some Western researchers saw this as a kind of class-alignment system when in fact it was not that but a pattern of behaviour based on these individuals' faith.[10] This was also the case when the *ulama* were needed to teach in Qur'anic schools or help manage family relationships, and so on. The *ulama* class, however, played a more important role in Saudi Arabia where the state was founded on an alliance between a religious leader, Shaikh Muhammad bin Abdul Wahab, and a political leader, Muhammad Ibn Saud, a situation that gave the *ulama* a prominent position in the country early on.[11] Their role in Saudi Arabia was not limited to the religious domain, that is, bestowing religious legitimacy on the Saudi ruler; many *ulama* had played a role in the wars that led to the creation of what we know today as the Kingdom of Saudi Arabia. In other words, they played a jihadist role in the Kingdom, if we can use this term to describe the wars of expansion that Ibn Saud waged in order to establish the Kingdom, in 1932.[12] After the discovery of oil, however, the *ulama*'s fate was not all that different from that of the merchants. When Faisal Bin Abdul Aziz assumed power, the Saudi government reduced the *ulama*'s role and made the position of the chief expert in Islamic law (*mufti*) part of the executive authority which is led by the King's leadership. Thus, in a country founded on Islamic legitimacy, the *ulama* could no longer rely on their independence to bolster their credibility. We will revisit this subject later in the book.

Second: After the discovery of oil

The discovery of oil in the Gulf led to a fundamental shift in the governments' relationship with their people. The governments saw their oil revenue, and the foreign protection that came with it, as an opportunity to extricate themselves from commitments made to the people. The balance of power started shifting in their favour, and the merchant class, the *ulama* and other sectors of civil society, like the professionals and intellectuals, became more like the employees of governments that used their oil revenues to coax them into professing loyalty to them and accepting their autocratic rule and warned them against displaying any opposition.[13] The governments also used all means available to control the people's assets, including the institutionalisation of the one-family rule system, i.e., turning their families into institutions whereby the main members secure the best positions in the state administration, coupled with an agreement among them on some form of hereditary succession. This institutionalisation could be construed as a move to concentrate power and decision-making in the ruling family's hands, in other words, ensuring that strategic decisions are the exclusive domain of ruling family, albeit a little less exclusionary in Kuwait.[14] Jill Crystal says that these families were once like all other families in the Gulf, with their members performing a number of administrative and social functions whenever Britain needed people to represent it locally. Gradually, however, they managed to garner a certain level of political influence, which grew exponentially after the discovery of oil and their successful attempt to put their hands on it, with help from the British. They began merging their political and economic power, distinguishing themselves thus from the rest of society and, according to Crystal, began withdrawing funds straight from the state budget and securing prime positions in the state administration. Eventually, their influence spread to the private economic sector, giving them the sense of being above society and the law.[15] Not satisfied with simply institutionalising themselves in power, i.e., setting themselves apart as separate entities, these families scrambled to protect their power by moving against civil society and weakening its position, through alternative enticements and scare tactics. They granted the merchants commercial agencies and allowed them to bid on big projects, with help from the countries' astronomical oil revenue, albeit in partnership with certain members of the ruling families.[16] This meant that this class was no longer independent like they were in the days of the pearl trade because the ruling families determined most of their economic activities in the post oil era. The latter granted commercial licences, called for bids on construction projects and financed infrastructure projects, and even the nature of the merchant class differed from one state to another after the discovery of oil.

In Kuwait, the merchant class was able to maintain some of the political acumen and dwindling influence of the pre-oil period, albeit under different circumstances and balance of power.[17] In Bahrain, Oman, the United Arab Emirates (UAE), Qatar and Saudi Arabia, the government succeeded in establishing a new merchant class, and took advantage of ethnic, sectarian and regional disagreements to integrate it into the official power structure.[18] As a result, many members of this new merchant class became enmeshed in relationships rife with corruption, patronage and self-serving interest, with their country's political and administrative leaderships. Thus, whereas in the past, the merchant class earned its income by financing and attending to different stages of the pearl industry, once the main reason behind the flourishing economies of the Gulf States, today it collaborates with people in power at the expense of the majority of the population. One of the ways this new relationship between ruler and merchant works is, for example, when a state official awards a government project, not to the most capable businessman who will execute the job in the most efficient manner and with the shortest delays possible, but to the one who gives him a commission. This means that this official, who might very well be a ruling family member or someone close to it, becomes at the same time a public sector employee and a private sector businessman. However, although a give and take relationship between the government and the private sector is both important and healthy, it should not develop to the point of mutual personal interests between the two, at the expense of society as a whole, because this will prevent the private sector, the political system and administrative institutions from further development.[19] Not only will such a relationship cause the entire development process to fail, it will turn it into theft of the country's assets by a handful of citizens, possibly with the involvement of outside parties. This is what sources say has been happening, to varying degrees, in the Gulf since the beginning of the oil boom in the 1970s.[20] The *ulama,* whose independence from the rulers once shielded the public from the latter's injustice as they moved to contain the merchant class, did not escape unscathed, either. Let us give a single example of that, despite the fact that the issue of the *ulama*'s containment and use of their religious edicts (*fatwas*) for political ends is not new at all. When the *mufti* of Saudi Arabia, Shaikh Muhammad bin Ibrahim bin Abdul Latif, an independent man who was not an employee of the Saudi government, passed away in 1969, his post remained vacant for almost a quarter of a century because King Faisal did not want a successor as independent as he was, a fact confirmed by later events.[21] In 1970, King Faisal established the Ministry of Justice and appointed one of the *ulama* as its head, which meant that the *mufti* and his ministry were now answerable to the prime minister who is usually a member of the royal family. From then on, the *fatwas* of the Saudi *ulama* were no longer separate from those of the political authority, meaning that the *mufti*'s prerogatives no longer involved any degree of independence. Later in 1971, the King established a seventeen-member Ulama Council, which, in the opinion of a Western researcher, signalled the death knell of the El-Shaikh era in Saudi history. The reason behind the move is the fact that a political-religious alliance, in which Shaikh Muhammad bin Abdul Wahab represented the religious side of the equation, i.e., the religious legitimacy of the regime, lies at the foundation of the Saudi State.[22] Subsequent events, including stationing American forces in Saudi Arabia after the occupation of Kuwait, the negotiations with Israel, the war on Iraq and events in Lebanon and Gaza, confirmed that the *ulama* in Saudi Arabia were not independent any more. It also confirmed that they were no longer a beacon of light guiding future generations, or a haven for a nation tossed around by the raging waves of globalisation. Not only did the *ulama*'s crisis end with the nationalisation of *fatwas*, it went beyond it to the actual nationalisation of the mosques and religious endowments, once a mainstay of the faith and educator of youth. People's everyday life was put in jeopardy, and students had no choice but to turn to the official education system or official sources of financing for help, which is how a new crop of the king's *ulama,* or his government's *ulama*, came to graduate and work among us.

With the merchants and *ulama* contained, it was the intellectuals' turn to fall into the trap set for them by an over-bloated state with vast oil revenues. Most employment opportunities in these countries were now in the public sector and its various institutions, especially given its higher salary scale, better insurance schemes and easier work conditions, compared with the private sector. The acquiescence of other sectors of society was bought through the provision of health and education services, and by subsidising a number of basic goods and services, such as fuel, telephones and food products.[23] Over and above establishing the ruling families as entities independent from the rest of society, containing the merchants, *ulamas* and intellectuals' role, and taking advantage of the people's necessities, like food and shelter, the region's governments resorted to yet a third option as a means of weakening civil society. They extended their authority over several civil society institutions, including social clubs, charitable organisations and unions, restricted their activities to domains that do not conflict with their policies, and prevented them from voicing their problems or calling for rights. Social clubs became a means of public entertainment to keep the people's attention away from their problems and other serious issues, with large sums devoted to this endeavour and made conditional upon a member of the ruling family sitting at the head of these clubs' administration boards, a practice that has become the norm in recent years.[24] Charitable organisations that once acted as a channel for almsgiving and other donations to the less fortunate in the Arab and Islamic worlds became the object of official control in the wake of 11 September 2001. This was done, naturally, upon orders from the United States which, wittingly or unwittingly, linked charitable acts to terrorism. In fact, the Gulf's governments took advantage of America's arrogance to set their sights on yet another civil society sector, either by turning these charitable organisations into an arm of the state, just like the merchants, *ulama* and intellectuals before them, or by restricting their activities to the point of preventing them from doing serious work. In October 2004, the Saudi government dissolved the Al-Haramain Islamic Foundation, the largest charitable organisation in the Kingdom, with the ability to collect more than $40 million a year,[25] and a number of Gulf countries, including the UAE, followed suit. All this happened despite the fact that several Western legal authorities, especially in the United States, have recently indicated that most of the accusations levelled in the West against Islamic charitable organisations proved to be unfounded. Moreover, a number of lawyers in the United States have confirmed that this onslaught on Islamic charitable activities is politically motivated,[26] which again proves that decision-making in the GCC is not an independent process since, by doing so, these governments are simply making things worse for themselves. These charitable activities were once among the most worthy hallmarks of civil society in the Gulf, bestowing on their governments a credibility, repute and recognition by the world's nations they had never even dreamt of. Yet, here they are destroying all this with the stroke of a pen, upon a mere signal from the West, without a shred of evidence.

Finally, not satisfied with the above measures to cut the elite's role down to size, the Gulf governments went after all those who dared oppose these policies using the different means at their disposal. They began by threatening to fire them from their jobs, freeze them in their positions or stop their promotions, even investigate, detain, imprison and torture them, which is what happened to a number of reformers in Saudi Arabia and elsewhere in recent years. For example, in the 1970s when the opposition to the Bahraini government escalated,[27] a number of university professors and state employees were fired from their jobs, and in 1994, the Omani security forces detained around 200 people and accused them of conspiring against the regime, only to discover later on that most had nothing to do with the attempted coup.[28] In 2003, a group of Saudis called for reform of the political system and in March 2004, Saudi Interior Minister Nayef bin Abdul Aziz had them arrested and sentenced to prison terms of seven to nine years.[29] Likewise, several UAE sources confirmed to this author that thousands of the country's citizens were denied employment because either they or some of their relatives were devout Muslims. This happened at a time when the country is flooded with a sea of foreign workers with no link whatsoever to the region's people, except the pursuit of profit, sometimes very quick profit.

Third: The responsibility of the elites

There is no doubt, therefore, that the ruling families of the Gulf took advantage of the circumstances, provided by their vast oil revenues, to sideline different elites. However, they would not have succeeded in their quest, or kept pursuing that track, had these elites been competent, had a clear vision, were able to cooperate, and had a modicum of respect for the opinions of others and patience necessary.[30] It might be difficult to pass a collective judgement on all the elites in the GCC, especially if we bear in mind that the repression that the elite has to put up with in Saudi Arabia is more acute than in Kuwait, although size of the Saudi population is bigger than those of the UAE and Qatar. Although, in one way or another, these variables have an impact on the level of these elites' influence on society, this should not blind us to the fact that there is a set of common characteristics among them. These are the very characteristics that limit their ability to play an effective role in their societies or, according to Abdelilah Belkeziz, "in shielding political life from trouble and providing it with the requirements of stability".[31] Chief among these interconnected characteristics is, in our opinion, the absence of clear vision, disunity, loss of independence, marginalising the other and disinterest in the people, as we shall see below.

1. Absent vision and programmes

Elites in the Gulf lack clear vision and practical programmes that can inspire and mobilise society, and influence government policies. Their propositions are general, emotional and fanciful, thus deemed by most as unrealistic and inapplicable, given the autocratic and authoritarian nature of the regimes in power. Although many of the Gulf's intellectuals talk about freedom and the need to oppose despotism in all its forms, they have proved incompetent so far in the face of the Gulf governments' monopoly of both money and decision-making. They proved incapable of coming up with a political programme that could be an alternative to the hereditary systems currently in power, a programme that transcends all the general talk about consultation (*shura*) as a preferred system, or democracy and its universality. In this respect, Saudi researcher Madawi Al-Rasheed indicates that some Saudi *ulama*, or Wahhabi *ulama* as she calls them, would rather leave political matters to the government and focus on issues like the doctrine of right and wrong, and the doctrine of faith. As a result, they do not provide satisfactory answers to more basic and simple issues, like the means of selecting the ruler and holding him accountable, or Islam's opinion on hereditary succession, but continue to repeat old and general clichés that fail to provide convincing answers for this day and age.[32] Ismail al-Shatti, a member of the Kuwaiti National Assembly, says that Arab movements for change, including the Islamist movements, do not have political programmes but a series of slogans, adding that only the Marxists have such a programme, albeit an imported one.[33] Addressing the issue of Saudi elites, Saudi researcher Muhammad bin Sunitan reiterates the same view on the elites' lack of reformist vision, and says, "As to the intellectuals themselves, the same scene replays itself again: the repetition of statements that have already been said in other Arab or liberal societies, without adding anything new or creative. Thus, the tribal institution did not work diligently at finding solutions to current and future issues, nor did the intelligentsia come up with specific visions or delineate paths towards clear objectives."[34]

2. Subservience to the regime

Elites in the gulf are clearly subservient to the central authority, and many of their members are social climbers and profit mongers, ready to side with the governments against other elites. The regimes took advantage of these tendencies to divide and weaken these elites, and sometimes used the Islamists to attack the nationalists and, at others, used the nationalists and liberals to fight the Islamists. Gulf researcher Usama 'Abd al-Rahman describes the intellectuals' dependency, which makes them seem more royalist than the King, saying, "What is noteworthy is that very few among the hordes of intellectuals have remained true to their word and maintained their credibility. The majority are apologists who turn a blind eye to what is right, under the pretence that the prevailing climate is too unfavourable, and the deterrent too strong. At the same time, they vie against each other to enhance the image of the regime, to such an extent that it sometimes appears as if they are well ahead of the government's own efforts in that direction, even to the detriment of their own image and role."[35]

The *ulama*'s subservience to the regime is, in our opinion, the most dangerous form of subservience because this nation's history has repeatedly highlighted the pioneering role they could play in fighting for justice, and supporting its victims to the end of days. The *ulama* are the heirs to the prophets and should fear God above all others because He gave them superior knowledge based on the Qur'anic verse "Those of His servants only who are possessed of knowledge fear Allah; surely Allah is Mighty, Forgiving."[36] Today's *ulama* are akin to government mouthpieces, issuing favourable *fatwas* and justifying its policies, even those that conflict with the vital interests of the nation. They issue *fatwas* that justify a variety of repressive policies, the theft of public funds, fighting the forces of change and reform, legislating war and peace with Israel and accepting the presence of foreign forces in the Arabian Peninsula, as did a number of Saudi *ulama* in the 1990s, according to Madawi al-Rasheed.[37] Bin Snaitan describes this mutually beneficial relationship between the regime and the *ulama* that detracts from the latter's credibility: "This means that there is an interest-based relationship between the monarchy and the tribal institution. The latter gives the former the legitimacy it needs, thanks to its credibility among the public, and the former empowers and contains the latter, at the same time. It is as if the path that links the tribal institution to the royal family requires the former's total absorption into the body of the state. Not only could this render this relationship potentially unstable, in the eyes of certain sectors of the population, mainly the educated class and those who do not view this relationship with disfavour, it also turns the tribal institution into apologists for the regime."[38]

3.   Disunity

Differences are natural and tend to increase in countries that do not have mechanisms to check them, and turn them into a force for good, like in the developing countries which include the Arab and Gulf countries. The elites should have been aware of the chaos and instability that could ensue from the absence of safety measures, but they were not; their gatherings and debates have become zero sum games whereby a gain for one side is necessarily a loss for the other. Disunity thus became the order of the day for elites in the Gulf, just as it is for other Arab elites, and all strategic thinking that places the whole above the partial, and allows people to see the forest from the trees, disappeared altogether. This turned their debates into a dialogue of the deaf that aims solely at scoring points, delivering speeches and letting off steam. Therefore, instead of solving problems, this only deepened the divide between different elites, and forced some of them to seek the backing of more powerful parties, such as the regime and sometimes even outside parties. The best way to illustrate this deep divide and the elite's inability to forge common ground is to quote Balqaziz on the crises afflicting the Arab political opposition. He says in this context, "... we cannot understand the phenomenon of savage political violence in Arab countries like Algeria and Egypt, or the phenomenon of using religion to advance political agendas and activism, without linking them to the outcome of the current regimes' efforts to politically engineer this confiscated and monopolised space."[39] Munir Shafiq responded to this saying, "The absence of Islam from politics is the exception that prevailed on the Arab scene for a brief period of time. It is its return that should rather be seen as the norm, and what is natural and usual."[40]

However, regardless of our position vis-à-vis these two opinions and their proponents, both of whom we respect and have learned a lot from, we wonder about the ability to close the wide chasm between the elites. We should underline here that there are many reasons why the Arab elites (including those in the Gulf) were unable to manage their disagreements. These reasons include their level of knowledge, preconceived ideas that do not stand up to objective scrutiny, lack of serious intent behind calls for reform meaning they see these dialogues as mere venues for venting anger and/or making an appearance, the tendency to work in secret, and the rigid and controlling mentality that ensues from that. There is no doubt that the elites' fall into the trap set for them by the government that plays on regional, tribal and sectarian differences in each country to keep these differences alive has exacerbated these disagreements even further. We have even heard some claims, after the liberation of Kuwait, that the Kuwaiti elite has its own particular distinction, and should therefore not build bridges to other Gulf elites whose systems are less participatory than Kuwait's. Statements like these have been debunked especially when it became clear that the saying "it will happen when hell freezes over" applies to the Kuwaiti elite as well. It means that the Kuwaiti experiment will remain under threat of extinction, or at least stagnation, as long as the Kuwaiti elites do not forge close ties with other elites in the Gulf and the wider Arab world, to ensure the minimum required level of development and security in the region. Those wishing to learn a lesson would do well to learn this one, which vividly draws on the experience of the past three eras.

4. Eliminating the other

The elites' failure to manage their disagreements and forge common ground in the face of autocratic regimes has led to attempts to eliminate one another. The phenomenon starts by attempts at intellectual elimination, at meetings and conferences, then turns into attempts at political elimination, which eventually leads to bloody confrontations from which no one benefits except the autocratic regimes that these elites seek to change or, at least, reform. Here are some examples. With the recent growth of the Islamic movements' popularity in the Arab world and the Gulf, and their different interpretation of democracy from that of others, some have claimed that the Islamists cannot be integrated in a democratic system. These claims allege that if Islamists come to power they will never leave and will nourish the spirit of confrontation between Islamists and other movements. On the other hand, we see certain Islamists appointing themselves as arbiters of members of other movements, as if Islam were their exclusive domain. However, our appreciation and respect for all movements notwithstanding , we believe that this kind of dialogue, with its generalities, preconceived value judgements and weak excuses, is not conducive to genuine dialogue and rapprochement. Rather, it is provocative and leads to clashes among the elites, even if unintentionally. Fawwaz Gerges is correct when he says that "Unfortunately Arab political literature is dominated by the tendency towards violent verbal confrontation, and acute ideological rejection of the other's opinion. This happens despite the issue's sensitivity and importance that require vision, calm reflection, unequivocal recognition of the other's freedom of expression and the need to engage him critically and constructively instead of accusing him of treason and apostasy, or concocting false accusations against him."[41]

More ominous than this intellectual elimination, or perhaps as the result of it, is the political elimination that leads to bloody confrontations, at varying levels of intensity, as we saw happen in Tunisia, Algeria and the Palestinian territories. In the latter case, Hamas' success in the legislative elections, and its bid to form the government, had displeased Abu Mazen and his supporters in the region, prompting them to concoct an elimination plan against the movement. It started with the siege of Gaza and ended with the Israeli onslaught on that city, by way of the Dayton Plan that Hamas successfully thwarted, details of which were published in the American magazine *Vanity Fair*. Despite all the death and destruction wrought by this war, which the Goldstone Report described as a war crime, the government in Ramallah calmly sat and watched, without any reaction, all because of its political disagreements with Hamas. The latter had rejected the Ramallah government's agenda, which relies on negotiations as the only strategic option in dealing with Israel, on the premise that any negotiations not supported by the option of resistance will neither bear fruit nor achieve peace with an enemy who only knows the language of force. The Palestinian National Authority (PNA) went as far as to withdraw the Goldstone Report from the International Investigation Committee charged with examining it. It is surprising to see a Palestinian leadership negotiating with the very state that colonises its entire territory, or almost, yet, at the same time, attempting to weaken the opposition instead of using it to put pressure on the enemy in view of regaining the largest part possible of its usurped territory. With the arrival of the Arab Spring, events repeated themselves after the election of Morsi as president in 2012. This was an Egypt on the road to the militarisation of politics because of the short-sightedness of all the elites and their failure to set a threshold for participation and to work towards this to expand the circle of consensus. The Tunisian experience may be the high point of what has taken place since the Arab Spring until now as regards the cooperation of the Tunisian elites. This experience was one that proved there was a large participation base and that consensus was the only way to build common ground.

5. Ignoring the people

Despite singing the praises of the ordinary public and saying that their interest inspires everything they do, it is obvious that the elites often belittle the people, especially when they want to cajole those in power and get into their good books, or when the people express different opinions to theirs. Some elites justify the rulers' autocratic policies on the premise that the people are not mature enough yet to exercise their political rights, that the elections could bring extremist elements to power, or that the current development stage requires a firm hand at the top. The despots hear all this with glee and a little dash of scorn for these intellectuals. Everyone knows now that these and other justifications, that only serve to exacerbate autocracy and belittle the people's importance, have wrought nothing for the Arabs but more dependency, instability and disregard for the Palestinians' rights.[42] Although in saying that we are not excusing the people's shortcomings and negativity, even their demagoguery sometimes, we believe that among the elites' main responsibilities is raising the level of the people's understanding and teaching them how to make the right choices by providing them with specific information and honest analyses and being patient. The more skilled the citizen is in exercising his rights, the better he will vote, the stronger his call for his rights will be, and the more chance he has of electing the leader who will best reflect his hopes and aspirations. Therefore, the elite's role does not simply consist of sitting on one's high horse and passing judgement on others. Rather, it entails lowering oneself to the people's level and helping them improve themselves in terms of awareness and behaviour, until such day when participation become a reality, if it does not exist already, or becomes genuine and effective, if it exists but still needs to mature. This way, the roles of both the elites and the public will expand, and the circle of autocracy and corruption will narrow down and so on. The more the public is aware of and follows the example of people whose deeds match their words, and are ready to sacrifice for their principles, the faster the pace of change will become.[43] Despite all the above issues plaguing people in the Gulf and the Arab world, the outlook is not all that bleak; efforts by a group of citizens, concerned about the nation's security, prosperity and unity, to forge a rapprochement between the Islamist and nationalist currents is a candle beginning to light the path ahead. Dr Khair-Eddin Hassib, director of the Centre for Arab Unity Studies, is correct in his assertion that the nationalist and Islamist currents are like "two peas in a pod". He says, "What further reinforces this realisation are the recent initiatives by enlightened nationalist and Islamist groups that reject the fabricated clash between Arabism and Islam, and highlight the fact that Islam is a major cultural and spiritual component of the Arab nationalist movement. This grants Islam a prominent position in the lives of all Arabs, even non-Muslims, since they see in it a reflection of a civilisation, culture and history of which they can be proud. These groups also insist that the Qur'an's language, the Prophet's identity and most of the early religious pioneers have given both Arabism and the Arabic language a special prominence in lives of Muslims, even the non-Arabs among them. It is especially so since all the wars that the Arabs have waged against the invaders were waged on behalf of all the Muslims, and since by defending the holy sites they were defending the holy sites of an entire religious community (*ummah*), not to mention the role of both the Arabs and Muslims in weaving this nation's cultural fabric."[44]

Arab sociologist Halim Barakat provides an accurate description of the Arab intellectual's situation as being akin to someone "under occupation". He clarifies this saying, "The Arab world has not just one, but many samples of thought; there are those who do not care much and sing the praises of beauty, love and absolute truth. There are those who depend on the regime in power and repeat its slogans, make themselves part of their retinue, and foment against other intellectuals who refuse to give in, and there are the opposition members and critics who choose silence over prison and exile. We also have the exiles who attach themselves to an Arab authority opposed to their own, and use the slogans of one ruling class to attack the ruling class of another country. Finally, we have the revolutionaries who shout in the desert, but their voices make no waves in the Arab silence. The Arab intellectual is under occupation."[45]

The fact is that all the elites are under occupation, no matter what shape and form it comes under. This is why they should start with the common denominators among them, and gradually deepen them until the impact of differences on their forward path diminishes, or becomes natural and easy to sidestep. It is at that time that the ship of this nation will be able to set sail across the stormy sea, where all hands on board need to come together and all resources are put in place to make sure that it arrives at its destination unfettered by the shackles of autocracy.

CHAPTER FOUR

Institutions

Just as autocracy has distorted our true Arab Islamic culture and marginalised the elites in the Gulf by their own acquiescence, it has incapacitated the function of the region's institutions, turning them into decorative entities that serve the interests of despotism and its proponents, and preventing Gulf societies from forging ahead. Institutions are the frameworks through which people channel their efforts to achieve security and development, and differ in the degree of their complexity, ranging from the simple relationship-based institutions that rely on mutual trust, to the official, civil society and modern market institutions that are more inter-connected and complex. The more competent, credible and fair they are, the better these institutions can elicit people's cooperation in efforts towards a more prosperous and stable society. On the other hand, the less competent and fair they are, the more they lead to distrust, patronage, insecurity and the squander of people's efforts and their share of the social capital, i.e., the mutual trust among members of society which means that economic activities will cost more to undertake.[1] In this chapter, we will address the state of institutions in the GCC states, starting by briefly defining the institution as a concept and its function before moving on to the current condition of these countries' main institutions, i.e., their executive, legislative, media and judicial institutions.

First: The functions of institutions

Institutions perform three important functions aimed at building society, the first being the provision of information to guide the decision-making of people in their particular domain. Producers need information about the level of demand for their products, their input costs, the state's taxation and investment policies, the rate of inflation, borrowing costs and the available technologies. On the other hand, consumers need information on the products available, their prices, differences in their quality and where they are sold. Voters need to know the candidates' service record and election programmes. The government needs information on public and private sector companies regarding their expenses and revenues, the competency of their management, their debts and shareholders. This information is regarded as essential to impose taxation, organise the financial markets, protect workers' rights and other financial, monetary and trade policies. Finally, to hold the government accountable, the citizen needs information about the way it generates and spends its income. In short, it means that a country's progress depends on the collection of data and information, the analysis of this data and its dissemination to the public in a timely fashion, and then basing various policies on it. Any policies not based on sufficient, precise, timely and regularly updated information would be inevitably wrong and societies that depend on these policies are destined to lose their way and not advance.

The second function of institutions is to build society's capacity to exploit the country's resources by encouraging competition, preventing unjustified monopolies, managing natural monopolies and simplifying the procedures for establishing economic institutions. Competition compels people to lower their costs, upgrade their work methods, raise the quality of their management, adopt the most modern technologies and scientific inventions and buy their production inputs at the lowest possible prices. This, in turn, is liable to increase production and encourage generosity and creativity in all domains. It is also why the industrialised countries spend millions of dollars on the establishment of institutions designed to prevent the monopoly of any product or service, regardless who stands behind it, because monopoly inevitably leads to lower quality, higher costs, squandered resources and less creativity. The court case against Microsoft a few years ago is one such example. It is important to mention here that the Prophet showed the dangers associated with monopoly when he said, "Whoever strives to increase the cost (of products) for Muslims, God will seat him in the centre of the fire on the Day of Resurrection."[2] This means that any Muslim society whose members are deeply devoted to this religion's values need only hear these words to avoid monopolies, and need not spend millions of dollars to this end; at least this is how it should be. We should also remember that it is thanks to these values, whose renaissance we are calling for here, that millions of Muslims give alms (*zakat*) and go through untold hardships to find those who deserve it, at a time when Western societies squander hundreds of millions of dollars on the pursuit of tax evaders. This is the difference between those who perform a duty they are entirely convinced of, considering it an act of faith in their creator and a way to earn His approval, and those who perform a task for someone they dislike.[3] What applies to monopolising economic decision-making applies to monopolising political decision-making, as well. This is why holding a leadership position in Western societies depends entirely on competition between candidates and their programmes, on which basis the voters decide, and on the exercise of power. In our Arab and Gulf societies, leaders assume power, seize the country's resources from the very beginning, and continue to do so until the day they die. This explains why we live in stagnant, backward and corrupt societies despite our countries' plentiful resources that go to waste due to the monopoly of political power.

The third function of these institutions is to define the limits of property, contracts and their execution, because the loss of property, be it intellectual, material or professional, renders society akin to a jungle where the strong preys on the weak. A society like that loses its creativity, generosity and special distinction, and sees its resources evaporate and chaos reign in its midst, because protecting the people's honour, financial assets and soul is a vital prerequisite for their stability, generosity, distinction, ability to take calculated risks and diligent efforts in various domains. This is why the more protected these rights are by efficient and fair-minded institutions, the more society will prosper and the more its citizens' potential will bloom; and the reverse is true. History is rife with examples of societies that were once rich in resources but poor in the quality of their institutions, that ended up wasting these resources, being mired in internal conflicts and becoming the object of foreign ambitions, i.e., societies that witnessed the loss of their security and development, at the same time. These societies have failed to produce enlightened and wise leaders, and have instead succumbed to leaders who lack long-term vision because their main interests go no further than the immediate present, and the Gulf region is rife with such characters, unfortunately.[4]

Second: The state of institutions in the GCC states

What is the current condition of institutions in the GCC states? Those who look closely at these countries will realise that the condition of their institutions is further proof of their rulers' autocratic mentality. The choice of who leads these institutions is not determined by the appointee's level of efficiency and honesty, two vital criteria for humanity's prosperity on this earth, but by the extent of his loyalty to the ruler. Moreover, these institutions' performance depends on the will of unelected governments anxious to protect their agendas instead of reflecting the people's will. Therefore, from the point of view of their composition, employee quality, responsibilities, oversight and the way they use their resources, these institutions are confined to the narrow outlook of the ruling authority that sees these institutions as its private property, or a booty it needs to protect at all cost. However, despite the dearth of information regarding these countries, we will prove this fact by citing the example of the four most important institutions whose job is to provide the right conditions for any human society's development; we will do this to the extent allowed by the amount of information available. These are the executive institutions or councils of ministers, the legislative institutions, the media and the judicial institutions.

1. Councils of Ministers

The Council of Ministers, i.e., the executive authority in the GCC states, is a clear expression of the individualistic nature of governance in these countries, a state of affairs that has several negative repercussions, the most important among which are:

a) One of the main repercussions of these governments' autocratic outlook is the fact that all heads of governments, i.e., the heads of ministerial councils, are members of the ruling family. In the past thirty years, ever since these countries won their independence, no one outside the ruling family has ever been appointed prime minister in any of the GCC states. This cannot be explained simply through the prism of efficiency and honesty, since it would mean that for over thirty years no one outside the ruling family was capable enough to assume this position, a claim that even the ruling family shies away from.[5] Since this troublesome phenomenon extends to all councils of ministers in the region, we will give an example from Saudi Arabia, the largest and most important country in the Gulf. In 1995, the Saudi Council of Ministers comprised five members of the Al Saud family, all holding high positions, including the prime minister and his deputy, as well as the ministers of defence, interior, housing and foreign affairs, none of whom had an university degree save for the foreign minister. The other seventeen positions were held by individuals from outside the al-Saud family, all of whom had university degrees, mostly doctorates and some master's degrees, from the best universities in the world.[6] In other GCC states, the composition of these ministerial councils are not that different, if not worse sometimes, from the point of view of the ruling family's domination of ministerial positions, a phenomenon that, again, cannot be justified by quoting standards of competency, credentials and experience. However, we do not want to bore the readers by repeating information easily found in these countries' official gazettes.

b) Appointments to these councils depend above all on one's loyalty to the ruler, and it does not hurt if the appointee is also well educated, especially if he is one of those who do not care if they learn of their appointment and dismissal through the official media. A study on ministerial and other high appointments in Saudi Arabia showed that 86.6 per cent of these appointments were based on the appointee's loyalty, though first, and foremost, for security considerations.[7]

c) The fact that loyalty is the first criterion in ministerial appointments detracts from these ministers' ability to perform their duties according to what is in the best interest of their communities, because their main objective is to please the ruler who appointed them. They are, therefore, unable to carry out their responsibilities with honesty and according to the law, as do ministers in countries where freedom prevails. As the result of that, their decisions are usually individualistic rather than the outcome of consultations with advisors or technical experts.[8]

d). The autocratic nature of these regimes favours the tendency to keep people in their positions in perpetuity, whereby individuals stay for decades in the same position. This leads to stagnation and the absence of any mechanism to ensure that responsibility passes from generation to another and the failure to benefit from new abilities. This is typical of the nature of autocratic regimes which are incompatible with change and renewal. Muhammad Bin Sunitan's study on Saudi society shows that thirty-two ministers, or 30 per cent of the government, remained in their posts for between ten to forty-seven years.[9] A Western researcher likened this perpetual post phenomenon to leaderships in the former Soviet Union, where people like Andrei Gromyko, the former Soviet foreign minister, remained in their position for an entire era.[10]

e) Introducing some new faces to these councils every now and then is akin to cosmetic surgery whose effects soon disappear because they are usually rare, and their specifications do not differ much from those that preceded them in terms of loyalty or social and geographic affiliation.[11]

f) This exaggerated emphasis on loyalty is an inevitable outcome of despotism and its effect is detrimental to a country's social renaissance because it encourages hypocrisy, flattery and subservience. Moreover, it deals a blow to genuine development and the values that lie at its core, like competency, honesty, magnanimity and trustworthiness because in such a situation the only behaviour likely to preserve one's status and achieve results is to placate the despot, be it an individual or a ruling family.[12] The fear is that the monopoly of state positions could spread to other ministries, considered as sovereign institutions, like those of defence, security and foreign affairs. The condition of ministerial councils and executive institutions in other GCC states is not that different from their counterparts in Saudi Arabia, from the points of view of shape, content and responsibilities. Given these governments' autocratic nature, it is not so strange for them to be deficient in competency and rights. The latest report by Polity IV, one of the institutions that gauge the performance of governments around the world, confirms that on a scale ranging from -10 for the least efficient performance, up to +10 for the most efficient, the GCC states figure regularly on the minus side, albeit with some differences between them. From 2000-2003, Saudi Arabia, Qatar and Oman were at -10, i.e., the worst government performance, with Kuwait coming close at -8.5, the UAE at -8 and Bahrain at around -7.[13] This means that the GCC governments are even worse off than their counterparts in the other oil-producing countries.

2. Legislative Councils

Before we look at the condition of legislative institutions in the GCC, we should first mention a number of criteria used around the world to measure the level of political development in various countries. Among the most important indicators based on which the assessment of a country's political development is measured, is the presence of political parties that compete against each other and, more importantly, whether they enjoy equal opportunities. In other words, it seeks to ensure that no single party monopolises all the power and resources, and uses them to prevent its rivals from reaching power. Not only should political parties have the right to compete, this right has to be codified and applied within each party, in order for these parties to form the strong foundation of a free society in which all citizens are equal in rights and responsibilities, and where the opposition plays a highly effective role. The second indicator used to gauge the level of a political regime's development is its ability to hold free, fair and regular elections, through which power is exercised without resorting to violence to solve disagreements, whether before or after the elections; in other words, to ensure that all sides abide by the elections' results. It is also necessary to provide the right resources, sufficient level of freedom and absolute transparency to allow all citizens to exercise their right to vote, and any shortcomings in this respect detract from the fairness of the election process. In fact, many governments put all sorts of pressure on election officials to deter them from performing their duties with absolute neutrality.

Over and above the need for strong and competent political parties, and regular and fair elections, effective political participation requires that all those concerned abide by the provisions of the constitution respect the rule of law and recognise the equality of all citizens before it. This means that the executive authority should not attempt to either alter or interpret its provisions to suit its narrow purposes at the expense of other sectors in society; it should also not restrict the freedom of the press or civil societies' activities that aim to protect citizens' rights.[14]

Let us look now at the legislative institutions in each GCC country and gauge their closeness to or distance from the above criteria.

Kuwait

The absence of political parties in Kuwait is probably the main shortcoming of this country's political experience, although somewhat regular elections have been held there since the constitution was issued in 1962. The Kuwaiti National Assembly is the oldest example of participation in the region and, by the same token, the most developed and effective from the points of view of performing its legislative role and exercising oversight of the government. The assembly is an outcome of the 1962 constitution, and the result of several factors that together brought it out to light in such a developed form. The first factor was internal and had to do with the Kuwaiti people's ongoing calls for political participation since the early 1920s, which resulted in the establishment of the Legislative Assembly in 1938, headed by Abdullah Salem al-Sabah, followed by the election of a Founding Council to draft the constitution, in 1962.[15] The second factor was external, embodied by Iraq's claims over Kuwait and the Kuwaiti ruling family's response to that claim, embodied by efforts to strengthen the country's domestic front, which facilitated the appearance of the 1962 constitution, and the ensuing establishment of the National Assembly. The external factor also played a role in reinstating the county's parliamentary system after liberation, and helped launch other participation models in the region. Journalist Yusuf al-Jassim says in this context, "In my opinion, even the National Assembly's reinstatement after liberation was not a sign of eager anticipation on the regime's part; external pressure also played a role and was instrumental in the establishment of consultative (*shura*) councils in other Gulf countries."[16]

Some observers believe that the ruling family's poor performance, during the occupation, coupled with pressure from the United States were the main motives behind the reinstatement of political participation in Kuwait, after liberation.[17] In an interview with a Western researcher, Edward Ghoneim, the former US ambassador in Kuwait, confirmed the external factor's role in reinstating political participation in the country.[18] It is apt to draw the reader's attention here to the fact that the big powers' pressure on Kuwait to introduce reforms was, in fact, a coincidence of interests and a desire to avoid a potentially worse situation. When the British Foreign Office drafted a project to encourage political and social reforms in that country in the late 1950s, it was not exactly an act of generosity on its part towards the Kuwaiti people. It was rather an attempt to contain the potential fallout from events unfolding in the region, including the establishment of the United Arab Republic between Syria and Egypt, the Iraqi Revolution of 1958, and the preceding July Revolution in Egypt. This means that Western efforts at that time to recognise the independence of Kuwait and encourage Abdullah Salem al-Sabah to allow public participation, were an attempt to stop the nationalist revolutionary wave from spreading eastwards, and negatively impacting Western interests in the region. We should be wary of this when we hear calls for reform coming from the West, though we should also leave room for the possibility that some might be indeed sincere.[19] The third factor, which some believe has had a role in launching the Kuwaiti political experiment, is Abdullah Salem al-Sabah's exceptional personality, farsighted vision and rejection of autocracy, which made him approve the 1962 constitution without hesitation.[20]

If the reformist currents were sincere in their attempts to introduce significant reforms in the next few years, they would do well to reflect on these three factors. It is important to note, however, that many external factors can have a positive as well as a negative impact on reform in the region, and therefore one should be careful when employing these factors that they would indeed achieve the desired outcome, without any strings attached, which is rare indeed. Some observers believe that Abdullah Salem al-Sabah's approval of the 1962 constitution, and his willingness to allow the Kuwaiti people to take part in the country's political life, was not the outcome of a consensus among ruling family members. Some of them did not approve of the constitution and these, according to some observers, were the ones who to this day are obstructing the implementation of its provisions, and thwarting efforts to take the experiment a step forward, to make it more compatible with the constitution's provisions.[21] However, the Kuwaiti political experiment, rightly considered the best in the Gulf given the relative freedom and accountability it affords the country's citizens, is still limited to the way the regime sees it, i.e., booty for some members of the ruling family, namely those belonging to the same wing that did not approve of it, in 1962. The fact that Kuwait still does not have officially registered political parties, and that blocs in parliament are still unable to assume power, despite holding the majority in parliament, confirms that this experiment is still not up to par; it means in effect that there is no real exercise of power in the country. Thus, despite the presence of an elected parliament, the emir still appoints the governments, and the ruling family, represented by the emir, still dissolves parliament at will, constitutionally or otherwise, even when it is not responsible for the events that led to its dissolution. Finally, the members of the ruling family still monopolise major state positions, including that of prime minister and other important government posts. In an analysis of his country's political experiment, Kuwaiti activist and author Ahmad al-Dayyin describes it as follows: "All this clearly shows that despite what the constitution says regarding the nation being the source of all authority, elections in Kuwait, despite being a mechanism for public political representation at the parliamentary level, only allow for a limited representation at the exercise of power level. This is in the absence of organised partisan politics and a clear mechanism for a democratic exercise of power, and in the shadow of a system that places all major government positions into the hands of ruling family members."[22]

This inflexibility on the part of a segment of the Kuwaiti ruling family, and its refusal to allow the Kuwaiti experiment to advance in line with the provisions and spirit of the constitution, has produced a somewhat rigid political scene in Kuwait. This in turn has reflected on the country's ability, both ruler and people, to achieve the desired development goals and, in doing so, offer a model of successful democracy for others in the region to emulate.[23] Nor can one exonerate the opposition from blame in helping make this rigidity a fact of the country's political life; for besides lacking focus, programmes with clear priorities and effective implementation mechanisms, this opposition did not escape the incompetence and corruption of which the government is accused. There is need, therefore, to loosen up the tight controls, and find some type of effective political activism to launch the Kuwaiti experiment forward, and make it a model that other countries, both in the region and beyond, can emulate, instead of the stagnation or decline in which countries surrounding Kuwait find themselves in, today. What makes us optimistic are the reforms introduced in the past few years, expressly for that purpose, including a reduction in the number of electoral districts from twenty-five to five, allowing women to participate, granting the right of public assembly, giving licences to the written and visual media, and separating the positions of heir apparent and prime minister.[24]

There remain, however, a number of key issues that have obstructed Kuwait's path forward, and still do, and have become points of contention between the government and the opposition, sometimes even among members of the opposition itself; they include administrative and financial corruption and the abuse of state positions by ruling family members and their coterie. They also include issues like allowing people with ready-made commercial projects to own public lands, a clear avenue of personal profit; expanding the private sector's role, especially in matters related to the activities of foreign oil companies, without hurting national sovereignty; developing local oil companies and transforming political groups into political parties. Some of these reforms, or contentious issues, might require changing some provisions in the constitution, like the establishment of political parties, while others might require a higher level of awareness and understanding, and a little compromise on all sides, to ensure that the experiment is successful. We should remind the reader that working on common issues is the only way to narrow down and dispel existing differences, that time is part of the solution and that society has the final say in solving problems among its members. In other words, Kuwaiti society as a whole has the final say in settling, through the ballot box, all problems between its elites and representatives.

In our opinion, the greatest threat to the Kuwaiti experiment is to believe the unfounded theories, propagated by some, that the Kuwaiti experiment has impeded the country's development, and that Kuwait's neighbours that do not have elected legislative assemblies are faring better. Accepting such theories as fact is not only tantamount to destroying this pioneering experiment and taking the entire region a step backward, it is a claim that could cause the region's failure to prosper, and bring in more instability.[25] Political participation is a safety valve because it garners the entire nation's efforts behind the process of nation building, albeit at different levels of participation, and sidelines no one because everyone has the same citizenship rights. However, political participation is neither a remedy for all ills, nor a machine in a factory waiting for someone to push a button. It is a process to which all members of society bring their resources and personal convictions, meaning that to reap the fruits of participation, people should be able to respect one another, accept compromise solutions, refuse to focus on disagreements or blow them out of proportion, and allow the experiment more time to bear fruit and have an impact. Several studies indicate that many Western monarchies shifted from autocratic rule to constitutional monarchy where the monarch appoints the government, as is the case in Kuwait today, before becoming full parliamentary systems where political parties appoint the government rather than the king. It is what we hope Kuwait will do in the next few years.[26]

The Kuwaiti government should therefore not lose patience with the people when they ask for their political rights in a somewhat confrontational manner, call for accountability or attempt to change the internal balance of power because, as Robert Dahl says, democracy is about allowing citizens to express their choices and preferences. It is how a country also moves from individual to collective decision-making.[27] Many observers believe that the political rigidity the Kuwaiti experiment has been recently experiencing is due to several reasons. Among these is a government with no clear vision of the country's development path, a parliament incapable of garnering the minimum unity needed to pressure the government into changing its policies, and a Kuwaiti voter who dislikes the ruling family's control over his assets, yet hesitates to throw all his support behind parliament.[28] Softening this rigidity in the next few years will no doubt require either reducing the level of political participation and bringing Kuwait closer to other systems in the Gulf, or granting parliament wider prerogatives such as allowing parliamentary blocs to form future governments, which would be the best-case scenario not just for Kuwait, but for the entire Gulf region. No doubt the changes which the region is going through due to the Arab Spring necessitate that all parties cooperate in bringing about the desired political transition in the Kuwaiti experiment. Here the biggest fault lies with the Kuwaiti government since it wants to be at the forefront of society instead of having change imposed on it later.

Saudi Arabia

Despite Saudi Arabia's ideological and economic weight, both regionally and internationally, despite ceaseless calls by various sectors of Saudi society to reform the political system by allowing public participation in decision-making, separating between the powers, safeguarding public assets and other steps that lead to more social prosperity and stability, and despite foreign pressures on the Kingdom to introduce gradual and limited reforms, the country has remained the personal domain of the royal family, supported by a class of official religious scholars. Whether wittingly or unwittingly, the latter have helped distort the image of Islam by focussing on the minutiae of this religion, and turned their back on its tenets and intent, including human rights, justice and development. The current Shura Council, established by King Fahd in 1992 without legislative or oversight prerogatives, is akin to the council that King Abdul-Aziz established in the 1920s, despite granting it a number of additional prerogatives, including the ability to question ministers, offer suggestions to the council of ministers and other non-binding prerogatives.[29] To some observers, the fact that the Shura Council addresses issues related to women, terrorism and corruption, and has held municipal elections in 2005, established an independent human rights commission and allowed some civil society institutions to operate, is in itself a sign of political progress. However, the bitter reality is that these steps are more decorative than substantial, since they alter neither the core of the decision-making process nor the way resources are managed. These and all other major executive positions are still in the hands of the ruling family and the regional emirs, as are the judiciary and the media, and there is no separation between the family's fortune and society's financial assets, which are still directly or indirectly under the family's control. A researcher says in this context, "The reforms introduced in Saudi Arabia have not altered the autocratic nature of the political regime. The royal family and the Wahhabi religious establishment still maintain control over society's assets. Their ability to block, stall and even reverse these reforms has not diminished significantly, and in the absence of any centres of rival power, the reform process is likely to remain limited and vulnerable."[30]

None of the royal family's initiatives is indicative of serious intent or at the very least, a minimum desire for change. In 2003, King Abdullah initiated a so-called national dialogue in the Kingdom. However, no sooner had he alluded to the need for reforms, such as more government openness, restrictions on the royal family's control of the country's assets and the possibility of holding elections at a later date, than Nayif bin Abdul Aziz summoned a number of opposition members and told them, "What we won by the sword, we will keep by the sword." Soon after in March 2004, Minister of Defence Sultan bin Abdul Aziz made a similar statement saying, "Saudi Arabia is not yet ready for an elected parliament because voters may pick illiterate and unqualified candidates."[31]

In 2007, King Abdullah Bin Abdul-Aziz issued a decree ordering the establishment of a thirty-five member body, the Council of Allegiance (*bay'a*), whose members all hailed from the royal family, except for the secretary, as if there was no one else in society. Saudi researcher Madawi Al-Rasheed said in this context, "The *Bay'a* Council is proof that politics and leadership are the royal family's personal domain, out of the reach of any other institution in the Kingdom. However, regardless of any pressures, whether internal or external, although absolute monarchy dictates a wider scope of political integration and participation, the royal family has sidelined all of Saudi society, those we often call the 'movers and shakers', from an issue considered an exclusive family domain."[32]

In the absence of a clear vision regarding the effective participation of Saudi society in determining its own affairs, such as the transformation of the current regime into a constitutional monarchy, allowing the formation of political parties, barring royal family members from executive public office and instituting public oversight of legislation and resources, Saudi society will stay where it is regardless of the number of sessions the Shura Council will hold, the number of its members or the issues it is allowed to address. Therefore, everything that takes place in the legislative or municipal councils will be effectively worthless, from the point of view of progress and development, as long as these bodies' decisions remain neither binding nor supported by a legal framework that makes legislation and oversight every citizen's responsibility; i.e., without a preamble that divides society into first-class and second-class citizens. In other words, such an experiment will not develop further in the absence of a clear social contract that defines the rights and responsibilities of citizenship, as the Kuwaiti constitution does for example, instead of keeping Saudi citizens at the mercy of despotism and its whims, and its ebbs and flows.

Naturally, the proposed move towards a constitutional monarchy requires a process of gradual change, a requirement no one would object to once the vision of change and its path become clear. For example, one of these gradual steps could involve a system whereby some of the Shura Council members are elected, while others are appointed. We could also establish two separate councils, one elected and the other appointed, the latter comprising capable individuals whose opinion the state would benefit from in making decisions, and who, for one reason or another, cannot win a seat in the elections on their own. However, this council should not have the same legislative and oversight powers as the elected one, lest the experiment stagnates like the National Assembly in Bahrain. Another way of activating the current Shura Council is by increasing its oversight role of institutional performances, the provision of services, the fight against corruption and exploitation of resources, and by enhancing its legislative role in a manner that would gradually involve it in the debate and enactment of new laws. This gradual approach to increasing the role of the Saudi Shura Council could also be applied to the municipal councils, to draw them out of their current marginalisation and allow them to play a more active role. Some believe that electing all the councils' members, instead of only 50 per cent as it is done today, could help develop and activate it, and allowing its members to choose their leaders and hold them accountable, instead of appointing them, will no doubt lead to better political and administrative practices. Appointments from the top weaken these councils' performance, and make their appointed leaders more authoritarian in their decision-making, and therefore less competent.[33]

This gradual openness should spread to other sectors, to civil society in particular, including professional unions, charitable organisations and cultural and sports institutions. We should aim for a society led by a government that represents it, instead of a society reduced to a single family that owns it. Although there is no doubt that Saudi society will one day achieve this desired transformation, we would like the process to be peaceful. A society whose members actively call for their rights will see change happen, sooner or later; the danger remains, however, that the ruling family will not realise the magnitude of its restrictions, and thus fail to address them in the right way, and with the urgency required. This is particularly the case given the continued repercussions of the Arab Spring that show the unwavering rise in the hopes and expectations of the region's youth.

Bahrain

Bahrain is a case worth pondering, not only because it is the first GCC country to experience the post oil era and its challenges, but also because its political experiment is going through a period of ebb and flow due to majority calls for placing more limits on the ruling family's prerogatives. The motive behind these calls is the need to seriously address the country's declining oil revenues, fight corruption and create more employment opportunities for an ever-increasing number of university graduates. This is happening at a time when, according to some neighbours of Bahrain who provide it with considerable amounts of aid, like Saudi Arabia and the UAE, are calling on it to place additional restrictions on its political experiment, to prevent the region's chain of despotism from unravelling.[34] It is also worth paying attention to Bahrain because of its sectarian dimension, whereby the country's opposition is dominated, to varying degrees, by Islamist Sunni and Shi'a currents, making the country an ideal laboratory where this kind of interaction could be gauged, since the same could someday occur in more than one GCC country. Although Bahrain was a pioneer in establishing an elected parliament in the early 1970s, namely the parliament founded on the 1973 constitution, which in turn was based on the 1962 Kuwaiti constitution,[35] confrontations in the Assembly between the government and the opposition, both Sunni and Shi'a, led to its closure in 1975. Some believe that the experiment's failure is neither due to sectarian tensions nor to the ruling family's fear of losing control of the situation. It was the fact that the family did not want to relinquish any of its powers to parliament, and did not feel the need to it either.[36] Others say that Saudi Arabia actually persuaded it to dissolve the Assembly, with promises of aid to the tune of $350 million.[37] Bahrain's political life has been stagnant since this dissolution, except for the 1990s when several confrontations took place between the authorities and the opposition, until the advent of Hamad Bin Issa to power in 1999, upon the death of his father.

Hamad began his reign by releasing political prisoners and inviting the opposition to return home from abroad; he announced municipal elections and reformed the laws relevant to security and the courts. In December 2000 he announced that the Shura Council, appointed in 1992, would become an elected body within five years, and soon after the country enjoyed a period of detente during which a series of political dialogues took place. The Emir promised to reinstate the 1973 constitution after amending a number of its provisions, and special committees were formed to prepare for that.[38] It was followed by an announcement on the proposed National Charter, on which basis Bahrain would become a constitutional monarchy, to be followed by the establishment of a legislative assembly made up of two chambers, one elected and the other appointed, made up of competent individuals and experts, albeit with some murkiness regarding each chamber's prerogatives. Prior to the referendum on the Charter, Hamad met with opposition leaders who proposed that the elected chamber be granted legislative prerogatives, and that the appointed chamber play a purely consultative role. Sources indicate that Hamad accepted these proposals, and an official announcement made in this regard.[39] The referendum on the Charter won the approval of 98.4 per cent of the Bahraini population and, on 14 February 2002, Hamad declared himself King of Bahrain, and promised to hold municipal elections in May, and legislative elections in October of that same year. However, despite feeling that the reforms were not serious enough, especially in relation to the elected chamber's exclusive legislative role, and integrity of the amended constitution, the opposition decided to take part in the municipal elections. In these elections, which took place on the appointed date, the Islamists – both Sunni and Shi'a – won all fifty seats in an election in which 51 per cent of eligible voters went to the polls.[40]

While some decided to take part in the parliamentary elections that followed the municipal elections, others boycotted them. The disagreement on whether to participate or not centred round the extent to which Hamad saw the 1973 constitution as a point of reference. Before the parliamentary elections, details concerning the new parliament were made public, namely that it would have two chambers of forty members each, the first of which would be elected and called the House of Representatives, and the second appointed by the King and called the Shura Council. The amendments to the constitutions were also made public, as a result of which four different political parties decided to boycott the elections, including the Shi'a al-Wifaq Party, on the premise that the prerogatives granted by the constitution to the elected House of Representatives were too limited. Despite that, 53 per cent of eligible voters took part in the elections, a higher rate of participation than that of the municipal elections.[41] Four years later, many of the parties that boycotted the 2002 elections decided to take part in those of 2006, although some believed that the Bahraini government was trying to influence the course and outcome of the elections.[42]

In the 2010 elections, the opposition, especially the Shi'a block represented by the Al-Wifaq Party, scored a major success by winning twenty seats in the House of Representatives, though there was a complaint that the elections had been marred by some fraud.[43] In short, the state of participation in Bahrain up to the start of Arab Spring was represented by an elected House of Representatives with limited authority, either constitutionally, placing it on the same footing as the appointed Shura Council in terms of oversight and legislative responsibilities, or in practice due to the representatives' inability to put the national interest above personal and sectarian considerations. It might be too early to judge whether the Bahraini experiment is a success or failure, since the reforms that the ruler has launched could still prove to be a strong basis for serious political progress in the future, especially in light of the developments of the Arab Spring which we will discuss in Chapter Fifteen.

Qatar

Since the coup he mounted against his father in 1995, the Emir of Qatar, Shaikh Hamad bin Khalifa al-Thani, and the entire Qatari leadership have launched several initiatives that attracted the world's attention to their country. One of these initiatives is launching the Al Jazeera television station, considered a unique phenomenon in the Arab world, despite disagreements among observers about the reasons behind its creation, comprehensiveness of its coverage and nature of its programmes. The latter no doubt has played and still plays a pioneering role in providing valuable information to Arab and foreign citizens alike, a role we will come back to in the chapter on media in the GCC states. What is important here is to find out what the government of Hamad bin Khalifa has managed to achieve domestically, especially in terms of the Qatari people's participation in determining their own affairs. It is also important to find out, based on the available information regarding the municipal and consultative councils, whether statements made by the Qatari leadership, over the past few years, are compatible with facts on the ground, mainly about Hamad bin Khalifa's desire to implement genuine political participation. In the country's first municipal elections, held on 8 March 1999, around 50 per cent of eligible voters registered to vote, save for members of the security and armed forces who were not allowed to vote, and twenty-nine of the 227 candidates were elected.[44] However, according to several sources and some of the elected candidates, the fact that the Council had no significant prerogatives, prompted many of them not to run in the second round of the elections.[45] This negative impression, and the ensuing frustration of the Council's members and, by extension, of the Qatari people themselves, has had no doubt an impact on the level of public participation in the second round that took place in April 2003. Several sources estimate that in this second round, the number of candidates dropped down from 227 to ninety-three,[46] and the rate of public participation dropped from 50 per cent to between 25 to 40 per cent.[47] This unconvincing political start to allow the Qatari people the minimum level participation, pushed some observers to conclude that Hamad's government was not serious in this regard. They believed that he simply wanted to play the "municipal elections card" – the term used by the observers themselves – and appear in liberal garb in front of the West, by holding ostensibly free and fair elections, the real and ultimate aim of the entire process.[48] Subsequent events relevant to the formation of the Consultative Council confirm the belief that political participation in Qatar is still at best a pro-forma and cosmetic exercise, not only because the authorities are not genuinely interested, but also because there are no pressing demands to that effect by the Qatari people.

In 1999, the Emir of Qatar appointed a 32-member committee to prepare for an elected Council based on a permanent constitution, and asked it to submit its proposals within three years of that date.[49] In 2002, it was announced that the draft of the permanent constitution was indeed ready. The provisions of this constitution addressed a number of issues, mainly the organisation of the country's succession system, establishment of a royal family council under the King's leadership, and other issues that define the relationship between the country's executive, legislative and judicial powers. In this respect, the constitution states that the executive power rests in the hands of the Emir, that the legislative power is the Consultative Council's prerogative, and emphasises the judiciary's independence. However, though the constitution highlights other rights, including the freedom of assembly, self-expression and economic activities, it bans the formation of political parties. As for the Consultative Council for which the constitution provides, it has forty-five members of which thirty are elected, and other fifte appointed by the Emir. However, a scrutiny of this constitution's provisions shows that the Consultative Council's prerogatives, as far as convening and dissolving it and its legislative and oversight roles, are entirely in the hands of the Emir.[50] Article 104, for example, gives the Emir the right to dissolve the Council albeit with a justification for his actions, Article

106 allows him to reject draft laws, with a justification for his actions as well, and Article 107 states that the Council cannot amend the draft budget except with the government's approval. In short, by making the Council's legislative and oversight prerogatives conditional upon the executive authority's approval, the constitution makes its decisions more "advisory" than "binding" and, in the process, voids it of its legislative and oversight responsibilities.

In April 2003, the Emir approved the permanent constitution and called upon the Qatari people to vote on it, amidst a wide promotion and mobilisation campaign; the vote took place on 29 April 2003, and reports indicated that around 96 per cent of the people voted in favour.[51] However, although the constitution went into effect in June 2005, the Consultative Council is yet to see the light of day. Therefore, despite its various weaknesses, we are still not in a position to pass final judgement on it, until it is actually implemented on the ground. However, our hope is that many of its articles will be reviewed so that it is more expressive of the will of the Qatari people, particularly with regards to, firstly, the events of the Arab Spring and, secondly, the new generation of youth which took over power after Hamad bin Khalifa abdicated his rule to his son Tamim in 2014. In short, this means that the young leadership in Qatar is taking the initiative and making serious steps towards the Qatari people's participation in government. Thus, this step will be of added value for Qatar's foreign policies, chief of which are those concerning the people of Gaza because the power of the government ultimately stems from its domestic front and cohesion with its people. This is the lesson learnt from the Arab Spring.[52]

Oman

Before 1970 and Sultan Qaboos' coup against his father, aided by the British, Oman was almost isolated from the world and the wider Arab milieu, and Qaboos himself was akin to a prisoner in the region of Salalah. Soon after assuming power, Qaboos announced a general amnesty for all Dhofar rebels and members of the opposition, both in and outside the country.[53] In his first speech to the Omani people, he said that his father had decided to remove his father from power after regretfully realising that he was unable to use the country's assets to serve the interests of his people, and promised to devote himself to forming a modern government.[54] Despite all that, the Omani experiment is still defined by the gap between the development level of the country's basic and social infrastructure, and the level of political development, although the slow pace of progress has remained both gradual and consistent. In 1991, the Sultan replaced the State Consultative Council of the 1980s with a Shura Council and, in 1997, the voters, whose number was limited to around 51,000, went to the polls to choose from among 700 candidates of both sexes. The final choice was in the hands of the Sultan who selected two of the candidates with the highest number of votes in the larger constituencies, and one of the candidates with the highest number of votes in the smaller constituencies.[55] Official Omani sources indicate that in the 2003 elections, between 750,000 and 800,000 Omanis, of twenty-one years of age and above, were allowed to vote, meaning that the participation rate in these elections had gone up 100 per cent.[56] Nevertheless, the level of enthusiasm for these elections, whether from the candidates or voters, was quite low since the number of people who registered to vote did not exceed one third of those eligible to vote, which is close to the rate of the 2000 elections. The number of candidates for the Council dropped down from 736 in 1997, to 540 in 2000 and to 506 in the 2003 elections.[57] This low rate of participation in the Shura Council elections could be due to a general feeling among the Omani people that the Council's prerogatives are too limited, based probably on the experience of previous councils whose role was confined to a number of economic and social issues. The appointed 48-member State Council, established in 2001 to form with the Shura Council what is known today as "The Council of Oman", has restricted the Shura Council's role even further.

It is actually true that Oman went from a totally appointed to a totally elected Shura Council and that, throughout the years, there was never any doubt as to the elections' integrity. It is also true that the Council has tried to hold a number of ministers accountable, like the Ministers of Information and Communications; that the number of those who registered to vote in 2007 had risen to 60 per cent, thanks to the use of information technology in promotion campaigns; and that the Council's composition has shifted in favour of younger members. However, although these are all positive signs, and no doubt reflect the Omani people's desire to take part in decision-making at all levels, yet, despite being a reflection of the Omani popular will, the Council's legislative and oversight powers are still dependent on the will of the Sultan. He is the one who decides what the Council can or cannot review, which projects and policies it should or should not accept, and decides who heads the State and Shura Councils.[58] In its present form, the Omani Shura Council is similar to the Municipal Council in Qatar, from the points of view of holding regular elections, diminishing voter numbers and limited prerogatives. But given the increasing rates of unemployment, decreasing oil reserves and heightened awareness by the Omani people of their right to participate in decision-making, does the Omani government realise that the road ahead requires more rights, more accountability and faster development of the productive Omani citizen who will one day be an alternative to oil? This is what we wish to see in Oman.

The United Arab Emirates

The UAE's experiment in political participation is the weakest in the Gulf region, since the constitution at the basis of the country's foundation calls for a Federal National Consultative Council whose forty members are all appointed by the rulers. In 2006, attempts to develop the experiment further were, in the words of Robin Wright,[59] more akin to a "political charade" than a serious effort to establish some kind of participatory decision-making system. According to the new formula, the rulers choose 6000 individuals, aged eighteen years and over, from among the country's 300,000 citizens and these in turn selected twenty of the forty National Council members, while the rulers themselves appoint the other twenty, meaning that 2 per cent of the country chooses half the Council members. It also means that the ruling families not only choose these 20 members but also guide and control the election of the other twenty.

In the meantime, the Council's prerogatives are purely cosmetic, embodied in approving everything the federal government puts in front of it, while the latter retains the option of accepting or rejecting any of the Council proposals.[60] Moreover, although attempts to improve political participation in the UAE came later than in other GCC states, it was weaker than theirs; even Saudi Arabia, which has the most stringent political system in the region, held elections in 2005 to fill half the Municipal Councils' seats.[61] Many observers believe that this political system is the reason why the UAE is at the bottom of the region's list in terms of political and civic rights.[62] The question is what holds this country's political system back compared to other countries in the region, and compared to its pioneering development in the economic field, especially Dubai? There is more than one possible answer; some believe that the UAE's citizens have acquiesced to trading in their political rights, even if implicitly, in return for the social and economic benefits that the government affords them, such as public employment, education and health services and other forms of support.[63] Those who uphold this view choose to forget, of course, that the benefits that the UAE government gives and withholds are public assets to begin with, rather than the ruling family's property.

Some believe that the UAE's development model rests on the assumption that economic development is both the mainstay and conduit to political development, and should therefore come first. According to these people, the integration of the UAE's economy into the global economy is liable to culminate in a series of reforms in the political and civic rights domain. To prove their point, they refer to the fact that the country has allowed some foreign worker groups to organise and elect their representatives, and changed some of its laws to encourage foreign investors.[64] Here again, the latter choose to forget that these relative rights are the result of foreign pressure and apply only to foreign residents, at a time when the local population lacks the minimum freedom to organise, call for their basic rights or form independent unions. This begs the question as to the kind of reforms that exclude a country's own population. Finally, some believe that introducing political liberalisation to the UAE, at a time when the majority of its inhabitants are foreign nationals, will have a catastrophic effect on the country's future identity and path, and this is a valid point. However, its proponents want the local population to make a sacrifice twice: firstly, when the policies of their government made them a minority in their own country and, secondly, by ceding their basic rights to ruling families who have surrounded them with foreigners. Instead of asking the people to give up their basic rights, it is incumbent on the UAE's government to be creative in the next few years, and find ways to involve their citizens in decision-making and oversight of the country's assets. A more important question is whether there is cause for optimism that the UAE's experiment will develop in the post 2010 Council sessions, whereby citizens, aged eighteen and over, would elect all forty of its members, except for the deceased, some of whom voted from their graves in 2006, according to UAE government figures?[65] If we assume, for the sake of argument, that these free and fair elections do actually take place, could the current experiment develop further when the Council's responsibilities, according to the constitution, are purely consultative?

In fact, the events of the Arab Spring imply that there is no reason for optimism since the current leadership's statements and policies show that they are not ready for any kind of serious political reform. Moreover, the great majority of the younger generation of society remains negative and has not embarked on any demands for reform except for the small section of them who presented a petition to the president of the state in March 2011. This is a subject to which we will return during our discussion on the Arab Spring.[66]

3. The Media

In democratic countries where people elect their governments and there is a genuine exercise of power, the press is the fourth estate that competes with the other powers – legislative, executive and judicial – to steer society's decisions in the right direction by providing it with accurate information. This is why, in order to play its role and lead society's forward march, this fourth estate relies

on a set of factors, chief among which are independence, quality of its information, its scope of influence, and the values that determine the final journalistic
product. The media's independence is determined by its ownership, the laws it
operates under and main sources of financing.[67] The quality of its information
depends on the level of transparency, availability of data, level of its employees'
training and competition between different media outlets. The kind of competition we are talking about here is not the kind that encourages consumerism or
teaches immoral behaviour, as many satellite channels targeting Gulf and Arab
audiences do, but the kind that offers quality public service programmes with
a valuable cultural content.[68] The question here is where do media in the Gulf
stand in relation to the above-described high-value media?

In 2009, a Freedom House study on the media that ranked 195 countries based
on their level of press freedom named five countries in the Gulf whose media
were not free and described the Kuwaiti media as partly free. This ranking has
remained unchanged according to the Freedom House report issued in 2013.
However, the UAE, Bahrain and Kuwait have fallen by two points between 2011
and 2012 because of the restrictions on all the media since the beginning of the
Arab Spring. Hence, the ranking of these countries ranges between zero, which
is considered the highest score for press freedom, and 100, which is regarded
as the worst score. The countries are then divided into those states with a free
press, rated between 0-30, those that are 'partially free', rated between 31-60,
and, finally, the 'unfree' press, rated between 61-100. Table 4-1 shows the classification and score for the countries of the GCC with regards to freedom and
their position among the 197 countries in the report of 2013.

Table 4-1
Rankings of Press Freedom in the GCC states by Freedom House, 2013

Country	Score	Rank among 197 countries	Classification
Kuwait	59	128	Partly free
Qatar	67	153	Not free
Oman	71	160	Not free
UAE	74	164	Not free
Saudi Arabia	84	182	Not free
Bahrain	86	188	Not free

Source: Freedom House, Freedom of the Press 2013, pp. 39-40.

These rankings do not surprise us since these countries' media are of the "government loyalist" type, as a Western researcher describes them.[69] Furthermore, they saw more restrictions with the start of the Arab Spring because of their possible inclusion of anything that might be influenced by the past and ongoing events in the countries of the Arab Spring. In addition to the nature of this press and the influence of the Arab Spring, there are also other factors explaining the lack of freedom in the media of the Gulf region.[70] These include whether the media is government-owned, whether this ownership is direct or indirect and the multitude of written and unwritten restrictions, rules, regulations and instructions it has to abide by.[71] This media also suffers from the lack of a positive environment in which it can develop and rise to the level of the citizens' expectations, an environment that provides it with precise information that allows it to hold the government accountable, and helps it adjust its course. This can only exist in countries where there is a real separation of powers, where the people elect their institutions and where the media is indeed the fourth estate. It is therefore not surprising at all to learn, in light of the above, that the media in the Gulf is not free but designed to serve the agendas of governments that do not draw their legitimacy from the people. It fails to address any of the people's priority issues, like political participation, protection of public assets, job creation for fresh graduates, human resource training including for journalists, economic integration, Gulf regional security and the governments' position vis-à-vis the Palestine cause, the public's number one issue. This has cost the media its credibility and forced the people to seek alternative sources of information, a fact, that many people believe, could explain the exponential spread of satellite dishes, since the 1990s.[72] Not content with setting aside issues of interest to the public, the official and semi-official Gulf media, especially the visual media, acted irresponsibly and destructively on numerous occasions by allowing their programmes to deviate from established values and moral codes, by appealing to people's basic instincts for the sake of publicity and material gain. More ominously, these channels that benefit from Gulf financing, target Arab viewers and obtain their operating licences in foreign countries, have started broadcasting in languages other than Arabic, so much so that some studies estimate that Arabic language broadcasts in the Arab world do not exceed 48 per cent. On the other hand, English language broadcasts and those in other languages, catering to non-Arab audiences, account for 41 per cent and 11 per cent of the total, respectively.[73]

Gulf journalists do not fare better than other elements of the media. Ibrahim al-Ba'iz writes, "Journalist cadres in the Gulf have a real problem; 62 per cent are non-professional, 59 per cent were never trained, 65 per cent earn less than 5,000 Saudi Rials per month, 50 per cent never travelled on assignment, and

78 per cent say that their role is to protect the public from opinions contrary to official state policies."[74]

The above opinion on the state of the media in the Gulf confirms the view of former Qatari Culture and Information Minister, Abdul Aziz al-Kawari, on the subject. He said that the media "insists on ignoring the objective realities that make it a waste of effort and money. It is autocratic, with strictly defined discourses, topics and path; it is individualistic, it negates the other and does not recognise pluralism, and it is official, it covers official events and hardly has anything to do with society, or its problems and aspirations. It lacks transparency, it is rigid, it failed to catch up with technological and social advances, and it aims to maintain the status quo, quarantine people's minds and cover up corruption."[75]

About the private media, which we call semi-official because it is mostly financed by members of ruling families, the Qatari former minister says, this media "relies on instructions from its owners and their policies and, despite being more advanced than the official media, it is still hostage to government policies. Most of those who own the media either belong to the circle of power or revolve in their orbit, meaning that their main objective is to make money by promoting consumerism. We have to recognise, however, that some private media outlets, mainly offshore audio-visual, written and electronic media, have had the courage to breach the region's official media codes by displaying a certain level of transparency and objectivity, and addressing serious issues."[76]

In a pioneering field survey of a number of Arab satellite stations, including Al Jazeera, Al-Arabiya and Dubai TV, one researcher tried to gauge the quality of news, political, social and entertainment programmes, their contribution to building a non-rigid and authentic modern culture, and whether they pave the way for genuine renaissance. The researcher said about her findings, "In short, these satellite stations have stopped at the threshold of dismantling the prevailing traditional culture, each in its own way and from its own vantage point, and most were unable to advance to the building stage. This is perhaps due to several reasons, among which is the fact that new structures need an underlying infrastructure to rely on, and also need reliable sources of information, actual facts, a genuine democratic environment and productive societies, both economically and in terms of knowledge and culture, all of which Arab societies unfortunately lack, so far."[77]

Thus, today Gulf citizens find themselves stuck between the rock of the official media's rigidity and the hard place of the commercial semi-official media, and it is unlikely that the current environment in the Gulf will produce media outlets like the BBC and America's PBS. The fact that these two outlets do not depend on advertising and address issues of importance to society, puts them out of the reach of despots and business people. However, although the Qatar-based Al Jazeera is close to this model, it is different from the point of view of operating in a controlled environment that prevents it from playing an effective role, especially in Gulf-related issues, though it remains the best of what we have in the region. Unfortunately, it is no more than a drop in the ocean.

Gulf researcher Usama Abd al-Rahman summarises the Arab media's negative role in development, saying, "Next to education, the media are a vital cornerstone of development, and it is impossible to imagine the media in the Islamic world as being in harmony with Islam's core values of honesty and objectivity. In these countries, the media is akin to a tool designed to enhance the official image; monopolise opinion; eliminate the other, and spread falsehoods, cover-ups, lies and hypocrisy, a variety of ills that cannot in any way be in harmony with Islam and its principles."[78] Perhaps the best assessment of the media in the Arab and Gulf region is by Kenneth Pollack, researcher at the American Brookings Institute. He says, "So subservient is most of the Arab press that it rarely requires violence on the part of the regime to intimidate it into doing something; the regime's control over their livelihoods, coupled with the knowledge that the regime could imprison, beat, or kill them, is more than adequate to ensure they do as they are told."[79]

Most ominous still, in the domain of publishing information and making it available to citizens, is the ugly and strict censorship that Arab governments impose on the freedom of thought in higher education institutions and university research centres. The United Nation's 2003 *Arab Human Development Report* states that, "Most laws governing higher education and university scientific research institutes include statutes and regulations that curb the independence of these institutions and place them under the direct control of the ruling regimes. This leads to the curtailment of academic freedoms, and encourages academics and researchers to avoid embarking on creative or innovative endeavours that may lead to controversy or political problems."[80]

Saudi Arabia is perhaps the GCC country that tries hardest to censor the media, and the Saudi media is the least accurate and slowest of all the GCC's media in making information available to its people. This is not because the country lacks human or material resources, but because the ruling family insists on maintaining tight control on the political scene. For example, five days went by before the Saudi media announced that Iraq had invaded Kuwait, and several days passed before they mentioned the fire during the pilgrimage to Mecca in 1997, although hundreds of pilgrims had died in the incident. The same media that failed to carry the two above important incidents was very quick to cover up the truth in an incident involving the regime. In 1996, 9000 copies of *Readers' Digest* were destroyed because of an article criticising the ruling family.[81] A former British diplomat in Jeddah at this time confirmed the Saudi government's excessive censorship of publications saying that, "[i]n practice the [Saudi government's] control is still wider-reaching than in theory because many of the members of the [privately-owned] newspaper corporations also hold senior positions in the Government."[82]

Abdel-Bari Atwan, former editor of the London-based newspaper *al-Quds al-Arabi*, was right when he said in 1996, "[The House of Saud] definitely want to cover up their domestic affairs. The Saudi press doesn't discuss anything about Saudi Arabia. No-one has any sense of how many people are in prison or any statistics on road accidents for fear that such reporting might be construed as a criticism of the king or his government."[83]

In recent years, even the Friday sermons, supposed to address a variety of issues and tailored to a specific audience, have fallen victim to the censor in all the GCC states. Imams began receiving made-to-order sermons whose subjects toe the government's line, even if they do not address any of the day's issues, or topics of interest to the faithful.[84] The Saudi regime's fear of free speech and its attempts to obliterate all opinion uncover the reality of what is taking place in Saudi Arabia; not only did this phenomenon involve the Kingdom itself, it also involved most of the international media, especially the Arab-speaking media, either through owning them or advertising in them. Suffice it to mention here the case of the BBC's Arabic service, founded in 1994 with funding from the Saudi Al-Mawared Group, in cooperation with the Orbit Television Network, owned by a member of the Saudi royal family. Available information indicates that as soon as the service began to address issues not to the Saudi government's liking, like the interview with Saudi opposition member Muhammad al-Mis'ari, addressing King Fahd's health and referring to human rights issues in the Kingdom, not only was Saudi financing withdrawn, the government tried to stop others from taking the project over.[85]

4. The Judiciary

No society can become stable and prosper without legal institutions that adjudicate conflicts among the citizens, and between the citizens and their government, and reassure them that their rights, property and talents are safe and secure, thus allowing them to give generously and build while taking full responsibility for their actions, and looking forward to reaping their due rewards. Without this legal safety net, society will remain at the mercy of conflicts that not only squander the country's assets, but also give rise to various forms of instability, starting with crime and ending with civil war, a fact that many old and new countries attest to. The judiciary evolves in tandem with society's evolution; therefore, when a society is small and simple, from the point of view of human resources, size of the economy and foreign relations, its tribal rules, laws and custom are sufficient to deal with conflicts among its members. The more complex and diverse the above aspects become, the more complex and diverse are the legal institutions that society needs to develop. Nevertheless, just like its simpler counterpart, this complex society's aim is to foster civic calm and economic prosperity among the citizens, and between itself and other societies.[86] What makes these legal institutions more efficient is that they are compatible with their society's values and traditions, rather than imported ready-made models that developed in an alien environment, which would have transformed them from development mechanisms into obstacles that lead to chaos and instability, like planting a seed in an inhospitable soil. Competent legal institutions render society more stable and prosperous in two different ways, firstly by protecting public freedoms and rights and, secondly, by protecting property rights and the execution of contracts.[87] The above two outcomes of the rule of law undoubtedly complement one another; a society that does not protect the rights of individuals will not make any effort to protect their property, and the reverse is true, to a certain extent. We indicated earlier, in the context of addressing legislative and media institutions, that the GCC states neither enjoy genuine political participation nor uphold freedom of expression. This is why we will focus on the ability of different laws to protect property rights and contract execution, without which no serious development can take place. For example, a recent study on a group of Eastern European countries in the process of moving from a centralised to a market economy shows that when Poland decided to establish a financial market, it began by establishing an independent oversight committee to monitor market activities, and gave it every possible incentive to perform its responsibilities well. In the nearby Czech Republic, on the other hand, oversight responsibility of the financial market was entrusted to one of the Finance Ministry's departments, and what was the outcome? The Polish financial market prospered and increased its capital, including its foreign capital, as well as the number of companies registered on it, while the capital of the Czech market, and the number of companies registered on it, continued to decline.[88] This confirms the belief that the more effective and independent laws there are governing the performance of financial institutions, the better is the exploitation of financial resources, and the higher the economic growth. But how about the banks, the second and most widespread source of funding in the world? If the importance of financial market contracts centres round protecting the shareholders' rights vis-à-vis the management and small investors' rights vis-à-vis large company shareholders, then the role of banking contracts and their execution is to protect the depositors' rights vis-à-vis the bank's management, and the banks' rights vis-à-vis borrowers who for some reason are unable to repay their debts. Laws that organise banking activities, especially in the developing countries, face more serious issues and challenges than similar laws in the developed world. Among these challenges are governments that steer the banks' resources towards self-serving projects, despite their uselessness and lack of productivity from a developmental point of view. An issue as well is the patronage system that grants easy loans to people linked to the banks' board members, which constitutes a significant obstacle to development because, as field studies show, these loans are without collateral, their interest rates are lower than the market rate and their terms are longer than other loans. Studies clearly show that the rate of default on these loans is higher than on commercial loans.[89]

Successful legal institutions are those that that open their doors to people who have a complaint to make, and hold the supposed offenders accountable with the shortest possible delay, at the lowest possible cost, and as equitably as possible. In other words, without giving in to pressure from the executive authority or those who wield economic power, while at the same time holding themselves accountable to other institutions, if they fail to perform their duties. Factors that ensure the judiciary's independence include their appointment for long periods of time, transferring them to new positions with their approval, giving them generous salaries and submitting their judgements to review by courts independent from the state. Judges should also be involved in the enactment of laws instead of being limited to only interpreting them, and the side which watches over judicial affairs should be independent from the state executive.[90]

Therefore, what does the record of judicial institutions in the GCC states look like, from the point of view of fair and efficient protection of property rights and execution of contract? Despite the dearth of published information regarding the effectiveness and time required to expedite various procedures in the GCC region, we will use data from the International Monetary Fund (IMF) and the World Bank, which are usually more precise and up to date than what these countries produce, if they do this at all. Table 4-2 shows the values of four different indicators that measure the effectiveness of legal institutions in settling commercial disputes in the GCC region. For the sake of comparison, we included on the list other countries that differ from the points of view of geographic location, development level and population size. These four indicators are the number of legal procedures, number of days required to execute contracts, the cost of executing these contracts compared to their total cost, and each country's rank in terms of efficiency in executing these contracts.[91] Naturally, the lower the number of procedures, of days required to execute contracts, of court judgments and of the cost of executing these contracts, the better the conditions were for launching economic projects, the higher the number of these projects and, by extension, the level of economic growth.

Table 4-2

Efficiency of Contract Execution

Country	Number of procedures	Number of days	Percentage of contract value	Rank
Singapore	21	150	25.8	12
Thailand	36	440	15.0	23
Malaysia	29	425	27.5	33
Tanzania	38	462	14.3	36
Turkey	36	420	24.9	40
Botswana	28	625	28.1	68
South Africa	29	600	33.2	82
Qatar	43	570	21.6	95
The UAE	49	524	19.5	104
Oman	51	598	13.5	107
Bahrain	48	635	14.7	113
Kuwait	50	566	18.8	117
Saudi Arabia	40	635	27.5	124

Source: Doing Business 2013

The above table leads us to a number of conclusions, the most important of which are:

a) The number of procedures required to execute commercial contracts in the GCC states is higher than in other countries on the above list, meaning that legal institutions in the GCC region are beset by routine and weakness. This high number of legal procedures undoubtedly has a negative impact on these countries' economic growth and on the flow of foreign investments; in this respect, we find that Qatar fares the best, while Kuwait and the UAE bring up the rear.

b) When we consider the number of days required to execute contracts, or rulings, it appears higher in the GCC states than in most other countries, including Singapore, Turkey, Thailand and Malaysia. This is another proof of the judiciary's incompetence in the GCC states, despite the small size of their populations and rich material resources, which again is a sign of poor administration systems and absence of accountability.

c) There is an obvious disparity between the cost of executing contracts in the GCC states and the other countries shown in table 4-2. These costs include lawyers' expenses, court fees, cost of enforcing the court's ruling and the bribes paid, if any. As the first two indicators show, the cost of executing contracts is higher in Saudi Arabia, the UAE and Qatar than in other countries like Tanzania and Thailand, given that these latter countries represent taxation as a main source of the imports for the state and not oil imports like the GCC states. Oman is considered the least expensive of the GCC states for executing contracts.

d) Finally, it is clear from the above rankings that out of 185 countries, Qatar's is in 95th place, followed by UAE in 104th, Oman in 107th, Bahrain in 113th, Kuwait in 117th and lastly Saudi Arabia in 124th place is the country with the lowest judicial efficiency. However, all the GCC states come after the other states in table 4-2 with regards to the global ranking. Other studies show that the execution of contracts in the Arab countries is the most significant obstacle to the launch and growth of economic activities in the region.[92] Others believe that one of the reasons for the poor performance of legislative institutions in the region is that many of the laws in effect are imported from Britain and elsewhere, and therefore often conflict with the principles of Islamic shar'ia law, which studies indicate is favoured by people in the region.[93] In a survey of six Arab countries, including the UAE and Saudi Arabia, it became clear that the majority in four of these countries were in favour of basing business laws on shar'ia principles.[94] This is not just a theoretical issue; several Western sources confirm that this was one of the reasons behind Saudi Arabia's delayed accession to the World Trade Organisation.[95]

In the above paragraphs, we tried to assess the situation of the executive, legislative, media and judicial institutions in the GCC states, based on the available data, and found that they do not perform in balanced ways based on advocacy, oversight and regular adjustments. They are rather sidelined and dysfunctional institutions because, in these autocratic countries, the executive institutions dominate and obliterate all the others. This state of affairs meant that, instead of protecting the citizens' rights by performing their legislative and oversight duties, these institutions were enacting laws that serve the government's agenda. The media became spokespeople for the regimes whose main concern is to maintain the status quo and attract advertisements, even if it means fragmenting the nation, robbing future generations of their potential and wasting the country's assets. As for the judiciary, it became more of a tool used by governments to further boost their power and privileges, silence all and any opposition, and maintain the existing balance of power, instead of helping settle conflicts among the people, and between the people and the government, to ensure the country's stability and prosperity. The institutional paralysis that has plagued the GCC states in recent years has distorted their development and security path because the interaction and advocacy that are the result of an efficient institutional environment, have never materialised. This means that instead of reflecting a comprehensive social vision, these countries' development and security policies have only reflected the government's vision. This is a vision that does not go beyond the narrow confines of the desire to stay in power and keep the current political entities in their present condition, as will be made clear later on when we address policies related to oil, development and security.

PART II

Oil Policies

In Part I of the book, we showed how the hereditary succession system, with its tendency towards autocracy, has weakened the constituent elements of development in the GCC by marginalising civil society, distorting our culture and turning its institutions into decorative incompetent façades. In this part we will show the previous developments have weakened the bargaining position of the GCC states vis-à-vis the international oil companies and their respective governments resulting in lower gains from their oil policies over the years. Thus, despite the fact that the first oil discovery in the Gulf happened over seventy years ago, Arab Gulf oil is still Western not Arab-owned, as many of us would like to believe. There are numerous reasons for that; some are historical and have to do with the long history of international companies' domination of this industry from the very beginning; others have to do with the political economies of the oil-producing countries, and the fragile relationship between the oil-producing countries, themselves. However, despite the fact that these oil variables and their local, regional and international dimensions have changed since the discovery of oil, the outcome of their interaction is still in favour of the West and small groups of Gulf society. In the meantime, most of the Gulf's and the Arab world's population is still waiting for the day when this crude oil will become an engine for sustainable development, in both the GCC states and the Arab world beyond. The international oil companies, once known as "the seven sisters", have always been in control of the world's oil industry, both vertically and horizontally. Vertically, they control all aspects of the industry, starting with discovery and exploration and ending with production, pricing, manufacturing and distribution; horizontally, they cooperate to maximise their profits and maintain control through the coordination of their production, pricing and marketing.[1] According to reports published in the USA, in 1949 these seven oil companies controlled 82 per cent of all oil reserves, 80 per cent of production and 76 per cent of the overall refining capacity outside the USA and Russia.[2] Their records show that their policies always aimed at maximising profit with no regard whatsoever for the oil-producing countries, if not at their detriment.[3] Moreover, these companies reaped their highest profits from this region due to the low cost of production, compared with other regions of the world. Hence, this part is devoted to showing how these variables have interacted with each other, and how the ensuing imbalance of power in the oil policy-making domain has skewed this policy in favour of Western governments and their oil companies, at the expense of the region's future prospects. To this end, we will focus on the most important oil policies, namely on the contracts relevant to exploration, pricing and production, based on the available data.

Chapter Five

Discovery and Exploration

The first thing to ponder when assessing the GCC governments' performance is the level of their success in protecting their countries' oil wealth, particularly in contracts with the international oil companies that were, and still are, largely in control of the overall industry, from discovery and exploration, to the production, transport and marketing of petroleum products. By success, we mean the oil-producing countries' ability to manage their relationship with the oil companies in a manner that allows them to secure fair and stable revenues, and to help local human resources gradually acquire the skills and technology necessary to eventually indigenise this industry, and reap added value from most of its stages.[1] In fact, there are many indications that these governments have lost a considerable amount of oil revenue to the international companies, and that the latter have failed to help these countries indigenise the industry, as done by other oil-producing countries, Malaysia for example. The fact that the relationship between these governments and the international oil companies was never fair and equitable meant that the oil companies' revenues were higher than what these governments have been able to achieve for their people. Therefore, before looking at the development of oil contracts since the discovery of oil, and how this has affected other aspects of the industry, we should address the main reasons behind the unequal relationship between the oil companies and the oil-producing countries. This inequality has secured more profits for these companies and their governments than the rightful owners of this valuable asset.

First: Inequality between the parties

Since the early 1930s, several factors that govern the relationship between the oil-producing countries and the oil companies rendered it inequitable. Among these factors, or what we call here the reasons behind the lack of parity between the two sides, are the legitimacy of political regimes in the oil-producing countries, their knowledge of the oil industry and the level of transparency that has governed this relationship over the years. We will address all these issues in brief as a prelude to following the course that these oil policies have pursued, be it in drafting these contracts, pricing, producing or manufacturing petroleum products.

1. Political legitimacy

The oil-producing countries' experience shows that oil companies were always careful to have the upper hand in all decisions related to the oil industry, and would never have relinquished any rights had the oil-producing countries not pressured them and made constant demands. This usually only happens in countries whose governments submit to the will of the people and pressure from them, coming to power and leaving it by the people's will. Unfortunately, the GCC states do not belong to this category. Therefore, it is not surprising to see the relationship between them and the oil companies as being exploitative and one-sided, if not outrightly dishonest on the part of the oil companies. The reason is that these companies have continued to deal only with a handful of rulers motivated mostly by personal interest and not accountable in any way to their people, while they themselves enjoyed the backing of their powerful governments. Some of these governments were even shareholders in these companies and had their own representatives on their boards, like the British government which in 1914 owned around 51 per cent of the Anglo-Persian Oil Company, which later became the British Petroleum Company (BP).[2]

Nothing is more telling about the international oil companies' lack of regard for the oil-producing countries than the words of Juan Pablo Pérez Alfonso, former Venezuelan oil minister, who complained that the oil companies treated them "like children"[3] in reference to the governments' weak negotiating position vis-à-vis the oil companies. Paul Collier, Professor of Economics at Oxford University, further clarified this conundrum that the GCC states faced, and still face, in the domain of oil contracts. He states that there is more than one reason for the unfair treatment of those who own these resources, whether by the governments or the companies, which always ends in the latter paying less than they should for discovering these natural resources. In Collier's opinion, the main reason is corrupt governments not accountable to their people, who collude with foreign companies motivated to pay the necessary bribe, while these governments are motivated to accept them. Collier describes the workings of the endemic corruption of recent decades: "The company is negotiating with a person, or a small group, whose responsibility it is to represent the interests of citizens, both living and yet to be born. Although the job of those representatives is to safeguard the public interest, they also have individual private interests, and ordinary citizens may have little control over them. Citizens may not be able to scrutinize deals, and even if one appears to be suspect they may have no effective recourse. Knowing this, companies have an incentive to offer bribes, and representatives have an incentive to accept them. The amount of money at stake is so enormous and the effective scrutiny so limited that any other type of behaviour would be quixotic."[4]

When a government is not subject to public oversight, it is usually unable or unwilling to stand up to the oil companies. This is because its calculations are not based on the national interest but on the personal calculations of a ruler and his agenda. Beyond this, it does not matter whether society develops or retrieves its assets from the oil companies. In Venezuela, most of the policies aimed at nationalising the oil sector and limiting the oil companies' ability to squander this finite resource, were adopted by elected regimes subject to public oversight.[5] In the same context, sources indicate that in 1949 the King of Saudi Arabia received around $90 million in gold, in return for oil, and that in December 1950 he received an additional $70 million, officially earmarked for raising the country's standard of living. In fact, the King gave 10 per cent of this sum to the tribal chiefs to win their support and spent the remaining revenue from oil on himself and his entourage. Revenues from the pilgrimage (*hajj*), amounting to around £4 million per annum at the time, went to finance the Kingdom's simple administration system.[6]

2. Knowledge

The second reason, which observers believe lies behind the inequitable relationship between parties involved in the oil industry, is what economists call the "asymmetric knowledge" of the contracting parties that allows producing companies to take advantage of countries that own this resource. Oil and other resource companies sit at the negotiating table with the governments of oil-producing countries, secure in their long experience in the field of oil exploration, and in the knowledge that they have the best means to evaluate the presence of oil, the cost of its extraction and its potential profits based on precise estimates of its expected price. On the other hand, the oil-producing countries do not have any of the above information, which inevitably allows the companies to make large profits at their expense. Collier says in this context, "Asymmetric information is likely to lead to the more informed party benefiting at the expense of the less informed party. The result is always the same: the company underpays."[7]

Abdullah al-Tariki, the first Saudi oil minister, underlined the oil companies' ability to exploit their strong negotiating position vis-à-vis the oil-producing countries by falsifying the accounts in a manner to maximise their profits. In a paper he presented at the Second Arab Petroleum Congress held in Beirut, in October 1962, al-Tariki said about the sales of the Arabian American Oil Company (ARAMCO), "there is an estimated sum of $5.5 billion, deducted by the companies as transportation costs and miscellaneous expenses."[8] On the issue of sharing the profits equally, he said, "Of its 50 per cent share, Saudi Arabia received only 32 per cent in net profit, because 18 per cent was deducted in favour of the companies."[9] The Saudi newspaper *Okaz* reacted to al-Tariki's statement, concerning ARAMCO's falsification of the accounts, saying, "It is Okaz's pleasure to grant this week's medal of the people to Mr. Abdullah al-Tariki, Director General of Oil and Minerals, for the significant role he played at the Arab Petroleum Congress in Beirut. He drew the world's attention to Saudi Arabia's efficiency level, and highlighted the giant sums taken out of the Arab petroleum companies' share as imagined transportation costs. Okaz salutes al-Tariki on his excellent speech that unveiled the secret policies of the companies that exploit Arab oil."[10]

It was therefore not surprising that al-Tariki was sidelined from the oil-related decision-making circles two years after making this statement, and this is not mere speculation on our part. The words of the American ambassador to Saudi Arabia and to King Faisal, at the time, confirm this theory; he is quoted as warning him, "unless Tariki is checked in his accelerating course, relations between the Saudi Arabian government and ARAMCO will become steadily and probably rapidly worse and there will be adverse effects on relations between our two countries. Tariki's policies and aims are not economic but political. He has told ARAMCO's people and members of this Embassy that he believes in the principle of Arabization of the company and does not care whether there would be loss of profits for the government thereby."[11]

When Venezuela obtained the right to share half the profits with the oil companies, the Mosaddegh government in Iran asked BP for a similar arrangement. The latter refused, claiming that the Iranian government's share was already close to the company's 50 per cent share, but this statement was clearly based on falsified accounts. In fact, between 1947 and 1950, BP paid the British government around 40 per cent of its total profits, at a time when the Iranian government received a mere 20 per cent. The company was able to play around with the numbers because it kept some of its activities out of the accounting books and prevented the Iranian government from auditing them to verify their accuracy.[12] The Mosaddegh government's insistence on correcting the situation led to a confrontation with Western oil companies and their governments, culminating in Mosaddegh's downfall and the reinstatement of the Shah in 1953.[13]

3.   Transparency

Over and above the lack of political legitimacy and the asymmetrical knowledge and skills, there is a lack of transparency in the terms of the agreements relating to the governments' and companies' share of profits from oil, as well as other terms. The more transparent these terms are, the more society is able to evaluate them and express its opinion regarding their fairness and validity. This phenomenon is liable to strengthen the oil-producing governments' negotiating position vis-à-vis the oil companies and allows them to obtain a larger share of the profits. Transparency also serves the interest of those financial institutions that either are shareholders in the oil companies or help finance them, and helps governments impose taxes on oil companies. Transparency also helps both shareholders and tax agencies exercise their accountability and oversight responsibilities of these companies' management and reduce corruption, which is one of the reasons behind the recent collapse of the American housing and stock markets which almost led to the collapse of the entire global financial system.[14] In the early 1960s, the Venezuelan government learned that a number of oil companies operating in the country were selling Venezuelan oil at prices lower than the international market price, thanks to generous discounts to their agents, and promptly stepped in to put an end to the practice. This experience, and others like it, taught the Venezuelan government that companies would always be able to play with numbers, accounts and quantities, and that only a collective effort by the oil-producing countries could put an end to that. This is when former oil minister Juan Alfonso and Abdullah al-Tariki began working on the establishment of the Organisation of the Petroleum Exporting Countries (OPEC).[15]

The Kuwaiti people realised the importance of transparent oil contracts when on 26 January 1965 the Kuwaiti parliament rejected an agreement proposed by the big oil companies to sell off any of its revenue when it realised how unjust the agreement was to the Kuwaiti people. Ahmad al-Khatib, a member of the Kuwaiti parliament, commented on the extent to which the oil companies were exploiting the government by saying, "This information provoked us and made us angry. The agreement that the Kuwaiti government has approved is shameful, a humiliating ploy by the companies and a debasement of the nation's integrity and sovereignty. It shows the extent to which these oil companies have belittled us and treated us like ignoramuses all these years, thanks to our region's unique and wise leaders who claim to be 'experts in all matters.'"[16]

It is worth noting that the very agreement that the Kuwaiti National Assembly rejected had been approved by three different countries in the region, Iran, Saudi Arabia and Qatar, perhaps because none of them had an elected parliament with a say in important matters.[17] What confirms this fact is that the Assembly produced by the 1967 elections, which many sources believed to be fraudulent, later approved the same agreement that the Kuwaiti National Assembly had rejected, in 1965.[18]

Second: The evolution of oil contracts

Given the amount of changes introduced to the contracts that regulate the relationship between the oil companies and oil-producing countries since the October 1973 War, we decided to divide the subject into two phases: the first starts with the first oil discovery in the early 1930s up to 1973, and the second starts in 1973 until the present.

1.   Period up to 1973

Those who ponder the nature of oil contracts between the oil companies and the unelected GCC governments, since the 1930s, including the amendments introduced to them, will realise the extent to which these companies have exploited the oil-producing governments that continued to negotiate without public accountability. Up until the early 1970s, the contracts that governed the relationship between the two parties were mainly "concession contracts" which, in the best-case scenario, were tantamount to selling concessions to oil companies by public auction to explore for oil in specific areas and for limited periods and, if found, to develop, produce and export it. According to these contracts, the oil-producing country's revenue would accrue from concession fees, which the producing country keeps regardless whether oil is found or not, in addition to the fees on total revenues and from income taxes if oil is found. Moreover, although these contracts do not require the same level of skill or technical and accounting expertise as other contracts, which we will be addressing later on, they nevertheless involve many injustices towards the producing countries. Among these injustices are the very wide concession area granted to the companies;

the length of the contract period sometimes reaches ninety years and gives these companies total control over the quantities produced and their price. The companies are also not obligated to refine the oil locally or invest their profits in the local market, or to employ local labour or purchase their production input from local markets, nor are most of their activities subject to the laws of the land. This helped to isolate the oil sector and disconnect it from the rest of society, except for those revenues that the government spends locally once it receive its share from the oil companies.[19]

The political changes that took place in Venezuela in the late 1940s could be behind the Venezuelan government's demand that the oil companies amend the terms of the oil concession contracts in favour of the Venezuelan people. The fixed income that Venezuela received for each barrel of oil was replaced by a 50 per cent share of the profits. This only confirms that conditions prior to the adjustment were less fair, and that change happens only when people ask for their rights. In the GCC region, change began in Saudi Arabia in 1950 in the wake of Abdullah al-Tariki's visit to ARAMCO during which he asked for a similar 50 per cent share, followed soon by other Gulf countries.[20] Even after Saudi Arabia and ARAMCO had agreed on the 50 per cent share, the latter kept manipulating the Saudi government's share. This went on until al-Tariki discovered, soon after the government appointed him as financial controller in the early 1950s, that the company was actually quoting lower values for oil prices than the official market price, and calculating the government's share on that basis, meaning that the government was getting a 22 per cent rather than 50 per cent share of the profit. Al-Tariki's role in uncovering ARAMCO's accounting manipulations forced the latter to start seriously applying the 50 per cent agreement and, in 1952, compensate some of the Saudi government losses.[21]

In 1959, Venezuela led the way again in adjusting its oil contracts, by obtaining a 60 per cent share of the profits. That same year, Saudi Arabia signed a concession agreement with the Japanese-owned Arabian Oil Company and this was a much more advantageous contract than the ones before it. According to Abdullah al-Tariki, the man who engineered it, the agreement gives Saudi Arabia 20 per cent of the crude oil produced, compared to no more than 16 per cent in other agreements, and gives it between 56 per cent and 57 per cent of the profits. The agreement also allows the Saudi government to sit on a committee that oversees all concession-related purchases, and the company agrees that 70 per cent of its local staff will be either Saudis or other Arab nationals, and that Saudi nationals will make up 30 per cent of its foreign branch employees.[22] However, just as Venezuela's initiative to change the terms of its contracts was a turning point in correcting the balance between the oil-producing countries and the oil companies and their governments, the spread of Arab nationalism, especially Nasserism in the 1950s and OPEC's establishment in September 1960, impacted positively on the independence of the oil-producing countries' policies.

In 1959, the international oil companies lowered the benchmark price, on which basis the oil-producing countries' profits were calculated, by around 10 per cent, claiming that the move was aimed at preventing an increase in Russian oil sales to the European market.[23] The move came just prior to the First Arab Petroleum Congress in Cairo in April 1959 and in the shadow of growing Arab nationalist sentiments in the wake of the Tripartite Agression, or Suez Crisis, in Egypt in 1956. The oil companies' decision, however, gave the oil-producing countries the opportunity to start preparing the ground for future joint action aimed at stabilising oil revenues, and gradually taking control of their petroleum industry. The Congress' consultative meeting in Cairo was an important step towards the establishment of OPEC in September 1960. It was probably the oil companies' second attempt to lower the price of oil by 7 per cent in August 1960 that prompted the representatives of five oil-producing countries, Saudi Arabia, Venezuela, Kuwait, Iraq and Iran, to announce four days later from Baghdad the establishment of OPEC, on 14 September 1960.[24] These countries were soon joined by Qatar, Abu Dhabi, Indonesia, Libya, Algeria and Nigeria. However, although the creation of OPEC put an end to the oil companies' monopoly on pricing, it did not bring prices back to where they were before, nor prevent the decline in their real value. The reason is that despite having all the right elements to survive, disagreements among OPEC's members, and the fact that the Arab regional order had begun to erode from within, prevented it from having any significant impact. Iraq's announcement of its intention to occupy Kuwait in 1960 resulted in tense relations between the two countries, followed by a decision to suspend Iraq's membership in OPEC. Also playing a role was the power struggle between princes Saud and Faisal in Saudi Arabia which ended in Faisal being crowned King and marked the end of the Kingdom's reformist wave of the late 1950s.

Abdullah al-Tariki, the man who played a pioneering role in calling for the liberation of Arab oil from Western control, the big thorn in ARAMCO's side, and builder of an advanced technical administration system admired even by the enemy, was the first person to be excluded from the decision-making process in Saudi Arabia.[25] Sources indicate that although King Faisal was the one behind al-Tariki's rise, he was nevertheless instrumental in sidelining him from power. Some blame King Faisal's change of heart on an incident when al-Tariki accused the King of personal involvement in certain oil deals, and after these accusations appeared in a Lebanese newspaper, Faisal denied them and asked their proponents to produce the evidence. Al-Tariki did indeed produce some evidence, namely that Kamal Adham, Faisal's son-in-law and head of the Kingdom's future intelligence service, was receiving a fixed share of the Arabian Oil Company's profits, the same company that was established with Japanese participation. It was on that basis that the Council of Ministers decided on 14 November 1961, under the personal chairmanship of King Faisal, to annul the contract relative to the company's establishment. The irony of the matter is that although Faisal was right to annul the contract, instead of rewarding al-Tariki on his honourable stand he punished him a few months later by dismissing him from his post, and replacing him with Ahmad Zaki al-Yamani as the new Oil Minister.[26]

At that time, Iran and Saudi Arabia were in a race to gain America's favour by raising their oil production levels. In other words, they behaved in a selfish and short-sighted manner without any regard for the long-term interest.[27] Moreover, prior to the establishment of OPEC, Iraq had witnessed a revolution that brought down the regime and it became clear, with time, that this regime had been the object of exploitation and double-crossing by the oil companies on account of its oil policies.[28] This explains why the negotiations between the new Iraqi government and Western oil companies proved unfruitful, prompting the former to issue what became known as Law 80 of 1961. This law allowed Iraq to reclaim concession land where oil had either not been found, or had not been exploited, estimated at around 99.5 per cent of the main concession area. The move was not an attempt to nationalise the industry per se, but rather to reclaim land where the companies had not lived up to their commitment to explore for oil, based on the terms of the original concession contract. However, the oil companies refused to recognise this law for fear that it might set a precedent that other Arab countries with similar concession contracts could emulate.

This decision left the Iraqi Petroleum Company (IPC) with a small concession area around the oil field of Kirkuk, and another north of the newly discovered al-Rumaila field in the south, i.e., around 2000 square kilometres in total. However, even this land was nationalised in 1962, after the IPC refused to accept terms more favourable to the Iraqi government.[29] Even then, the Iraqi government was unable to exploit the areas reclaimed under Law 80 because these foreign companies put considerable pressure on other oil companies to deter them from signing contracts with the Iraqi government regarding these lands. In 1967, after the reestablishment of the Iraqi National Oil Company, the Iraqi government was able, for the first time, to sign an agreement with the French state-owned group ERAP, to exploit for oil in the "Amara region". Soon after, it issued Law 97 of 1967, banning all oil exploration contracts, and took the decision to allow the Iraqi National Oil Company to explore directly for oil in the field situated north of al-Rumeila, and a technical cooperation agreement was signed to this end between the Iraqi company and the Soviet government. The Iraqi National Oil Company also embarked on negotiations with a Yugoslav government-owned company to exploit other oil fields, but the Ba'ath Party's coup of 17 July 1968 put an end to that. In 1972, the Iraqi government completed the drive it launched in 1961 and 1976 to nationalise all foreign company assets in the country.[30]

In the meantime, the Shah's Iran was less inclined to stand up to the foreign companies, which is not at all surprising given that it was the CIA that reinstated the Shah to the throne, in August 1953 after bringing down the government of Prime Minister Mohammad Mosaddegh. The latter had tried to nationalise Iranian oil after BP refused to increase Iran's share of the profits, as it had done with Saudi Arabia and Venezuela.[31] Meanwhile, the international oil companies did their best to foment disagreements between the oil-producing countries themselves, for example, by threatening to reduce their investments in Venezuela and move them to the Middle East where costs were lower. They did the same in the late 1940s in their negotiations with Venezuela's dictatorial government, in an attempt to lower the taxes imposed on their oil.[32] They insinuated to countries with considerable oil reserves like Saudi Arabia and Kuwait that they ought to increase their output to deter the search for energy alternatives since this could eventually rob them of the ability to benefit from their oil. This is a mantra we still hear today. Moreover, they repeatedly reminded Iran that the Arabs took advantage of their move to nationalise oil in the early 1950s by raising their own production. In his writings, Abdullah al-Tariki was careful to detail many of the ploys that these companies have used.[33]

The June 1967 War dealt a final blow, or almost, to the Arab regional order, and strengthened the international oil companies' resolve with regards to the oil-producing countries, just as it strengthened the resolve of forces opposed to change in the region. These were the reasons that led to the OPEC countries' failure to exert minimum control over the pricing and production of their oil, until the October 1973 War gave the Arabs the opportunity to forge a more independent oil policy.

2. After 1973

The October 1973 War was a key moment in the process of readjusting the formulas and terms of different oil contracts signed between the oil-producing countries and international oil companies. From 1970 to 15 October 1973, the oil-producing countries were in constant negotiations with the international oil companies to improve the terms of oil contracts, especially regarding compensation for the drop in the price of the dollar and the increase in the rate of inflation, but to no avail. Meanwhile, in a press conference on 15 September 1973, President Richard Nixon waved his "big stick" at the oil-producing countries by warning them that they risked losing Western markets and facing the same fate as former Iranian Prime Minister Mosaddegh, whose downfall was engineered by the CIA for having rejected the unfair oil deals in 1951 and trying to nationalise Iranian oil.

However, for the very first time in the history of their relationship with the oil companies, the Arabs decided to take the initiative away from these companies and use it to rectify the situation. They called for a meeting of oil ministers on 16 October 1973, while the war was still raging, and decided to raise the price of oil by 70 per cent, thus raising the price of oil from $3 a barrel to $5.12. The following day, the Arab oil-producing countries held a private meeting where they decided to lower monthly production levels by 5 per cent, which meant that decisions on oil pricing and production were out of the hands of the international oil companies.

In 1973, there took place the accelerated implementation of a partnership agreement between the oil-producing countries and foreign companies which allowed the producing countries to own around 25 per cent of the crude oil-production facilities, with the proviso that this share would rise to 51 per cent by 1982. This not only drew a distinction between the producing countries' oil and foreign companies' oil, the latter also had to adhere to the benchmark price and pay royalties and taxes to the producing countries. In 1974, the producing countries decided on their own to raise this tax to around 85 per cent, and the royalties to 20 per cent and, instead of waiting for 1982, raised their share to 60 per cent.[34] The 1970s were, therefore the decade during which the oil-producing countries reclaimed their oil sector. However, the foreign companies did maintain control over most of the industry's technical production stages because the governments, rather than continue to take the initiative, reverted to their former reactionary policies.

Third: Oil-related industries

The oil-producing countries' experience with the international oil companies shows that the latter were always careful to maintain control over all stages of the oil industry, starting with production and ending with transportation and marketing, by way of the refining and petrochemical industries. Thus, despite the above-mentioned gains by the oil-producing countries in their relationship with the companies, including reclaiming ownership of their oil industry, raising their margin of profit and having a say in matters of pricing and production, these countries' performance in so far as the stability of oil revenues and indigenising this industry's various stages is still far from satisfactory. In the rest of this chapter, we will address these governments' failure to achieve significant progress in the oil industry, and in the next chapter we will examine their failure to adopt pricing and production policies to stabilise the income from oil.

Although the oil companies' record as far as indigenising the oil industry in the GCC and other countries is rather shameful, part of the blame should be shared by the local governments who have been prone to bend under pressure because they isolated themselves from the people, the very source of their power. Let us take the example of ARAMCO that operates in Saudi Arabia, the largest GCC country and presumably the best able to force the company to indigenise various stages of this industry. Did the Saudi government succeed in doing that? To answer this question, we should go back to the company's early beginnings and see how it treated its Saudi employees compared to other nationalities, and how it blocked all steps to indigenising this important industry.

1. Working conditions and wages

Robert Vitalis describes how in the 1940s ARAMCO's residential compounds in Dhahran were divided along racial lines. White Americans lived in compounds with full educational, health and recreational facilities and received the highest wages, even when their skills were equal to those of other nationalities, followed by the Italians and Asians who received lower wages and had the use of fewer facilities. The Saudi employees were the worst off at every level; they lived in structures of what seemed like corrugated steel and brush, were not allowed to go close to where the Americans lived, had the least number of facilities and received the lowest wages, even lower than the diggers and other workers with similar skills.[35] Even Abdullah al-Tariki who, in the mid 1950s was the Finance Ministry's representative to ARAMCO, was not spared this racist treatment by the company, which insisted at the beginning that he live outside the American compound, but failed.[36] However, after several years of strikes, confrontations and sacrifice by the local workers, coupled eventually with a reaction on the part of the Saudi government, ARAMCO had no choice but to introduce gradual reforms to its employment, salary scale, residential, nutrition and health policies, though these reforms remained rather timid.[37] It is worth mentioning here that there was no noticeable change in the way ARAMCO treated its Saudi employees until al-Tariki visited Venezuela, appraised this country's experience in this respect and on his return put pressure on ARAMCO to introduce a number of reforms.

These included adjusting the Saudi employees' wages as well as educating and training them, integrating them within the company structure and improving their living conditions. Among al-Tariki's demands was the appointment of Saudi nationals to the company's administration board, the response to which came several years later in 1959 when Hafiz Wahbi and al-Tariki himself were appointed as the Saudi government's representatives to ARAMCO's administration board. However, the company's headquarters remained in New York, where the board held its meetings until recently.[38]

Again, it is not that surprising that ARAMCO, the Western press and even the CIA mistreated Abdullah al-Tariki, whom they sometimes accused of being a communist and mocked by twisting his words. At the same time, many Western sources admit that al-Tariki knew the oil industry inside out, was a true patriot and faithfully carried out his responsibilities towards his people and the Arab nation as a whole.[39]

ARAMCO was not the only oil company in the region to mistreat its local employees compared with other nationalities. In 1952, Kuwaitis working for the Kuwait Oil Company, a British-American company, decided to make a stand for their rights, chief among which was doubling their wages to make them equal to those of foreign workers, replacing their hot, corrugated-steel living quarters with more suitable accommodation and providing them with a proper dining room. When the company rejected these demands and the workers went on strike, the government intervened, broke up the strike and arrested the leaders, without heeding any of their demands. This happened several years later, when the government again intervened and some improvements did take place.[40]

2. Education and training

As indicated above, given that ARAMCO was not eager to either employ or promote Saudi nationals within the company ranks, it was not that surprising that it objected to their education and training, especially if it felt a certain receptivity to that by the authorities, and data from that period confirm this. Several sources indicate that the American ambassador to Saudi Arabia, after meeting King 'Abdul-'Aziz, had the impression that the King did not want the Kingdom's education system to be as comprehensive as America's, but preferred some kind of vocational and business training system to help the people raise their standards of living. In other words, he did not want a new generation of politicians and lawyers, like in Egypt.[41] As this book makes clear, this particular way of thinking on the part of the region's governments was not particular to Saudi Arabia. It was rather a deeply ingrained conviction by all governments in the region who realised, unfortunately, the danger of raising the public's awareness and the ensuing calls for change and readjusting the balance of power between the government and the people. However, even the King's wish to limit the level of the Saudi people's education was not good enough for ARAMCO who learned from other oil companies' experience in Mexico and Venezuela that educating the people will eventually help them take control of the country's oil sector, which automatically means a decline in the company's control. This is why ARAMCO had no desire even for the type of vocational training proposed by the King, especially since they employed Saudi nationals mainly for their low wages. Even when the company finally did make available a number of training programmes, these focused on a single technical skill not useable in other domains, which made the Saudi employees' jobs both boring and without hope of further development.[42]

In Kuwait, the terms of the oil agreement with the Kuwaiti government committed the company to send Kuwaitis abroad for education at its own expense, but the company kept its part of the agreement only on occasion. When it did so, it sent one or two individuals to Bahrain to train in skills like carpentry and ironwork, rather than skills that would allow them to attain leadership or advanced technical positions in the company. In other words, the British-American company operating in Kuwait was no different from its sister ARAMCO in that respect.[43]

The situation in Iraq was somewhat different. The agreements signed between the oil companies and the state in 1951 called for thirty secondary school graduates to learn a variety of skills in Britain, at the company's expense, and upon graduation to replace foreign experts working in the country.

3.   Refining

Types of crude oil differ from the points of view of density, sulphur content, ease of transport and other characteristics. What is important for us to know here is that crude oil can be refined and turned into a variety of petroleum products, chief among which is benzene for engines, naphtha for the petrochemical industry, kerosene for airplane fuel, diesel for transport and agricultural equipment, and other derivatives like lubricants, asphalt and so on. There are also different forms of refining and of refined petroleum products; the more sophisticated the refinery, the wider the variety and higher the quality of its products from crude oil are.[44] Therefore, when we talk about refining as a stage, we are in fact talking about human resource training, modern technology integration, more value-added products and the promotion of other industrial domains, especially the petroleum industry.

This is why, ever since the discovery of oil, the international oil companies have been careful to locate their oil refineries in consumer rather than producer countries, and even after the oil-producing countries took control of this sector, there is yet to be significant progress in this domain. As these countries were reliant on the West and failed to keep in touch with their people, the foreign companies had no reason to cooperate with efforts to indigenise the industry, and the industrialised countries did their best to thwart all attempts in that direction. According to recent reports from BP, the total global refinery capacity equalled 92,531 thousand barrels per day in 2012 whereas the refinery capacity for the total Middle East region did not exceed 8255 thousand barrels per day or 8.9 per cent of the total refinery capacity in the world.[45] This is in view of the fact that out of the global production of oil of 8652 thousand barrels per day in the same year, the share for the countries of the Middle East combined reached approximately 28,270 barrels a day or around 32.5 per cent,[46] oil having been discovered there as early as the 1930s. Even the latter countries' effort to export their refined oil to the West has met with a barrage of obstacles, some tax related while others had to do with administrative procedures, like claiming that the quality of these products does not meet the industrialised countries' specifications. In fact, the refining industry failed to develop locally because the oil-producing countries did not negotiate collectively with the West. Furthermore, the fact that some of them bought refineries in the West, at a time when refining had become less profitable and environmental laws more stringent, was no substitute for locating the industry in the region. Had they done that, they would have provided cheap crude oil and gas, indigenised the technology, provided employment opportunities, encouraged forward and backward economic linkages, and benefitted from the economies of scale in the Arab-Islamic region, especially since demand for oil will hitherto mostly come from Asia. This requires a kind of cooperation that safeguards the interests of all parties.[47]

In brief, locating refineries in other countries' economies is, in some way, akin to investing oil surpluses in international financial markets. Despite reaping financial gains or losses, this kind of investment deprives the producing country of a genuine development process that would help it build its human and technical resources, vary its economic structures and expand the market, and through that, reduce costs, increase employment opportunities and bring stability and prosperity to the Arab region.

4. The petrochemical industry

We showed earlier how the oil refining process results in a number of products, which in turn become inputs for several other industries, and that naphtha is one such product used in another important stage of the petroleum industry, the petrochemical industry. This is an important tool in the oil-producing countries' development because it has backward and forward economic linkages with several other sectors, like construction, agriculture and transportation. It is also known for its variety of products, whereby some sources indicate that around 80 per cent of its products are used in the plastics, industrial fibre, rubber and other industries.

Moreover, compared to refining, the latter is a high value added industry; whereas the value added from refining is no more than $3 per barrel, the petrochemical industry adds between $36 to basic products, like ethylene, and around $2600 to multi-purpose products.[48] Furthermore, just as cheap Arab oil played a pioneering role in the development of modern means of transportation, after WWII, it also played a role in the establishment and expansion of the petrochemical industry, in particular the plastics industry. However, this industry's added value and other benefits have remained in the West because both the refineries and their output, like naphtha, that go into the production of petrochemicals, remained there as well.[49]

Moreover, despite their relative advantage in this domain thanks to their vast oil reserves, the GCC and other oil-producing countries have so far failed to indigenise this industry. This is either because of their weakness and lack of cooperation amongst themselves, or the obstacles the industrialised countries have put in their path as these countries possess a relative advantage in their production due to having crude oil. Even when some oil-producing countries like Saudi Arabia, Kuwait and Qatar, tried to produce a number of basic petrochemicals in the 1980s, the European Union imposed customs duties on these products, despite unsuccessful attempts to make it change its mind, which ranged between 13 and 15 per cent and impeded the industry's progress. There seems to be no way out of this conundrum, for either the petrochemical or petroleum refining industry, except through regional integration, at least among the GCC states and their wider Arab milieu. This is because these industries' success depends on a minimum market capacity that would allow them to produce at a competitive cost. Moreover, mastering the technology and skill required for these industries' success makes it imperative that these countries unite their efforts and negotiate collectively with the oil companies from a position of strength. This strong negotiating position is also essential in negotiations with Western countries so that the latter open their markets to these products, given that the success of this industry depends on fostering the right conditions for both supply and demand.[50] If this collective effort does not take place, then there is the strong possibility that in future the centre of mass for these industries will move from the industrialised nations to the Asian countries that have successfully developed the necessary infrastructure for these industries. According to the data for 2010, the Middle East region as a whole had a share of no more than 15.6 per cent of the global production of ethylene. From 2009-2010 meanwhile, there was an increase in the production of ethylene in the Middle East, equating to 4 million tonnes because of the increased production in both Qatar and Saudi Arabia. The increase in the Asian countries was 4.8 million tonnes.[51]

Chapter Six

Pricing and Production

As explained previously, the international oil companies still control most stages of the oil industry, starting with discovery and exploration and ending with the transport and distribution of the final product, by way of refining and the petrochemical industry, even if it all takes place under the umbrella of the so-called national oil companies. The reason is the international oil companies' monopoly of the oil industry's intricacies, advanced technology and the highly advanced technical and administrative skills involved. The producing countries have failed to indigenise these aspects for various reasons, mainly the lack of political will on their part, as indicated earlier. However, the oil-producing countries' biggest failure, so far, is their inability to stabilise oil prices and revenues in order to implement various development projects, although the main objective behind OPEC's establishment in 1960, and efforts to control the industry's management after the October 1973 War, was to stabilise oil revenues by controlling prices and output.[1] In this chapter, we will try to clarify the developments that affected the price of oil since the early 1970s, before looking at the reasons behind OPEC's failure to stabilise the price of oil, and whether these are specific to the region, or not.

First: Evolution of oil prices

Until the establishment of OPEC in 1960, the international oil companies, known as the "seven sisters", controlled the world's oil industry both vertically and horizontally. They understood the strategic importance of the Gulf region's oil for developing the transportation technology, building the petrochemical industry and implementing the Marshall Plan to rebuild Europe after WWII. However, the main impact of the increasing importance of oil as a source of energy was the cost it exacted from the GCC states in terms of the depletion and pricing of this finite resource. The oil companies increased their production levels in Saudi Arabia, Iran, Kuwait, Iraq and the UAE from around 1.7 million barrels per day (bpd) in 1950, to 13.3 million bpd in 1970, then to 20.5 million bpd, in 1973. What helped them do that was the low price of production in the region that dropped from around 20 cents per barrel in 1948, to around 11 cents in 1970, compared to over one dollar in other parts of the world.[2] This steep increase in Gulf oil production led to a drop in the price of "Arabian Light crude oil" from around $2 per barrel per year, in 1950, to $1.80 in 1960, and $1.21 in 1970.[3] In the words of a Western oil company official, these prices were lower than 1920 prices, both nominally and in terms of purchasing power.[4]

This nominal and real drop in the price of oil, especially after 1960 the year of OPEC's establishment, is proof that the organisation had a limited impact on oil prices and production. The fact that the price of "Arabian Light" went up from $1.21 per barrel per year in 1970 to $2.90 per year in 1973, in the aftermath of negotiations between the oil-producing countries and the oil companies, confirms that a unified position by the these countries actually bears fruit and protects their rights. However, the drop in the value of the dollar and increase in the rate of inflation eroded most of this nominal increase, considered quite modest at the time.[5] On 16 October 1973, a few days after the outbreak of the Ramadan War and the Egyptian army's breach of the Bar Lev Line, representatives from six Gulf countries met in Kuwait City and decided to raise the price of the "Arabian Light" from $2.90 to $5.11 per barrel. It was a one-sided decision on their part, meaning that they did not consult the oil companies, and a historic move that laid the ground for future independent decision-making in matters of pricing and production.

Soon afterwards, prices began to inch gradually upwards due to a drop in Arab production and the impact this had on consumer expectations, and in December 1973, OPEC decided to raise the price of "Arabian Light" to $11.65, that is, a four-fold increase in the span of four months. However, the decision to lower production levels, and make its increase contingent upon Israel withdrawing from the Arab territories it occupied in 1973, began to weaken when Israel failed to withdraw.[6] Nevertheless, OPEC's decision to act independently in determining oil prices and production was a historic turning point, and a confirmation of the need for solidarity among oil-producing countries. Until the establishment of OPEC in 1960, the oil companies decided autonomously on matters of pricing and production, and only afterwards did they begin to consult the producing countries on such issues. The events that followed the October 1973 War marked another adjustment in the balance of power between the two sides as decisions on pricing and production became the exclusive domain of producing countries. This transformation created a new de facto situation in the oil market, whereby oil prices began to interact with this new reality, including a raise in the price of oil up to $13 per barrel, in 1978.[7] In late 1978, early signs of the impending Iranian revolution began to appear at a time when the country produced around 5.5 million barrels, or almost 10 per cent of the world's production, 80 per cent of which was for export. Subsequent events in the region, starting with the Shah's downfall and outbreak of the Iran-Iraq War, and ending with, among others, the Iranian students' occupation of the American embassy in Tehran and the Soviet occupation of Afghanistan, led again to an increase in the price of "Arabian Light" to $42 per barrel at the end of 1980.[8]

After reaching that peak, oil prices began a long downward trend because their sudden big rise had clearly left its mark on supply and demand, and this, in turn, wrested control over the oil market away from the producers in favour of the consumer. The rise in prices encouraged several non-OPEC members, like Mexico, Russia, the North Sea and Alaska, which were not producing before due to the high costs of production, to raise their production thus increasing the supply. Russia alone raised its production in 1973 to around 11 million barrels per day, a rise of 40 per cent. On the demand side, changes also happened in favour of alternative sources of energy, of a more economical use of energy in homes and factories and other such policies, leading to a global drop in the demand for oil of around 6 million barrels per day. The combination of more supply and less demand started a downward trend in oil prices, which did not help dispel divisions among OPEC's ill-prepared members, a subject we will come back to later. For the first time in its history, OPEC had to impose production quotas on its members, in response to the new market conditions, and in March 1982 imposed a production ceiling of around 17.5 million barrels per day, half of OPEC's production in 1979, estimated at 31 million barrels per day. To retaliate against the Arabs who supported Saddam Hussein in his war with Iran, Khomeini's Iran decided not to abide by the quota and increased its production to 3 million barrels per day, by the end of 1982, i.e., three times the quota imposed by OPEC, and Nigeria soon followed suit. At the time, Saudi Arabia was a "swing producer", i.e., the party that made up the difference between OPEC-imposed quotas and amounts actually produced by member countries, meaning that Iran and Nigeria's overproduction had forced Saudi Arabia to lower its production.[9] However, none of these policies made any difference, especially since non-OPEC members were bringing their oil prices down to increase sales in the now highly competitive market. What helped exacerbate the problem and weaken OPEC's control over pricing and production, was the fact that most OPEC members were producing above their quotas, and that the Iran-Iraq War had increased tensions among these members, making any agreement exceedingly difficult to achieve. In an attempt to control the situation, Saudi Arabia continued to decrease its production to reach 2.2 million barrels per day, in May 1985, from a high of almost 10.5 million barrels in 1980. However, when it realised that it was useless to continue playing the swing producer, Saudi Oil Minister, Shaikh Ahmad Zaki al-Yamani, announced his country's intention to give up this role, since OPEC was no longer able to control oil prices, which meant that Saudi Arabia wanted to reclaim its share of the market.[10]

Thus, in 1985, OPEC's share of the world's oil production dropped by around 25 per cent from the early 1980s level, and its revenues became a quarter of their 1980 level.[11] Oil prices fell steeply to reach $10 per barrel in May 1986, and Dubai's oil even fell to $7 per barrel.[12] This collapse in oil prices convinced OPEC members of the need for a minimum level of cooperation among them. Thus, in December 1986, they set a new average reference price of $18, based on a basket of OPEC oil prices, with the opportunity for adjustment every three months, which allows for certain flexibility. However, although this helped stabilise the nominal price of oil at $18, from 1987 to 1999, prices did not go back to their former high levels, and the real price of oil during that period remained in decline.[13] From 1999 to 2003, oil prices continued to fluctuate between $19.3 and $31.1 per barrel, before starting to increase again after the occupation of Iraq to reach over $140 in 2007. They stabilised again at around $75-$90 per barrel, and were still at that level at the time of writing this book. It is worth mentioning that the future oil markets have begun to play a more significant role in defining prices, particularly since the start of the twenty-first century. This in turn has led to the declining role of the oil-producing nations and the oil companies in setting these prices. Furthermore, it has led to increasing fluctuations in these prices, in addition to deepening the conflict surrounding the responsibility for pricing oil between the producing and consumer states. President Bush and Prime Minister Gordon Brown blamed OPEC for the rise in oil prices from $68.71 per barrel in August 2007 to around $128.33 per barrel in June 2008. They both demanded that OPEC increase production. The organisation's response was that the responsibility lay with the speculation in the financial markets and likewise the inadequate investment in refinery capacity, especially for crude oil.[14]

The above survey shows that the real price of oil has gradually eroded since OPEC's establishment in 1960, except in times of crisis and war. However, the October 1973 War was the exception since it witnessed the transfer of control over pricing and production to the producing countries. This begs the question as to why OPEC failed to stabilise oil prices and revenues, one of the main reasons for its creation in the first place. We will try to answer this by looking at OPEC and the role of the external factor, i.e., foreign influence on these policies.

Second: OPEC between reality and ambition

In our opinion, the drop in oil prices and revenues is due to several factors, some related to the supply side, like the development of alternative energies, more economical usages and global economic growth rates. Other factors relate to the demand side, including the oil-producers' pricing and production policies, especially OPEC members led by the GCC states, the subject of this book.[15] As we mentioned earlier, since its establishment in 1960, OPEC has failed to achieve the minimum level of stability in oil prices thanks to its division into two groups, due to several reasons, some of which are economic, others not. The first group comprises countries with big populations, small oil reserves and a high absorptive capacity, like Iraq, Iran and Algeria, and usually leans towards lowering production and raising prices. The second group comprises countries with large oil reserves, small populations and a limited absorptive capacity, like Saudi Arabia, the UAE, Kuwait and the other GCC states, and usually leans towards increasing production and lowering prices. The latter countries justify their policies by claiming that their opposition to high prices is due to several factors,[16] including the fact that their pricing and production policies take into account their oil large reserves, which force them to increase their production and maintain moderate prices to deter the early search for alternative sources. Some also say that their policies are based on realism and the desire to avoid causing any harm to the closely connected global economy, especially given that any harm to this economy will also harm the oil countries' assets in the West. They add that the marginal $3 per barrel cost of production is quite low in these countries compared with the rest of the world, and conclude that any increase in the price of oil is a burden on the developing non oil-producing countries, many of which are Arab and predominantly Muslim. However, such justifications cannot be taken in isolation from the high price that the region's people have paid as a result of these policies which these countries have mostly adopted. These policies have not only led to the erosion of oil prices, as we have seen before, but also thwarted these countries' ability to forge a unified position vis-à-vis the oil companies and Western nations. Moreover, these policies were not governed by the above considerations as much as the desire to revolve in the West's orbit, as we will see later. Furthermore, these governments would not be able to withstand the opposition's scrutiny, which would involve the following issues:

1. These countries are fully capable of increasing their revenues, either by increasing their oil prices without increasing production levels, or by simply reducing current production levels, because the development of alternative sources is still far off. Even if alternatives did exist for all energy usages, including fuel for transportation and aviation, their prices would not be anywhere near the price of oil, even in the medium term. Moreover, adopting policies similar to those of other OPEC countries will not only result in a higher income, it will also make these countries' pricing and production policies closer to those of OPEC members with large populations and limited reserves, countries whose prosperity means the prosperity of GCC states as well.

2. The oil-producing countries should link the level of their oil income to the absorptive capacity of their economies; in other words, the quantity of oil produced should not lead to a surplus of oil and money that the domestic economy cannot absorb in a productive manner. Like the above-mentioned policies, this policy will preserve the oil underground and increase its price in the future. Moreover, not only is this policy compatible with the objectives of the other OPEC members, it is liable to strengthen these countries' position vis-à-vis the international oil companies and Western consuming nations who have not stopped trying to weaken and dismantle OPEC since the International Energy Agency was established in the 1970s.

3. Accumulating oil revenues and investing them abroad carries with it a number of risks, including lower currency values, inflation and diminishing revenues, not to mention various political risks. Moreover, because it also carries with it the danger of a financial meltdown, producing countries should refrain from producing more than their economies can adequately absorb, as they transition from one development stage to the other. For example, one study showed that the same assets invested by OPEC members abroad and estimated at $129.5 billion, based on 1974 prices, were worth no more than $75 billion in 1979, due to the drop in the value of the dollar alone. In the meantime, the losses incurred by these countries' sovereign funds due to the recent financial crisis, to which we will come back later, are astronomical.

4. The policy of keeping oil prices low is based on a false assumption which

says that since the Western consumer is the main beneficiary of these prices he will undoubtedly increase his consumption. The proponents of this policy, however, ignore the fact that consumer governments impose exorbitant taxes on imported oil, meaning that they fill their coffers with huge revenues at the expense of the producing countries that badly need it. For example, oil experts Joseph Stanislaw and Daniel Yergin say that in 1992, the European Union earned a yearly income of around $200 billion from taxes on oil consumption amounting to 11.8 million barrels per day. This sum is almost three times the $75 billion that the oil-producing countries earned from selling that same amount of oil, which simply means that in that same year, 1992, the consumer countries' revenue from taxes on oil imports was higher than the oil-producing countries' revenue from oil sold to the EU.[17] Oil expert Leonardo Maugeri points out to the gap between what oil-producing countries earn and Western consumers pay, and says that when the per barrel price is $60, the European consumer actually pays $200-$250, meaning that the difference is the amount of taxes that Western governments levy on oil and its derivatives, which sometimes reaches 70 per cent.[18] A Western research organisation undertook a comparative study of oil prices compared to other consumer goods, and the results showed that if other products were priced by the barrel, like oil, and the barrel was 42 gallons, the price of these goods would be much higher than oil. It gave a number of examples including one saying that if Coca Cola were sold by the barrel, it would cost $119 per barrel; if Perrier was sold by the barrel, it would cost $426; if "Stop and Shop's" anti-dandruff shampoo was sold by the barrel, it would cost $1469 and, if "McIlhenny's" Tabasco Sauce was sold by the barrel, it would cost $4542.[19] All this clearly shows how unfair the per barrel prices are to the countries of origin, especially at a time when the poverty rate in the Arab world stands at 30 per cent. With that in mind, would a good and honest government accept seeing such a huge amount of wealth taken away from its needy population, just to line the coffers of Western countries that have the highest standards of living in the world?

5. Some also believe that current production levels accelerate oil's depletion rate, because once extracted a barrel cannot be replaced. Therefore, reducing production levels will make this resource last longer, and give the producing countries more opportunity to benefit from this vital resource, not only by selling it in crude form, but eventually by using it to manufacture the above-mentioned petroleum products.[20]

Third: The foreign factor

Now that we know that the GCC states' pricing and production policies, since the 1970s, cannot be justified economically, how should we understand them? The answer again lies in these governments' weak negotiating positions. Since they do not draw their legitimacy from their people, these countries remain subject to pressure and exploitation, and their policies end up serving the consumer countries' interests at the expense of their own people, a fact confirmed by observers from all over the world, especially the Western world. Kenneth Pollack, a former advisor to the Clinton administration, confirms that the United States is protecting the Saudi regime in return for services rendered, which includes selling it oil at prices lower than the official market rate.[21] William Quandt, a well-known researcher and Middle East expert, says that justifying Saudi Arabia's oil policy in the 1980s, which consisted of maintaining high production levels and low prices, by claiming that it was moderate, conflicts with the fundamentals of economic analysis in the mind of many experts. He says that several Saudi technocrats believe that lowering production, preserving the country's reserves underground, hoping for higher prices in the future and avoiding the accumulation of oil surpluses in the form of cash, is better than producing large quantities at low prices. These technocrats also believe that, in the 1980s, Saudi Arabia could have produced between 5 and 6 million barrels of oil a day and earned a higher revenue, instead of the actual production level of between 8 to 10 million barrels a day, which does not serve the country's long-term interest.[22] Moreover, just as it is impossible to explain Saudi Arabia and other GCC states' oil policies from the perspective of their societies' interests and the interest of the wider Arab milieu, it is impossible to explain their pricing policies. In December 1976, the OPEC countries decided in their conference in Doha to raise the price of oil by 10 per cent, then by another 5 per cent in the middle of 1977. However, Saudi Arabia and the UAE decided not to comply with that decision, and instead raised their price initially by a mere 5 per cent, then by another 5 per cent in the middle of 1977, with a Saudi proviso that the other countries freeze their prices until the end of 1977. To make sure that this freeze actually took place, Saudi Arabia increased its own production by around 9.2 million barrels per day, which led to an oil glut in 1978. Several observers believe that Saudi Arabia's main motivation was its desire to win the Carter administration's good will and support.

The late Professor John Kelly reminds us that an agreement of sorts was reached between Saudi Arabia and the USA in 1974, according to which the former guaranteed uninterrupted oil supplies to the latter at a fixed price and committed not to withdraw its investments from the US, in return for American protection. Kelly also says that when King Fahd visited Washington D.C. in 1977, the two sides agreed to increase Saudi oil production to 10.4 million barrels of oil per day, after January, and place any surplus over 8.5 million barrels at the United States' disposal.[23]

In 1979, under pressure from the USA in the form of a visit by Ambassador Robert Straus to the region, and his meeting with the Saudi crown prince Fahd Bin Abdul-Aziz, Saudi Arabia agreed to increase its oil production from 8.4 million barrels to 9.5 million barrels of oil per day.[24] Thus, despite an oil market surplus in the early 1980s, Saudi Arabia continued to produce 9.5 million barrels per day at $28 per barrel, at a time when other OPEC members were insisting on $32 or more per barrel. Former American Deputy Secretary of Energy, John Sawhill, confirmed the presence of a political angle to Saudi Arabia's production policy when he told a Congressional committee that, "Future Saudi production is primarily a political decision. For its own foreign exchange needs, Saudi Arabia has to produce less than 5 million bpd. However, Saudi Arabia has a great interest in the political stability of the West and the stability of our financial markets."[25]

Saudi Arabia's above "political" position helped dismantle OPEC's pricing policies, and just as it increased its production at the outbreak of the Iranian Revolution, it did so again at the outbreak of the Iran-Iraq War. In October 1980, Saudi Arabia announced that it was raising its production by around 1 million barrels to compensate for the interrupted Iraqi and Iranian supplies. Who knows whether the collapse of oil prices in the mid 1980s would have still taken place had it allowed prices to go up after the war broke out? The price of Saudi oil continued to be low compared to other OPEC members, a deliberate policy confirmed by former Saudi Oil Minister, Shaikh Ahmad Zaki al-Yamani, in an interview with NBC in 1981. He said in the interview that Saudi Arabia had engineered the rise in supply to cause an international oil glut and bring prices down. Saudi Arabia thus continued to saturate the market by producing at full capacity, and prices continued to decline, dropping from around $38 per barrel in 1981, to around $11 in 1986. This compelled George Bush senior, Ronald Reagan's vice president at the time, to pay a visit to the region and pressure the Gulf governments to raise their oil prices to above $12 per barrel.[26]

This shows the reader the reality of this "noble" stance, which made it seem as if the United States cared about the GCC's economies and the low oil prices. In fact, asking these countries to raise their prices above $12 per barrel was actually meant to save Texas-based oil companies and others from bankruptcy. The reason is that in some American states, including Texas, the per barrel extraction cost is no less than $12, meaning that any drop in the world's per barrel price below this figure makes it is impossible for these companies to continue to produce, and they will therefore lose out. These companies borrowed money and dug wells with the hope that prices would be high enough to cover their costs, including their borrowing costs, and guarantee a return on their shareholders' investments. Asking the Gulf countries to raise their prices deprived them of the only advantage from maintaining low prices, namely the departure of many non-OPEC oil-producing countries from the scene, which gave OPEC members a larger share of world production. Once again, this failed to materialise thanks to Saudi Arabia and other GCC states' political decisions which were not the kind that protect the people's interests, but the kind that spelled submission to the strong blackmailing the weak, in a world devoid of morality. Moreover, Bush senior had no interest in seeing OPEC regain its strength, nor in it imposing its control over the oil market, and was thus able to kill two birds with one stone. He gave the American oil companies back their strength and kept OPEC's share of the world production low compared to the 1970s, which negatively affected the price of oil. On his way to Saudi Arabia, Bush made a statement that he would tell the Saudis "the protection of American security interests requires action to stabilize the falling price of oil" and his words only confirm this move's positive implications for the Western world.[27]

Kuwait officially acknowledged that Iran was to blame for the sabotage to its oil installations in June 1986, because, according to official sources, the Kuwaiti government's decision to lower its oil prices was due to Saudi pressure rather than its support for Iraq in the war against Iran.[28] Even when Iraq emerged from the war with its economy on the brink, due to an accumulated debt of over $150 billion,[29] and the destruction of its basic infrastructure and economy, the Gulf countries, especially Kuwait and to a lesser extent the UAE, did not hesitate, according to Western sources, to flood the market with oil. To this end, they went above their OPEC quotas, producing well over 80 per cent of the production above OPEC's quotas.[30] This might have been the straw that broke the camel's back in its relations with Iraq and other Gulf states, since soon after came the occupation of Kuwait and the ensuing disaster for the entire region.

When George W. Bush declared his so-called "war on terror", the Saudi ambassador in Washington, Bandar Bin Sultan, pledged his country's support for the war and confirmed Saudi Arabia's intention to maintain the stability of oil prices. To prove the point, Saudi Arabia sent around 9 million barrels of oil to the United States, a move that led to a sudden drop in the price of oil from $28 to $22 per barrel.[31] Naturally, the Saudi ambassador did not care much about the repercussion of his move, or care to ask the United States what the terror he pledged to fight actually meant. He was simply content to adopt the American position wholesale, which later events proved included the destruction of Iraq. Even this particular outcome the ambassador had no objection to, if not supported, as we will show later on in the context of looking at the GCC's security policies. It is worth noting that in the course of preparing for the war on Iraq, George W. Bush had asked one of his advisors about the "additional oil production capacity of the UAE and Saudi Arabia". The fact that he asked this question at all indicates that it was no longer a matter of these countries' sovereign or independent decision-making, but that it all boiled down now to a simple technical issue, as if Saudi Arabia and the UAE had become private plantations for Bush, the United States and these countries' governments.[32]

One is hard-pressed to find a neutral and honest oil expert who endorses the pricing and production policies of Saudi Arabia and other Gulf countries. Author Daniel Yergin admits there was "a general meeting of the minds between Riyadh and Washington"[33] on matters related to oil policy. Anton Sarkis, an expert who worked with former Oil Minister al-Tariki, one of OPEC's founders, said that the Saudi government was always ready "to protect US interests, even if it means sacrificing their interests and the rest of OPEC".[34]

This, of course, reminds us of the injustice towards the oil-producing countries between the 1950s and the early 1960s. At that time, the international oil companies sold the oil barrel at around $1.78, which reduced the oil-producing countries' share to no more than 80 cents, i.e., 45 per cent of the total price, with the remainder going to the companies and their governments, which divided it among themselves.[35] In this context, an Arab oil expert reflects on the unfair division of oil revenues and asks, if the price of a barrel of oil product to the final consumer is $100, as was the case in Europe and Japan before prices began to rise in 2004, why is the difference between the total cost and the consumer price (i.e., the revenue), distributed in such a way that the owners of this finite natural resource get no more than 15 per cent of the revenue, while the rest goes straight into the coffers of consumer countries, whose per capita income is tenfold that of most oil-producing countries?[36]

In the twenty-first century, the GCC governments are still practising the same unfair pricing policies towards their people and, if history is anything to go by, we do not expect this to change as long as the same regimes remain in power. The Saudi move to flood the oil market in the early 1980s, which led to a price collapse in the mid 1980s, happened again just over a decade ago, as the well-known *Washington Post* columnist Bob Woodward confirms. Woodward says that when George W. Bush met with Bandar, the Saudi ambassador in

Washington, in February 2004: "He then thanked Bandar for what the Saudis were doing on oil – essentially flooding the market and trying to keep the price as low as possible. He then expressed appreciation for the policy and the impact it could have during the election year."[37]

PART III

Development Policies

We mentioned earlier that policies related to the discovery, exploration, pricing and production of oil that the GCC states have pursued over the past thirty years were, in the main, neither motivated by a nationalistic nor even a national vision. Rather, they were motivated by the vision of regimes that seek to remain in power and maintain their privileges, by any means. We also showed how these policies allowed international oil companies and Western governments to take advantage of this narrow vision, and get the lion's share of oil revenues. However, not only did the ruling families give up the country's oil wealth through the mismanagement of oil contracts and submission to Western pressure to keep prices low and production high, they failed to manage their own share of the revenue in a manner that serves the interests of their people and the Arab world at large. They spent this revenue as if it were booty with a single objective in mind, to remain in power; in other words, maintain the status quo.

One of the core strategies of the world's societies is using their public revenue to promote development and security. This strategy assumes even greater importance in countries whose economies depend on oil, a sector not structurally linked to other sectors, except in how governments spend its revenues; i.e., it has no forward and backward linkages to the rest of the economy.[1] In the nineteenth century, for example, the wheat sector in North America played an important role in the transportation and agricultural equipment sectors' development, which helped the latter sectors achieve significant progress. In Peru, the fish canning industry of the 1950s and 1960s promoted the manufacture of fishing boats, and this in turn helped the growth of several related industries.[2] The reason for the weakness of the oil sector's backward linkages is the failure to use it as input material in other sectors; the sector is characterised by its significant amount of capital and special skills, most of which is imported from abroad. This is why the oil sector does not stimulate other sectors by using their products as input, a phenomenon known as weak backward linkages. On the other hand, the weakness of this sector's forward linkages comes from the fact that no industries use its products as input for the manufacture of various petroleum products for example, meaning that most of its products are exported for such use abroad. Even the refining and petrochemical industries, established by a number of GCC states, are still limited compared with the world's overall production and not compatible with the amount of crude oil and gas in the region.

The failure to develop the region's petroleum industry is due to these governments' failure to agree on an integrated development path, a path that unifies their resources, avoids duplication and strengthens their negotiating position vis-à-vis the oil companies who monopolise all the technology and skills. It would also strengthen the governments' negotiating stance vis-à-vis the consumer countries that, in addition to other impediments, never stopped trying to impede this industry's development by imposing high taxes on imports from the GCC states. In any case, more important to us here than the oil industry's isolationist nature is that the important role of oil, whose revenues are accumulating in the coffers of unproductive governments, has made the manner in which the region's governments spend these revenues the main definer of their countries' developmental and security paths.

This economic characteristic, particular to the Gulf region, is what compelled many researchers to characterise these countries as "rentier economies" because their revenue comes mostly from exporting oil.[3] The accumulation of oil revenues in their coffers, especially since the 1970s and in the shadow of unaccountable governments, led to certain patterns of spending which, in turn, resulted in distorted development, characterised by waste, marginalised citizenry, acute dependency on foreign labour, private sector erosion and endemic corruption. On the other hand, there is a number of positive aspects as well, including spending on basic infrastructural projects and improved, though unsustainable, standards of living; it is unsustainable because this improvement is linked to the presence of oil, to the exclusion of all other sources of income. This will become clear in the next paragraphs when we address whether these governments have achieved the country's main development objectives.[4]

CHAPTER SEVEN

Diversification of Economic Structures

Nothing condemns these governments' record more than the failure to diversify their economic structures and find alternatives for oil, after more than thirty years of "development efforts". The diversification of economic structures should be the main objective of the region's governments, not simply because oil is a finite resource in the middle and long terms, or its prices and revenues fluctuate in the short term, but also because it is an isolated sector which requires a substantial amount of capital and advanced technological skills. Consequently, it cannot provide enough employment opportunities for an ever-increasing local workforce. Were these countries able to use their oil resources to achieve self-sustainable development in terms of Gross Domestic Product (GDP) and per capita income? Was there any significant change in their productive infrastructures to indicate a reduced dependency on oil? Did they develop an industrial sector worth its name, capable of contributing to the GDP and creating employment opportunities? Finally, did the GCC states succeed in diversifying their export products in a tangible way? The answer to all these questions, based on the available data, will likely give us a clear picture of the extent to which these governments have succeeded or failed to achieve their development objectives.[1]

First: Erratic economic growth

The kind of economic growth that leads eventually to self-sustainable development and structural transformation is a high growth rate, i.e., higher than the population growth rate. This helps to increase per capita income and savings, which raises the standard of living and contributes to expanding the economy's productive capacity. Economic growth should also be stable and sustainable to avoid obstructing or slowing down various development projects. For over thirty years, the GCC states have failed to initiate this kind of growth, and we will show, through growth-related data from the Arab Monetary Fund, the IMF and the World Bank, how economic growth in the GCC states has remained in flux, due to their continued dependency on oil and its fluctuating prices and revenues. Table no. 7-1 shows the rate of GDP and per capita income development in the GCC states, between 1978 and 2011.

Table 7-1

Development of Gross Domestic Product and Average per Capita Income in the GCC states 1978-2011 (at current prices)

Year	1978	1998	2011
GDP (Billion US Dollars)	106.5	231.7	1368.7
Average Per Capita Income (US Dollars)	9266	7937	29375
	1978-1998	1998-2011	
GDP Growth Rate per cent	8	19.4	
Average Per Capita Income Growth per cent	-1.5	13.9	

Source: *Al-Hisabat al-qawmiyyah li-l-duwal al-ʿarabiyyah 1978-2011* [National statistics of Arab States, 1978-2011] (Abu Dhabi: Arab Monetary Fund, 2012)

Table 7-1 clearly shows that the GDP in the GCC region as a whole increased from $106.5 billion in 1978, to $231.7 billion in 1998, an annual increase of 8 per cent. However, the per capita income during this period fell from 9266 to 7937, i.e. a decrease of 1.5 per cent, and this reduction is attributed to two reasons. The first is that oil prices and revenue in this period were lower compared with the 1970s, and this caused the rate of economic growth to fall while at the same time the growth in population continued. This meant that the modest increase in income did not cover the population growth, thus there was a decline in per capita income. Conversely, the first period of the twenty-first century saw a third oil boom that materialised as a steady increase in oil prices and revenue in the late 1990s. Hence, the GDP of the GCC states rose from $231.7 billion in 1998 to $1368.7 billion in 2011, i.e. an annual 14 per cent increase. There is no doubt that this increase in per capita income was caused by the surprising increase in oil prices and revenue. However, this is a worrying growth as it was not a result of any change in the production framework of these countries. Consequently, the per capita income may fluctuate in the future if oil prices and revenue fall. Indeed, reports by the IMF confirm that the GCC states will require the price of oil to be $100 per barrel in the coming years, otherwise they will begin to suffer deficits in their public budgets and a fall in trade balance surpluses in view of their current spending.[2]

It is worth mentioning that the above growth rates conceal several facts that make reality less positive than it seems. We will underline the most important of these facts before looking at the picture drawn by the data from the international organisations.

1. The above growth rates indicate a continued link between these countries 'GDP and per capita growth, on the one hand, and oil revenues whose prices are determined by the international oil market, on the other. This link has spread to other economic variables, including drafting public budgets, trade balances, foreign currency reserves, the sustainability of development projects and foreign aid. We saw how, when the price of oil dropped sharply in the 1980s, budget deficits compelled the GCC states to rein in spending, mainly in the development domain. Some countries had to borrow money, while others opted to liquidate part of their foreign investments, and give up their interests.[3]

2. As we will see later, these countries past growth rates were not the result of structural transformations or establishment of industries based on highly productive human resources. They were, in fact, the result of transforming finite material wealth, i.e., oil, into financial wealth, or paper wealth that could be spent, if that was desired. This means that the major part of these countries' GDP is no more than the consumption of an existing asset, rather than generating new ones through hard productive efforts. This is why figures relevant to the national income of GCC states do not reflect the finite nature of oil, and this leads to significant exaggerations that need constant reviewing and adjustment, if we want to know the real dimension of these countries' economic activities. Some studies indicate that such an adjustment of figures might well reveal that these countries' actual GDP is no more than 25 per cent of its current value.[4] A researcher who, after calculating real growth rates taking into account the finite nature of oil, showed that between 1980 and 2000, these countries growth rates were actually negative.[5]

3.   Most GDP figures are at current prices, including those of the Arab
      Monetary Fund, which we used to calculate the rates shown in table
      7-1. In other words, some of the above growth rates are due to price
      changes, meaning that the real increase in GDP and per capita income
      in these countries is less than the increase shown in the above table.[6]

Thus, if we consider the GDP and per capita income growth rates in these
countries while taking into account the inherent inflation and depletion factors, it would not surprise us if a detailed look at the above figures shows that
these countries have actually grown economically, but without any significant
development. Reports by the World Bank, the IMF and other agencies confirm
this and show that between 1975-2000, the GDP growth rate in the Middle
Eastern oil-exporting countries (excluding Qatar) was around 3.2 per cent per
annum, while that of the East Asian and Pacific countries was around 3.1 per
cent and 7.4 per cent, respectively. Even this low growth rate witnessed fluctuations due to oil price changes, during that same period.[7] Thus, with the oil price
boom that accompanied the October 1973 War, this price and revenue increase
simultaneously led to an increase in these countries' economic growth rates by
around 4.3 per cent per annum during 1975-1980. However, according to figures
published by various international agencies, even this rate was lower than growth
rates elsewhere in the world, which reached 6.7 per cent in the rest of the Middle
East and 7.3 per cent in Asian countries, during that same period.[8] When the
price of oil dropped in the mid 1980s to under $10 a barrel, the oil-producing
countries showed negative growth rates, in 1980 to 1985, at a time when other
Middle Eastern and East Asian countries registered growth rates of 5 per cent
and 6.5 per cent, respectively. When the price of oil stabilised at around $20 per
barrel, in the 1990s, growth rates in the oil-producing countries returned into the
black, but at rates lower than in the above-mentioned two groups of countries.
In the period 1995-2000, the growth rate in the oil-producing countries was
around 3.3 per cent per annum, compared to 4.5 per cent in the other Middle
Eastern countries, and 5 per cent in East Asia. The decline in the world's growth
rates in 1998 led to a drop in real oil prices to where they were in 1973-1974,
i.e., prior to the first oil price boom, and this in turn led to a drop in the price
of petroleum products by around one third. This again led to a decline in the
GCC's growth rates.[9]

With the onset of the twenty-first century, particularly after 2003, the oil
market witnessed a boom in oil prices due to an increase in demand by China
and India, a shortage in refining capacity because of instability in a number
of producing countries, like Venezuela, Iraq, Nigeria and Iran, and oil market

speculation.[10] This in turn led to successive increases in the price of oil, from around $30 per barrel, in 2003, to over $140 in 2007. With the emergence of the financial crisis, these prices then dropped to under $40 per barrel in 2008, before rising again to approximately $100 in 2011.

Again, developments in the oil market affected economic growth rates in the oil-producing countries, this time positively, since 2003-2008 witnessed a real growth in GDP of 6.8 per cent per annum. However, this economic growth remained in flux and registered lower rates than in other regions of the world, namely in low income and developing countries[11] according to the IMF's classification, as well as the Caucasus and Central Asia. However, regardless of the manner and speed of these countries' recovery from the current financial crisis, the obvious lesson to learn from this economic survey, spanning three time-periods, is that these countries' growth rates have remained in flux and closely linked to the price of oil. This confirms that these countries' economies are still heavily dependent on oil, and have failed to achieve significant progress in the effort to diversify their sources of income, exports and GDP.

It is not surprising that this erratic and slow economic growth is reflected on the GCC states' growth and real per capita income during the same period. According to some sources, the per capita income in these countries was either stagnant or in decline in 1975-2000, at a time when the real per capita income growth in East Asia was at 5.9 per cent per annum, at 2.3 per cent in the other developing countries and at 1.3 per cent in the world overall. In short, this means that these countries had lower standards of living than the rest of the world, despite short economic booms every now and then, due to changes in oil prices and revenue.[12] In Saudi Arabia, the largest GCC country, the per capita income dropped from $28600 in 1981, to less than $6800 in 2001, which proves the fragility of this country's economy and its lack of diversified economic structures.[13] However, though this income might increase eventually, as happened during the oil boom which began in 2003, it will no doubt drop when the price of oil declines again. This is owing to the fact that growth is still dependent on a single finite resource at a time when the country's population continues to increase.

Despite the fact that the development indicator for the GCC states is higher compared with many other countries, the comparison of the economic boom in these nations to their developmental achievements as regards the quality of education and health services and the diversification of sources of revenue reveals a huge failure. In order to distinguish between the rates of economic growth resulting from the oil booms and the efficacy of development policies, international organisations like the United Nations are trying to measure the difference in a country's wealth and the development of its human resources. This is because countries may have equal wealth but differ in their rates of development. The data indicates that most of the oil-rich nations of the Middle East have a negative value for the difference between the GDP per capita minus the Human Development Index (HDI) rank. This value is -75 in Kuwait, -50 in Oman, -36 in Qatar, -27 in the UAE and -19 in Saudi Arabia whereas it is +9 in Jordan. This positive figure indicates the fact that Jordan was more effective in converting its revenue into a developmental programme, especially in relation to human development which is considered a condition for economic development.[14]

Second: The continuing dependence on oil

The diversification of economic structures in the Gulf requires a gradual decrease in the economies' dependence on oil and its replacement with renewable goods and services which can act as an economic motor once oil is depleted. Even before this inevitable depletion happens, there are a number of factors influencing the continued demand for oil. Shaikh Ahmad Zaki al-Yamani, the former Saudi Oil Minister, was right when he described the problems associated with an eventual decrease in the demand for oil, saying, "On the supply side it is easy to find oil and produce it. And on the demand side there are so many new technologies. The hybrid engines will cut gasoline consumption by something like 30 percent. . . . Thirty years from now, there is no problem with oil. Oil will be left in the ground. The Stone Age came to an end not because we had a lack of stones, and the Oil Age will come to an end not because we have a lack of oil."[15]

Naturally, numerous factors could lead to a decrease in the demand for oil, including a more efficient exploitation of oil and development of alternative sources of energy. Did the region's governments succeed in reducing their dependence on this finite resource? At least three indicators help us gauge a given economy's dependence on a single commodity, like oil; these are, this commodity's share of the country's GDP or total economic activity, the percentage of oil exports to the entire amount of exports, and the percentage of petroleum revenues to total revenue. The higher these indicators are, the larger and more central the role that petroleum plays in this country's economy, and the reverse is also true. Did the GCC states succeed, over more than thirty years, in reducing radically their dependence on oil, in accordance with the above indicators?

The role of oil in these economies remains pivotal, as is clear from Table 7-2 which illustrates the contribution of the oil sector in the economies of the GCC states since the 1970s until the present time. The major part of the fluctuation in these relationships is due to the repercussion of developments on the oil market and not because of the declining importance of the oil sector. For example, the percentage share of the extractive industry fell between 1978-1998 in all the GCC states, then it went up again in 2011. This confirms the power of the link between what happens to oil prices and their revenues on the one hand, and economic activity in these countries on the other. The fall which took place in these percentages in 2011 was likewise because of the effects of the third oil boom during which prices reached their peak in 2008 then lowered somewhat during 2009 as a result of the financial crisis. They then recovered and began to increase after that to reach around $100 in 2011.[16]

We calculated the extractive industry's share of the GDP in the GCC states, over a number of years, to know in which direction this industry is heading and the changes it underwent. The results are shown in Table 7-2 below.

Table 7-2

Development of the extractive industry's share of the GCC countries' GDP 1978-2011 (in percentages)

Country	1978	1998	2011
Saudi Arabia	56.4	27.4	53.2
Kuwait	59.3	30.7	62.1
UAE	54.1	21.0	38.6
Bahrain	23.3	15.1	31.0
Qatar	55.1	34.8	57.7
Oman	55.6	31.1	51.2

Source: National statistics of Arab States, 1978-2011 (Abu Dhabi: Arab Monetary Fund, 2012)

This is the contribution of the oil sector to the GDP. The share of oil revenues to the total revenue confirms the role of oil once again. The data from the IMF for 2011 indicates that these percentages are as follows: 61.4 per cent for the UAE, 92.6 per cent for Saudi Arabia, 95.6 per cent for Kuwait, 69.6 per cent for Qatar, 85.3 per cent for Bahrain and 82.7 per cent for Oman.[17] In fact, the level of these countries' dependence on revenue from oil is higher than what these figures reveal, since the contribution of non-oil revenues[18] is still marginal, and reflects another failure of these governments, namely the failure to establish an efficient taxation system. Even the current taxation systems rely on oil revenues because custom duties and taxes on companies depend on the level of economic activity, and the latter in turn depend on the amount of oil revenue these governments spend. Therefore, when oil revenues drop, public spending, including spending on revenue, begins to decline and causes a drop in customs revenue.[19]

In addition to the role of oil in the GDP and public revenues, it also represents the largest part of the exports of these countries. According to the data from the IMF, the percentage of fuel exports to all exports during the period 2005-2011 was as follows: Bahrain 62.9 per cent, Kuwait 59.6 per cent, Oman 86.5 per cent, Qatar 86.6 per cent, Saudi Arabia 89.7 per cent and the UAE 54.1 per cent. The fall in the percentage in the UAE is attributed to the size of re-exporting which takes place from the ports of Dubai to the outside world. [20]

Even the services sector, whose figures have improved in all the GCC states thanks to the growth of the real estate, trade and financial markets, in recent years, is no more than a temporary bubble resulting from either spending the oil money or attracting speculative funds. This means that these figures do not actually reflect real progress, stability or sustainability, as shown by the recent crisis. [21]

Third: Limitations on the share of manufacturing

The ongoing dependence by the GCC states on oil and its revenue, and what this means in terms of economic fluctuations, is proof of these governments' failure to correct the imbalance in their economic structures by increasing the manufacturing share and reducing their dependence on extractive industries. The higher the manufacturing share of a country's economic activities, the more diverse are its products and its workforce, and the more employment opportunities there are, whether these products are for the local market or for export, which bring in foreign currency. Likewise, the more diverse the country's sources of revenue and sources of export and import are, the more stable is its economy and the less vulnerable to shocks are its economic projects, thus making growth permanent and self-sustaining. The industrial sector's development is no doubt vital for economic stability, and it is not possible to compensate for it by an excessive expansion in the services sector, particularly those non-producing services. The recent financial crisis highlights the fact that when the cancerous expansion of the financial sector is not accompanied by a similar expansion of the productive sector, mainly the industrial sector, it is considered an unhealthy phenomenon that could lead to disaster. The experience of Western and Asian countries shows that the manufacturing development happens in stages. It starts with the production of light consumer goods that uses intensive labour and relies on simple technology, then proceeds to durable consumer products, and ends with capital goods that require advanced technology and economies of scale, to reduce production costs and raise the products' competitive edge, in a competitive world headed towards more openness.[22]

However, this transformation has not yet taken place in the GCC states due to several reasons. The most important is the absence of a clear development vision, effective environmental structures and sound policies, coupled with the failure to make significant progress in integrating the Gulf and Arab regions, thus depriving the GCC of a market large enough to accommodate such transformations. Moreover, the overwhelming reliance on foreign labour has seen much-needed funds fleeing to the workers' home countries instead of being spent locally, which would have helped generate local demand, encourage more production and ensure sustainability. If we examine official figures published by various GCC states, whether they are relevant to the manufacturing share of the GDP or share of creating employment opportunities, it becomes clear that their role is still limited despite thirty years of development efforts. For example, whereas the manufacturing share of the GDP in the United States, Japan and Korea is around 20 per cent, 30 per cent and 40 per cent, respectively, the share of this sector is still around 12 per cent in the GCC states, with the exception of Bahrain. Similarly, its share has not changed much since the 1970s, as shown in table 7-3.[23]

That is unsurprising if we consider the failure of these countries in various industries, particularly the hydrocarbons industry in which they have a relative advantage. Except for the petrochemical, fertiliser, and iron and aluminium industries, these industries have remained mostly consumer-oriented, while capital and intermediate goods have made no significant progress. Furthermore, the petrochemical and refining industries' contribution to the industry as a whole is still not commensurate with these countries' oil and gas reserves. This is due to the protectionist policies of the industrialised countries, limited local market capacity, the lack of regional and inter-Arab coordination, the high cost of regional wars and lack of adequate human resource training. According to the report by BP issued in June 2013, of the global refining capacity that amounts to 92,531,000 barrels per day, the GCC states' share is no more than 3768 barrels per day or 4 per cent, most of which is concentrated in three countries, namely Saudi Arabia, Kuwait and the UAE.[24] As for petrochemicals, the Middle East's share of the global production of ethylene of 138.5 million tonnes in 2010 did not exceed 15.6 million tonnes since its production is concentrated in Saudi Arabia and Qatar.[25]

Table 7-3

Development of the manufacturing sector's share of the
GCC states' GDP 1978-2011 (in percentages)

Country	1978	1998	2011
Saudi Arabia	4.4	9.9	1.1
Kuwait	6.6	11.9	4.6
UAE	3.6	12.9	8.0
Bahrain	10.5	12.4	16.8
Qatar	3.8	7.9	9.9

Source: League of Arab States, *Al-Taqrir al-iqtisadi al-'arabi al-muwahhad* [Unified Arab Economic Report], (Abu Dhabi, Cairo: Arab Monetary Fund, Arab Fund for Economic and Social Development, League of Arab States and Organisation of Arab Petroleum Exporting Countries, [various years])

The petrochemical industries are considered the most important source for development in the GCC states. This is not only because they possess an abundance of the inputs for this industry and are situated close to the Asian markets, which are expected to have the lion's share of the increasing demand for petrochemical products in the future, but also because this industry can be an effective solution for the growing unemployment crisis among the youth in the region. However, that requires the availability of several conditions, including the acquisition of technology, the training of human resources, the adoption by these countries of supportive policies and their cooperation for entering the markets of other nations, such as China, India and others. These are nations in which production capacity has begun to replace production in the United States, Europe and Japan. In 1980, around 75 per cent of the production of raw petrochemical resources was in this group of three countries. However, their share fell in 2010 to approximately 37 per cent of the global production, while the share of other regions increased. China alone began to produce around 17 per cent of the global production and the Middle East as a whole produced 13 per cent, and the remaining share was produced in other developing countries. The fear remains, as we have mentioned previously, that the global production of petrochemicals will gradually move from the West to East Asia. Consequently, the GCC states will lose their ability to compete because they do not offer the necessary conditions for competitiveness because the abundance of oil and gas in itself does not guarantee the development of these industries.[26]

This is the picture with regard to the share components of the industrial sector in the GCC states. Similarly, the share of industrial workers compared to the total labour force is low with the exception of Qatar where it was 54.4 per cent in 2011. The percentages in the rest of the GCC states were as follows: 9.5 per cent in the UAE, 24.9 per cent in Bahrain, 19.3 per cent in Saudi Arabia, 8 per cent in Oman and 14.4 per cent in Kuwait. Even these modest amounts in most of these countries represent foreign workers, and the available figures do not allow a more accurate grasp of the size of the native labour force in the industrial sector because these governments do not publicise them since they would reveal another failing relating to the predominance of foreign labour in these countries.[27]

Fourth: The weakness of interstate commerce

When the economic structures of a group of neighbouring or distant countries produce a diversity of goods, i.e., they each offer different sets of goods and services, an economic network will develop among these countries unless political reasons prevent this from happening. When trade among these countries increases, the indicator for interstate trade, i.e., the percentage of interstate commerce to the overall volume of these countries' foreign trade, will increase as well. This is what we are witnessing currently in Western Europe, East Asian and Latin American countries where these percentages reach up to 67.3 per cent in the EU countries and 49.5 per cent among the NAFTA countries (the US, Mexico and Canada).[28]

The GCC states are close to each other geographically but distant in terms of trade since their interstate exports and imports do not exceed 4.2 per cent and 7.6 per cent respectively according to data from 2011.[29] This is further proof that the GCC states have so far failed to diversify their economic structures in any tangible way and, thirty years on, they are still exporting oil and using its revenue to import all their intermediate, consumer and capital goods, including their workforce, meaning that their economies are similar rather than integrated.

The above indicators, which include erratic economic development processes, the overwhelming domination of oil revenues, limited conversion industry sectors and marginal interstate trade, indicate without the shadow of a doubt that the Gulf's economies are still all about oil. Oil is still the main driver of economic growth, and of imports, exports and foreign trade in the GCC states, meaning that these countries' economic structures did not change at all despite this being the main objective of whole development process. This is because the diversification of production infrastructures is precisely what will prepare these countries for the post oil period. The fact that they have not yet achieved this diversification proves that the development policies they have been pursuing have failed, despite claims to the contrary. In addition to this being one of the reasons for the failure of these governments' development efforts, it is also the result of other development failures, which we have already addressed or will address in later chapters. These failures are in human resources, the private sector and in the many aspects of the waste of the people's resources, and all of these issues are central to any development process.

Chapter Eight

Human Resource Development

Colonial countries, like Britain formerly and the United States of America today, were careful to prevent any genuine resource development in the region, because they saw it as a readjustment in the balance of power between themselves and the host countries. The reason is that raising the Gulf people's awareness and allowing them to play an active role in the management of their resources, by holding their governments accountable and seeking closer ties with their wider Arab environment, was not in the West's interest. The latter preferred to make deals with unelected governments on which they could impose their own conditions, in return for promises of protection. This is evident from the policies that the great powers and the region's own governments have pursued both before and after independence. Given this issue's importance, and the fact that it is deeply ingrained in the way governments do business in the region, we have decided to divide the subject of human resources into two time-periods to show the real reasons why they remained marginalised and ineffective in this particular region.

First: Before Independence

Colonial countries, like Britain once, and the United States today, have always tried, directly or indirectly, to sideline the region's people from the decision-making process, to isolate them from their Arab milieu to prevent any integration between the two, and to avoid any potential demands for readjusting the balance of power between themselves and the region's governments. This dual policy, i.e., locally reducing the ceiling of public freedoms and participation, and isolating the GCC states from their Arab and Islamic milieus, has no doubt served the colonial powers' interests well because it allowed them to control the region's governments and dictate their policies. This fact is attested to by these countries' experience. The protectorate agreements which Britain and the Trucial Coast rulers signed in 1835 and codified in 1892, continued to be in effect until the mid-twentieth century, and categorised these emirates as protectorates with no internal sovereignty or external independence. Moreover, the agreements barred the rulers from signing agreements with any party other than Britain, and forbade them from allowing any visitors to the emirate other than British subjects and from leasing or selling land except to British concerns, a provision that no doubt had to do with oil concessions.[1] Other provisions of these agreements ban the importation of almost all kinds of technology, from diving gear to equipment for radios, given the latter's role in potentially raising the locals' awareness and allowing them to know what is happening elsewhere in the world.[2] Nothing highlights the fear of raising the people's awareness in the region more than when the local population went to the streets to express its support for the nationalisation of the Suez Canal in 1956. This led to confrontations between the British and local governments on the one hand, and supporters of the Nasserite current on the other. The National Front, established in Dubai in 1953, is an apt example of this confrontation since its members were supporters of the Nasserite current and opposed to the British government and its policies in the region. This prompted the British Resident to describe Dubai's inhabitants at the time as being "partially hostile to Britain and capable of jeopardising the oil operations",[3] adding that "Britain could not afford a hostile regime to take root, especially one that would 'nationalise the oil industries ... or seek the degeneration of administration in the hands of an irresponsible ruling family of the kind prevailing in Saudi Arabia.'"[4] Perhaps these statements were made at a time when Saudi Arabia showed some signs of reform, signs that were promptly put down, however. The British government, in coordination with the region's rulers, thus began to pursue policies that aimed at containing the nationalist wave, including lending military support to governments, and placing revenue from British bases and ports and other aid sums in the hands of the countries' rulers. The aim was to gain their loyalty, entrench their power and reduce their dependence on the taxes they collected from merchants, to free them from any authority save that of the foreign power.[5] The British also forbade Arab delegations from visiting the Gulf and even prevented Arab airlines, like Egypt Air, from flying to the region.[6] Not content with that, they turned their attention to the region's educational institutions and removed from the curricula anything which exhibited nationalist tendencies to prevent the emergence of a new, highly aware and nationalist-leaning generation, influenced by events unfolding in the Arab world.

In Dubai, for example, the British government appointed Banaga al-Amin, a Sudanese national and friend of the British Political Agent, as the Director of Education. They asked him to draft a politics-free curriculum to steer the youths' energy towards innocuous activities, like card games, and forbid everyone from bringing political publications to school.[7] Two like-minded, pro-British men were appointed to assist him[8] and Britain assumed all the costs. In Qatar, when anti-British demonstrations took to the streets in support of the nationalisation of the Suez Canal, including many of the Shaikhdom's notables and members of the ruling family, the reaction of the ruler, Ali al-Thani, was to try to contain the movement by incorporating provisions into the labour law banning political activism. He also asked the director of education to hire "non-politicised", even non-Egyptian, teachers. The reason was again the fear that such activism would harm British oil concessions in the country, and lead to a readjustment of the relationship between the ruler and the people, especially since the oil workers who took part in the demonstrations had previously gone on strike to ask for their rights.[9] To this end, a security service under the command of British officers was formed and tasked with keeping order, and protecting compounds and installations belonging to the oil company.[10] Dr Ahmad al-Khatib, a veteran Kuwaiti politician, confirms this British tendency to oppose reform in the region, saying that the British encouraged the rise of opposition movements but, once they became strong, urged the rulers to strike them hard. This, he believes, has occurred in almost all the Gulf countries since the late 1930s.[11]

How much today resembles yesterday, for in the shadow of the growing Islamist renaissance, the region's governments are today pursuing the same policies as they did so long ago against the nationalist Nasserite current. They keep the Islamists away from education and other fields, and review their curricula with help from Western experts and under Western supervision, to distance the region from its Arab-Islamic identity that began acting like a conduit to the renaissance in this and other regions. It should be mentioned that for a major power like Britain, and for most of the region's rulers, education was never a priority to begin with, because it meant awareness, aspirations, efforts towards change, better conditions and a fair distribution of the country's assets, none of which was desirable either to the rulers or to the colonialists, to say the least. Some studies indicate that until the National Front's establishment in Dubai in 1953, the British government was not interested in education because some ruling family members feared that it would lead to calls for political reforms. In the 1950s, the British Political Resident voiced similar fears on his government's part, when he said "it is inevitable that with a spread of education there will in due course be demands of modification in the existing patriarchal forms of the government. There may even be some anti-British agitation."[12] However, when they could no longer put it off, the British and local governments, together with the great powers, opted for a closely guided education system that would preserve the status quo, in other words, a non-politicised and politics-free system. We already know ARAMCO's method of choice to educate the Saudis, as well as King Abdul-Aziz Bin Saud's idea on what kind of education is best for the country. It is the kind of education that could happen only when some economic and social development has already taken place, and provided this education does not impact on the political balance of power between the ruler and the people, in a manner that would make the latter partners in the decision-making process.

Second: After Independence

The views of regional governments on the importance of developing the potential of local citizens, and considering them partners in the development process, did not change all that much after independence. These governments still fear an educated citizenry even after being forced, for internal and external reasons, to increase their spending on various public services, including education. However, any benefits from an improvement in the education system remained hostage to the fear that better educated generations would become a conduit for change in the political status quo, and the spearhead for efforts towards integration and cooperation with the larger Arab milieu, which would inevitably loosen their grip on power and control over the people. This is evidenced by the policies that the region's government have pursued to offset the shortage in human resources ever since they launched their development plans after the rise of oil prices in the early 1970s until today, as will be made clear in the following paragraphs.

1. Labour supply

Human resource shortages in the GCC[13] mean that the local workforce is limited, and there is a need to import workers from abroad; this policy could have remedied the problem, to a certain extent, had it been implemented within the context of efforts to integrate the Gulf and Arab regions. It would have also succeeded had these countries' academic curricula been better able to prepare the local work force to compensate for this shortage, as they did in Singapore and other Asian countries. What happened, however, was that these countries' governments chose the worst possible option to deal with the problem; they neither gave enough attention to a potential Gulf and Arab integration, nor developed advanced academic curricula, despite having the ability to do both. Even the drive to naturalise a number of foreigners was not done on a proper selective basis, i.e., trying to attract a skilled Arab workforce; it was rather an attempt to build coteries of loyal and obedient followers seeking to earn their livelihood. Every year, countries like the US and Europe introduce new and talented elements from all over the world to their workforce, and use all sorts of incentives to entice them into coming over and helping their societies flourish. On the other hand, our governments' naturalisation policies are not selective enough, unfortunately, meaning that the newly naturalised citizens have become an added burden on the economy instead of shouldering their share of the responsibilities. Once their integration, education and naturalisation policies proved to be failures, the region's governments had no choice but to flood their markets with foreign workers from every field, and the ratio of foreign workers to local workers continued to rise. Available data indicates that the number of foreign workers in all the GCC states together was 1.4 million, in 1975, jumping up to 2.9 million in 1980 and to 4.4 million in 1985, i.e., 70 per cent of the GCC's total workforce.[14] The impact this had on culture and security in the region became quite serious, as billions of dollars continued to flee to these workers' home countries. In recent years, there was a fundamental shift first towards workers from Asia, then workers from Europe, at the expense of the Gulf and Arab economies' wellbeing. With the drop in oil revenues and the impact this drop had on reducing government spending, on the governments' inability to cover the expenses of foreign workers and their families and on the rise of unemployment among local citizens, the region's governments began leaning towards indigenising employment and reducing their reliance on foreign labour. For several reasons, however, these intentions were not translated into fact mainly because the region's citizens shun certain jobs, especially those considered socially unacceptable or pay low wages, like in the fields of construction, domestic service and other commercial and services. Other reasons include the private sector's tendency to employ foreign workers because of their low wages, their high productivity and self-restraint, the local graduates' lack of scientific and technological knowhow and ease of importing skilled workers from anywhere in the world.[15]

In the mid 1990s, the GCC states reiterated their resolve to reduce the role of foreign labour in their economies and increase local recruitment, due to rising unemployment rates among the local citizens. They adopted a series of policies including stricter rules concerning the employment of foreign workers by the private sector, allocating quotas for the employment of local citizens in various sectors and professions and reducing the salary gap between the public and private sectors. To this end, they increased the cost of importing foreign labour, and encouraged the private sector to employ more locals by covering part of their training costs and salaries. They focused the need to steer education towards more scientific and technical fields, began deporting undocumented workers and diversified economic structures by paying more attention to fields favoured by the local workforce, like tourism and finance.[16]

However, the number of foreign workers in the Gulf countries continued to increase, and still does to this day, despite all these policies and regardless whether they were actually implemented or not. The latest available figures indicate that in 2008, foreign workers accounted on average for 41 per cent of the GCC's total population and 66.9 per cent of the total workforce, most of which were in the private sector and a small percentage in the public sector. However, a detailed examination of these figures reveals a stark reality, namely that the countries with a majority foreign population have ceded one of the basic elements of their survival, and the others are very close to that red line. Figures for 2008 show that in the UAE, foreign workers account for 81.3 per cent of the population and 85 per cent of the workforce. The percentages for the rest of the GCC states are as follows: 27 per cent and 50.6 per cent in Saudi Arabia, 87 per cent and 94.3 per cent in Qatar, 31.4 per cent and 74.6 per cent in Oman, 67.9 per cent and 83.2 per cent in Kuwait and 51.4 per cent and 76.7 per cent in Bahrain.[17]In a related context, these estimates show a parallel rise in unemployment among local university graduates. According to data from the Arab Monetary Fund, the rate of unemployment among citizens in the UAE reached 14 per cent in 2011, it was 3.7 per cent in Bahrain according to the 2010 data, 10.5 per cent in Saudi Arabia in 2009 and 2.3 per cent in Qatar. In Kuwait, the unemployment rate was estimated at around 5.9 per cent in 2010 and recently.[18]

Of course, these are public figures. If we scrutinise them in detail, then we will see that they paint a bleak picture. For example, some sources show that the rate of female unemployment in Saudi Arabia reached approximately 27 per cent in 2008. Among males aged 24 years old, this rate varies between 29 per cent and 56.[19] The above figures clearly show that the local workforce in many of these countries is a minority that is likely to be increasingly sidelined. In spite of that, the unemployment rate is rising and the local workforce is concentrated in the governmental sector where recruitment usually does not rely on skill and productivity. The fact that there are very few of those local employees in the private sector is proof that these countries' education systems did not provide them with the required expertise, and also that the training and indigenisation policies have failed.[20] However, the United Nations Human Development Report shows that despite the quantitative expansion of their education systems, the quality of these countries' graduates is still lower than that of middle- to high-income countries. Their education indicator is also lower than the overall average human development indicator, which measures three different indicators: income, health and education, particularly in the UAE and Oman.[21] Thus, when these countries' human development indicator is high, it does not mean that their education systems are more advanced, or that they have more freedoms and good health services. It is simply due to the increase in income and this is income which is not turned into productive human resources. We should also remember that this high income is not the result of self-generated growth and diverse sources of income in these countries, but the result of depleting the country's oil by converting it into financial assets and spending it on unproductive ventures.

2. Market size

Small populations are usually not conducive to the type of market that is amenable to the establishment of successful and productive projects. As we indicated earlier in our discussion on manufacturing industries, industry and production begin in the local market and then develop in terms of price competitiveness and product quality on the global market. This is a proven fact, even in a globalised world with its openness and various reduced trade barriers; for had it not been for local markets and their protection through industrial policies, we would not have heard of the historically proven success of the Asian Tigers, or that of the United States and Western Europe.[22] One cannot resolve the problems associated with small markets, and the serious development opportunities they provide, by flooding them with foreign workers who tend to have low consumption levels. The fact that these workers spend only a fraction of their income surpluses on local goods and services and send the rest back to their home countries reduces local demand on goods and services and, in turn, stunts local production due to the small size of the market.

3. The impact

The GCC states' overdependence on foreign labour, especially from non-Arab countries, has its costs, some of which have already become evident like cultural distortions, the flight of millions of dollars from the region in the form of remittances and the increasing costs of services that these workers receive. Other costs are starting to make themselves felt, including those related to workers' rights and the ensuing potential restructuring and reconfiguration of the nature of these societies, not to mention the ongoing trade in visas associated with the vast numbers of incoming workers. We will briefly address the impact of these phenomena and raise the alarm with the hope that those listening will seize the initiative and address these issues, in the next few years, with the due diligence they deserve. Although Gulf and other Arab researchers have been raising the alarm for quite some time now, for one reason or another, the ears of decision-makers in the Gulf are listening to other voices.[23]

a) **Cultural distortions**

It would be hard for visitors to the GCC states, particularly to the UAE, Qatar, Kuwait and Bahrain, not to notice the challenges that the Arab-Islamic culture is currently facing, whereby the local citizens are becoming strangers in their own countries as far as facial characteristics, mannerisms and language are concerned. People's homes are full of non-Arab domestic workers because the driver is Indian, the farm labourer is Pakistani and the domestic helper is from the Philippines. This forces them to speak their languages differently and practise their long-held customs in the most intimate of settings. These citizens find themselves compelled to speak in a broken or hybrid form of Arabic so that their foreign workers can understand them,[24] and the situation in the street, the marketplace and in public institutions is no different from the situation at home. Commercial venues boast a variety of languages, and cinemas brim with films targeting the largest minorities and ignoring the smallest minority, and the same goes for restaurants and private schools. These schools have become places where other people's cultures are unloaded, while Arab culture, with all its wealth, is kept at bay, with the same thing happening to newspapers, clubs and the other institutions.[25] However, the worst of these distortions starting to spread to these countries could well be the decision by local education institution to make English the teaching language in lieu of, instead of alongside, the Arabic language. This is no doubt tantamount to a treacherous stab at the language of the Qur'an and its culture, because it isolates students from their Arab heritage and cuts them off from their values. If they dare utter one word about their languages and values, they sound like parrots repeating what they hear without any understanding, spirit or appreciation. Since these students have never read a poem or literary piece in their mother tongue, there is no longer reason to translate any foreign texts into the Arabic to enrich this language with words from other cultures, deepen contacts or foster a cultural renaissance. Today, university professors are compelled to publish in foreign languages, mainly in English, to avoid being retired. This and other forms of cultural distortion in the GCC states have led to the loss of any sense of belonging to an Arab nation. Students today no longer hear the lyrics of the famous song "The Arab lands are my nation, from Damascus to Bughdan, from Najd to Yemen to Egypt to Tetouan" or other similar songs that deepen their Arab identity. The voices of these songs have become so low, if not completely muted, because they relegated the sweet-sounding language they once embodied from the centre of gravity, and replaced it with other languages.[26] These students might even make fun of the above lines, or of this or that poem, as if they have no memory at all, or as if their memory has been erased or totally disfigured. It is no doubt a sad reality the price of which will be paid by future generations, unless matters are quickly remedied.

b)   **Flight of assets and wasted resources**

The second impact of foreign labour is the flight of billions of dollars in the form of remittances to the workers' home countries, thus depriving the Gulf economies of their benefit. We should remember, in this context, that foreign non-Arab workers tend to have low consumption levels, meaning that they spend only a small fraction of their income in the local market and send most of it back to their home countries, which impacts negatively on local markets. Bahrain's Employment Minister, Majid al-'Alawi, is quoted as saying, "Foreign workers take out of the country an estimated $25 billion a year, not to mention the social and political threat they pose given the potential for global pressure to naturalise them."[27]

The GCC states' losses do not end with the flight of funds, but are compounded by squandering the country's resources in the form of services provided by the state to foreign workers, especially those with low-level skills and productivity, an amount currently estimated to be in the billions of dollars. For example, the cost per foreign worker in Bahrain is around $106,[28] a figure likely to be higher in other GCC states like Saudi Arabia, Kuwait and the UAE, where the government's subsidy of basic services is higher. In the UAE, the annual cost of foreign workers is estimated to be around $180 billion.

c)   **Political and security threats**

In addition to the above cultural and economic impacts, foreign labour brings in its wake a plethora of political and security issues. Regional governments that do not draw their legitimacy from the people could well use the presence of vast numbers of foreign workers as an excuse to avoid any form political participation, meaning that the same autocratic regimes and their security and developmental failures, which this book addresses, will stay where they are. Moreover, the high and cheap foreign presence in these countries encourages citizens to look more towards income-generating activities, away from productive projects with a majority foreign labour force, thus placing these countries' economic security in the hands of non-citizens.[29] No doubt, the moves by governments in the region, like Saudi Arabia, Kuwait and the UAE, to expel Arab workers in the wake of Iraq's occupation, has only exacerbated the problem; Saudi Arabia expelled mostly Yemeni workers while other GCC states expelled Palestinians whom they blamed for their leaders' political positions, and replaced them with non-Arab workers.[30] These practices were repeated after the start of the Arab Spring. Another impact of the over-reliance on foreign labour is these countries' loss of their independent decision-making ability given the competition among labour-exporting countries to secure the lion's share of the Gulf's labour markets.

This competition and the ensuing pressure on the region's governments no doubt negatively affect these governments' ability to make independent decisions, and could cause tensions among different minority groups, or between their respective governments and governments in the region. However, given globalisation and international law, the most ominous political danger ensuing from this phenomenon has to do with these non-Arab workers' political and social rights, rights that are beyond reproach in principle, but which, in the context of the GCC, actually means the end of these countries' Arab identity. Western countries could grant foreign workers their rights, even the right to take part in the country's political life, without fear of destabilising their societies because they are small minorities and could therefore melt into the host country's political and social fabric and be influenced by its culture rather than the other way around. On the other hand, for the GCC states to grant foreign workers their rights means dissolving the local population in a sea of foreigners, which, in short, means turning this population into a numerical minority, and a minority voice in the decision-making process; in other words, it makes them strangers in their own homeland.[31]

d) **The endemic trade in visas**

One of the worst aspects of corruption associated with the large number of migrant workers in these countries since the beginning of the oil boom is the trade in visas. The phenomenon usually involves persons or institutions that obtain visas for foreigners not because they want to employ them, but in return for money. Once these workers are in the country, they are either allowed to work at a place of their own choosing or a place chosen for them by the party that obtained the visa, based on a prior agreement with the prospective employer. In Saudi Arabia, the visa for a domestic worker costs between 5,000 and 6,000 Saudi Rials, and those who pay these sums are usually individuals who cannot get an entry visa by any other means.[32] It would have been slightly less harmful had this been done by people who earn very low wages. But alas, the bitter reality is that this trade was, and still is, the domain of people in high places who do not trade just in a handful of visas but thousands of them, often leaving these poor people to wander the streets of an unknown country, which sometimes leads them to a life of crime. Ruling family members often use this trade to win supporters and curry favour.

A Western researcher says, in this particular context, that a Saudi regional prince gave one of his business friends 3,000 such visas just before addressing a conference on that particular subject, i.e., naturalisation or "Saudification".[33] The trade in visas or people can take other forms: instead of keeping the visa in the original importer's name, they transfer it to the name of the immigrant's prospective employer within months of his arrival in the country, in return for a fixed price that sometimes reaches 10,000 Saudi Rials. A Saudi businessman estimates that in 2004, 70 per cent of all visa transfers, i.e., 600,000 visas in total, happened within two months after the worker's arrival in the country.[34]

In a 2004 meeting with the Council for Saudi Chambers of Commerce, former Saudi Labour Minister, Ghazi Algosaibi, condemned the visa trade and confirmed that 70 per cent of all visas were sold on the black market.[35] However, although Minister Algosaibi tried to end this practice by banning all visas transfers except for the highly skilled categories, preventing companies with less than ten employees from obtaining visas and sending all the princes' visa requests to King Abdullah, the endemic corruption in the Kingdom and various deception tactics caused his efforts to fail. That same year, the Saudi Labour Ministry admitted that some people owned no less than fifty companies "on paper", while other sources said that the corruption associated with the visa trade had infiltrated the Interior Ministry, once responsible for the workers' portfolio before its transfer, and had even infiltrated the Passports Department.[36] The Saudi Shura Council's decision to endorse temporary seasonal visas has weakened the credibility of the Labour Ministry's decisions and, at the same time, uncovered the haphazard nature of decision-making and the absence of coordination among different state institutions.[37] In recent years, some companies abandoned their original activities and joined the visa trade, and in May 2008, the Saudi Labour Ministry discovered that no more than six companies had resold 14,000 visas in total.[38]

As portrayed in Saudi Arabia, this phenomenon and all its complications is replicated in all the Gulf countries, especially the UAE, Kuwait, Qatar and, to a lesser extent, Oman. It has no practical solution in the long term except through the adjustment of current development models by increasing Gulf and inter-Arab integration. In the short term, the ideal solution would be to quell the source of endemic corruption in this domain, by putting an end to the current "sponsor system", and finding another formula to regulate foreign labour by mitigating opportunities to exploit the system, while providing these countries with the workforce required. Bahrain's pioneering experience in this domain might be a case in point.[39]

4. Where does the problem lie?

We could say, therefore, that all the policies that these governments have pursued in their attempt to address the population deficit, and its impact on the labour market and its size, were wrong and short-sighted, and failed to achieve the desired objective, whether in terms of naturalisation, education or importation of foreign labour. They were also costly culturally, economically and in terms of security, and the GCC states were too slow to adopt the best solution available to them, namely more integration among themselves and between themselves and their wider Arab milieu, a point we will return to later on. As mentioned earlier, the problems ensuing from the above situation, currently plaguing the GCC states, are the result of a mixture of reasons. These include the education system's failure to adequately equip the graduates with the skills required, because Gulf citizens gravitate overwhelmingly towards the humanities, and other fields not compatible with local market needs. They leave behind all the scientific and technical specialisations that reflect their country's current priorities, forgetting that acquiring an education in these fields is the sine qua non of development. What further exacerbated the problem is that Gulf citizens tend to stay away from jobs that require low technical skills and earn low wages.[40] The real reason behind this and all the above-mentioned problems, however, is the distorted development models chosen by unelected governments that care neither about their people's interests, nor about achieving comprehensive development for the benefit of all, by integrating the region economically, and integrating the region with the wider Arab world. These governments' main concern is to keep their monopoly on decision-making, state positions, the country's resources and all what ensues from this main objective, as evidenced by their chosen development path from the 1970s to the present.

It is really unfortunate that these governments do not realise, do not want to know or do not even care, that the current population imbalance is no longer just an economic or social issue, but is now linked to their countries' very security and Arab identity. To continue on the development path of the past thirty years means more marginalisation of their own population in the face of increasing waves of migrant workers, whose second and third generations will have entirely different calculations. They will not continue to simply ask for fair wages, healthy living conditions and humane treatment, all justified demands that we support based on our religious values, but will ask, based on the length of time they spent in the country and their demographic weight, for rights akin to full citizenship, which means permanent and fundamental transformations in our society's values and identity.[41]

In turn, we wonder, as do no doubt our readers: is the manner in which the region's governments have dealt with the shortage in labour the result of a lack of knowledge and skill, which means we have a catastrophe on our hands, or it is much bigger than that? Are they so greedy for power and profit that they are willing to do anything, including flooding the country with foreign labour and turning the local population into a minority incapable of asking for the rights that total citizenship and partnership entitle them to?

There are those who believe that these governments intentionally did not pursue policies which would have led to the emergence of a native working class, arriving at the erosion of their legitimacy. Thus, these governments are content to rely on foreign workers who will not demand nationalisation, or so they believe. If this is the governments' ultimate motive, i.e., to sacrifice the citizen for sake of personal power and profit, then we have an even greater catastrophe on our hands. It would confirm what *New York Times* columnist Thomas Friedman said mockingly, namely that such autocratic governments do not explore for local brains and potential as long as they can explore for oil, use the revenue to buy loyalties and avoid political participation at any cost.[42] A foreign researcher recounts an even more telling incident which shows that one of the reasons for the failure to adequately prepare human resources in Saudi Arabia, is due to the wrong polices of the early 1970s. Not expecting the oil boom that was soon to follow, officials at the Saudi Ministry of Finance proposed to the government and the King two different development options, one focussing on building the country's material infrastructure, i.e., roads, seaports and buildings, and the other on human resource development. The foreign researcher remembers one official at the Ministry of Finance telling him at a meeting that they had opted for the first option, i.e., material development, which in fact means prioritising stones over human beings.[43]

We have to remember that this is happening in a country in which, as available data shows, over 100,000 people enter the job market every year, of which no more than 50 per cent are fortunate enough to find employment.[44] No doubt, that, in such countries, prioritising inanimate objects over human beings has continued unabated, even after enough funds became available to adopt both options together, as evidenced by the real estate boom these countries have witnessed, to varying levels, particularly since the onset of the twenty-first century. It is a boom that only the international financial crisis, which began in 2007, could dampen and whose repercussions were still being felt as these lines were being written, just as they will surely not be the last.

CHAPTER NINE

Private Sector Development

Private sector development, reflected in its increased share of the GDP, employment opportunities, total exports and paying taxes to the state, is considered to be one of the most important engines of development in advanced countries. In the GCC, the fact that this sector's role is still marginal partly explains why these countries' economies are still dependent on oil and the public sector, with all the price fluctuations and economic instability that come in their wake. This is why we decided to devote this chapter to the private sector, as one of the mainstays of development in the GCC states. We will explain the sector's importance and relationship to the public sector, the obstacles that impede its development, and how best to address them in the coming years so that this sector plays a more active role and complements the role of the public sector in order to achieve these countries' development objectives.

First: Importance of the private sector

Those who have followed the continuous increase in the rate of unemployment among university graduates in the GCC states over the past twenty years will notice that the public sector is no longer capable of absorbing the ever-increasing population size, yet the private sector's contribution to a self-sustainable economy and the creation of new employment opportunities is still limited. This problem and its economic and social consequences are expected to worsen in the future if we bear in mind that the region's governments can no longer continue to expand their administrative institutions due to oil revenue fluctuations in the short term and to the decreasing importance of oil in the long term. We already see the impact of Bahrain's closeness to that critical stage, and the inability of Saudi Arabia and other GCC states to continue providing the services they provided in the 1970s. That is because oil revenues are dropping and population rates are increasing and this will no doubt have political, social and security repercussions.[1] Moreover, the private sector is usually more competent than the public sector in using the country's resources, especially if there exists a healthy legal environment, good governance system and a certain amount of foreign competition for this sector.[2]

This is why there is a need to develop the private sector in the next few years to act as an engine of growth in the GCC, as far as the volume of production, employment opportunities and exports are concerned, in order to allow these countries to maintain a good standard of living after the depletion of oil. Despite the fact that the post World War II experiences of economic systems in the industrialised countries confirm without a doubt that the success of any economy depends on public and private sector integration, there remains a difference in the size of these two sectors. In some countries, the private sector becomes the main driver of economic growth once the public sector has provided the right environment for a healthy multi-layered economy to grow, including legislation, sound and comprehensive economic policies, less distorted prices of goods and factors of production, and basic infrastructure like roads, transport, means of communication, education, health and environmental protection laws. However, when the public sector is itself the driver of development, as in the case of the Asian Tigers, the state's role expands to incorporate the selection of strategic industries and to encourage them with protection, funding and marketing to render them more competitive and ready for privatisation to help the private sector grow.[3] This is the model that most industrialised countries followed, to varying degrees, in the early years of their development, despite the World Trade Organisation's attempts to reduce the state's developmental role today, forgetting the above historical realities and taking advantage of the weak negotiating positions of developing countries, including the GCC. It is worth calling to mind the fact that rather than being dogmatically delineated, the size of both the private and public sectors is defined by a set of factors, chief among which are the stage of development that the country has reached and the size and nature of its resources. In the GCC states, where the economies are dependent on oil revenues, it is only natural for the public sector to play a leading role in development at the beginning, given that the government decides how these oil revenues are spent.[4] However, if the political leadership's vision for development is clear regarding the finite nature of oil and, hence, the need to develop the private sector as a main driver of economic growth, then the public sector's role will no doubt decline in favour of the private sector.

In light of the above, the growth of the private sector and the performance of its intended developmental role depend on the nature of the government in power or the public sector with which it deals. In this context, development literature distinguishes between two kinds of governments or states. The first kind is what we know as the developmental state in which a relationship develops between the public and private sectors, one that leads to genuine development based on the industrial sector's growth. This is what actually happened in the East Asian countries where the state had a clear development vision and maintained highly professional administrative institutions because their staff were hired based on ability and given worthwhile incentives, which made them eager to make the country development programmes a success.[5] The second kind is known as the predatory state (or weak state) in which a relationship of mutual interest prevails between the political leadership and the private sector but of the kind that does not lead to genuine development. The reason is that the political leadership steers the country's resources towards a specific segment of the private sector with which it shares certain economic interests, in return for shielding it from any competition by other private sector groups.[6] The potential for such governments to exist is greater in rentier countries where the revenue comes from oil or any other commodity, including the GCC states. As the governments of these countries control the oil revenue they do not feel compelled to abide by society's hopes and aspirations because they do not depend on society for the implementation of their plans and programmes. Rather, society needs the government to respond to all its needs, like health and education services, employment and other forms of support, which leaves the government free to choose who benefits from these revenues and who is left by the wayside, making reform in these countries more difficult to achieve.[7] Some rentier governments, like Norway and Botswana, are not predatory governments but developmental governments. That may be because they were elected governments and, therefore, their policies reflected the voters' will, which explains why they were, and still are, successful in achieving genuine development for all social classes. On the other hand, Zaire under Mobutu is a good example of the predatory state.[8] As we will see below, the relationship between the private and public sectors in the GCC states shows these countries are increasingly acquiring the characteristics of the predatory state. Researchers Cypher and Dietz describe this state as follows: "The predatory state is one wherein the appropriation of unearned income via rent-seeking has become endemic and structural. Everything is for sale: the courts, the legislature, the military, the taxing authority, etc. Government employees use their authority to maximize, in the shortest possible time, their accumulation of wealth. Political offices are held not for the reason of providing service to a nation, but for the purpose of individual gain in a society which may offer few alternative avenues to wealth accumulation." [9]

Therefore, we could say that in order to become a development state rather than a predatory one, two conditions must exist relating to the private sector. The first is that instead of being partial to any particular private sector group, the state should be guided by the interests of society as a whole. The second is that the government should consult the private sector to forge a partnership that would ensure sustainable development to the benefit of all sectors of society. Moreover, private sector efforts should be directed to achieving the public interest and not to maintaining trade privileges and concessions and government support, reducing competition or evading laws for employing nationals (e.g. "emiratisation"), as the private sector in the GCC states is currently doing.[10] It will be clear later how these two conditions are pivotal to ensuring that government policies and legislation are translated into actual practices that instil confidence into the private sector and motivate it to play an important role in development.

Second: The real contribution of the private sector

To gauge the private sector's contribution to the GCC's economies, we should first look at a number of indicators that include, among others, the size of domestic and foreign investments, their impact on exports, their variety and their role in creating jobs. Based on the most recent World Bank data, the amount of private sector investment in the Middle East region is still the lowest in the world, which is further proof of the public sector's dominance over these countries' economies. Moreover, this ratio is even lower in the oil-producing countries than in the non-oil producing countries of the Middle East due to the serious and deep private sector reforms that the latter have recently introduced.[11] Even the increase in private sector investments between 1995 and 2006 was mostly in the oil sector.[12] Since 2000, the annual growth rate of private investments was 11 per cent in the Middle East, including the GCC states, which is lower than the 16 per cent annual growth rate of these investments in the developing countries as a whole.[13] Except for the Latin American countries where private investment grew at a rate of around 3 per cent, the corresponding growth rates in the rest of the world were better than in the Middle East region, namely 12 per cent in sub-Saharan Africa, 25 per cent in East Asia, 16 per cent in Europe and Central Asia, and 14 per cent in South Asia.[14] The Middle East's failure to attract foreign investments is no less serious than its attempt to increase local private investments. According to World Bank reports, apart from the oil sector, this part of the world has remained the least attractive region in the world for foreign investment, with rates staying the same in relation to the GDP for over thirty-five years. The reasons for that might include the unsuitability of the local environment, whether due to the scarcity of investment opportunities, the level of risk involved or poor legal conditions. Even the modest investments outside the oil sector were concentrated mainly in sectors that do not have much impact on the diversification of these countries' industrial exports, such as real estate, tourism and communications.[15]

Similarly, the private sector in these countries does not significantly contribute to these countries' export structures. Studies on many of the countries that have achieved constant self-sustaining growth, like the East Asian Tigers, highlight the essential role of the private sector in increasing and diversifying industrial exports; export diversification influences economic growth in various ways, including increasing productivity, encouraging new industries and expanding existing ones and mitigating fluctuations in export revenues.[16] However, the Middle Eastern countries' record over the past forty years in this respect does not invite much optimism because the share of industrial exports as a percentage of these countries' GDP is still low in comparison with other regions of the world. Prior to the oil boom of 2003, the rate of non oil-related exports to the GDP was 16 per cent in the non oil-producing countries of the Middle East, whereas it was 9.1 per cent in the oil-producing labour importing countries and approximately 3.5 per cent in the oil-producing countries with a plentiful domestic workforce, compared with the overall global figure of around 17 per cent.[17] Data for 2010 reveals that the share of industrial exports to total exports was 79 per cent in Asia, 76.4 per cent in Europe and 68.8 per cent in North America. This ratio was no more than 22 per cent and 18.6 per cent in the Middle East and Africa respectively. The industrial exports of most of the Arab countries according to the 2009 data did not exceed 10.2 per cent of the total exports.[18]

Even this low percentage of non-oil related exports by Middle Eastern countries, including the GCC states, does not involve high technology or diversified products, like the exports of industrialised nations in East Asia and the West. The high and medium-high technology exports do not account for more than 21.2 per cent of the non-oil producing Middle Eastern countries' exports, and less than 5 per cent of the Middle Eastern oil-producing countries' exports, compared with much higher rates in other parts of the world. These are 37 per cent in Latin America, over 55 per cent in Eastern Europe and East Asia, and over 60 per cent in Korea, Taiwan and China.[19] In terms of export diversification, the record of Middle Eastern countries compared with the rest of the world is no different from its record in the above domains. The number of exported goods worth over $100,000 was 3,500 in the UAE and no more than 2000 in Saudi Arabia, the largest GCC country. The products exported from the UAE are not even produced in that country but imported to Dubai's free zone then re-exported to the region's other countries. In the rest of the world, the number of exported goods ranges from 3,500 in Malaysia and Thailand, and 4,000 and 5,000 in India and China, respectively.[20] Moreover, it is important to confirm that even this marginal role of the private sector in the GCC states does not rely on a local workforce but on a foreign one. This adds another problem to the many already afflicting the private sector as it has no connection to the citizens because it does not provide them with employment due to its short-sightedness and desire to increase its profits by relying on foreign labour, the majority of whose income goes abroad. Similarly, it is an obstacle to raising work productivity which has declined since the 1980s because cheap Asian labour have taken the place of semi-skilled Arab workers, and the increase in production in these countries is happening with the increase in the numbers of workers and capital instead of an increase in the competence of workers and the development of technology.[21] The contribution of the private sector to the economic activity in the GCC states has remained low, even compared with other Middle Eastern countries. The sector's contribution to non-oil based GDP does not exceed 60 per cent in the GCC states', while the same rate goes up to over 80 per cent in other countries of the region.[22] Finally, the private sector in the GCC states even now is almost an obstacle to society rather than a contributor to growth and guiding decision-making in the Gulf. Hence, it still depends on obtaining government projects and support for energy, water and electricity but it does not pay taxes to the state in order to remain independent of it and influence its decisions.[23]

Third: Obstacles to private sector performance

A quick survey of the actual role the private sector plays in Middle Eastern economies, including the GCC states, clearly shows that it is still marginalised, which compels us to try to understand the obstacles that impede its development. We should remind the reader here that the oil boom, and the ensuing accumulation of oil revenues by the public sector, led to the unchecked expansion of the public sector at the expense of the private sector. The latter became dependent on the state, with its role limited to the domains of trade and services, after being entirely independent from the state in the days of the pearl trade. The GCC states, however, started paying attention to the private sector's role only when oil prices and revenues began to fall, and signs of a deficit in the general budget began to appear in the mid 1980s. This turned the governments' attention to the need to expand the private sector to lower the public sector's expenses, and provide employment for the ever-increasing numbers of graduates. However, this awareness of the private sector's role has not been translated into actual policies capable of fostering an environment amenable to this sector's development. Several economic studies confirm that the government's role is to provide an environment amenable to economic growth, and the private sector's role is to invest and create wealth,[24] while economists believe that this environment should comprise several interacting elements. These elements include pursuing comprehensive economic policies that help fight inflation, ensuring stable borrowing costs, responding to local market demands and formulating policies that reduce trade barriers and deepen the local economy's integration into the global economy.[25] It is also incumbent on the government to enact laws that protect the people's rights, help in the execution of contracts and liquidate companies at the lowest cost possible, in terms of both time and money. Finally, governments should formulate policies that help regulate factors of production markets including, among other, employment, capital and land.[26] However, finding the right environment that allows the private sector to develop and perform its role does not solely depend on the enactment of laws and legislation, because this is much easier than the following step, which involves the translation of these policies and laws into tangible realities that businessmen can see and feel. This requires a highly efficient, fair and transparent administrative system that inspires the private sector with confidence in government policies and measures.[27] Although it is true that in order to develop, the private sector needs comprehensive laws and legislation, the experience of both industrial and developing countries confirms that the weaker and more corrupt are the state agencies and institutions that translate these policies into fact, the wider the difference is between these laws and actual daily business practices.[28]

However, though it is difficult to say for certain whether the private sector crisis is the outcome of absent laws and legislation or their poor implementation, available data shows that this sector suffers from an array of problems, most of which are due to the large gap between laws and their actual implementation on the ground. There is almost no competition within this sector because economic activities are mostly the domain of powerful families with close connections to the political leadership that ensures that they do not face any competition in their particular fields. This means that the latter reap exclusive benefits that reflect negatively on the rest of the population and on economic development as a whole, not to mention the fact that it deters serious and able business people from starting new businesses.[29] For example, most private sector companies in the GCC do not employ local citizens, pay taxes or assemble their products locally, which, incidentally, would have helped train the local population, all for the sake of making a quick profit. There are also no serious laws that compel these people to strike a balance between maximising their profits and helping achieve genuine development. What further exacerbates this sector's fragility is the unelected governments' use of oil revenues to control the businessmen's activities. Oil revenues finance the largest and most important projects, and funding comes from financial institution under the governments' financial and administrative control. The importation of foreign labour is subject to labour laws and state legislation, and the state has the major say in the procurement of commercial licences, distribution of land for housing and commercial projects and the enactment of import and export laws, in addition to its control of the media, security and defence, among others.[30]

Over and above all that, the ruling families who were once content with maintaining political power and leaving trade matters to others are now up to their ears in competitive commercial activities, and use their power to obtain the most advantageous projects and commissions. Today, ruling family members take advantage of their political power to gain economic advantage, since they could easily be ministers, contractors, foreign company representatives, partners in a local company, investors in a financial institution or presidents of investment fund boards.[31] This means that the business class remains at the mercy of government policies and will not play an independent and pioneering role in decision-making, as they do in the developed countries; and the fact that it remains dependent on the government, in the absence of fair competition, means that it will also not be able to develop, diversify or expand.[32] Even these countries' trade with the outside world has not escaped either the government's control or measures that ensure that no class capable of competing with it ever emerges. In these countries, commercial licences and trade restrictions are meant to help groups loyal to the governments. Nevertheless, these groups can never become a competent and able trading class, with influence over the economy, as long as they remain agents for foreign companies and ruling elites, at the same time.[33]

On the other hand, when these economies were largely dependent on the pearl trade, the merchants, private sector and tribal chiefs played the most important role, and the ruling families were largely dependent on the merchant class and other social sectors. They deferred to them in all matters not only because of the revenues they brought in, but also to ensure their own security and survival. In the post oil period, however, the business class and tribal chiefs became more like government employees rather than elites with power and influence, and community representatives.[34] Other signs of the private sector's weakness include the excessive routine, complicated procedures required to start a business, poor execution of contracts, difficulty liquidating businesses and the failure of small businesses to obtain financial aid.[35]

In a research study by an expert on Saudi society, based on meetings she held with thirty Saudi businessmen in 1999, it became obvious that although the Saudi private sector suffers from all the above-mentioned problems, the main problem lies in the control that ruling family members, and other powerful administration officials, wield over the private sector.[36] According to these businessmen, tenders are not awarded based on the best price available but rather on one's connection to powerful individuals, especially ruling family members. However, worse than needing an intermediary to win small tenders, large tenders are not even publically issued, but agreed upon behind closed doors among powerful stakeholders. The aid intended originally to ensure the fair distribution of the country's assets and helping the poorer classes went to people in power, and the agricultural aid that targetted the farmers and poor desert dwellers went to rich people and large farms. As well as these practices, which rob the people of their rightful assets, businessmen in the study group said that ruling family members acted as middlemen between decision-makers and the private sector, because the success of any new project depends on the support of certain princes in return, of course, for a percentage of the new company's profits.[37] In addition to the corrupt relationship between the government and the private sector, businessmen in the sample referred to several shortcomings in the effort to provide the private sector with the right environmental conditions. New graduates are ill-equipped because their skills are limited and expertise unsuitable for the local market, and laws are remiss in protecting property rights, executing contracts and rules and resolving conflicts.[38] Many laws are inadequate for managing bankruptcy procedures, debt payment or the relationship between companies and their employees, and even when the relevant laws do exist their implementation is not transparent, meaning that they remain susceptible to the influence of people in power, especially to members of the ruling family.[39]

The Saudi businessmen also complained about the financial market's weakness and insufficient infrastructural services, especially in industrial areas, such as telephone, electricity and internet services, even about an inadequate sewage system.[40] They also point to the fact that the administration system suffers from excessive routine and incompetence, its expansion to such an extent that it is not justified economically even if seen as a means of providing employment, and its size has become costly in terms of number of necessary formalities, endemic corruption and delays in implementing people's paperwork. Establishing a company now needs between three to six months to complete and requires the owner to deal with several ministries, each of which asks for a different set of documents. This compels many Saudi businessmen to invest in neighbouring countries, like Dubai, where such procedures could be conducted over the telephone, and if approved at all, procuring a commercial licence could take up to six months.[41] Such impressions by members of the private sector agree, to varying degrees, with what one hears from similar groups in other Gulf countries.

Fourth: Means of developing the private sector

From the above analysis, it is clear that the future development of the GCC states will depend on the private sector's ability to play a pioneering role in the process. However, for this to happen, the environment in which this sector operates needs to be reformed, starting by bridging the gap between the laws and legislation that help manage the private sector's activities, and their actual implementation on the ground. This should be done in a way that encourages the emergence of a business class eager to engage in productive activities, in a competitive atmosphere that raises performance levels, develops knowledge and diversifies products. This requires, in our opinion, a series of efforts on several fronts chief among which are:

1. Activating economic integration

Although we will address Gulf economic integration in more detail later on in the book, what we would like to reiterate here is that activating the provisions of the Gulf Economic Agreement, announced in Muscat in 2003, will expand the market and increase competition among Gulf companies. It will also commit the region's governments to abide by conditions likely to weaken various aspects of unproductive and illicit gain by people in power, who collaborate to this end with merchant groups in each Gulf country. The implementation of several World Trade Organization (WTO) provisions, and what this means in terms of integration and openness to the world, will mitigate many of the aspects of theft perpetrated by those in power, a phenomenon that currently afflicts the GCC states, simply because the reliance on openness and competition is one of WTO's core concepts. Despite being an unfair competition, it will compel many Gulf leaders to reconsider the way they deal with the private sector; otherwise they would have to put up with heightened levels of social and economic malaise, and various challenges, especially when oil prices are on the decline.[42] There is no doubt that, if done collectively, i.e., within the Gulf and Arab contexts rather than individually, the GCC states' integration into the world economy, whether in the context of WTO or through the establishment of free trading areas, will reap higher profits and reduce costs.

2. Promoting good governance

Although we already addressed accountability and the fact that it needs transparency at all levels, we shall address it here in the context of the relationship between the public and private sectors. All countries with highly developed private sectors that act as engines of economic growth, and have maintained different types of accountability mechanisms, which, despite their differences, agreed on the ultimate objective. In the industrialised countries, political parties exercise power, the judiciary is independent and treats everyone equally, the media is free and does not hesitate to address any topic that serves the public good, and parliaments respond to voter pressure. Regardless of their shortcomings, these countries' institutions have proven to be the best of what is available in terms of fostering an atmosphere of accountability that steers the public and private sectors towards serving the interest of society as a whole. They also steer society's resources towards the best available options, and reduce revenue that accrues from rentier activities that use government policies and institutions to further the interests of a small group of people. Even Asian countries that do not have advanced political participation systems have instituted other forms of accountability to achieve results similar to those of Western countries, thanks to the presence of alert political leaders with serious intentions and clear vision. In other words, in both Western and East Asian countries the private sector was able to develop because the political leadership was committed to fostering an atmosphere amenable to institution building. The fact that their decisions were clear and responsible, that they responded to society's aspirations and that they were not monopolised by a small minority, instilled in the private sector the confidence that those able and willing have an equal opportunity to contribute to building of a productive private sector.[43] Furthermore, the businessmen in these countries had a high sense of national responsibility. They were able to take the initiative in proposing policies and discuss them with the political leadership. This led to the success and development of their countries at the same time, given that some of them used to manage family business enterprises with a similar structure to the private sector in the GCC.[44]

On the other hand, the institutionalisation of such mechanisms, and the concomitant restrictions on the political leadership, do not exist in the GCC and other Arab countries. This means that their policies, including those related to the private sector, are in the hands of the ruler and a small group of his advisors and friends. Not only does this make their decisions whimsical, temperamental, unsustainable and skewed exclusively towards government loyalists, it weakens these governments' credibility in the eyes of local and foreign potential investors.[45] This means that private sector development will depend on the ability of these societies, especially their elites, to ask for more rights and political participation, for press freedom and an independent judiciary, and for the ensuing transparency of decision-making and oversight of decisions by the political leadership. The Qur'an tells us that only advocacy is the safety valve against social decline and endemic corruption, when it says, "And were it not for God's repelling some men with others, the earth certainly would have been corrupted."[46]

3.   Raising the administrative system's capacity

It is not enough for the political leadership to be aware of the private sector's important role, and of the need to provide it with a suitable environment to grow. Even honest and aware leaders cannot ensure the private sector's success on their own, in the absence of a highly capable and fair administration system, because this system selects the projects and implements laws and legislation relevant to this and other sectors. Since much has been said about Singapore's model administration system, we decided to take a quick look at it to find out what distinguishes it from the others, and pinpoint areas that the GCC states could learn from in developing their own private sectors.

The first and foremost characteristic of Singapore's administration system is the integrity and fairness of the country's political leadership; it has a clear development vision and the conviction that only a capable administration system can make this vision a reality. Lee Kuan Yew, Singapore's former prime minster, said in this context, "After several years in government I realized that the more talented people I had as ministers, administrators, and professionals, the more effective my policies were, and the better the results."[47] What confirms this focus on talent and skill is that, beginning in 2007, Singapore's public sector salary scale granted high-ranking administration officials annual salaries of up to $1.5 million, which is substantially more than the $400,000 annual salary of the American President, or the around $351, 000 salary of the British prime minister.[48] The second most important characteristic of Singapore's administration system is that its promotions and benefits scale relies on ability and performance. Since early in 2006, 40 per cent of all benefits granted to ordinary administration employees, and 50 per cent of all benefits granted to administration officials with seniority, were based on performance.[49] The third characteristic is the decentralised nature of the system; it has the flexibility and ability not just to make decisions, but also to use available resources including, for example, transferring surplus funds from one area to close the deficit in another. This was made possible thanks to this system's crystal-clear objectives, transparent decision-making and easy movement of precise information from one department to the other, which reduced opportunities to engage in corruption and misuse of power.[50] These and other characteristics of Singapore's administration system earned it credibility in the eyes of both local and foreign investors, and turned the country's private sector into a pioneer of sustainable development that led to a rise in the per capita income from around $1000, at the time of independence, to over $30,000 at the beginning of the twenty-first century.[51]

We shall see below how the Taiwanese and South Korean private sectors also played a pioneering role, not that different from Singapore's, which paved the way for an industrial revival whose outcomes included the development of an efficient private sector.

Fifth: The public sector's role in developing the private sector

Before ending this chapter on the private sector, we should mention once again that our recommendations regarding this sector's development in the GCC and Arab countries, are not in line with what the international organisations recommend, including the IMF and World Bank. This is not only because these organisations follow the big powers' agendas, as we will show later, but also because their formulas usually ignore the advanced countries' experience and the recent experience of the Asian Tigers, that contradict many of the policies they are trying to impose on the developing countries. We, therefore, decided to take a close look at Taiwan and South Korea's experience in industrialisation, because it sheds light on the public sector's pioneering role in laying a solid foundation for development and growing the private sector, lessons that we have mentioned several times earlier due to their importance in paving the way for genuine development in these countries.[52] Since the early 1970s, Taiwan and the other East Asian countries, better known as the Asian Tigers, managed to achieve high economic growth rates, by all international standards, accompanied by a series of structural transformations. These include an increase in the share of manufacturing of these countries' GDP and of the percentage of industrial export of the total exports, a rise in productivity levels and the reduction of income disparities among different social sectors. We are compelled to ask here, in light of these successes, what was role of the public sector in these remarkable economic achievements, and is it the same role that the World Bank and IMF are trying to impose on the developing countries, today? To answer these questions, we should look closely at the two above experiences to understand the development tracks they pursued, and elicit from their experiences and those of other countries some of the examples and lessons that help us recognise what role the private sector should play to ensure sustainable development. We will start with Taiwan's experience.

1. Taiwan's experience

In his evaluation of Taiwan's industrial development, Ezra Vogel, social science professor at Harvard University, said that in 1947, the ruling Nationalist Party began pursuing the policy of replacing foreign imports with locally produced goods, and fulfilling local demands for agricultural products, to reduce the country's dependence on China and Japan. Moreover, in 1949, when the government felt that local consumer products were facing stiff competition from Japanese products, it imposed restrictions on Japanese imports, and, in 1952, promoted and subsidised a number of products on which local demand was increasing, including bicycles, flour and cement.[53] The promotion of local agricultural production has no doubt paved the way for the country's industrial development, by providing foreign currency for the importation of industrial input and reducing inflation rates thanks to the low cost of food products. Taiwan benefitted from the infrastructure that the Japanese colonisers had left behind, including transportation and communications systems, a banking system, a railway network, a stable and efficient legal system, good quality health services and a modern irrigation system. The United States helped train local political leaders and technocrats, and the World Bank provided different kinds of funding and technical aid.[54]

Naturally, America's efforts and the World Bank's assistance to Taiwan were in the United States' interest, because it helped it contain the spread of communism and ensure the capitalist project's success at a time when the Cold War was at its height. In the mid 1950s, Taiwan completed its import-substitution strategy, i.e., domestic products covered almost all the local market's needs, and began looking towards establishing export-oriented industries, taking advantage of advanced technological equipment, and tools and machinery imported from the industrialised countries. Overseeing this strategy was a group of highly skilled and well-trained Taiwanese technocrats, known for their fight against corruption and for their insistence on the state's role in obtaining the most advanced technology, and in choosing and implementing strategic projects capable of lifting up the entire economy.[55] Later on, the country established other industrial projects like steel manufacturing, shipbuilding, electricity generation and nuclear energy production. At the same time, the government began privatising a number of companies with proven potential, that were established in the 1940s, which helped raise the private sector's share of the GDP from 28 per cent, in 1947, to 84 per cent in 1985.[56]

Not content with simply establishing an industrial base by imposing restrictions on imports and controlling foreign labour, the Taiwanese government established a number of industries that provided input for the private sector, like cotton, iron, steel and refined petroleum products. It sold these products at subsidised prices to promote private sector products earmarked for export, such as textiles, fertilisers, plastics and machinery, all products that the country began exporting in the 1960s. The government reinforced its above policies with others, including tax exemptions, establishment of free trade areas, promoting scientific research, developing the country's basic infrastructure, providing all forms of funding at low cost and promoting exports.[57] Also helping the Taiwanese development process succeed were laws that helped manage the relationship between the public and private sectors, the generous compensations awarded to technocrats, and forbidding the latter from establishing their own businesses or accepting gifts from the private sector, even a mere lunch invitation.[58]

2. South Korea

South Korea's experience with development began around 1961, i.e., somewhat late compared with Taiwan. Among the factors that helped the country's industrial drive were the presence of a military regime that sought to create a successful development model as a tool in its fight against its enemy, North Korea, and the impact of Japan and Taiwan's successes. The first stage of South Korea's industrialisation drive began with the imposition of restrictions on imports to promote local production, followed by other policies designed to encourage exports and locate industries that deserve assistance and support. This is how the country's exports, in general, and industrial exports, in particular, began to increase rising from $42 million per year, in 1962, to $1 billion dollars per year, in 1971, then up to $20 billion in 1981, most of which were industrial products.[59] Korea's political leadership, embodied by a group of highly talented and well-trained technocrats, then embarked on a series of steps that began with the protection of local industries, provision of the necessary infrastructural projects and encouragement of the agriculture sector, before turning its attention to the export-oriented industrial sector.

At the same time, public banks controlled the funding of industrial projects and the state imposed restrictions on wages to avoid any exponential increase in prices. Korean industrialisation began with the manufacture of fertilisers to lower the country's dependence on imports from North Korea, and this industry, in turn, required the establishment of an electrical energy generator and an oil refinery. The state also established an agriculture equipment industry and strengthened various basic infrastructural installations like seaports, road and communication networks. It was also able to set up, in coordination with Japan, a variety of industries like textiles, shoes and household goods, and, once it acquired the necessary skills and knowledge, it began assembling ships, and electronic equipment locally. The country then turned its attention to reducing Japan's control over its economy by lowering the level of Japanese investments in it, until it became certain that its own industries would be able to compete in terms of cost and quality. Even after that, the Korean government resisted opening the country up totally to the global economy.[60]

The experiences of Taiwan, South Korea and other East Asian countries, of which China is the most recent, teaches us a number of lessons about how the public sector can contribute to development, in general, and to private sector development, in particular. Their experiences undoubtedly confirm that building an advanced economy, which comprises an effective private sector, can only be achieved if the public sector plays a pioneering role in paving the way for comprehensive development, and guides economic activities in a manner that safeguards the country's economic and social objectives. This is a fact the World Bank itself recognises. In one of its report, the Bank says that based on experience, neither abandoning its role in development nor totally controlling the economy will help the state achieve development.[61]

Another World Bank expert confirms that one of the most important reasons for economic growth in certain countries, like Japan, South Korea, Singapore and Taiwan, is the right intervention by the government in the economy.[62] As Paul Streeten, professor and distinguished theorist of development economics, argues, "countries could learn from the East Asian countries' experience where governments did not only choose profitable industries, but established these industries and strengthened them with other selected industries."[63] Furthermore, in a meeting of the World Bank and the IMF, the Bank's Deputy Director and CEO said that the industrialised East Asian countries, and those who have copied their experience, are a strong proof that the positive and active role by the state could be a major factor in industrial progress.[64] It is also worth nothing that to develop their industrial base, Western Europe and Western industrialised nations like the United States and Japan pursued policies similar to those of the Asian Tigers. The recent financial crisis that has rocked the world since 2007 and whose full dimensions are so far still unknown, is another confirmation that it is the "visible hand" of the state, rather than the "invisible hand" of the market, that lies behind sustainable development. It is the state that ultimately determines the economy's stability and prosperity, provided its hand is clean and it sees and understands how the country's assets should be managed; in other words, provided it is a developmental rather than a predatory state. However, the WTO, which is under the industrialised nations' control, is trying to prevent the developing countries, including the GCC, from pursuing these same policies under the banner of "trade liberalisation". This means that the developing countries end up paying the price even for the unfair laws imposed by the international organisations, while the industrialised world has managed to escape this fate.[65]

CHAPTER TEN

Foreign Investments and Aid

Given the GCC states' limited absorptive capacity due to their small populations and scarcity of non-petroleum resources, they established sovereign wealth funds to invest their oil surpluses and develop sources that complement their income from petroleum exports. They also established development funds to grant soft loans and aid to other countries. We will first address these countries' foreign investments, and then evaluate the aid they grant to other countries, based on the data available to us.

First: Investments

The IMF estimates that in 2008, i.e., prior to the current financial crisis, the foreign investments of the GCC's sovereign wealth funds amounted to $1 trillion dollars, a figure expected to rise to at least $3 trillion in the next five years.[1] Estimates for 2011 show that the Abu Dhabi Investment Authority which is the biggest sovereign fund in the world is worth $627 billion, the funds for the Saudi Arabian Monetary Agency abroad reach $472.5 billion, the Kuwait Investment Company has funds estimated at approximately $296 billion, and the funds of the Qatar Investment Authority equal $85 billion. Libyan investments are around $85 billion, the funds of International Petroleum Investment Company owned by Abu Dhabi government are estimated at $58 billion and the Algerian National Revenue Fund owns about $56.7 billion.[2]

These funds had their positive dimensions including absorbing the economic shocks resulting from the drop in oil prices and revenues and, in Kuwait's case, helping pay the cost of the country's liberation and reconstruction. Until recently, these funds also helped avoid the inflation that could have resulted from the rise in the real value of these countries' currencies, better known as the Dutch Disease. This is because had these countries not invested this surplus abroad, changed it into the host countries' currencies and spent it there, a steep rise in price levels and in the value of the local currency vis-a-vis other currencies would have ensued, reducing the industrial sectors' ability to compete. This phenomenon is known as the Dutch Disease because it was first observed in Holland when the country developed its natural gas sector.[3] Regardless of this, however, the gist of these funds' role, i.e., what people actually expect from them, is to achieve genuine development in the GCC states and the Arab region. This development would involve diversifying the region's sources of income: expanding economic interstate networks, developing real sectors like agricultural and industrial production and information, raising the per capita income and laying the ground for a regional revival to benefit future generations. These sovereign funds have not done that.

The assets accumulating in these funds, in which annual revenue sometimes exceeded revenue from oil in certain countries,[4] have been more advantageous to Western countries than the Gulf or Arab countries. For example, instead of addressing the growing unemployment among GCC and Arab citizens, they opened new employment opportunities for speculators in the world's financial markets. However, a large part of these accounts was consumed by successive wars in the region, and the fact that they existed at all could have itself been a motive for purchasing weapons and increasing tensions in the region. What war did not consume of these liquid assets was consumed by other means, including the high rates of inflation and drop in the price of the dollar. According to Morgan Stanley, a 10 per cent drop in the price of the dollar against other major currencies, cuts the GCC's assets purchasing power by about 5 per cent.[5] On the other hand, the collapse of financial markets, which has been ongoing for the past twenty years, poses the biggest threat to the GCC's investments abroad, and the current financial crisis that began in the American real estate market is the most recent such incident. The fact that it spread from one sector to the other, and from one region to the next, could make it as big as the great depression of the 1930s, in the West, if not bigger. This crisis' impact is still unfolding and there seems to be no quick solutions. So far, the sovereign funds' losses from this crisis are estimated at around $400 billion, or more, and according to the IMF, could well be over 40 per cent,[6] excluding the cost of rescuing the global economy to which these countries will no doubt contribute, without any return on their money. According to some Western sources, the amounts which the Gulf funds pumped to rescue Western financial institutions like Citibank, UBS and Merrill Lynch were about $60 billion.[7]

The *Financial Times* reported that the United States and the United Kingdom asked the Gulf states to pump approximately $500 billion to deal with the recent financial crises and the governments of the Gulf states pledged to help but did not announce a specified amount.[8] We should still remember that prior to that, Arab investments had suffered losses to the tune of approximately $20 billion in the financial market crisis of 1987.[9] In 1992, Abu Dhabi's investments in the United Kingdom and Kuwait's investments in Spain sustained heavy losses, with Kuwait's losses alone, which many suspect were stolen, being estimated at around $4 billion.[10] Over and above that, there is fear that these accounts could eventually be either frozen, for one reason or another, or used to remedy various Western financial crises, especially since it has already happened before, although the region's governments have so far not learned their lesson, unfortunately. We still remember how at the beginning of the current financial crisis, the value of Citibank's shares dropped by around 80 per cent due to speculations in high risk investments. A Western economist says that these shares were headed for a worse fate had former American Treasury Secretary, Robert Ruben, not asked Middle Eastern officials to pump in billions of dollars to rescue the Bank from its gambling directors' errors, and we recall how Abu Dhabi had pumped in no less than $12 billion to extricate it from its woes. [11] If we dig deeper still in our memories, we will also remember that these investments were constantly at the mercy of the West's unfair policies. Do we not still remember what happened when Margaret Thatcher put the British government's shares in BP up for sale during Britain's privatisation drive in 1979-1987, and the Kuwaiti government bought around 21.6 per cent of them, to benefit, as numerous others did, from this good investment opportunity? The British government did not like that at all, and asked Britain's anti-trust agency to look into the matter and help it find a way out of this conundrum. The latter did indeed find that Kuwait's total share of BP had become a threat to British national interests, and that these should not exceed 9.9 per cent, thus forcing Kuwait to sell the difference back to the company.[12]

Even the extreme generosity shown by the Arabs towards the West during the recent financial crisis did not find appreciation among the West which spoke in the language of its interests. The former French president Sarkozy warned the industrial countries of the danger of Arab sovereign funds, saying, "I do not want European citizens to wake up a few months from now and discover that European companies belong to non-European capital which has bought at the lowest point of the stock exchange."[13]

In brief, on paper this wealth is not a serious income diversification effort since, as we said before, it did not provide employment for Gulf or Arab citizens, although it did provide such opportunities in the West, for a very low return.

These assets did not provide food or clothing for the region's inhabitants, weapons with which to defend themselves and their lands, communication or transportation systems, or road networks to help them stay in touch with their wider Arab milieu. It helped establish neither scientific institutions that graduate highly skilled experts nor modern hospitals that satisfy the Arab region's need for doctors. Except in very rare cases, these funds were not even manned by well-trained and capable local staff, which made them more like another link in the chain of dependency on international financial markets.[14] This does not surprise us, however, because these institutions are not much different from other GCC institutions that the ruling families see as their private property. Moreover, these assets are not accountable to the citizen, meaning that the public has no idea about their real size, the currencies used to buy them or vehicles through which they are invested, and no one knows their geographic distribution or nature of the intermediating institutions that help invest them.

Hence, the above institutions are managed like all other GCC institutions; withdrawals from them are not subject to clear and specific laws and the important decisions that concern them are not taken by institutions that represent the will and interest of society, as a whole. Their activities are neither straightforward nor transparent, which puts them in the same boat as other public assets that the ruling families, in the absence of any social developmental vision and clear public oversight, have turned into their private domain, as they did the country's state positions, lands, islands and deserts. Under no circumstance can this behaviour lead to prosperity and stability in the region.[15] Actually, the estimated size of these sovereign funds' assets confirms what we said above, namely that Gulf governments do not link oil production to the public interest, otherwise why the need for all these surpluses and why expose them to all these risks? Why not keep the oil underground instead of converting it into paper assets for the sole benefit of speculators, consumers and few beneficiaries in these countries, like all the spending on armaments that only leads to astronomical losses? Western sources also confirm, moreover, that these investments are actually useless in their present form and do not hide the fact that the best way to use them is to invest them in real projects, though they prefer that these projects be in their own home countries, just like the petroleum industry. Over and above the low returns on these assets, America's increasing debt and what it means in terms of a future drop in the value of the dollar means the possibility that these assets might witness additional losses in the coming years.[16] However, we would not have objected to these accumulated assets had the region's governments shown that their decisions were independent, or launched an Arab Marshall Plan to transform the Arab region into a prosperous, secure and peaceful economic belt that protects the GCC from destructive conflicts and foreign invasions, like in Iraq and Afghanistan, and earlier in our beloved Palestine. Given the above, can we still talk about sustainable development and security in this region?

For all the above reasons and others, and under the present circumstances, we do not pin much hope on these assets being an alternative or substitute for oil, and believe in the need for a fundamental change in current investment strategies. We advocate a shift from cash investments to real investments in agriculture, industry, trade and knowledge-based projects, and from investments in Western markets to investments in the Arab and Islamic region, followed by Asia. We also advocate a shift from hidden investments, like secret private accounts, to clear and specific account statements to the assets' real owners, i.e., the local citizens and the Arab-Islamic people that surround them, or to their representatives, who should ensure that only institutions that represent all social sectors in the GCC decide these assets' fate.[17] We could learn a lot from Norway's experience with sovereign funds, namely their transparency, investment instruments, geographic distribution of their portfolios, investment currencies and other relevant aspects.

Second: Aid

Prompted by humanitarian and development concerns, the GCC governments, and especially Saudi Arabia, the UAE and Kuwait, have granted a lot of official aid to other developing countries, the size, type, constituent elements and geographic distribution of which have varied along the years. We will briefly address all of this below using the available data. By official aid, we mean here the funds that developing countries get from donor governments to help them implement their development projects, part of which, usually no less than 35 per cent of their value, is in the form of grants.

1. Size and development of aid

The aid given by three GCC states, Saudi Arabia, the UAE and Kuwait, has accounted for over 90 per cent of all Arab official aid over the past forty years. However, although changes in oil prices and revenue have affected the size of this aid, which is another proof of these countries continued dependence on oil, its absolute value and share of these countries' GDP has remained, according to World Bank figures, higher than in any other country. Estimates show that in the period 1973-2008, these countries' official aid amounted to around $272 billion, based on 2007 prices, representing on average around 1.2 per cent of their GDP. The latter ratio is higher than the 0.7 per cent of the GDP that the United Nations suggested rich nations should give in aid, a suggestion that largely remained unheeded. In 1973, i.e., at the beginning of the oil boom, this aid rose to over 12 per cent of the GDP for the UAE and to around 8.5 per cent of the GDP for Saudi Arabia and Kuwait, declined in the 1980s in tandem with the drop in oil prices, and then rose again at the beginning of the twenty-first century.[18] This means that in these three countries, the ratio of aid to the GDP remained higher than in the rich industrialised nations, even when it decreased in tandem with the drop in oil prices, or in times of war when there was need for more spending on security, defence or reconstruction.[19]

In terms of official aid, Saudi Arabia headed the list of Arab countries in 1973-2008, accounting for around $172.9 billion, or around 63.6 per cent of the total, most of which was in the form of soft loans. Kuwait came in second with an overall figure of around $44.3 billion, or 16.3 per cent of total official Arab aid, and the UAE in third, with around $31.4 billion, based on 2007 prices, or 11.5 per cent of official Arab aid. Over 89 per cent of this aid was bilateral, i.e., given either through direct transactions between donor and recipient countries or via these countries' finance ministries, while the remainder was channelled through different local, regional and international agencies.[20]

Though this aid was distributed between grants and soft loans, available data shows that the number of grants was decreasing in comparison with soft loans. In the period 1990-1999, 70 per cent of official Arab aid was in the form of grants, and 30 per cent in the form of loans, whereas in 2000-2008, the ratio of grants dropped to 36 per cent and that of soft loans went up to 64 per cent.[21]

2. Geographic and sectoral distribution

Official Gulf aid came in various shapes and forms as far as geographic and sectoral distribution were concerned. Its geographic distribution extended to countries like Syria, Jordan, Palestine, Sudan, Senegal, Bangladesh, Cambodia and Pakistan, even to Europe and Latin America, although the ten countries that benefitted the most from this aid were Arab countries. For example, this aid accounted for 70 per cent of all official aid to Syria, Bahrain and Oman, though in Syria's case it dropped from over 90 per cent, in the 1970s, to under 20 per cent in recent years. In the case of Morocco, Jordan, Lebanon and Yemen, this aid accounted for 20 per cent to 40 per cent of the total aid they received, and for 10 per cent to 20 per cent of total aid for the West Bank, Egypt, Turkey, Sudan and Somalia.[22] In the 1970s and 1980s, assistance focussed on infrastructure building and payments for imported petroleum products, but then expanded to cover the agricultural sector, natural resource management, social project development, debt reduction, productive capacity-building and emergency crisis management.[23]

3. Motives and effectiveness

Some believe that the motive behind official Arab aid, whether bilateral or channelled through regional and international agencies, emanates from the fact that most poor Arab and Islamic countries do not receive aid from other sources. Others believe that this aid is an expression of Arab and Islamic solidarity, while a third group believes that since the GCC states are weak security-wise in a region plagued by instability and war, this aid helps them win friends and ensure a measure of security.[24] However, regardless of motives, what is important for us here is the extent to which these Arab and Islamic countries have benefitted from this aid. One of the ways of finding this out is by gauging Arab attitudes to the Iraqi invasion of Kuwait in 1990, though this is difficult to ascertain with precision. Thus, despite the unprecedented large amount of aid from the Gulf countries, according to international standards, the majority of Arabs did not side with Kuwait and even actually supported Iraq's invasion of that country, as did eight different Arab governments, as many sources indicate.[25] Should we blame these people for their ingratitude or is there another reason behind this phenomenon? Moreover, given this large amount of aid, by any standard, why are Arab League countries like Sudan, Yemen, Somalia, Palestine, Djibouti and the Comoros Islands still plagued with a 30 per cent poverty rate, according to the Arab Monetary Fund's latest figures?[26]

In our opinion, the problem lies in the manner in which the GCC states give this aid; in other words, what are its advantages, if any? They give it neither in an institutionalised and transparent manner, nor with clear objectives in sight in order to serve the region's people, but give to autocratic governments which are not accountable to their people. Several sources indicate that because this aid was channelled through the ministries of finance and shrouded in secrecy, it actually raised many suspicions as to the real motive behind it.[27] This also explains why these funds never went into real projects like schools, hospitals, bridges and jobs, which ordinary citizens can see and feel, because most of it went straight into private pockets, and the few exceptions here do not negate the rule. This why most development-related literature says that to effectively achieve the desired objective, recipient regimes should be held accountable, and there should be clearly defined development programmes to which this aid can be channelled. In recent years, the African countries have become aware of this fact and started to address the issue, to make the best use of the aid they receive.[28]

Chapter Eleven

Oil and Corruption

The oil boom and the astronomical revenues it brought in for the GCC states, coupled with the absence of public oversight of government spending, led to both endemic corruption in these countries' administrations, and the squandering of resources. That partly explains, as mentioned before, their failure to develop properly. Therefore, this chapter will begin by clarifying the relationship between oil and corruption before discussing some of the forms of this corruption in the GCC states.

First: The relationship of corruption to oil

The development literature indicates that there is a strong relationship between the economy founded on oil and the spread of corruption which is considered the most important obstacle to the path of development. Corruption here entails the misuse of public power to achieve personal gains, either politically by passing legislation to serve the interests of a specific group, or administratively by misapplying laws for personal gain. For example, the money that was wasted or plundered in Nigeria by successive governments since independence in 1960 is estimated at around $380 billion. In Angola, some sources indicate that approximately $1 billion has disappeared annually from the state's oil revenues since the beginning of the 21st century as a result of corruption.[1] There is no doubt that the rest of the oil states, including the GCC states, suffer this phenomenon which has taken root in these societies since the start of the oil boom in the 1970s.

Corruption spreads through two ways in the oil states and both have a negative effect on growth in these economies. The first way is via the rentier behaviour or the characteristic behaviour of members of society who vie and compete to obtain the largest part of the oil rent instead of utilising their skills or time to undertake productive activities. As a former Angolan planning minister commented, "This has nothing to do with a capitalist system. This is not about production, but about a cake to fight for."[2] Many studies confirm that in the oil society where the institutional structure is weak, businessmen are more likely to put more effort into obtaining oil rent through their business production activities but in the long term such behaviour means the decline of society's productivity and the small slice of the "cake" over which the struggle began. This exemplifies the importance of the existence of effective institutions to prevent the spread of this unproductive behaviour. It is these institutions which change the incentive system in the private sector, primarily maintaining ownership rights, applying laws and so on.[3] The second way in which corruption spreads in these states is by governments channelling oil revenues to buy loyalties or practise favouritism through offering support or setting up baseless plans that nonetheless gain supporters. Alternatively, these governments spend enormous amounts on security equipment to contain the emergence of any opposition seeking change. It is undeniable that this kind of spending prevents large sections of these societies from obtaining basic services, such as education, health and employment, and that it is more widespread in countries where accountability is absent, like the GCC states. Once again, we see that the remedy might be to build effective institutions, although the institutions mentioned here relate to creating an oversight system for the government and its spending of society's resources. This requires political participation and the existence of governments that express the will of all of their societies.[4]

This relationship between oil and corruption is one of the most important obstacles to the process of growth in the Gulf region. It is this relationship that explains a large part of the phenomenon of the "oil curse". Consequently, we must define the manner in which rentier behaviour has an impact on the different variables of growth. That is because the rentier behaviour of individuals in addition to the oil governments' dependence on relationships of favouritism, and results largely in disabling the economy's passage from its reliance on oil to its reliance on diverse economic structures and equal political and social relationships.[5]

While the lowering of rentier income in the non oil-producing countries creates positive dynamics that lead to effective growth, the presence of this income in the oil-producing countries engenders negative dynamics which impede the development process. In those states characterised by a low oil rentier income, the governments find that they need a strong connection to their people in order to achieve economic growth by directing investments to productive aspects and through market forces, with an emphasis on the system of competitive incentives and the prevalence of law and equal opportunities in funding and marketing. This is what induces members of society to direct their energies, time and efforts to productive activities. In turn, this leads to the establishment of industries that have a large part of their production consumed domestically while the rest is exported abroad. With the expansion of the industrial sector's role, there is an increase in wages, skills development and job opportunities and the gap in income between the different strata of society is not so obvious. At the same time, alongside these economic developments, there are other developments. These include the evolution of a class of businessmen who are independent of the government and wish to protect their industries and investments through the demand to create an institutional environment with various dimensions to oversee the government's performance. Another development is the emergence of civil society institutions to balance the power of the state and express the aspirations of the people, and the emergence of a taxation system based on the earnings of individuals in society, especially the private sector, instead of on rentier income as is happening in these states today.[6]

Conversely, we see that in those societies with an increasing oil rentier income, as is the case in the oil states, dynamics are forming which obstruct the process of growth described above. The political leadership in this kind of society does not possess the desire, will or need to connect with other sections of society in order to generate new wealth. Rather, most of the leadership's interests are concentrated on the distribution of existing wealth and achievement of timely political gains from this process. Thus, these leaderships do not wish to direct society's resources to the forces of supply and demand, the prevalence of law and the creation of integrated institutions because that would reduce their ability to use the rentier income in order to preserve their own interests. Therefore, they substitute institutions with a network of personal relationships founded on a reciprocal "give and take" favouritism. This situation results in a lower ability to exploit society's resources and an economy that does not start out in manufacture, skills development and exportation, and hence forces economic growth to focus on oil rentier income alone. Furthermore, a class of productive businessmen who are independent of the government does not emerge, nor is there any opportunity to develop society's civil institutions. Similarly, the state prevents the development of the taxation system because of the lack of a productive private sector. In this case, the state is compelled to continue spending an increasing part of the oil rentier income to employ new graduates who have no place in a rentier private sector that relies on brokerage and reselling the products of others.[7]

In view of this relationship between corruption, oil and development, the true starting point for reducing corruption in these states, and thus improving their development opportunities, may be in building effective institutions that help to rectify the rentier behaviour among individuals and governments alike. A number of intellectuals and decision-makers in the West have for years adopted an initiative for transparency and demanded that oil companies and oil-producing governments disclose their oil accounts. This initiative, excellent though it is, does not deal with the fundamental corruption in the GCC states because it focuses on revenues, whereas the main problem in these countries is hidden in the expenses side, as we have seen in our discussion on the rentier behaviour of individuals and governments.[8] The remaining discussion in this chapter will attempt to present three examples of our previous analysis: the bloated administrative system, allocations to ruling families and military expenditure.

Second: Forms of waste and corruption

1. Bloated administration system

The lack of legitimacy plaguing the GCC governments has affected their institution building efforts, whether in terms of the objectives, employment conditions, resources allocated to them or level of transparency at which they operate. A close look at these institutions will show that the aim behind their establishment is to control society, and allow ruling families to remain the final arbiters of society's destiny. This, according to one Western organisation, has robbed their employees of any national sentiments and awareness of a concept such as public assets.[9] As we mentioned in the section on institutions, these bodies are usually managed by ruling family members who may or may not be qualified to hold such positions, meaning that employment in these institutions does not depend on honesty, experience and ability, as in modern countries, but on the individual's closeness to the agendas of the governments. They expand these institutions to allow government control over the private sector, and increase their expenses accordingly, even if there are more worthy avenues on which to spend this money. A Western researcher drew attention to this phenomenon, saying that "The fragility and irrationality of Middle Eastern political systems makes it hard, if not impossible, to address the structural problems of Arab economies and educational systems or to present acceptable pathways to deal with social and cultural change."[10]

Oil revenue has helped exacerbate the problem by making employment in government and the public services sector state-funded, including positions in the health, education, housing, security and defence sectors, in appointed bodies and those with limited powers. This means that the government has turned the above institutions into vehicles through which it can tighten its grip on society by granting or denying these services to the public.[11] The question is, however, what happened to the institutions established with this vision in mind? They began by guaranteeing positions to all new graduates which led to an imbalance in the students' choice of specialisation and the quality of their academic performance resulting in a surplus of students in the liberal arts and a shortage in the sciences. This imbalance led to employment practices that moved away from expertise, ability and need, and favoured loyalty over ability, which ultimately worsened the state of the administrative machinery, and gradually raised unemployment rates to exceedingly high levels.[12] However, the vicious circle did not stop there; employees with the wrong specialisations, who were not hired for their skill and expertise, were coming to work late, making the minimum effort, leaving the office early and occupying themselves with alternative pursuits like financial market speculations.[13] Furthermore, in the absence of transparency and accountability, many of these employees began using their positions to help themselves, their regions or their ethnic groups, encouraging more corruption, patronage and routine.[14]

The negative impact of these politicised institutions found its way into the education system and the private sector, with the education system continuing to produce the same quality of graduates, due to the absence of proper employment conditions in public institutions and the lack of employee evaluation. The private sector also suffers as a whole from a shortage of local staff, especially highly skilled educators, because the majority gravitate towards the public sector despite it being plagued by underemployment and low productivity rates.[15] The impact of this unjustified public sector expansion on these countries' budgets is starting to be felt; budgets are showing deficits whenever oil prices and revenues drop, while the incompetent government agencies continue to grow. With the advent of the twenty-first century, the GCC states realised that they could no longer maintain their bloated public sectors and gradually began to pedal back from these policies. They no longer guaranteed jobs for all new graduates, reduced the rate of public employment and, in the process, succeeded in reducing government spending. This resulted in a distorted drive to privatise a number of public institutions to the advantage of people in power, and some countries attempted to freeze the salaries of their public employees, which led to a drop in their purchasing power. This raised the rate of unemployment among the category of new graduates that the public administration system could no longer absorb, and who, at the same time, were rejected by the private sector due to their poor abilities and high salaries compared with foreign workers.[16] This turned the bloated administration systems into hubs of profiteering and corruption, meaning that these governments were able to turn their administration systems, often described as nests of patronage and corruption, into protective shields for them and their illegal pursuits.[17]

2. Allocations to ruling families

All the GCC's ruling families deduct a percentage of their countries' financial assets for their personal use. This practice, which differs from one country to another, one time period to another and one emirate to another, is in our opinion an illegal and unjustified way for the rulers to put their hands on the people's assets, as they do in the UAE, for example. Some of these families openly take a certain amount out of the country's funds. In Kuwait, for example, parliament has earmarked the sum of 50 million Kuwaiti Dinars, equivalent to US$137 million, for the personal use of the al-Sabah family.[18] It sees no need to justify the decision, or say whether this sum is an acquired right that has a moral, legal and logical justification, or if it is simply a means of acquiring wealth based on power and authority. In the other GCC states, including the UAE, Qatar, Saudi Arabia, Oman and Bahrain, these deductions are even worse since the citizens' wealth is plundered without their knowledge, and without any set limits or controls over this theft, a process which, in some countries like the UAE, has reached levels of unrestrained and unmonitored plunder.

Gulf researcher Ali al-Kawari says that in the early 1970s, the percentages that the ruling families deducted from their countries' budgets were as follows: 25.7 per cent in Abu Dhabi, 29.3 per cent in Bahrain, 32.8 per cent in Qatar, 2.6 per cent in Kuwait and 12 per cent in Saudi Arabia.[19] Parker Hart, a former US diplomat in Saudi Arabia, said that when Faisal became prime minister, in the early 1960s, he learned that the ruling family was deducting 60 per cent of the country's oil revenues for its personal use,[20] and many believe that the actual percentages were much higher than the above figures.[21] Peter Wilson and Douglas Graham say that, in the early 1980s, Saudi princes received annual salaries of between $50,000 and $200,000, in addition to trade commissions and profits from unofficial oil sales. These sources confirm that in the 1980s, one of King Abdul Aziz al Saud's sons used to receive around half a million barrels of oil a day. Over and above that, ruling family members own large tracts of land that they resell to the government to build roads and erect building and other facilities.[22] Said Aburish says, in the same context, that a number of Saudi princes holding major state positions used to receive around $100 million per year.[23] Daniel Byman and Jerrold Green confirm the existence of this financial burden in Saudi Arabia due to the ruling family's generous allocations, saying that the twenty thousand Saudi princes and princesses take out of the country's budget monthly salaries amounting to thousands and millions of US dollars.[24] Another Western researcher said at the beginning of the twenty-first century, that the sums paid to Saudi princes and tribal chiefs allied to them totalled between 15 per cent and 20 per cent of the Kingdom's budget.[25]

A recent study by Ali al-Kawari on the estimated gap between the value of four GCC states' crude oil and gas exports and figures recorded in the general budget showed that billions were missing from the budget and that the lost assets indicator, or the percentage of lost funds to the total exports, i.e., "the theft indicator", was indeed high. For example, in 2007, the amount of lost or stolen funds in Saudi Arabia reached $56.4 billion, or 27.4 per cent of the total amount of oil and gas exports. In the other GCC states, based on what little information is available, these amounts were $14.6 billion or 17.3 per cent in the UAE, $20.5 billion or 50.4 per cent in Qatar, and minus $5.1, or minus 8.5 per cent in Kuwait. Al-Kawari explains Kuwait's negative figures saying that the revenue from oil recorded in the general budget was higher than the amount of exports by around 8.5 per cent, because the general budget's share of the local oil and natural gas consumption was added to its share of the exports.[26] Egalitarian-minded people are mainly put off by the fact that the sums that these ruling families take out directly from the people's assets, and other such privileges, have transformed them from families equal to others in rights and responsibilities, as they were in the past, to families that seek to entrench their particular privileges. Many observers believe that this kind of behaviour has already eroded these families' credibility among the people, and will no doubt continue to do so in the future.[27]

However, since we are writing for generations that could confuse between these families' transgressions and our authentic Islamic heritage, especially in a country like Saudi Arabia where the regime persists in claiming that its legitimacy draws on the true tenets of Islam, we should end this section on the ruling families' allocations with examples from the first four caliphs, known as the rightly guided caliphs. The manner in which the latter dealt with public funds embodies the best and most wholesome of what Islam has to offer, and reveals the width of the gap between the way they managed the Muslim people's assets and the way current Gulf governments manage them today, and leave it for the reader to judge. There are various narrations (*hadiths*) that attest to the actions of the rightly guided caliphs in this context. One narration says, "When Abu Bakr became Caliph, the companions of the Prophet, said 'Give the successor of God's Prophet that which will enrich him'. They answered, 'Yes, the clothes he wears, his mount when he travels, and his family expenses as they were before he become caliph.' To that, Abu Bakr said, I accept."[28] Another narration says that when Abu Bakr fell ill with the disease that eventually killed him, he said, "See what has been added to my wealth since I entered office and send it to the caliph who comes after me."[29] In another narration regarding Umar Bin al-Khattab it says that "Umar gathered the people and said to them, 'You have preoccupied me with your affairs. What is your opinion, how much of this wealth is allowed to me?' Ali replied 'Whatever will keep you and your family, but you can have no more than this amount.' The people responded 'Ali has spoken rightly.'"[30] Umar also said, "By God, no one is more deserving of this money than anyone else, neither do I deserve it more than any other. Every Muslim has a right to a share of this wealth. If I live a long life, the shepherd from the mountains of Sana'a will have a share in this wealth even if he does nothing but stays there and rears his goats."[31] Likewise, Umar used to say, "'Do you know who is like me and you? Like you and me are those who travelled and paid the expenses of others with them.' They replied, 'Then pay for us, why should this man be an exception?' They said, 'No, O prince of the faithful'. He replied, 'Then we are like you and me as well'."[32] When sedition mounted under Uthman bin Affan's caliphate and its propagators accused him of favouring his family from the Muslim's treasury, he answered them saying, "I allow nothing for myself from the wealth of the Muslims, nor for any other person. I have only received the fifth [the caliph's allocation]. The Muslims administer its placement to those who deserve them without me."[33] Before being acclaimed caliph, Ali said to the people, "'I have no authority which excludes you, other than holding the keys to your treasury and that I will not take even a dirham from it without your permission, does that please you?' They replied 'Yes' so he said, 'O God bear witness' and they swore allegiance to him on that."[34] Mu'awiyah bin Abi Sufyan, the fifth caliph, said in one of his speeches, "In the treasury there is a surplus from your grants. I am distributing that among you. It is not our wealth but a booty that God has bestowed on you."[35]

It is, therefore, not surprising to see countries that do not understand either accountability or transparency, and whose decision-makers abuse the people's assets, becoming fertile ground for rampant corruption. This is shown by table 11-1 that reveals Transparency International's findings on corruption levels. It is worth noting that the level of corruption that this organisation has unveiled is limited to what its representatives could see and read, which makes their task all the more difficult in countries like the GCC where there is no transparency whatsoever. This suggests that the levels of corruption are actually higher than those shown in the following figures.

Table 11-1

Corruption Indicator in the GCC states for 2013

State	Rank	Score	2012 Score
UAE	26	69	68
Qatar	28	68	68
Bahrain	57	48	51
Oman	61	47	47
Saudi Arabia	63	46	44
Kuwait	69	43	44

Source: Transparency International Corruption Perceptions Index 2013. (The figure 100 indicates the lowest level of corruption and 0 indicates the highest; the above order is among 177 countries).

It is clear from the above table that all the GCC states are beset by corruption to varying degrees. The UAE is the least corrupt country and Kuwait is the most corrupt, while the remaining countries are ranked between them. Moreover, the table shows that corruption fell in some of those countries between 2012 and 2013, such as UAE and Saudi Arabia, that no change has happened in some of them during this period, like Qatar and Oman, and in others corruption increased, like Bahrain and Kuwait. It might be surprising to know that despite Kuwait's political openness, corruption in that country is higher than in most of the other GCC states. This is in Kuwait's favour, however, since it means that level of transparency that the country's political participatory system allows for has made corruption easier to detect. This means that the remaining countries, for example the UAE and Saudi Arabia, might actually suffer from higher levels of corruption than Kuwait, especially when major weapons deals and public projects are involved. However, the lack of effective participation in these two countries, and the relative lack of transparency, makes uncovering corruption that much more difficult. At the same time, we should also not exclude the other possibility, namely that Kuwait did indeed witness higher levels of corruption during the aforementioned period.

3. Military expenditure

Military spending is the largest drain on the GCC states' assets, caused by both local and Western governments represented by the manufacturers and sellers of weapons. Having lost all public legitimacy, these governments have tried for decades to make up for this deficit by seeking the backing of foreign powers, which forced them to pursue several policies that do not necessarily serve their people's interests. Among these policies is spending money on weapons, weapons that neither target the region's main enemy nor are manufactured locally, meaning that they neither promote local development nor ensure these countries' internal security. They have remained, instead, a constant cause of regional conflict, existing for no other reason except the protection of Western interests and those of local illegitimate political entities.

Tables 11-2 and 11-3 below give an idea of the size of this waste which has continued since the early 1970s and clarify the total amount of revenues from oil that went back into the coffers of Western countries through the military expenditure of the GCC states. The tables reveal the average amount that these countries have spent on weapons between 1990 and 2012, in billions of dollars, given that the values for 1990-2008 are based on 2008 prices, while the values for 2009-2012 are based on 2011 prices. Additionally, the tables point to the rate of military expenditure to the GDP of each country for the same period. Complete data for Qatar's military spending is not available. data for the UAE does not include the spending of all separate seven emirates for arms, and which if added the UAE's expenditure would increase greatly , as confirmed by reports from the Stockholm International Peace Research Institute (SIPRI).

Table 11-2

Average expenditure on military equipment by
GCC states (in billions, based on 2008 prices)

State	Saudi Arabia	Kuwait	UAE	Oman	Bahrain
1990-2000	17.64	7.58	16.42	2.41	0.32
2000-2009	29.73	4.47	1.98	3.86	0.54
2009-2012	48.97	5.2	16.96	5.17	0.83

Source: SIPRI Military Expenditure Database

Table 11-3

*Average military expenditure as a percentage of the
GDP (per cent) for the GCC states*

State	Saudi Arabia	Kuwait	UAE	Oman	Bahrain
1990-2000	11.0	25.3	5.8	13.9	4.8
2000-2009	8.3	4.5	7.2	12.3	3.0
2009-2012	9.6	3.5	5.1	7.9	3.6

Source: SIPRI Military Expenditure Database

A close look at these tables makes clear several key points.

1. Not only are these countries' military expenditures high by all regional and international standards, they are unjustified from the security point of view because they are neither confrontation states nor capable of standing up to any regional threat, from countries like Iraq or Iran for example, given their current defence systems. This became amply clear when the United States and other foreign powers had to intervene repeatedly on their behalf, when conflicts broke out in the region. From the perspective of absolute values, Saudi Arabia spent an annual average of $17.64 billion, or 11 per cent of its GDP, on weapons, from 1990-2000, while, during that same period, Egypt, Israel and Turkey spent an average of $3.34 billion, $11.89 billion and $17.75 billion, respectively. The latter sums accounted for 3.9 per cent, 10.5 per cent and 4.5 per cent of these countries' GDP, respectively.

    This means that during that same period, a country like Turkey with a considerable population size, and key to NATO in the region, has spent barely 4.5 per cent of its GDP on armament, while Saudi Arabia spent 11 per cent of its GDP. In the period that followed, i.e., 2000 to 2009, the average amount spent by Saudi Arabia was $29.73 billion, or almost 8.3 per cent of its GDP, which means an increase in absolute value and a decrease in ratio. This drop in the ratio of military spending in relation to the GDP is due to a sudden rise in GDP value caused by an unexpected rise in oil prices, during that same period. Expenditures by the above three countries, Egypt, Israel and Turkey, during that second period amounted to $3.89 billion, $13.95 billion and $18.46 billion, respectively, with percentages of the GDP equal to 2.7 in Egypt, 8.0 in Israel, and 2.5 in Turkey, rather low percentages when compared to Saudi Arabia's 8 per cent. During the period 2009-2012, the average spent by Saudi Arabia on arms rose to $48.97 billion, or equivalent to 9.6 per cent of the GDP. In contrast, Egypt, Turkey and Israel spent around $4.38 billion, $17.46 billion and $15.5 billion respectively. This spending represents 1.9 per cent, 2.4 per cent and 6.5 per cent of these countries' GDP. This excessive spending on arms by the remaining GCC states is evidenced by the figures in tables 2-11 and 3-11.

2. These expenditures rise and fall in tandem with the ebb and flow of oil prices and revenues, with the economic situation in the West and with wars and crises in the region. Thus, the more there are crises in the region and the higher oil prices and revenues go, the more opportunity Western countries and weapons dealers, who are also members of the ruling families, have to maximise their share of these countries' oil revenue. Nothing is more indicative of this link than former British Prime Minister Tony Blair's refusal in 2007 to launch an investigation in the corruption case that the British press had uncovered, regarding the arms deal between Britain and Saudi Arabia, the al-Yamama deal worth $84.4 billion. A report by the Centre for Arab Unity Studies entitled "State of the Arab World", usually written by several Arab intellectuals, gives the details of the al-Yamama deal and the corruption associated with it. The report says that when the details of the deal became public, former British Prime Minister Tony Blair warned that an investigation would lead to the "complete wreckage" of British national interests, and would damage the two countries' close cooperation in the fight against terror and the cause of peace and security in the Middle East. In early 2007, a number of ministers in Blair's government went even further by asking for the dissolution of the anti-corruption office, the same office that had previously revealed that the Saudi ruling family had received bribes to facilitate the weapons deal with Britain, in 1985. In 2007, in return for this kind gesture, Saudi Arabia signed a new contract with the same British group for the purchase of seventy-two fighter jets, at the cost of £10 billion, the equivalent of US$19 billion.[36]

3. The squandering of the GCC's assets continued unabated even when spending was curtailed to coincide with lower oil prices, because this spending acts as a cover for the ruling families' theft of the region's wealth. Just as it is happening now, curbs on spending always target development projects, as well as health and education services, but never touches spending on weapons and security.[37] Western researchers

David Holden and Richard Johns say that because the budgets of the Saudi defence and national guards are neither transparent nor accountable, this has made Sultan Bin Abdul-Aziz the richest man in Saudi Arabia, and there are rumours that his brother Fahd used to take 40 per cent of all arms deals.[38]

The squandering is still going on as these lines are being written. In September 2010, Saudi Arabia signed a contract with the United States to the tune of $60 billion, for the purchase of advanced weapons over the next ten years. In 2012, a report issued by the US Congress showed that the GCC states are considered the biggest buyers of American arms since their purchases between 2007 and 2010 reached more than $26.7 billion. This report also mentions that the US agreed in 2011 to sell fighter planes to Saudi Arabia worth $29.4 billion, making this the biggest deal in the history of the kingdom.[39] The alliance between the region's governments and the arms dealers has no doubt found in the current Western financial crisis, and the Iranian nuclear issue, a new opportunity to do what it does best, namely steal the people's assets at a time when poverty and backwardness are on the increase in the Arab region. Some sources say that the recent Saudi arms deal will create 77,000 new jobs in the West,[40] at a time when Saudi Arabia itself suffers from unemployment rates of over 25 per cent and rising, as previously indicated in this book. It is also worth noting that though we chose to give the reader an idea about what takes place in the biggest and most important GCC country, the corruption associated usually with Saudi arms deals is quite common in other countries of the regions, especially those with significantly large deals, like the UAE and Kuwait.

In closing, we would like to end the section on squandered assets by pondering the gigantic sums these countries spend on weapons, and wondering what justifies, if anything, all these expenditures. If these countries are not in direct confrontation with Israel, are neither convinced nor willing to engage in cross-borders wars, are not ready to establish a united Gulf army and cannot, given the above, stand up to powerful regional countries like Iraq and Iran, then spending all this money can only be justified by the desire to please Western governments. The aim is to keep the Western weapons industry alive, protect the local weapons dealers' commission, most of whom are members of ruling families or people who turn in their orbit, and provide weapons for the Western forces' use if, and when, it becomes necessary.[41] Thus, instead of bringing security, this spending on military equipment has led to instability in the region, increased chances for war and locked these countries in a destructive vicious circle that starts with producing irrational amounts of oil, leads to huge amounts of money being spent on weapons, which, in turn, leads to more war. The vicious circle goes on and on destroying the region's wealth and reducing its basic infrastructure to rubble. Those who ponder this fact will realise that neither the ruling families nor Western countries incur any losses from this situation because the cost is always borne by the people, and by future generations whose wealth has been squandered and will remain mired in backwardness and poverty. We will show later why the current spending levels will not serve the people's interests or bring security to the region; what will do that are the policies that steer revenue towards highly productive agricultural, industrial, trade, educational, health, communications and transportation projects, all over the Arab world. Policies such as these will provide the minimum level of dignity and peace of mind not only for the Gulf and its citizens, but for the wider Arab region as well. The prosperity of the Arab world that surrounds the GCC is the only safety valve likely to reduce conflicts in the region, guarantee the GCC's stability and free the region from Western extortion and theft that has lasted far too long. Not only has this failed to provide security, stability and prosperity in the past, it is also unlikely to provide them in the future. Furthermore, it will continue to wreak havoc on every inch of the Arab-Muslim world, as we see happening today in Iraq, Afghanistan, Palestine, Somalia and elsewhere in the Islamic world.

PART IV

Security Policies

The Gulf region will remain, as it was in the past, an arena of regional and international conflict. That is due to several reasons, not least its extensive natural resources, mainly oil and gas, for which international demand is increasing at a time when new sources of energy are proving hard to come by. According to figures from 2012, the GCC region has the world's largest oil and gas reserves. Its oil reserves are estimated at 494.6 billion barrels, 29.6 per cent of the world's reserves, and if we add to that Iraq's reserves of 150 billion barrels and Iran's reserves of 157 billion barrels, the total reserves for the region reach 801.6 billion barrels, 48 per cent of the world's total reserves.

Compared with the oil and gas reserves owned by the countries of the region, the United States' oil reserves accounted for only 35 billion barrels in 2012, or about 2.1 per cent of the global reserves with a lifespan of 10.7 years (this is conventional oil of course).[1] The GCC states together with Iraq and Iran produce approximately 27.7 million barrels a day, equivalent to 32.2 per cent of the global production of around 86.2 million barrels a day.[2] In 2012, the GCC's natural gas reserves were estimated at around 1494.4 trillion cubic feet, equivalent to 22.6 per cent of the total global reserve of 6614.1 trillion cubic feet. If Iraq and Iran are added to this, the reserve becomes 2808.4 trillion cubic feet, 42.5 per cent of the global reserve.[3] It is worth noting here that the ratios published by BP which are cited here include their estimates of the proven reserve of oil with both conventional and non-conventional oil in both Canada and Venezuela which in total reached around 471.5 billion barrels of oil. Accordingly, if we exclude this figure from the total reserve, the percentages mentioned previously would be greater than they are now.

The above figures underline the Gulf region's vital importance to the rest of the world, and this will continue to be the case as long as these energy reserves continue to exist, and as long as alternatives to oil are hard to come by, either because there are none, or because their cost is high. This makes crude oil the chief energy source for a period estimated at approximately 52.9 more years on the basis of current production, and this is the expected life of the current reserve. With this continues the importance of the Gulf region as a "lake of oil" for the rest of the world. Moreover, the West only sees Saudi Arabia in terms of the size of its reserve which, according to the figures for 2012, is equivalent to 265.9 billion barrels of oil, approximately 15.9 per cent of the global reserve of oil. The West views the country only in terms of its ability to increase or decrease its productive energy if the market demands it. This is exactly what happened when Iraq occupied Kuwait, and Saudi Arabia and the UAE compensated the 4 million barrels or so that Kuwait and Iraq used to export, and the same happened during other conflicts.[4] However, having and using this flexibility is probably not in the Saudi economy's interest, as indicated earlier, but rather in the interest of Western nations. A Western oil and gas expert says in this context that, "Not only is Saudi Arabia the leading foreign supplier of crude petroleum to the United States ... In return for providing the United States with so much of its oil, the Saudi government – which is to say the Saudi royal family – relies on the United States for defense against its adversaries, both foreign and domestic. Over the decades, we have provided the kingdom with vast quantities of sophisticated weaponry, along with large numbers of military advisors, instructors, and technicians."[5]

Several observers underline the fact that the Western countries would not have achieved such a level of economic prosperity since the end of WWII, nor been able to develop the military capabilities that helped them defeat the Soviet Union and its allies, had it not been for GCC and Saudi oil. Oil and security expert Michael Klare supports the view that without Saudi and the GCC states' oil, the United States and its European allies would not have been able to achieve such high levels of economic development, in the post-war era. Likewise, Washington would not have been able to maintain such a large army, navy and air force in the face of a potential threat from Russia and its allies.[6]

This is why everything we hear from the big powers, in terms of policies on terrorism, freedom, military bases, or other forms of interference in the region, are no more than variations on the theme of getting their hands on this oil and, of course, ensuring Israel's security. Several Western research projects and studies clearly confirm this fact.[7] However, the interaction between the Western countries and the Gulf to ensure uninterrupted oil supplies and protect other Western privileges does not happen in a vacuum; rather, it affects and is affected by other vital issues, as well. Foremost among these is the big powers' attitude towards the political rights of the region's people, and their interaction with neighbouring countries, especially Iraq and Iran. The reader will clearly see that what the West says about security, and what the region's governments say about that, has in fact nothing to do with the security of people in the Gulf, or the Arab world, i.e., with the so-called "Arab regional order". This means that the subject we are addressing here, namely security policies in the region, is closer to being the West's vision of security for the region than the local population's vision. We will, therefore, try to draw an accurate picture of various conflicts that have unfolded in the region between the oil-seeking big powers and their economic interests, and the countries of the region that compete with each other and with the big powers, in the total absence of any independent security vision by the regions' governments and people.

In the past few years, developments in the region, especially the occupation of Iraq and the removal of its regime, have certainly not been in the region's best interest because they gave Iran the upper hand at the GCC states' expense, and weakened the Arab regional order vis-à-vis Israel. As we shall see later, if the Arab regional order is not revived, the above developments will no doubt have negative repercussions on the region's security. This is why this section will focus on the geopolitical game the big powers play in the region which aims at controlling it and securing a number of advantages. This is carried out under hereditary regimes that disregard the people's interests and an Arab regional order that has been in a process of gradual disintegration since the June War of 1967, and unfortunately still continues to be so even after the Arab revolutions.

The section is made up of three chapters that address the West's view of the Gulf as a mere oil reservoir, and how it has dealt with neighbouring countries over the past thirty years to ensure its supply of oil. We will also look at the manner in which countries in the neighbourhood have dealt with each other, and with the GCC states. Finally, we devote an entire chapter to the Iranian nuclear reactor, and the possible repercussions of an eventual Iranian nuclear weapon, including a further destabilisation of the Arab-Iranian balance of power in favour of the latter, and the impact this will have on the GCC and Arab countries' security.

Chapter Twelve

The Gulf as an Oil Reservoir

The relationship between the United States and the West in general and the GCC governments is complicated and interconnected, thanks to its multi-layered dimensions that sometimes clash with each other. The West holds onto certain principles that it seeks to propagate, most importantly democracy and human rights. Moreover, it also has interests that sometimes compel it to establish military bases in the Gulf region, or elsewhere, to protect unelected regimes and sell them weapons. Therefore, any assessment of the relationship between the West and the Gulf's regimes should take place within the context of principles and interests, so that people in the Gulf understand this relationship and how it is managed. Those who look closely at this relationship's history will realise that the West's interests have more often superseded their principles, especially when oil and Israel are concerned. No doubt the extent of Western achievements in our region, whether oil or non-oil related, have primarily depended on the balance of power between us and them, although, as we shall see later, this balance has itself been affected by several variables. This is why the equation between us and them is not a rigid but a dynamic equation, and could therefore be changed. For example, whenever the region's governments have been able to bridge the gap between them and their people, they also strengthened their negotiating positions vis-à-vis the East and the West, gained more advantage or, at the least, lowered their costs. This means that the West's policy of prioritising interests over principles, or creating an imbalance between them in this region, depends as much on us as on the West.

There were at least two visions regarding the type of policies that the West should pursue towards the region, its oil and its governments, after the collapse of the Soviet bloc. The first vision believes that there is no longer any reason for the United States to interfere in the region, whether militarily or politically, because the main objective, which is to ensure the flow of oil, can be achieved by political means as much as by mechanisms of supply and demand. Those who uphold this view say that even if the region's regimes were opposed to the United States, and had Saddam Hussein even remained in Kuwait, both he and they would still have had to sell their oil to the West. They call for more oil exploration in other parts of the world, like Asia and Russia, and for more cooperation among oil consumers, via the International Energy Agency, to mitigate the GCC states' impact on the oil market.[1] Events since the downfall of the Soviet Union, including American attempts to secure a foothold in Afghanistan, Eastern Europe and more recently the African continent, seem to support this view. Upholders of the second vision believe that the first vision is detrimental to American interests, including, first, the inability to deal with the shortfall in supply, in the short term, as happened when Saudi Arabia compensated for the oil shortage after the Iraqi occupation of Kuwait. The latter say that there is also the possibility that the Arab-Israeli conflict might spill over into the oil production domain leading to circumstances similar to those that followed the June 1967 War. At that time, the GCC states had cut off their oil exports in support of the countries in confrontation with Israel, despite the latter group's belief that this possibility is quite remote, due to the ongoing Arab-Israeli peace negotiations. It is worth attracting the readers' attention here to the manner in which the West was able to separate oil from the Palestinian cause when it dragged Arab governments into separate peace negotiations whose outcome brought neither peace nor an interruption in oil supplies, but only continued occupation and deeper inter-Arab discord. The third danger regarding the risks involved in America distancing itself from the region has to do with the advantages it gains from its current relationship with the GCC governments. This relationship brings the United States billions of dollars in government and private funds, especially in the form of investments in US treasury bonds, in the financial market or in large arms deals that keep the American economy running, as we saw earlier. More important than the above-mentioned losses, in the opinion of those who uphold the second view, is the potential risk that the oil-producing countries, lead by the GCC states, would price their oil exports in a currency other than the dollar. This would lead to a fall in the price of the dollar and to an increase in the cost of American energy imports, not to mention the negative impact it would have on the economy of the United States.[2]

The above makes it clear that a number of interests compel the United States to stay involved in the Gulf region, and those who look closely at its attitude towards the region, since oil was discovered, will realise that successive American governments were not very interested in the political rights of local citizens, but rather the opposite. To protect their oil and non-oil related interests, American governments have stood strongly against most attempts at political change in the region, not only contrary to what is in the best interest of the local population, but despite the very principles on which their country was built. For although political participation would lead, in the long term, to stability in the region, to the benefit of the region and the world, the West, including the United States, has only focused on the impact this participation would have on the balance of power between the people and their governments and, by extension, on Western interests in the region. Thus, the closer the GCC governments came to their people, the better they were able to confront the others, including the big powers; the more independent were their decisions regarding oil, investments and military policies, and the better relations they had with their neighbours. Political participation would therefore gradually turn the triangle of hereditary succession, oil and foreign powers into a triangle of participation, productive human beings and Arab integration, a path that the West would find hard to digest. It does not hide its conviction that any public political participation in the GCC would mean that many of the above-mentioned interests will be amended to reflect the interest of the local population, at the expense of their own. It also means that the West prefers to deal with the governments that are currently in power rather than with those that draw their legitimacy from their people, and whose survival depends on their defence of this people's rights.

The most vivid example of the United States standing against the people's freedom to choose, when it comes to oil, was its policy towards the Mossadegh government, in Iran. The latter government had decided to nationalise BP in the 1950s, in response to which the company refused the elected government's request that it train, promote and improve the working conditions of its local employees, and accept a 50/50 profit sharing system. The CIA, in cooperation with British Intelligence then contrived a plot to topple the Mossadegh government and reinstate the Shah, who had left the country during the crisis, and this is exactly what happened. It put an end to Iranian democracy and created a new role for the Shah, that of Gulf's policeman and guardian of American interests in the region, until he was brought down by the Khomeini revolution of 1979.[3] What confirms the West's endorsement of the Gulf's hereditary regimes is, for example, its role in establishing the Saudi National Guard and Royal Guard among other similarly named agencies in the other GCC states designed to keep the citizens in check rather than safeguard their rights and to eliminate any opposition to the existing regime, a fact that several Western sources, alas, confirm.[4] Former US President Franklin Roosevelt is supposed to have promised to defend the Saudi government against "internal" and external enemies, which explains America's very long security presence in Saudi Arabia.[5]

In 1981, US President Ronald Reagan reiterated the promise to protect the Saudi ruling family because, as he was quoted as saying, he did not want them replaced by a regime that would cut off the oil supplies.[6] Reagan and others know, of course, that even the most anti-American government would not cut off the oil supply because it needs the revenue to build up the country. What Reagan therefore meant was that he did not want to see the current Saudi regime replaced by another that would place the people's interests ahead of others', because all the present regimes care about is, unfortunately, their personal interests and those of their supporters in the West. Such declarations by Western leaders radically conflict with the very principles of freedom on which the United States was founded and enshrine the people's right to choose their own leaders. This means that when American leaders make such statements they are not only interfering in other people's affairs, they are also insinuating that GCC governments do not draw their legitimacy from their people, since they need America to defend them against the so-called "internal threats". Furthermore, what the Gulf's citizens resent the most about their governments, that reject any criticism from their people, are the very shortcomings that the West highlights when it sees fit to put pressure on these governments to sign an arms deal, lower oil prices, raise production levels or pursue policies in support of the United States and the West.

Thomas Friedman of *The New York Times*, who was received by Emir Abdullah before he became King, and is said to be behind the Saudi initiative that became known as "Emir Abdullah's Initiative" to solve the Arab-Israeli conflict, named Saudi Arabia among the worst countries in the world today, in terms of human rights and opportunities for progress.[7] *The New York Times* also underlined in one of its editorials that the Saudi regime is plagued by endemic corruption, opposes human rights, squanders its resources and is subservient to the West, according to the opposition, because it receives military and security assistance from the West.[8]

In the UAE, Union Defence Forces intervened to reinstate Sultan al-Qasimi after his brother 'Abdul-'Aziz's attempted coup against him, in 1987,[9] and in Oman, the army waged a war from 1970 to 1975 against what was known then as the Dhofar Rebellion, with the assistance of Iranian forces. Just as the United States took care to protect GCC regimes against internal threats, it took care to protect them against external threats, as evidenced by the various strategies it pursued since the end of WWII, to counter any potential threat to the region. In WWII, Britain and Russia occupied Iran to prevent it from falling into enemy hands, and part of the post-war agreement was for Russia to withdraw from Iran by mid-1946, but Russia did not comply. This greatly worried the Americans and their allies who feared for their interests in that country, and even more for their interests in the Gulf region as a whole, and forced the United States to increase its naval presence in the East Mediterranean, to compel Russia to withdraw from Iran.[10] This incident was the first spark of the Cold War because it raised suspicions in the West regarding Russia's intentions in the region. This gave rise to what we know today as the "Truman Doctrine", announced by President Truman in a speech, on 12 March 1947, which stated that, "The free peoples of the world look to us for support in maintaining their freedoms. If we falter in our leadership, we may endanger the peace of the world."[11] As we will see later on, this was followed by a series of Western strategies aimed at controlling the region, and preventing developments from changing the balance of power in favour of the region's people, or any other regional or international party.

Chapter Thirteen

The Neighbouring Countries

The West views Iran and Iraq as key states in the region not only because of their oil and natural gas reserves, but also because of the potential trouble and instability they could bring to a region deemed vital for the interests of the United States and its allies. Kenneth Pollack, of the Brookings Institution, confirms this and says that: "the United States is not simply concerned with keeping oil flowing out of the Persian Gulf; it also has an interest in preventing any potentially hostile state from gaining control over the region and its resources and using such control to amass vast power or blackmail the world."[1]

If we wanted to simplify America's view of these two countries, i.e., Iraq and Iran, we could say that its preferred option is to have them both as allies, just like the GCC states are. If this is not possible, and one of these countries has to be anti-American, then the Americans would prefer that one of them stay an ally to deter and counter-balance the other. There is no doubt that the United States does not want both these countries as enemies, at the same time, since they would form an alliance against it, and against the GCC states. The worst scenario for the United States, however, would be if one of these countries occupied one or more GCC country, like Iraq's occupation of Kuwait. Another worst-case scenario would be if one of these two countries ended up having a lot of influence on the other's decisions, similar to Iran's influence in Iraq after Saddam, where the current regime is almost a strategic ally of Iran's. Those who ponder America's security policies in the region after the departure of Britain, will realise that these policies have changed in tandem with different challenges to the region, which proves that Western visions for the region are not inevitable, requiring us to submit to them, but rather aspirations that could impact positively or negatively. In the 1970s, the United States relied on Saudi Arabia and Iran to protect its interests in the region and, in the early 1980s, after the Shah's downfall at Khomeini's hands, a rapprochement took place between Iraq and the United States to contain and deter Iran and control its assets. The United States has undoubtedly benefitted from the war between these two countries because it weakened them both, at the same time. However, Iraq's occupation of Kuwait, after the Iran-Iraq War, compelled the United States to stand against the two countries at the same time, by adopting the so-called "dual containment policy" that sought to weaken them both. Yet, here we are today, with Iraq occupied, its military power destroyed, the country squarely in the hands of a government loyal to Iran and the latter's fortunes rising on account of its promising nuclear programme, watching the United States as it tries to keep Iraq weak while attempting to contain the rising power of Iran. In the following section, we will try to explain these policies in some detail, to understand how they really affect the GCC states. We will also show why, while these policies succeeded in protecting Western oil interests, they only wrought more instability and violence throughout the region, more dislocation for the Arab world and more losses in the Arab-Israeli conflict. Perhaps this subject's importance and complexity are what prompted us to devote the longest chapter in this book to it.

First: British withdrawal

Those who follow the United States and its allies' relationship with the GCC states will notice that since Britain's departure from the region in the late 1960s, the US has been the main power trying to fill the vacuum, and manage the conflict in the Gulf in a manner that serves its interests and those of other Western nations. The Shah of Iran, who fled the country after Mohammad Mossadegh nationalised the country's oil sector, and was reinstated by the CIA in 1953, owed a major debt to the West for reinstating him, and was therefore more amenable to playing the role of the Gulf's policeman.[2] However, before looking at the developing role of the United States in the region, we should look briefly at the circumstances that surrounded Britain's withdrawal from the area, because it involves numerous examples and lessons. As we mentioned before, the Gulf has large strategic oil reserves that make it strategically very important to the world's nations, an importance that has turned the region into an arena of ongoing war and conflict. What exacerbated these conflicts is the fact that the GCC states have always fallen between the rock of foreign powers, and the hard place of regional warring countries, like Iran and Iraq, due to the absence of a clear security strategy based on the will of the people, and in line with the requirements of the Arab regional order. In the late 1960s, and in the shadow of difficult economic circumstances and a drop in the value of the pound sterling, Britain decided to withdraw from the region, in March 1971, which helped it save some £12 million. It sent Lord Goronwy-Roberts to inform the region's rulers of Britain's decision before it became official, and he visited Iran, the Shaikhs of what was then the Trucial Coast and Saudi Arabia, for that purpose, although two months earlier Britain had confirmed its intention to stay in the region, and ensure its security and stability.[3] Both Shaikh Zayed of Abu Dhabi and Shaikh Rashid of Dubai told Goronwy-Roberts that they were prepared to cover the British forces' expenses, and the rulers of Qatar and Bahrain expressed their readiness to share the burden, as much as their budgets would allow.

The British government's response to the Shaikhs' offer to cover British expenses in the region had a tone of disapproval and mockery. When asked during a television programme why Britain had rejected the offer, Dennis Healey replied saying: "I don't very much like the idea of being a sort of white slaver for the Arab Shaikhs ... And I think it would be a very great mistake if we allowed ourselves to become mercenaries for people who would like to have a few British troops around."[4] This is how the British government dealt with the emirates' Shaikhs who kept their money in British banks and in pound sterling during the 1967 crisis and incurred huge losses when, without prior notice, the British government decided to devalue the pound. It is worth noting here that Britain had previously accepted deploying its troops in other countries in return for payment, as it did in Hong Kong and West Germany, a fact confirmed by historian John Kelly.[5] More important, however, is why these Shaikhs were so anxious to maintain Britain's occupation of the Gulf, at a time when it obviously diluted the region's sovereignty. The short answer is that they feared other countries' aspirations in the region, especially Saudi Arabia in light of its border dispute with Abu Dhabi, and Iran with its claims on Bahrain, meaning that in these Shaikhs' eyes, Britain's departure would leave a security vacuum where their neighbours were much stronger than they were, as later events have shown. This is why the British government began to encourage the Gulf's Shaikhdoms to form a nine-member union, which would both help protect themselves, and make it easier for the West to deal with them. However, as soon as Iran got wind of the efforts towards unification, it began openly expressing its aspiration in the region, which only served to heighten the Shaikhs' fears of their regional neighbours. The claim over Bahrain, which lay at the core of Iran's aspirations, became the subject of long negotiations between Iran and Britain, at the end of which both sides agreed in 1969 to ask the Secretary General of the United Nations to hold a general referendum that would allow the Bahraini people to determine their fate. The referendum's results showed that the Bahraini people preferred to remain independent from Iran, and the Shah announced he would renounce his demand for Bahrain.[6]

However, although Bahrain succeeded in putting Iran's aspirations behind it, the proposed nine-member union failed to materialise due to the number of unresolved conflicts among its potential members. Bahrain and Qatar later announced their independence, and the UAE announced the birth of its seven-member union, in December 1971. However, Saudi Arabia refused to recognise the newborn state because its dispute with Abu Dhabi had not yet been resolved, and negotiations between the two sides on the issue continued until an agreement was reached between the two parties at the end of 1974.[7] The nature of the agreement was determined by the balance of power on the ground, as well as Shaikh Zayid's desire to launch the UAE, an agreement that many observers believe was unfairly skewed against Abu Dhabi. According to John Kelly, the specialist in the region's history, Zayid gave the Saudis almost everything they wanted, including a passage to the sea west of Sabkha Matti, a wide area in the west of the emirate, and most of the Zarara field in the south, all in return for Saudi Arabia agreeing to relinquish its claim over Burimi. This Saudi claim on Burimi, Kelly believes, is no less nonsensical than its claim over the Western areas that Zayid ceded to them.[8]

Yet, the nascent UAE, which escaped the need to pay a tax over its borders with "big brother" Saudi Arabia, could not escape paying another kind of tax over its borders with Iran. Just one day before British forces withdrew from the Gulf, Iranian troops, with the tacit approval of an American government deeply mired in Vietnam, occupied three UAE-held islands in full view of the British forces, taking advantage of the lack of any Gulf or Arab security network in the region. These three islands were not strategically significant to the Americans, who had decided to put the region in the Shah's hands for the time being, which confirms that the United States' relationship with the region is based, above all, on interest and balance of power, a fact that many of the region's leaders have not yet come to terms with.[9]

Second: The Shah as the Gulf's policeman

Western documents confirm, beyond the shadow of a doubt, that the United States under President Nixon believed that Britain's withdrawal from the Gulf, in the early 1970s, would leave a security vacuum behind, especially with America preoccupied with Vietnam. The American president therefore decided, based on the "Nixon Doctrine", to supply the Shah with a large quantity of advanced weapons and entrust him with the role of "Protector of the Gulf's security", i.e., from the perspective of Western interests, a role that he took very seriously, between 1970 and 1979, when his regime fell to Khomeini's revolution.[10] The Shah's role was an actual translation of the "Nixon Doctrine", which relied on the twin pillars of Iran and Saudi Arabia as protectors of Western interests in the region. The Shah's Iran succeeded, however, in retaining the upper hand due to the weakness of the Saudi regime and its inability to be the main initiative taker in the region.[11] The American president had reiterated on numerous occasions that the United States intended to supply its allies in the region with the necessary weapons to defend themselves, and Congress was told, "We especially look to the leading states of the area, Iran and Saudi Arabia, to cooperate for this purpose."[12]

In the 1970s, the Shah received American weapons worth $14 billion, most of which were used to help the Omani forces put down the rebellion in Dhofar. Saudi Arabia received similar weapons which it spent on the development and training of its Internal Security Forces and National Guard. However, since the military capabilities of the Saudi and Iranian forces were not developed enough to handle these advanced weapons, the United States sent between 4140 and 6250 military experts to train the two countries' military on how to use them.[13] However, the Shah, one of the pillars of America's security policy in the region, according to the Nixon Doctrine that provides weapons to its allies to help protect its interests in the region without the need for direct American intervention, was toppled in 1979 by Khomeini's revolution. The Shah's era had thus ended, brought on, no doubt, by his brutal and autocratic domestic policies, by all the injustices he had inflicted on his people and by his blind subservience to the West.[14] Not only was the Shah the Gulf's policeman, he was also an ally of Israel; this means that his role was not confined to maintaining security in the Gulf, but went beyond it to playing a negative role as far as the Arab regional security was concerned. He cooperated closely with Israel in secret to avoid damaging his relations with the Arab-Islamic world, because Iran had discovered that it shared many interests with Israel, mainly resistance against communism and the spread of Arab nationalism, especially under Nasser. In other words, Iran saw Israel as a means of containing and mitigating Arab power and a bridge to the West, especially to Washington.

For Israel, the rapprochement with Iran was based on Ben Gurion's "Periphery Strategy", which relied on the presumption that the Arab-Israeli conflict is eternal and will not be solved anytime in the near future. Based on that premise, therefore, and in order to weaken the Arabs, Israel had no choice but to forge alliances with non-Arab countries like Iran, Turkey and Ethiopia and with minorities in the region, like the Kurds and the Christians. Mosaddegh's government had recognised Israel's existence without any diplomatic fanfare, and the Iranian embassy in Israel operated under the name "Bern 2" in Iran's diplomatic files, as if it was just another office based in Bern, Switzerland's capital. The Israeli embassy in Iran, on the other hand, remained without a name and its diplomats refrained from taking part in any diplomatic functions in Tehran, although these two embassies performed full diplomatic duties.[15]

Among the aspects of Iranian-Israeli cooperation were reciprocal visits by these countries' prime ministers, including Ben Gurion's secret visit to Iran in 1956. Iran also funded a pipeline running from the port of Eilat, in southern Israel, to the Mediterranean Sea, via Bi'r el-Sabi', to ship Iranian oil to Israel at the cost of $1.3 per barrel, without passing through the Suez Canal.

Other aspects of cooperation included Israeli military training of the Iranian security forces, known as the Savak, on the most advanced forms of torture, and training Iranian air-force pilots and agricultural engineers.[16] However, no sooner had the Arabs been defeated in the June 1967 War and Israel occupied even more Arab territories, that the Shah began to feel that Israel's role in the region had become much too obvious, especially since Iran did not support the acquisition of land by force, in light of its border dispute with Iraq.

Signs of a detente in Egyptian-Iranian relations began to appear, especially after Anwar Sadat expelled the Russians from Egypt and turned towards the West. Iran never abandoned the feeling, however, that it shared a common enemy with Israel, namely the Iraqi regime whose relations with the Soviet Union had recently improved. Furthermore, the entente that took place at the time between East and West prompted the two countries to each seek a new foothold for itself, especially Iran in light of its well-known historic aspirations.[17] As we shall see later on, Iran's search for a regional role did not end with the 1979 Revolution, even if this required that it take a stand against the Arabs, and contradict the Islamist slogans often repeated by successive Iranian governments.

Third: The Iran-Iraq War

After the downfall of the Shah, the United States found itself in need of new security policies to contain the Iranian Revolution, and ensure that it did not influence the balance of power in the region; it did not see the Saudi regime as a strong pillar of power, and Iraq was in the Soviet orbit. Then the Soviet Union invaded and occupied Afghanistan, raising America's fears for its interests in the Gulf even further, and prompting President Jimmy Carter to announce his "Carter Doctrine", on 23 January 1980. The Doctrine rested on the premise that the United States had vital interests in that region, and was ready to defend them by any means, including the use of military force. The Doctrine's announcement was soon followed by the formation of a Rapid Deployment Force, expected to be the centre-point of America's military presence in the region, and the United States began acquiring military facilities in the wider region, from Oman and Kenya to Diego Garcia, by way of Somalia.[18] The Reagan administration kept the "Carter Doctrine" alive but amalgamated it with the "Nixon Doctrine", which allowed it to supply Saudi Arabia with advanced weapons and military experts. It also did its best to influence the outcome of the Iran-Iraq War, with its position changing in tandem with the ebb and flow of battle.

American-Iranian relations deteriorated after the Shah's downfall, especially after a number of Iranian students broke into the American embassy in Tehran, on 4 November 1979, and took its diplomats and staff hostage. This was not only a loss for the United States, but also for Israel who saw Iran as a regional ally with which it shares common geopolitical interests vis-à-vis the Arab countries and Soviet expansion in the region, based on Ben Gurion's above-mentioned "Periphery Strategy", especially in light of the Soviet Union's 1979 occupation of Afghanistan. Saddam Hussein felt that the Iranian Revolution posed a threat to him and to the region, a feeling shared by the West and the Arab world, as a whole, including the GCC states. This gave him the opportunity to abandon the 1975 Algiers Agreement, imposed on him under a different balance of power set-up, as we shall see later on, readjust the balance of power with Iran and regain Shatt al-'Arab, by taking advantage of the instability in Iran following the revolution. The GCC states stood behind Saddam and helped him financially and diplomatically and, in return, he closely coordinated with their governments.[19]

Thus began the Iran-Iraq War that lasted eight years without producing a decisive winner, as Saddam had hoped. This prompted him to make a peace overture to Iran, in 1983, which Khomeini promptly rejected, insisting on continuing the fight until victory. The United States then decided to initiate a rapprochement with Saddam Hussein, and sources indicate that towards the end of 1983, President Reagan sent his personal envoy, Donald Rumsfeld, to Iraq to look at a possible American-Iraqi rapprochement. These same sources also say that Rumsfeld carried with him a letter from the Israelis offering Saddam help against Iran, but that Iraqi Foreign Minister, Tariq Aziz, had refused to take it.[20] During that time, the United States gave Iraq loans, information and weapons.[21] Thus, in light of the American-Iraqi rapprochement, the American ban on arms sales to Iran, the growing number of Americans kidnapped in Lebanon, and Iraq's success in beating back Iran's counter-attack using long-range missiles and, some say, chemical weapons, it seems that Israel saw an opportunity to revive its "Periphery Strategy". It put the Arab countries in a bind by playing a leading role in breaking the embargo on Iran, with the hope that a moderate wing would emerge within the Iranian post-revolutionary government.

The result was the Iran-Contra scandal that proved, once again, that Iran's geopolitical considerations supersede its principles, and that all the Islamist and revolutionary slogans were nothing but publicity stunts designed to dupe the Muslim world, and hide Iran's pragmatic streak guided above all by self-interest. The Iran-Contra story begins with Israel and a number of arms dealers persuading the Reagan administration to supply weapons to Iran, in secret, in return for its help in releasing the American hostages in Lebanon. According to the agreement, profits from the deal would go to the Contras fighting the government in Nicaragua, at odds with the American government at the time. However, individuals close to Ayatollah Montazeri revealed details of the deal between the American delegation and Rafsanjani's people to a Lebanese newspaper, forcing President Reagan to apologise to the American people for his actions. Shimon Peres, for his part, claimed that Israel had taken part in the deal solely upon the request of the United States, while Khomeini kept appealing to Arab and Muslim sentiments by denying the claims' veracity.[22] Nevertheless, prompted by Iran's need for weapons and Israel's need for a strategic ally, Israeli-Iranian contacts continued even after the scandal had become public.[23]

While the Iran-Iraq war was still raging to determine the main power in the region, revolutionary Iran was putting all sorts of pressure on other Gulf countries to make them accept its leadership and control over the area. Just as the Shah had asked the region's governments to consult him on important issues facing the region, Khomeini's first statement after the revolution was to ask these same countries to follow Iran's example and break their relations with the "Great Satan", the United States. He did not hesitate, however, to say that the Gulf's monarchies were the worst symbols of revisionism and the reason for America's presence in the region, and to accuse the Saudi regime of betraying its religion and acting as a foreign agent.[24] This revolutionary rhetoric did not get any traction either in the Gulf or on the Arab street, except for a few limited protests by Shi'a minorities, protests put down by using the carrot and the stick approach, i.e., by arresting demonstrators while promising better economic and social conditions for minorities.[25] Perhaps these slogans' failure to have an impact on the majority of Sunni Arabs is due to what they perceive as the pronounced Shi'a-Persian character of the Iranian revolution, especially when its constitution highlights the supremacy of the Shi'a sect and doctrine as reference points, and the ill-treatment of Sunni and non-ethnic Persian minorities in Iran. When the revolutionary rhetoric failed to work, Iran used more violent means to drive its point home, including blowing up embassies, industrial projects and oil instal-lations in those GCC states with Shi'a minorities, like Saudi Arabia, Bahrain and Kuwait, using the Da'wah Party, which was part of the post occupation Iraqi government, to do its bidding.[26] However, while the slogans generated no sympathy for its revolution, the use of force generated revulsion and did not topple any regime in the Gulf, as Iran had hoped.[27]

Fourth: The occupation of Kuwait

On 20 August 1988, both Iran and Iraq accepted United Nations Resolution 598 calling for an immediate ceasefire, thus bringing to an end the eight-year war that cost over one million lives, caused hundreds of billions of dollars in material damage and destroyed both countries' infrastructures, without changing the status quo on the borders. What is important from the GCC's perspective is the path that each of these two countries chose to pursue after the war, and their fallout on the region, in particular the Iraqi occupation of Kuwait and its impact on the balance of power in the region, and the wider Arab world. Let us start with the path that Iran chose to pursue.

1.   Pragmatic Iran

Iran did not only incur human and material losses as a result of the war, it also incurred a moral loss because its revolutionary rhetoric failed to win either the Arab or the Islamic street, which caused internal divisions regarding the course that the country should pursue after the war, especially after Imam Khomeini's death in 1989. The country was divided into two camps; the first was the revolu-tionary camp whose main concern was safeguarding and exporting the revolution, which required the country to rearm by any means possible. The second camp, one of whose protagonists was Ayatollah Rafsanjani, believed that rather than try to topple other regimes, Iran should correct its course, break out of its isolation, build a strong economy and forge a tightly knit society protected from Western dissolution by Islamic religious values, thus making it a model to emulate.[28] Lead-ers that succeeded Khomeini focussed their attention on rebuilding the economy by opening up to the West, and obtaining the loans necessary for that endeavour. This openness, however, did not come without a price, since it required Iran to reconsider its foreign policy vis-à-vis other countries, and no one was surprised when one of President Rafsanjani's first steps was to help release the American hostages in Lebanon, with help from Italy.[29] He then turned his attention to the GCC and Arab governments, and Iran's discourse began targeting governments instead of people, signalling the beginning of a process that again placed interests ahead of principles. This policy did in fact achieve some progress, especially in relations between Iran and the GCC states, whereby it seemed that some of the latter would not object to a future Gulf security system that includes Iran.[30] The Gorbachev era in Russia, and the ensuing decrease in that country's support for Iraq and the communist opposition in Iran and Afghanistan, helped ease relations between Russia and Iran.[31] However, not all of Iran's attempts to remedy its relations with the outside world were successful; the United States, whose president had promised to improve his country's relations with Iran if it helped release the hostages in Lebanon, did not keep his word. It is worth noting here that Iran, at the time, did not support jihadist movements and was content to support the Palestinian cause without lending it any material assistance. This is either because these movements were Sunni, because they had supported Saddam Hussein in the War or because Iran still hoped that the West would depend on it as a regional power with impact on the region.[32]

2. Iraq's wrong calculations

The Iraqi regime made a dangerous and risky move, which, regardless of the reasons, proved disastrous for GCC security, the Palestinian cause and, eventually, for Iraq itself, and the GCC governments were instrumental in pushing Iraq in that direction. The end of the Iraq-Iran War with a cease-fire agreement, in mid 1988, and onset of negotiations between the two parties did not bring stability to the region because the seeds of a new crisis had already been sown by external influence and internal short-sightedness, i.e., by both the GCC and Iraqi governments. Iraq emerged from the war burdened by a $65 billion debt to the West and the Soviet Union, and by another debt of $80 billion to the GCC states, mainly to Kuwait, the UAE and Saudi Arabia;[33] the country's infrastructure was in tatters and its army made redundant. However, regardless of whether we agree or disagree with Saddam's regime, the policies that the GCC governments pursued at the time contributed to Iraq's decision to invade and occupy Kuwait. In saying that, we are not trying to justify Iraq's actions in Kuwait, but simply trying to avoid a repetition of what happened as the result of these policies, since in this day, and age, values do not determine geopolitical calculations. The reason we say that the GCC policies were wrong is because these countries' governments helped Saddam in his war with Iran, and saw his stand against the new Iranian regime as both deterrent and protection against its ambitions in the region. These governments should have pursued a smarter policy towards Saddam Hussein after the war and, had they taken into account what is best for the people and stability of the region, they would have accommodated Saddam by waiving Iraq's debt to the GCC, and pursued a wise energy policy to help Iraq rebuild itself. This is what these countries should have done even if Saddam's regime was foreign rather than Arab, if only because it was the wise thing to do given the situation on the ground and the existing balance of power in the region, as evidenced by the series of destructive events that followed.

Unfortunately, these governments decided to pursue the exact opposite policy, a policy that not only showed a lack of both civility and understanding as to what the balance of power means for the region, but also one dictated by the big powers' special agenda in the region, as later events have shown. The GCC governments insisted that Iraq repay its entire debts, and the series of meetings that followed, between Iraq and Kuwait, failed to reach a solution amenable to the parties. The GCC governments' oil policies made things even worse, especially in Kuwait and the UAE, when they pushed oil prices down, at a time when Iraq had increased its production in order to pay its debts. These countries could have chosen, under such circumstances, to reduce their own production to keep prices up and help Iraq out, but did not. Oil prices and revenues remained low, compelling Saddam Hussein to utter his famous statements "cut off necks not [our] livelihood" and "If words fail to afford us protection ... then we will have no choice but to resort to effective action to put things right and ensure the restitution of our rights."[34] This put the disagreement between Iraq and the GCC on a downward spiral. In his meeting with April Glaspie, the American ambassador to Iraq, on 25 July 1990, the Iraqi president complained about several matters. They included the low price of oil, the size of Iraq's debt, the fact that several Arab countries were asking Iraq to return the funds originally granted as aid, the groups opposed to him inside the American administration and Kuwait's ill intentions towards him. Ambassador Glaspie reassured him that the Bush administration wanted to maintain good relations with his regime, and did not support the economic boycott of Iraq. Regarding his conflict with Kuwait, Glaspie insisted that the American administration did not take sides in inter-Arab disagreements, including the one between Iraq and Kuwait. However, the letter Glaspie sent to her government, entitled "Saddam's Message of Friendship to President Bush", was proof that she had completely misunderstood Saddam's intentions and view of the situation."[35] Did Glaspie misunderstand Saddam's words? Was she laying a trap for him? Did Saddam misunderstand her response regarding his country's border dispute with Kuwait?

There are still no clear answers to these questions, but what is certain is that the events that followed were totally unexpected; on 2 August 1990, the Iraqi forces crossed the Kuwaiti border and occupied the country in less than twenty-four hours. Soon afterwards, the Iraqi government published the minutes of President Saddam's meeting with Glaspie, which made a number of Western and Arab observers suspect that the Bush administration had implicitly approved this invasion, for strategic reasons of its own, not least the desire to weaken Iraq as a regional power.[36]

Slowly, the American war machine began creeping into the region to oust Saddam from Kuwait and destroy Iraq; and, again, the importance of oil comes to the fore as the one and only reason why another country would intervene in the region. On 8 August 1990, six days after the occupation of Kuwait, Bush senior announced his intention to use military force to drive Iraq out of Kuwait. He justified the decision saying that since the United States imported 50 per cent of its oil, its economic independence could be in jeopardy, adding, "The sovereign independence of Saudi Arabia is of vital interest to the United States."[37] In a meeting with Congress' Defence Committee, on 11 September 1990, then Defence Secretary Dick Cheney reiterated that same objective, saying that the occupation of Kuwait would allow Saddam's to dictate oil prices in the future, and that this would affect America's economic independence.[38] Of course, new reasons for the war were added to the America's discourse, later on, to cover the real reason behind the intervention; there was talk, for example, about wanting to liberate Kuwait, getting rid of weapons of mass destruction (WMDs), spreading democracy and, of course, combating terrorism. Nevertheless, as American energy expert Michael Klare says, preliminary documents show beyond the shadow of a doubt, that President Bush and his advisors viewed the occupation of Kuwait from the "Carter Doctrine" perspective, meaning that they saw Iraq's invasion as a threat to Saudi Arabia and oil supplies to the West.[39] American journalist Bob Woodward confirmed this in one of his books.[40] The United States thus began to prepare for the deployment of its forces to Saudi Arabia, and reports show that King Fahd agreed to this only when the American defence secretary showed him pictures of tanks supposedly heading towards the Kuwaiti-Saudi border. According to these reports, Fahd relented only on condition that these troops withdraw as soon as the danger from Iraq dissipated, thus giving the green light for Operation Desert Shield to proceed, an operation that ended with Iraq's ousting from Kuwait.[41]

It is worth mentioning here that, according to some sources, Osama Bin Laden had proposed to King Fahd that the liberation of Kuwait and defence of Saudi Arabia be entrusted to the Arabs youths returning from the war in Afghanistan, i.e., the "Arab Afghans", but that the King had refused.[42] However, regardless whether this is a logical proposal or not, if true, Fahd's refusal could have been the catalyst behind Al-Qaida's rise, and hence the prelude to 11 September 2001, and everything that ensued in the region, including the occupation and destruction of Iraq and the impact it had on the balance of power vis-à-vis Israel and Iran. American air raids on Iraq began in January 1991, went on for five weeks, followed by a ground offensive that lasted from 24-28 February, and culminated in Iraq's withdrawal from Kuwait. The American forces did not attempt to cross the border into Iraq, because their declared objective was the liberation of Kuwait. The American administration was afraid of the consequences of such a move, either for fear that it might provoke a costly anti-American resistance, or because it believed that expanding the campaign's objectives to include an incursion into Iraq would dismember the alliance, particularly by the Arab allies.[43] However, the "containment" policy kept Iraq under siege and isolated it from the world. The American government imposed a no-fly zone over the south and America made its presence in the region felt by positioning its forces in Kuwait, and storing stacks of weapons in Kuwait and Qatar to facilitate their eventual reuse. To implement the no-fly zone, the Americans needed no less than 5,000 American air force pilots and their assistants, availing itself for that purpose of the Sultan Bin Abdul-Aziz base in Saudi Arabia. Moreover, the American sold Saudi Arabia, between 1991 and 1999, weapons worth $40 billion, four times what it sold to Egypt and Taiwan together.[44] This meant that the United States would remain in the region, mostly in Saudi Arabia, and that all Cheney's promises to Fahd would come to naught. There is also no doubt that this American presence had begun to erode the credibility of the Saudi regime, and strengthen different opposition groups in the country, in particular the Islamists. In a speech, Bin Laden called for toppling the Saudi regime, by any means possible, and ousting the Americans from the region. He said, in this context, "The United States has maintained its occupation of the holiest place in the Muslim world, the Arabian Peninsula, and has plundered its wealth, subjugated its rulers, humiliated its people, scared its neighbours and used its bases as a spearhead to attack other Muslim countries."[45]

To underline his words, Bin Laden began by attacking the symbols of America's military presence in the region, before moving on to its very heart with the attacks of 11 September 2001, the reasons for which are still the subject of debate. Some see these attacks as the beginning of the clash of civilisations between the Muslim East and the Christian West, based on former Harvard Professor Samuel Huntington's predictions,[46] others see them as a negative impact of economic globalisation, and others yet see them as a reaction to the United States' support for Israel. However, there are those who say that none of the above justifies the action, and that one should see it as a part of the anger and resentment against the American alliance with the Saudi ruling family, an alliance whose cornerstone was laid in 1945 by American President Franklin Roosevelt and King Abdul Aziz Bin Saud. At the core of this alliance is an agreement that, on the one hand, secures America's control over the oil, and, on the other, ensures America's support for the Saudi ruling family's survival in power.[47] In our opinion, the reason behind the events of 11 September 2001 is a mixture of all the above, at varying levels of importance, however. The American alliance with the region's autocratic governments to divide the oil wealth between them, at a time when the Arabs and Muslims are mired in ignorance and poverty, the Zionists still occupy Palestine and American bases still detract from these countries' sovereignty, are all part of the reason. These factors contributed to the already growing hatred in the region for the United States, and the West in general. However, instead of helping improve the situation, the United States disregarded these factors and continued, as usual, to behave on the basis of the language of force and to beat the drums of war against Iraq and Afghanistan. On the other hand, the GCC and the other Arab countries failed to forge a common position to end the deterioration in inter-Arab relations, choosing instead to remain hostage to the big powers' vision and narrow interests in the region.

3. Israel, Iran and the division of influence zones

Before moving on to the next and more ominous stage as far as the region is concerned, namely the occupation of Iraq, we should end this section with a few words about the impact that the Iraqi occupation of Kuwait, and the ensuing events, have had on Israel and Iran. There is no doubt that Israel was the main beneficiary from the demise of the Iraqi Army, whose members dropped from 1.4 million in 1990 to 475,000 at the end of the Gulf War, not to mention the drop in Iraqi military spending, during that same period, from $26.4 billion to $2 billion.[48] Despite it not being a country of confrontation, Iraq's military power has always frightened Israel because of its rapid deployment ability, had the political will and cooperation among the confrontation countries really existed. This is exactly what happened when Iraqi-launched missiles hit the Iranian capital, during the Iraq-Iran War, and hit Israel during the occupation of Kuwait.[49] The other beneficiary from Iraq's occupation of Kuwait and the ensuing war on Iraq, was Iran; the occupation of Kuwait had created a serious rift among the Arabs and, for the very first time, Iran felt that the GCC governments might turn to it for help in the future to counter-balance Iraq's influence in the region. Some in Iran even rejoiced at the GCC states' conundrum and thought that they got exactly what they deserved for their short-sighted support of Iraq in its war with Iran.[50] Some sources also say that the Iranian security forces had even warned Kuwait about the impending Iraqi invasion a few hours before it happened.[51] Iran also used the Iraqi invasion to tell the world that Iraq, not Iran, was the main source of instability in the region, and President Rafsanjani was even clearer when he said, right after Iraq's ousting from Kuwait, that "only one power was capable of ensuring peace and stability in the Persian Gulf, and this power was Iran."[52] Nor did the Iranians hide the fact that their attitude towards this war could be described as one of "positive neutrality", which in fact means that they supported the American action, given that they had even refused to help Iraq when it requested their assistance. The fact that Iran, at the same time, was accusing the United States of looking for excuses to remain in the region does not alter any of the above facts.[53]

While all this took place out in the open, in secret Iran was in fact helping the United States in more than one way. Among other things, it allowed American airplanes to use Iranian airspace, and refused to return the military aircrafts that Iraq had sent to Iran for safekeeping, early in the air campaign, a decision that prompted American Secretary of State James Baker to laud Iran's positive role.[54] With this policy, Iran hoped to kill two birds with one stone; it aimed at weakening Iraq as a rival power in the region, and hoped to persuade the United States to allow it the freedom to put some order in the region's affairs, as it did when the Shah was in power. However, the rapprochement between Iran and the GCC states in the wake of the war on Iraq did not last long because, under pressure from Washington, these governments concluded bilateral security agreements with the United States, instead of establishing a Gulf-based security system that included Iran.[55] What made things worse was that right after Iraq's ousting from Kuwait, the Americans tried to build on the Western-Arab alliance, and the end of the Cold War, to launch peace negotiations between Israel and the Palestinians, and this is what they actually did. The Madrid Conference was held in the presence of several regional and international parties, except for Iran whose presence was deemed unnecessary, since its influence on the Palestinians was rather limited at the time. This could explain why Iran eventually sought closer ties with jihadist movements in Palestine.

In any case, sidelining Iran at the Madrid conference, after it helped release the American hostages in Lebanon and playing an indirect role in the successful outcome of war on Iraq, no doubt humiliated it.[56] The sidelining of Iran in the Middle East region as a whole, compounded by its failure to establish a Gulf-based security system, put an end to Rafsanjani's era of Real-politic, and took the country back to its former confrontational style, including acts of sabotage and attempts to thwart America's policies in the region. The first thing that Iran did was organise a conference parallel to Madrid, that brought together in

Tehran different Palestinian and Lebanese opposition groups, and the Iranian government's tone changed from moderate to hard-line. This might be the point at which Iran began to seek a foothold for itself not just in Lebanon, but in Palestine as well. Several experts on Iranian affairs believe that Iran would not have gone down this path, i.e., opposed the Madrid Conference and adopted a hard-line position vis-à-vis the United States and its own regional neighbours, had it been invited to Madrid.[57] The United States accused Iran of blowing up the American military barracks in Khobar, Saudi Arabia, in 1996, although some believe that it was the work of Al-Qaida.[58]

Just as in the past, Iran's sabotage operations failed to achieve their objective until President Khatami came to power, in 1997, and opened the door to a new era of relations between Iran, the GCC and the Arab countries. Khatami began his tenure as president with an admission that the way his country had dealt with its neighbours in the past had failed because of Iran's insistence that the GCC governments adopt an anti-American position, which they had refused to do.[59] The Khatami administration was thus forced to live alongside these governments in the shadow of an American presence that maintains the balance of power in the region. President Khatami made this conciliatory stance official in a speech he delivered at the Islamic Summit Conference in Tehran, in 1997, when he said that, "Iran is not a threat to any Muslim country." He added that his reformist vision recognised the sovereignty of neighbouring countries, the inviolability of their borders and the commitment not to intervene in their internal affairs. The Supreme Guide of the Revolution approved this new vision, although many sources indicate that his position vis-à-vis the region's governments, as well as Khatami's before he assumed the presidency, were entirely different.[60]

Here we come face to face again with the geopolitical dynamics that make a country shift from principles to interests then, once again, from interests to principles. During that period, the Iranian leadership must have felt isolated and decided to take a little rest before resuming its attempts to control the region, the country's ultimate strategic objective. In fact, regardless of the reasons behind it, Khatami's new position had a positive impact on Iranian-GCC relations, and the fact that Iran signed a number of trade and other agreements with various countries in the region allows us to say that President Khatami's policies were more pragmatic and interest-driven than ideological and confrontational. However, did this trend survive Khatami's departure from power? We will know the answer to that later on.[61] In the meantime, Iran's growing role in the region raised numerous fears in Israel, because the Arab regional order had fallen apart and Iran had taken the first steps in its attempt to infiltrate the Arab region. This not only meant that Israel had now a rival trying to dominate the region, especially if Iran succeeded in reaching some sort of understanding with the United States, it signalled the beginning of a rift in the strategic alliance between the two countries that lasted several decades. Many also believe that it was Israel's fear of Iran's ascendance in the region that made Shimon Peres, who was elected in a landslide in 1992, propose the "New Middle East Project" idea. The project centres round the creation of an entity, following the European Union's model, made up of the Arab countries and Israel, in which Israel, with its advanced technological knowhow, would be the main engine of development while the Arab world would supply the necessary financial and human resources. The project, which implementation was supposed to start with the resolution of the Palestinian issue in the shadow of an imbalance of power skewed in favour of Israel, would make the Red Sea region and Israel the core of the Middle East area, while simultaneously reducing the importance of the Arab Gulf and Iran's influence in the region.[62]

Israel also no doubt realised at that time that the balance of power was shifting in favour of Hamas, and other jihadist movements, at the expense of the declining PLO, or, as Peres said, either making peace with a weak PLO now or preparing for another confrontation with Hamas, in the near future.[63] Of course, Peres saw nothing wrong with his plan to make peace with the Arabs to Iran's detriment, which in fact meant putting an end to the "Periphery Strategy" that made Israel and Iran strategic allies at the Arabs' expense, a shift about which Peres said that though his ideas had not changed, what surrounded him did.[64] It was therefore not that surprising to hear an Iranian observer say, while commenting on the New Middle East Project, that the role Peres had ascribed to Iran in the new configuration was so marginal that it prevented it from achieving even the least of its historical aspirations.[65] The Clinton administration did not support Peres' new proposal, or Yitzhak Rabin's, whom Israel had widely promoted on the world stage, nor did certain circles within Israel or the Arabs themselves. Speculations abounded, at the time, as to the reasons behind this sudden shift in Israel's position towards Iran. While some speculated that Israel could not live without a real or an imaginary enemy, others believed that it wanted to scare the Arabs with a potential future enemy in order to bring them closer to it, and make them accept it as one of them, which would then make them more amenable to signing a peace treaty with it. Others speculated that Israel wanted to remind Washington that it was still an important strategic ally and, yet others thought that it was just being cautious against any potential move by Iran to dominate the region, especially in light of Iraq's demise and Iran's attempt to develop a nuclear weapon.[66]

On 18 May 1993, the United States announced its "dual containment" policy that aimed at simultaneously weakening Iran and Iraq, in lieu of its previous policy of using one to weaken the other.[67] Many tried to explain the reasons behind the new policy; while some thought that the aim was to deter Iran from taking advantage of Iraq's weakness to achieve advantages detrimental to US interests in the region,[68] others saw it as an attempt to create the right environment for Arab-Israeli peace negotiations.[69] However, regardless of whether these two explanations are correct or not, the policy only served to widen the gap between the United States and Israel, and Iran, and pave the way for closer ties not only between Iraq and Iran, but also between Iran, some Palestinian factions and a number of anti-American groups in the region. This means, in short, that after the demise of the Soviet Union and Iraq, a shift took place in Israeli-Iranian relations that turned the conflict into a race as to which country will eventually control the region, since the Arabs in the Gulf and wider region chose to sit and watch as events threatening them and their future unfolded. The question remains, however, as to whether Israel is capable of maintaining its "Periphery Strategy" and pursuing peace with its Arab neighbours at the same time. We will let future developments in the region give us the answer.

Fifth: The occupation of Iraq

It is worth noting that although the United States used the events of 11 September 2001 to justify its invasion of Iraq, the plans to configure the Middle East were formulated much earlier. In 1992, former Under-Secretary of Defence Paul Wolfowitz designed a strategy at the Pentagon entitled "Defence Planning Guidance", which called on the United States to launch a pre-emptive attack against any threat to its control, whether the target is a friend or foe. Seen from a Middle Eastern perspective, this strategy means that the United States and the West should maintain their control of the Gulf by preventing the emergence of any regional or international power that threatens their control, and oil supplies at low prices.[70] In 1996, Richard Perle, Chairman of Defence Policy Board, presented with the help of Douglas Feith, then Wolfowitz's Under-Secretary of Defence, a paper entitled "A Clean Break" to Israeli Prime Minister Benjamin Netanyahu, in which he proposed that he tear up the Oslo Agreement and topple Saddam Hussein from power. In 1998, the neo-conservatives, including Paul Wolfowitz and Douglas Feith, sent a letter to President Clinton asking him to topple Saddam Hussein's regime in Iraq.[71] Furthermore, in September 2000, i.e., a year before the events of 11 September 2001, some neo-cons, including Cheney, Rumsfeld and Wolfowitz, issued a document at the end of their meeting entitled "Rebuilding America's Defenses: Strategy, Forces and Resources for a

New Century", among whose recommendations was that America maintain its forces in the Gulf,[72] The document stated that although the conflict with Iraq justified America's presence in that region, the need for a larger American force there went beyond Iraq, a proposition that can be seen as a prelude to what this group had in mind in terms of reconfiguring the Middle East from an American perspective.[73] This paved the way for what was to happen after 11 September, and later events proved that true. In a speech at West Point, President George W. Bush said that earlier strategies like deterrence and containment were no longer applicable in all cases, and added, "We must take the battle to the enemy, disrupt his plans, and confront the worst threats before they emerge."[74]

We now had a new strategy to contend with, the "Bush Doctrine", which gave the green light to Bush and Blair to begin preparing for the invasion of Iraq, including concocting stories and accusations to justify their plans. Some stories circulating in the West accused Saddam of having a relationship with al-Qaeda, others said that he had weapons of mass destruction and others claimed the need to free the Iraqi people from Saddam's tyranny. However, *Washington Post* columnist Bob Woodward points out to another reason yet, which he mentioned in the course of recounting a conversation that took place between Michael Gerson, George Bush's speech-writer, and Henry Kissinger, former US Secretary of State, at a meeting in September 2005. Gerson asked Kissinger why he supported the war on Iraq, and Kissinger replied, "Because Afghanistan wasn't enough," adding that, "In the conflict with radical Islam, they want to humiliate us, and we need to humiliate them."[75] If we look beyond what Kissinger has said, which is "justified" and has been often repeated by Western officials since the end of the Cold War, and pondered the reason put forth by the American administration, we would find that they are weak and without foundation. According to law professor and lawyer Philippe Sands, an expert in international affairs, who both knows about and was party to several issues that surfaced in the past few years, like the case of former Chilean President Pinochet, various terrorist incidents and the Iraq War, there is no doubt that the occupation of Iraq was an illegal act. The reason is that international law, which has evolved since WWII, does not allow countries to go to war except when there is just cause, like in cases of "self-defence", upon a "mandate from the United Nations" or for "humanitarian considerations", i.e., in cases of substantial human rights violations, although this last condition is the object of several interpretations. In Sands' mind, the occupation of Iraq does not constitute a just cause, because Iraq did not pose a threat,.in the legal sense, to any of the big powers.[76] What further confirms the fragility of these excuses is Paul Wolfowitz's statement saying that for "bureaucratic reasons", the WMD issue was the only one on which everybody agreed, which is why it was chosen as the main reason for the invasion of Iraq.[77] The United States never proved the veracity of any of the thirty claims that Secretary of State, Colin Powell, made in a meeting on February 2003, regarding the presence of WMDs in Iraq.[78] This brings us back to the real reasons why there was an occupation at all. These were to impose America's domination of the region, to combat the Islamic renaissance and its inherent spirit of resistance and rejection of the status quo, the need to keep oil prices down, and to protect Israel, objectives that the West does not deny. They had once appointed the Shah as policeman and protector of their interests in the region, and after his downfall and the outbreak of the Iranian revolution, they tried but failed to convince Saddam Hussein to assume that role, who instead had gone on to occupy Kuwait, a move they saw as crossing a big red lines.

Once its strategy was no longer effective or had become insufficient, the United States had no choice but to be directly and militarily present in the region.[79] However, the West was not the only party with the wrong calculations; the GCC states had also thrown in their lot with the West, in the sense that they had aided and abetted efforts to topple Saddam from power, a fact several Western sources confirm. Bob Woodward underlines this fact and speaks of repeated efforts by former Saudi ambassador Bandar Bin Sultan to convince President George W. Bush to get rid of Saddam. In a meeting in November 2001, Bandar handed President Bush a letter from Prince Abdullah, the former Saudi King, in which the request to bring down Saddam Hussein's regime was crystal clear. According to Woodward: "As instructed, Bandar then said formally, 'Since 1994, we have been in constant contact and touch with you on the highest level regarding what needs to be done with Iraq and the Iraqi regime. Throughout this time we were looking for a seriousness from you that should have been demonstrated in coming together for formulating a joint plan between the governments to get rid of Saddam.'"

In 1994, King Fahd had proposed to President Clinton a joint US-Saudi covert action to overthrow Saddam, and Crown Prince Abdallah in April 2002 had suggested to Bush that they spend up to $1 billion in such joint operations with the CIA. Bandar then told the American president that Saudi Arabia had begun to "doubt how serious America is about the issue of regime change".[80]

However, despite the Saudi attitude in support of toppling the Iraqi regime, Saudi Foreign Minister, Saud al-Faisal, blamed the United States for the situation in Iraq after the regime's downfall. In a lecture at Rice University, sometime later, the Saudi minister said that, "Now it seems that Iran is being handed to Iraq on a golden platter."[81] Bob Woodward also says that when King Abdullah Bin Abdul-Aziz criticised the American presence in Iraq, describing it as a form of foreign occupation, Condoleezza Rice, George W. Bush's National Security Advisor at the time, sent Donald Rumsfeld immediately to Saudi Arabia. On 22 April 2007, Rumsfeld met with the Saudi King, the same man who promised to pay $1 billion to topple Saddam Hussein when he was still crown prince: "The United States has handed Iraq to Iran on a platter," the King said. "You have allowed the Persians, the Safavids" – the Shi'a rulers of Persian in the sixteenth and seventeenth centuries – "to take over Iraq."[82] The American envoy's response was to reassure the King that the United States would stay in the region for another fifty years or more, and to make it real, he told him that they were taking a a series of steps and that "Giant arms sales packages for the Gulf states, for the Egyptians and even for the Israelis were in the works."[83] Indeed, this is what Bob Woodward quoted the Saudi King as saying, and what Donald Rumsfeld's response was, namely selling more weapons to the region, i.e., more destruction and theft of the people's assets, especially since Iran, with help from the United States, has already dug its teeth deep in Iraq's body. We ask ourselves, in turn, is it possible that the Saudi government, which aided and abetted the downfall of the Iraqi regime, never suspected that this would be the outcome, especially given the security vacuum in the Gulf? According to Western observers, and regardless of whether Iraq ends up going down the path of democracy or chaos, the country's new rulers have managed to change the balance of power, particularly as far as Sunni Arab influence is concerned.[84]

Iran did not hide its pleasure at seeing the balance of power change as the result of America's occupation of Iraq and downfall of Saddam's regime; nor was this its only gain from America's actions in Iraq. The Americans had already brought down one of Iran's main enemies in the region, the Taliban regime in Afghanistan, and it was therefore not surprising to see Iran effectively helping the United States, on both the Afghani and Iraqi fronts, and get rid of the Sunni security belt that surrounded it from two sides. Thus, despite Iraq's defeat in Kuwait liberation war, Iran never stopped seeing Saddam's presence as a threat, and its political and military leaders believed that there would be another fateful encounter with Saddam, during which the latter's use of WMD's would not be farfetched.[85] Therefore, when the Bush administration decided to topple Saddam's regime, Iran played an effective role in the process because Iraq was offered to it on a golden platter. Most of the opposition factions that the United States had relied on to gain access into Iraq and were now ruling that country, mainly the Da'wa Party and Islamic Supreme Council of Iraq, were allies of Iran, the country that supported them materially and diplomatically, and the place where the militia that rules Iraq today had been trained.[86] Moreover, when the American forces entered Iraq, in March 2003, Grand Ayatollah Sistani, the Shi'a Supreme Guide in Iraq and the Gulf, issued a *fatwa* (religious edict) calling on his followers not to resist the American forces, which prompted Paul Wolfowitz to tell Congress that the Iraqis had issued a *fatwa* in support of America.[87] As later events have shown, this *fatwa* was, of course, not a positive act in America's favour as much as a means of redressing the balance of power between Iraqi Sunnis and Shi'a , ahead of an eventual political system under Shi'a control.[88] This was perfectly in line with Iran's interests in that country, given the near consensus in Iranian political circles that as long as Sunni leaders controlled Iraqi politics, Iraq would remain an enemy of Iran.

This is why replacing the old leadership with a Shi'a leadership sympathetic to Iran is one of Iran's strategic interests in the new Iraq, as they call it today.[89] A month after the downfall of Saddam's regime, Iranian President Khatami was speaking to over 50,000 Shi'a in Lebanon, during which he called for a Shi'a government in Iraq, describing Saddam's departure as a precious opportunity to introduce reforms in the region, and render justice to the Shi'a people.[90] Naturally, Iran's sense of having benefitted from Saddam's demise does not mean that it had not been frightened by the speed with which the Iraqi regime had fallen, or by the possibility that it could be next in line on the neo-cons' agenda. This is evidenced by the Iranian regime's behaviour in the wake of Saddam's downfall, whereby some Western sources indicate that it sent a message to the United States, via the Swiss embassy in Tehran, which the Supreme Guide of the Revolution had previously approved,[91] in which it proposed an understanding between the two countries. In the message, Iran offered a number of concessions including its willingness to abandon Hezbollah in Lebanon and ask it to transform itself into a political party, to stop aiding jihadist groups in Palestine, accept international inspection of its nuclear installations, stop aiding and abetting terrorism, help establish a democratic system in Iraq, accept King Abdullah's initiative to end the Arab-Israeli conflict and hand over to the United Staes all the al-Qaeda members detained in Iran.[92] In return, Iran proposed that the United States hand over to it members of the opposition Mujahiddin Khalq in Iraq, end its animosity towards Iran, support its demand for war reparations from Iraq, respect Iranian national security, allow Iran to develop its biological, chemical and nuclear technology and grant it a major role in the Gulf region.[93] However, under pressure from the neo-cons, the United States refused this tempting offer believing that it was the winner, after having brought down Saddam Hussein's regime, and as such had the right to dictate the terms. Soon afterwards, however, the balance of power shifted against the United States due to the rise of the Iraqi opposition, on the one hand, and the influence of pro-Iranian parties on the Iraqi political scene, on the other, which made Iran the main winner from Saddam's demise. Perhaps it was these developments that prompted King Abdullah of Jordan to say, "If Iraq goes Islamic Republic, then we've opened ourselves to a whole set of new problems that will not be limited to the borders of Iraq."[94] In turn, Saudi Foreign Minister Saud al-Faisal said about the Iranian expansion, "We fought a war together to keep Iran from occupying Iraq after we drove Iraq out of Kuwait. Now we are handing the whole country over to Iran without reason."[95] Of course, what neither the Jordanian King nor the Saudi Foreign Minister have said is that the absence of a competent GCC and Arab role, if not their support for America's policies, is one of the main reasons for Iran's successful infiltration of Iraq.

Sixth: Who is responsible for Iranian expansionism?

It is clear from the above analysis that Iran is seeking to extend its influence not only in the Gulf, but also in the Arab region as a whole, an expansion that has now become a reality, and which Iran is using to achieve its objectives in the region. It is also using it, no doubt, in its negotiations with Israel and the West, which is not at all surprising for a regional country that has always had, and still has, national and sectarian strategic interests. A Shi'a-controlled Iraq is a source of strength for Iran and for Shi'a minorities in Saudi Arabia, Kuwait, the UAE, Lebanon and elsewhere, a fact confirmed by Iranian-American researcher Vali Nasr in his book *The Shi'a Revival*.[96] There is also no doubt that Iran's ongoing efforts to develop its nuclear reactor are one of the ways it hopes to extend its influence over the Gulf, the Arab region and the Caucasus. However, although we do not want to exacerbate current sectarian conflicts, whether in Iraq, the GCC, Lebanon or elsewhere in the Arab and Muslim worlds, and still hope that reason will prevail when addressing present challenges to our nation, we feel compelled to shed light on events as they unfold and their outcome, and not content ourselves with wishful thinking. Therefore, the important question that begs itself here is: who is responsible for the growing influence of Iran in the Arab regional order?

1.   Syria and Lebanon

We have already showed how the occupation of Iraq has removed this country from the regional equation as a deterrent to Israel and Iran, and how the conflict between these two countries has filled the vacuum left behind by Iraq's departure from the scene. We have also showed how, as the result of that, Iran has become the main player in the Gulf region, with no one to deter it except for America's presence and its rivalry with Israel, and how it has begun to spread its influence across the Arab world, even if based on well-defined geopolitical considerations. The relationship between Iran, Syria, Hezbollah and the Palestinian jihadist movements is closer to an alliance based on common apprehensions. Syria needs, especially now that Egypt is no longer part of the equation against Israel, a way to put pressure on Israel to regain its occupied Golan Heights, and has so far used Hezbollah as the instrument of pressure.[97] Iran, in turn, sees its relationship with Syria as a conduit through which it can influence events in the Arab region, and steer the conflict over power with Israel, Egypt, and even Saudi Arabia, although, for the time being, Israel is its only rival. For Iran, Hezbollah is the spearhead of its strategic and ideological interests in the region, while for Hezbollah itself, the main advantage from the alliance is above all domestic, i.e., particular to Lebanon and the Arab world. These three parties together have gained considerable popularity in the Arab street by standing, even if in name only, behind Palestinian jihadist organisations. As for the latter, including Islamic Jihad and Hamas, an alliance with these three parties is a way to bolster their military and political struggle against the Zionist enemy, especially in the absence of support from the GCC, Egypt and other Arabs.

The question is, however, does this quadripartite alliance have what it takes to survive, or is it doomed to fail because it is not a strategic alliance and its objectives are therefore only transient? The answer to this question depends, no doubt, on other regional variables, especially on what the Arabs, Israel and the big powers will do. If Syria sees the alliance only as a means of regaining its occupied lands, then Israel's withdrawal from the Golan Heights as part of a comprehensive regional peace agreement could end Syria's need for an alliance with Iran, particularly if this agreement involves a measure of Arab economic integration or a set of economic incentives to help Syria develop.[98] Events in Iraq could also help weaken the Iranian-Syrian alliance, whether these are related to its identity, the nature of its political system or its relationship with Israel, issues very difficult to predict at this stage. What is certain is that the increasingly religious character of the Iraqi regime is in direct contradiction with Syria's secular character, especially since the country's regime is currently a minority regime, i.e., the exact opposite of Iraq under Saddam.[99] In any case, we believe that as long as the Arab regional order remains as weak and dislocated as it is today, and as long as peace efforts in the region continue to stall, despite a number of difficult crises, the Syrian-Iranian alliance will neither unravel nor weaken, in the short term. What could eventually unravel the alliance between Hezbollah and Iran is the former feeling that the latter has become a burden to it, if the big powers agree to deal a blow to Hezbollah, either to weaken Iran and its nuclear programme or to reduce its role in the region. Events could also unfold in such a way as to persuade Iran to abandon Hezbollah, and other resistance groups in the region, in return for the big powers accepting a certain role for it in the region. On the other hand, the nature of the Palestinian struggle imposes on the Palestinian factions the need to keep all channels of communications open to everyone, until such time when their independent state is a reality. However, a fair solution to the Palestinian conflict, in the shadow of a competent Arab role, could reduce Iran's influence on the issue, though we believe this scenario to be rather farfetched given the current power imbalance between the Arabs and Israel. Let us look now at how this alliance has helped Iran achieve certain advantages from Israel's war on Lebanon in 1996, in the absence of any competent role for important Arab countries, like Egypt and Saudi Arabia. As we said earlier, Saddam Hussein's downfall had increased Iranian influence in Iraq, and Israel, alerted to the significance of this development, began with the help and support of other parties to plan for the 2006 attack, with the hope of dealing a blow to Hezbollah, the arm of Iranian influence in the region. Thus, although Hezbollah's kidnapping of two Israeli soldiers in Lebanon on 12 July 2006 gave Israel the excuse it needed to launch its 34-day war on Hezbollah, its leaders admitted that the country had been preparing for this day for over two years. According to several Israeli sources, Israel had prepared for this war more than it did any other war, since 1948.[100] In the meantime, American Secretary of State, Condoleezza Rice, said that the war represented the birth pangs of a new Middle East and the neo-cons urged George W. Bush to join the war on Israel's side, rather than only support it.[101] It was therefore a planned war launched with American approval, and its aim was to contain Hezbollah, which, as far as Israel was concerned, was the spearhead of Iran's expansion in the Arab region. In Israel's eyes, this expansion is a negative development likely to weaken its absolute domination of its Arab neighbours, a domination that Israel sees as a vital strategy for survival, based on the premise that the Israeli Army cannot be defeated. What we had here, therefore, was an expansionist Israel trying to maintain its domination of the region by occupying Arab lands and expanding into neighbouring Arab territories, facing a Hezbollah, which, regardless whether we agree or disagree with it on this or that issue, including its relationship with Iran, is resisting on its own territory and winning. Hezbollah's victory is above all a victory for the Palestinian cause, since it weakens a historic enemy of the Arabs. Does it make sense then when certain Arab and Gulf governments blame Hezbollah for having recklessly provoked a war with Israel, a statement that surprised many observers because it embodies the incomprehensible contradiction of Arab governments blaming someone fighting Israel on an Arab country's territory?[102] Even former

Israel Prime Minister, Ehud Barak, admitted that the Israeli invasion of Lebanon, in 1982, was the main reason why Hezbollah existed at all. He said in this context, "When we entered Lebanon ... there was no Hezbollah," a statement echoed later by Yitzhak Rabin who said that Israel's 1982 invasion of Lebanon had brought the "genie out of the bottle", by which he meant Hezbollah.[103]

Hezbollah was able to stand fast in the face of the Israeli Army because it enjoyed Iranian and Syrian support, and would not have achieved what it did had it not been for this support. The way the war unfolded, and its outcome, have confirmed that the same Israeli Army that the Arab governments had failed to defeat, except very briefly early on in the October 1973 War, could be defeated by a militia willing to sacrifice for its land and religion. When early on in the war Israeli planes attacked Hezbollah's bases, Dan Haluz, the Israeli Chief of Staff, called Prime Minister Olmert to tell him that all the long-range missiles had been destroyed and that the war had been won.[104] The Iranians, on the other hand, initially saw the event in an entirely different light. They believed that the attack on Hezbollah was a prelude to an attack on them, saw Hezbollah's eventual demise as the loss of one of their main trump cards in the region and understood the destruction wrought on Beirut as a warning to them.[105] This again confirms that Iran only thinks about Iran, and that everybody else is but a tool to use or discard, at will. Subsequent events in the War were far from being that optimistic for Israel, or that pessimistic for Iran. Hezbollah was able to resist heroically using advanced technology and, according to several sources, succeeded in breaching Israel's coded messages, learning a lot about Israel's military casualties and its performance in the war. Seven weeks after the war began, opinion polls conducted by the Israeli Army showed that around 63 per cent of the Israelis wanted Olmert to resign, and 74 per cent wanted the Minister of Defence, Amir Peretz, to do the same. By then, the Israeli people's expectations of a victory had been replaced by the willingness to accept a draw and a troop withdrawal.[106]

The war thus ended with the withdrawal of Israeli forces, and instead of achieving its objective of cutting Hezbollah's power down to size and, by extension, weakening Iran's role in the region, it produced the exact opposite. The myth of the unbeatable Israeli Army was torn asunder, the credibility of the United States was eroded and the Gulf and Arab citizens' confidence in their pro-Western Arab regimes plummeted to near zero.[107] It plummeted even lower when these governments refused to acknowledge the mistake of siding with the losing side and the oppressor, and some of them, like Saudi Arabia, added insult to injury when they accused Hezbollah of having embarked on an "uncalculated adventure". However, such accusations were no more than a flagrant expression of these regimes' failure, and their inability to make an impact on the course of events in the region.

In short, if Iran has helped Hezbollah resist the Israeli Army's mighty onslaught and, through that strengthened the Palestinians' position vis-à-vis Israel and secured a foothold in Lebanon and the surrounding area, then the Arab regimes are to blame for failing to fill the security vacuum that Iran has subsequently filled, and used to spread its influence throughout the region. In his description of Saudi Arabia's criticism of Hezbollah, Saudi researcher, Khalid al-Dakhil confirms this theory and admits that Saudi Arabia has strategic interests in both Lebanon and the surrounding areas. He then adds, "At the same time, we have to face the fact that what left the Arab arena open to the so-called miscalculated adventures is the absence of an Arab role in the struggle with Israel, as well as the absence of an Arab position towards America's presence in the region."[108] We agree with Khalid al-Dakhil, and add that if we really want to deter Iran from infiltrating the Arab region, we should mobilise our resources and abilities and use them to strengthen the domestic front; resolve all pending problems, mainly the Palestinian issue; and reduce our dependency on the big powers, an issue that Iran and others use as excuse to interfere in the Gulf and wider Arab region.

2. Palestine

The recent years have witnessed the spread of Iranian influence on the scene in Palestine and, in our opinion, this development is another reflection of the vacuum that the Arabs have left behind, and that Iran has begun to exploit successfully, albeit to a lesser extent than its relationship with Hezbollah. It is not at all surprising to find the GCC governments, who depend entirely on the United States and Western countries for their security, in an impasse regarding the Palestinian issue. The West has helped establish the Zionist state and is now protecting it, at a time when the Gulf's people support the Palestinians and consider Israel the enemy. Many Western observers recommend that, given the impasse in which the GCC governments find themselves regarding the Arab-Israeli conflict, the US government should refrain from asking these governments to contradict the majority view in their countries, openly. They should be content with these governments' undeclared, or behind the scenes, support, mainly in the form of financial endorsements to facilitate the implementation of US's policies in the region, in other words circumventing their people's wishes and demands.[109] In fact, the GCC governments have been showing their support in this roundabout way for quite a while; they funded and diplomatically supported various peace negotiations and helped thwart all forms of resistance, without which the peace negotiations would not have proceeded. However, these never-ending negotiations, which many would rather see fail, are Israel and the West's way to weaken and dismember the Palestinian people, a reality confirmed by the Oslo negotiations; yet the GCC governments still hold onto Oslo because they do not have a position of their own. The GCC's boycott of Israel, especially the bilateral track, began to weaken over thirty years ago thanks to US pressure on these regimes,[110] and today it is virtually non-existent in these governments' minds and behaviour, save for a few popular organisations that refuse to go down this path. Today, the Israelis attend conferences in the Gulf, especially in the UAE, and according to Western sources, they have even become partners in some of the Dubai Ports' projects, and active in a number of other businesses including restaurants and the diamond trade; and the same could be said about other GCC states.[111] The Zionists and their supporters never stopped trying to impose facts on the ground to force the land's rightful owners to give up their rights, gradually, so that Israel would survive and gain strength, a deliberate strategy that several Israeli and Western officials confirm. For those able to use their mind, the theory based on usurping other people's rights by force with total disregard for international rights and legitimacy, has become an ongoing phenomenon.

Henry Kissinger, considered one of the architects of twentieth-century diplomacy, says that international law alone does not help regain lost rights.[112] Former American President Jimmy Carter also reminds us that John Bolton, former American ambassador to the United Nations, believed it would be a big mistake for the US to grant any validity to international law even when it may seem in its short-term interest to do so, because it will constrain it over the long term.[113] Furthermore, Kissinger admits that Israel was created by force and is still dependent on it.[114] In turn, Richard Perle, former US Assistant Secretary of Defence, and David Frum, former special assistant to President George Bush, acknowledge this principle when they say that the Arabs refused to accept what six confrontations with Israel have dictated since its establishment, namely the need to make peace with it and settle the Palestinians in their own countries. The reason is that they will never get more than what President Clinton had offered Arafat at Camp David, in September 2000.[115] Moreover, in a joint article, Zbigniew Brzezinski, National Security Advisor to President Carter, and Brent Scowcroft, National Security Advisor to President Bush senior, called for a Palestinian state in order to win the Arabs' support for America's so-called war on terror.[116] Consequently, if we take the time to look at the borders of the future Palestinian state, as proposed by the West, we would inevitably find that they reflect the balance of power imposed by Israel, with help from the West. If this happens, this eventual state will not secure the minimum of what the Palestinian people aspire to, because it involves "most" of the West Bank and Gaza Strip and a trade-off between Israeli settlements and the Palestinians' right of return. It means, in effect, that the exiled Palestinians have to give up their land in return for territories that the Jews had occupied in previous wars, and end up with a mere 23 per cent of their historic homeland, i.e., less than what the UN Partition Plan had given them in the late 1940s, and the Arabs had rejected.[117] How could the Arabs accept less than what they rejected sixty years ago? For what purpose were all these wars, then?

The answer to these questions is that Israel and its allies have imposed a balance of power that allows them to either dictate their conditions or refuse to make peace, while knowingly insisting on pursuing a fruitless peace process with a weak Palestinian side, at a time when Israel is tirelessly trying to bolster its negotiating stance. The evidence is that when Hamas appeared on the scene saying it would neither negotiate for the sake of negotiating nor give up resistance as an option, the West, the Arab Quartet (Egypt, Jordan, Saudi Arabia and the UAE) and the Arab countries chose to forget that the Palestinian people had elected Hamas, and that it had the right to liberate its occupied lands. The above parties had focussed their attention on preventing Hamas from changing the balance of power, and forcing it to accept negotiations as the only option available, because both Israel and the West know that negotiations without parity between the sides would only benefit the strong. Michael Herzog, former senior military aide to the Israeli Defence Minister, admitted that much. He said that only financial and military pressure would force Hamas to give up resistance as a weapon and to accept to play the political game, i.e., the peace process the West promotes in favour of Israel.[118] Some experts even went as far as to proposing targeted assassinations against the leaders of Hamas, and other Palestinian groups opposed to the peace process, to allow Israel and the United States to impose a peace amenable to the West and ensure Israel's control over the region.[119] This is not a new weapon; the Zionist state has used it before in the worst possible way when it killed Shaikh Ahmad Yassin, a paraplegic man confined to a wheelchair who was on his way home from dawn prayers, and reserved the same fate for Abdul Aziz Al-Rantissi and others. Gulf governments close to the West just sat there and watched all this unfold, as if what takes place in the occupied territories did not concern them at all, and as if they have to sow discouragement and despair into the new generation's heart in order to maintain the status quo. These governments also know that any change in the balance of power with Israel means a change in the balance of power between the government and the people, in each Arab country, whereby these governments will start expressing the will of the people and make independent decisions. However, since this is not something that the current GCC and Arab governments would like to see happen, they chose the confrontation with Hamas and other forces of change in the region and put all their eggs in the US and Israelis' basket. The bitter reality, however, is that Hamas' very appearance on the scene, as late as 1987, was in reaction to Israel's twenty-year occupation of the West Bank, Gaza and East Jerusalem, which makes Israel, in one Western observer's view, "responsible for the creation of Hamas", and makes Hamas no more than a reaction to the injustice.[120]

It is indeed regrettable to see the Western countries vying with each other to defend and support the oppressor, in flagrant disregard of all international conventions, laws and resolutions. Regardless of the circumstances, however, the fact is that the United States and the West sympathise with the Jewish state and support it for ideological, economic and security reasons, and also due to the guilt complex resulting from the massacre of Jews in Europe, during the holocaust. A Western author admits that although the United States helps Israel for ideological and economic reasons, it does so also because they are both settler states, meaning that their citizens have built their society on the ruins of the land's original owners, namely the Native Americans and the Palestinians.[121] This means that although Western support for Israel is not inspired by goodness as much as by pure interest, and the need to make amends for past mistakes, today the Palestinians are being asked to pay the price despite having had nothing to do with what happened to the Jews in Europe. This is therefore the West's attitude towards Israel, an attitude we actually understand quite well. We understand it because for the West, principles are not only relative, they are sometimes superseded and led by self-interest, and we understand it because we know these countries' colonial history in our region and the hardship it wrought. What we do not understand is the attitude of Arab governments, including the GCC's, an attitude that conflicts with their religious teachings, their morality and their people's interests, yet their leaders wonder why Iran keeps expanding in the Arab region. Let us look at what the Centre for Arab Unity Studies (CAUS) said in the report entitled "State of the Arab World" on the fallout from Hamas' rise on the Palestinian scene, and how different parties have dealt with it, to understand how these countries gave Iran the opportunity to get involved in the Palestinian cause. The report states: "Hamas' spectacular success in the legislative elections of 2006 was a surprise to everyone, including to Hamas itself. The paradox is that Hamas' political agenda, i.e., which insist on certain national imperatives and on pursuing the armed resistance, is similar to Fatah's when the late Yasser Arafat was still in power, in 1969 and beyond, which makes it more of a return to the source than a new policy, at least in the political context. It dealt a blow to ready-made solutions and the parties involved scrambled to thwart the outcome: the United States and Israel actually made plans to do away with Hamas politically and eliminate its leaders physically (this being Israel's role). In Ramallah, the Palestine National Authority (the PNA based in Ramallah and led by Mahmoud Abbas) mobilised its forces against Hamas either for political reasons, meaning that they refused to recognise the results of the election, credited by the whole world as free and fair, or for material and personal reasons to safeguard the advantages reaped from the Oslo Agreement. The PNA's interests coincided, naturally, with the foreign parties' interests and, for some, the difference between negotiations, collaboration and treason became too narrow to tell."[122]

However, not content with ending all forms of support and assistance to the Palestinian people, the GCC governments actually tried to cause harm by taking part in the siege of Gaza. In a March 2008 report, *Vanity Fair* magazine confirmed the collaboration between the United States, Israel and the Arab Quartet in a bid to bring down the elected government of Hamas, by provoking a Palestinian civil war.[123] Here again is CAUS' report describing the siege of Gaza and subsequent events: "If it is usual for the United States and Europe to ally themselves with Israel in war, it is still unusual to see PNA cadres who lost in the elections taking direct or indirect part in besieging other Palestinians in Gaza. Some Arab regime played their part as well, at least by keeping quiet as the crimes were being committed. Moreover, security agencies led by Muhammad Dahlan and funded by the Americans and Israelis were involved, directly or indirectly, in the assassination of resistance leaders and cadres, in manner that could qualify as high treason. It came to a point where Dahlan and his associates were directly attempting to implement the Dayton Plan that sought to eliminate Hamas both physically and ideologically."[124]

Israel's all-out attack on Gaza, "Operation Cast Lead", which began on 27 December 2008, which used warplanes and naval vessels and was followed by an attempt to invade the city, was the crowning glory of Israel's barbarism against this valiant people. Although the attack, which lasted until 18 January 2009, left behind it death, pain and the destruction of the Strip's infrastructure, not to mention the homelessness, the world did not deem it reason enough to end the siege. Pressure on Hamas to give up the Palestinian people's rights, like others have done before, continued unabated, but the movement resisted and, in the process, won the support of many in the world.[125]

Chas Freeman, former American ambassador to Saudi Arabia, stressed that the negotiations between the Palestinian leadership represented by Mahmoud Abbas and Israel have lost credibility, especially after the Arab Spring, and that even if there is an agreement, the Arab people will refuse it because it is illegitimate. He says, "The very structure of the talks emphasizes their futility. Most Palestinians are unrepresented in them. The Palestinian Authority is on the Israeli and American payrolls. It has been appointed to represent the Palestinians by Israel and the United States but its authority to speak even for the inhabitants of the West Bank is in doubt. It certainly has no mandate to negotiate on behalf of those in Gaza, in the refugee camps, in diaspora, or living as second-class citizens in Israel. In the unlikely event that the Palestinian Authority were to come to some sort of agreement with its Israeli masters, few Palestinians anywhere would consider themselves bound by this."[126] Rather, we believe that the reconciliation discussed in May 2014 between the Palestinian Authority and Hamas is another manoeuvre by the Palestinian Authority which has legitimacy in neither the Arab world nor the West. Consequently, it does not express a strategic change in the position of President Abbas and matters will revert to the status quo, i.e., more negotiations while Israel expands its settlements and control. The war against Gaza in 2014 confirms the extent of the collusion between the global powers and Israel as well as a number of Arab governments, such that Netanyahu admitted that a number of Arab governments were aligned with his government ... therefore, the masks will have slipped completely.

This is what happened, and is still happening, to the Palestinian people in general, and to the people of Gaza in particular. Is it logical, therefore, for this Gulf and Arab silence to persist in the face of this slaughter, that only adds another chapter to the pain and suffering that this people has endured? Is it fair, given the above, to ask the Palestinian people why they accept assistance from Iran and forge an alliance with it, or with anyone else, for that matter?

Chapter Fourteen

Iran's Nuclear Reactor

We tried above to clarify the circumstances that led to the recent spread of Iranian influence in the Gulf and Arab regions, and found that the main reason behind it was the chronic incompetence of the Arab regional order and, by extension, its inability to face up to the challenges imposed on it by regional and international conflicts. It is important, in light of Iran's insistence on developing its nuclear reactor, and the ensuing potential imbalance of power in the Gulf and Arab regions, that we shed light on various policies relevant to this nuclear programme, and their possible repercussions in the coming years. Given the importance of this still unfolding issue, we have devoted an entire chapter to it in which we focus on four main points: the programme's development, how close it is to producing a nuclear bomb; its justifications and objectives; the options available to the world's nations on how best to deal with it in the next few years; and finally, recent developments in the programme.

First: At what stage is Iran's nuclear programme?

Iran's nuclear aspirations began under the Shah who was at the time the guardian of Western interests in the region. He had earmarked no less than $40 billion for the programme, which he developed mainly in cooperation with Germany and South Africa. Ardeshir Zahidi, the Shah's foreign minister, said that the programme's objective was to build the country's infrastructure, and train local human resources to build the country's nuclear capability within a short time, i.e., providing the right elements and conditions to produce a nuclear bomb within an eighteen-month period.[1] However, although the programme was put on hold after the revolution, on orders from Khomeini, Iran's experience in the war with Iraq, the Scud missiles that rained on its cities and failure of the millions it sent to the front to change the course of the war, forced Rafsanjani's government to reactivate the programme. It was still in its initial stages and lacked centrifuges and the ability to enrich uranium. Yet, although the West had helped the Shah develop his nuclear programme, this cooperation ended after the revolution, and Iran turned to Russia who agreed to build two nuclear reactors in Bushehr, despite its neglect of the programme during the war with Iraq,[2] according to some sources. In the 1990s, the programme succeeded in making considerable progress, despite Western pressure on Russia to stop its nuclear cooperation with Iran. However, since the world believed at the time that the programme was still in its early stages and posed a threat to no one, there were no calls for sanctions of any kind on Iran. In 2002, information out of Iran confirmed that the country now had the necessary facilities to enrich uranium in Natanz, south of Tehran, that it had acquired the skill and technology required, and that it already had around 160 centrifuges with 1000 additional units on the way. The number of these machines was expected to reach 50,000 within two years, which would allow Iran to produce several nuclear bombs.[3] The same source also indicated that Iran was equally active in another nuclear field, namely plutonium development, that it had taken considerable forward strides in that domain and that it was even on the verge of becoming self-sufficient in terms of what it needed to develop a nuclear weapon. In other words, the restrictions that the world had imposed on Iran to prevent it from importing the necessary expertise and equipment had failed to slow down the development of its nuclear reactor.[4] Gradually, Iranian officials began confirming the rumours and, on 25 May 2004, President Rafsanjani admitted to the Iranian News Agency that the country was close to owning a nuclear weapon, saying, "That we are on the verge of nuclear breakout is true."[5] That same day, Iran's representative to the International Atomic Energy Agency (IAEA), Ali Akbar Salihi, said as much when he declared, "We have found the way and we do not have any scientific problems."[6] In April 2006, Iranian President Ahmadinejad announced that Iran had succeeded in assembling a cascade of 164 centrifuges and that it was actually enriching uranium.[7]

If these reports are true rather than politically motivated, this means that Iran is now beyond the critical stage, and it is a matter of time before it produces a nuclear weapon. Realising this fact is important to the world so that it knows what options it has in dealing with Iran and its nuclear reactor, in the next few years. The progress this country has achieved so far in developing its nuclear reactor, clearly means that, as mentioned above, the boycott is unlikely to end the programme. The world's failure to take a firm position on this issue is unacceptable to several countries, which means that the remaining two options are either to try to contain it, or destroy its nuclear installations, each of which, as we shall see later, entails a myriad of complications.

Second: Motives behind the programme

Most, if not all, the countries that have built a serious nuclear programme have either felt threatened at some point, whether by a real or an imagined danger, or wanted it for peaceful development purposes; and Iran is no different. What are the motives behind Iran's nuclear programme? The motives behind the Middle East's desire to develop nuclear weapons, including Iran, are numerous, among which is the need to control and/or deter, develop the country's technology and knowhow and build its institutions.[8] Below, we will try to clarify Iran's motives in this domain.

1. Domination and expansion

The countries of the Middle East are beset by several elements of instability, including border disputes, autocratic regimes, income disparities and historic conflicts, all of which not only raises their apprehension regarding their interests, but their very survival as well. Because of that, possessing a nuclear weapon bestows on these countries status and respectability among their neighbours, and deters any ambitions these might harbour towards them, not to mention the pride they would feel in their country's technological ability and knowhow.[9] Iran is no different, since it is no doubt eager to extend its presence and influence across the neighbourhood.

a) As indicated above, Iran was and still is eager to dominate the Gulf region, and ensure that it plays an essential role in determining the region's policies, objectives that did not change even after the revolution that removed the Shah from power. As a regional Arab state, Iraq was a deterrent to Iran's ambitions in the region until the Kuwait liberation war and the country's occupation in 2003, which considerably weakened its ability to play that role. What increased Iran's fears even further was the fact that Iraq's Scud missiles had reached the main cities during the Iran-Iraq War, without it being able to protect itself, which is why it does not deny that the main objective is to ensure that no inimical Arab or Sunni regime rules in Iraq again.[10] Moreover, Iran is afraid that now Saddam is gone, the United States and the West will install a regime in his place that would serve as their mainstay in the region, and play the Gulf policeman as the Shah did under the "Nixon Doctrine".[11] This is why as far as Iran is concerned, having nuclear weapons means the ability to deter any future Iraqi regime and, at the same time, increase its status and influence in the region, not only to enhance its deterrence capability but also its ability to pressure states in the region. It will also use its newfound abilities to influence OPEC's decisions, secure a place in various regional blocs and impede any serious rapprochement between the GCC states and the Arab world. In brief, Iran's success in developing a nuclear weapon will make it the main power in the Gulf region and the Arab world, if the latter's situation remains unchanged. Moreover, this new power will not only strengthen Shi'a minorities in the Gulf and the surrounding Arab countries, it will lead to the establishment of militias similar to Hezbollah in Lebanon, and the Mahdi Army and Badr Brigade in Iraq. The latter were trained by the Iran's National Guard as support for Iran in its bid to extend its influence over the region, and the recent events in Bâhrain could well be a case in point.[12]

b) Iran is also interested in making its presence felt in the Arab world, not only to secure a foothold in the Arab regional order, but also to protect its interests and ensure that no Arab regional order inimical to it, led by Egypt and Saudi Arabia, will ever see the light. Iran also wants to contain Israel as a rival in the Arab region, and nothing in the history of the two countries' relationship makes us to believe that Iran's nuclear weapons would target Israel, because, as the Supreme Guide of the Revolution Ayatollah Khomeini said, "The Palestinian Cause is not a jihad for the Iranians."[13] This historic position could change, however, if there are new developments in the rivalry over who controls the region, given the absence of a common enemy, be it Iraq or any Arab regional bloc. Some in Israel do not discount the possibility that, in the next few years, Iran would try to assume Iraq's former aspirations by raising the banner of Islam and nuclear weapons, at the same time, which would automatically mean reducing Israel's role in the region.[14] We do not agree with this view, however, because pre-occupation Iraq and today's Iran are different on the national and sectarian levels, even the cultural level, which qualified Iraq to raise a banner acceptable to the region's people. Iran does not have the qualifications for that role, however, since it does not have what it takes to attract the support of the Sunni Arabs. In our opinion, and if history is anything to go by, even the Shi'a Arabs will soon realise that the wider Arab world will always be their first home because, for Iran, the national dimension will always be much stronger than the religious one. This is confirmed by the experience and evidence of history.[15]

c)   We saw earlier how Iran has helped the United States bring down the Taliban regime in Afghanistan, and if we remember the organic bond between Afghanistan and Pakistan, whether on the national or sectarian levels, we will understand why Iran will always see these two countries as a threat, especially in light of Pakistan's nuclear arsenal. Moreover, although former Pakistani Prime Minister, Zulfiqar Ali Butto, had called it "the Muslim Bomb" as opposed to the "Hindu Bomb", because it is supposed to protect all Muslims, Iran still sees it, in the words of Iranian researcher Vali Nasr, as a "Sunni Bomb" representing the Pakistani-Afghani threat on Iran's eastern borders.[16] This also means that Iran is anxious to develop its own nuclear weapons to deter Pakistan, Afghanistan, Russia and China, and extend its influence in Central Asia for strategic and religious reasons.[17] We could say, therefore, that Iran seeks to develop nuclear weapons in order to control events in the Gulf, spread its influence to the Arab world, deter any threat from neighbouring countries like Iran, Pakistan and the Taliban in Afghanistan, and ensure its presence in Central Asia for economic and security reasons.[18]

2.   The American supremacy challenge

The considerable inadequacy of the Arabs' conventional weapons vis-à-vis the big powers, especially the United States of America, has compelled many countries in the region to seek a nuclear deterrent, to bridge this gap and mitigate America's influence in the region. No doubt America's presence in Iraq and Afghanistan has promoted this kind of thinking in certain Middle Eastern countries, like Iran, who give credence to the words of an Indian military leader who, in the course of commenting on the outcome of the Gulf War, warned against going to war with the United States without having nuclear weapons.[19] As we saw previously, while the Western countries, mainly the United States, have been trying since the Shah's downfall to prevent any country in the region, whether Iraq or Iran, from imposing its control over the Gulf, the countries of the region have been trying to have a say in determining this vital region's fate, by any means possible. However, though the occupation has sidelined Iraq's role from this regional tug-of-war, Iran is aware that, today, the United States of America is still the main power and hegemony in the Gulf and Middle East regions.[20]

Iran's right to own nuclear weapons has been the object of much debate in the West, and many Western observers are sympathetic to its point of view. This means that despite the stern tone emanating from the West regarding Iran's nuclear ambitions, a future understanding that allows Iran to pursue its nuclear objectives in return for protecting American interests in the region, as it did in Iraq and Afghanistan, is not farfetched. Iran could also be persuaded to support the peace negotiations between the Arabs and Israel, especially if the West becomes convinced that stopping Iran's nuclear drive would be impossible, at this stage, without a costly military intervention. If this actually happens, a nuclear Iran will change the entire equation between itself and the United States, because the latter will be forced to recognise that as a nuclear power, Iran has the right to have a say in what happens in the region, although this can only be at the expense of the other Gulf states. Any alternative to America's recognition of Iran's role in the region would force the latter, now armed with a nuclear deterrent, to revert to its old confrontational stance, i.e., prior to 1996, against the American presence in the region. This confrontation could take several forms, such as encouraging resistance and violent acts, thwarting peace efforts, supporting countries opposed to the US and fomenting instability in those allied to it, and obstructing oil supplies through the Straits of Hormuz, without fear of American retaliation, except if the latter decides to use nuclear weapons, which is a very remote possibility.[21]

Third: The programme between containment and destruction

It is clear, from the historical development of Iran's nuclear programme, detailed above, that the programme has taken considerable steps forward towards its objective, i.e., the development of a nuclear weapon, although the time it still needs to reach the ultimate objective is still unclear. However, if we assume in light of the above that the United States decides that it cannot accept that Iran continue on this track, as evidenced by the economic sanctions on this country, then there are two options available regarding what to do with the nuclear reactor issue, each with its own supporters and detractors, and benefits and costs. The first option is if Iran actually advances from the stage of building the infrastructure required to produce nuclear weapons, to the stage of actually producing such a weapon, in the next few years, meaning that it has decided to take the risk, including the programme's possible destruction by the United States, Israel and their allies in the region. The second option is if the international community and Iran arrive at a formula whereby Iran is guaranteed the right to a peaceful nuclear programme, without progressing to the stage of producing an actual weapon. Here below is a summary of each option.

1.   Containment and deterrence

The international community, led by the United States, is currently trying to contain Iran's nuclear programme, steer it towards peaceful purposes and make sure that it does not lead to a nuclear weapon. To its supporters, the option is quite reasonable although its success depends on Iran's acceptance, which is largely contingent upon the guarantees that the world is prepared to offer, and its own calculations as to whether it is worth producing its own nuclear weapons versus the cost of jeopardising the programme and the country's infrastructure. Supporters of the containment option underline the importance of understanding Iran's position towards the nuclear option, in all its dimensions, because understanding it would help find a peaceful resolution to the crisis, and thus avoid the confrontation and destruction option. According to the latter, there are two camps in Iran regarding how best to deal with the crisis. On the one hand, there are the conservatives, led by the Supreme Guide of the Revolution Ayatollah Khamenei, as well as President Ahmadinejad, who want to use the reactor for military purposes because, as they see it, Iran faces numerous threats not least from America's ongoing attempts to topple the regime, and destroy the country. They believe that the present international order and current international conventions are incapable of protecting their country from the looming dangers – they point to the war with Iraq as an apt example – and see the IAEA's behaviour as a violation of Iran's sovereignty. Nor do they care that much about the international boycott, since they feel that it works to their advantage by strengthening the domestic front.[22] The conservatives believe that the opposition to their nuclear programme is not that different from the opposition that India and Pakistan's nuclear programmes had to endure, an opposition that quickly dissipated once the world recognised them as nuclear states.[23] The supporters of containment say, on the other hand, that Iran is not necessarily monopolised by the conservatives, since there is a more pragmatic current in the country, whose protagonists include former President Rafsanjani. The latter do not object to certain restrictions on their country's nuclear programme, in return for avoiding international isolation, integrating the country into the global economy and sparing it a potentially disastrous confrontation. These liberals believe that taking the programme a step forward, i.e., from being able to produce a nuclear weapon to actually producing one, will only force the GCC states to seek further American protection and to actively try to isolate Iran.[24]

This means that preventing Iran from using its nuclear reactor for military purposes is actually possible, provided the international community offer it the right incentives, including integration in the region on several levels, especially the security level, which implicitly means recognition that Iran has a special role to play in the Gulf region.[25] Those who advocate this position say that even if Iran does go on to produce a nuclear weapon, the West and others should resort to both traditional and nuclear deterrence methods, to ensure that these weapons are not used to change the balance of power with its neighbours, whether through war, transferring weapons and technology, or acts of sabotage. In our opinion, the latter option would pose the biggest danger to the GCC states, in the next few years. At the same time, the deterrence option raises a number of issues, including drawing the line between Iran's transgressions and violations that require a response using only conventional weapons, and those that require using nuclear weapons. Some observers believe that the West should threaten to use nuclear weapons even in response to acts of sabotage in the region,[26] while others believe that such threats are unrealistic, since there is more than one way to define sabotage, and numerous reasons why these acts actually take place. Therefore, the big powers cannot build their deterrence on murky concepts that could eventually force them to either retreat, and lose face and credibility, or use this weapon when it is not actually necessary, and wreak needless havoc on the region. Even responding to acts of sabotage with conventional weapons might not be the ideal response because, in these people's opinion, sabotage could be dealt with by directly addressing its root causes. Thus, since acts of sabotage are a mixture of finding weapons, consultations and training, fighting them requires collecting information, secret operations to thwart them before they actually happen and covert security activities; and if Iran takes advantage of the ill-treatment of Shi'a minorities in certain GCC states, then the solution is to give these minorities more rights. This means that using nuclear weapons can only be justified if Iran threatens to use them first, or actually uses them against others.[27]

Accepting the option of Iran's transformation into a nuclear country, which the United States and the West could very well do in the next few years, especially in light of what they had to endure in Iraq and Afghanistan, will have a major impact on the credibility of American policy in the region. It will also have serious repercussions on the GCC states and the Arab world as a whole, especially given the weakness of Arab regional order, and the illegitimate nature of the region's political regimes that exacerbates this weakness even further. If this happens, neither Washington's assurances nor the successive armament deals that drain the GCC states' resources would be enough to bring stability to the region, or deter Iran from exerting more control over the GCC states' domestic and regional policies. We are therefore not worried about Iran transferring its nuclear weapons to others in the region, as numerous observers would like to believe; what we are worried about is using these weapons to put pressure on countries in the region to pursue policies that serve its strategic interests.[28] Moreover, even if in order to deter Iran the Arab countries try to produce their own nuclear weapons, an endeavour of this magnitude is not simply a matter of policy decision that one could implement in a short time, but rather a long and complex process. It requires putting together the necessary resources, then building the reactor, searching for nuclear fuel, developing and learning the enrichment technology and, finally, being able to produce a weapon and finding the means of launching it towards the intended target.

Such a complex process would no doubt require a lot of cooperation among the Arab countries, though this does not mean that they will not finally opt to buy these weapons rather than manufacture them. Some wager on the two main Arab countries, Egypt and Saudi Arabia, choosing not to go down the nuclear path, because the former risks forfeiting American assistance to the tune of $1.5 billion per year, and the latter risks forfeiting American protection, a scenario that should not be dismissed given that the Arabs have ceded their strategic decisions to others.[29] Some in the West fear that Iran might use its nuclear weapons as an umbrella to protect the resistance in Palestine in its quest to reclaim Palestinian rights from Israel's hands, a development they see as negative since it would weaken the latter's position vis-à-vis the Palestinians. However, much as we wish these fears to be justified, the fact remains that Iran's historical record makes us hesitate before believing that such a scenario could actually happen, meaning that we should wait and see whether Iran will actually use its nuclear weapons in this manner, if it develops them at all.[30]

2. Destruction

If containment fails and the United States and its allies prove unable to deter Iran from its nuclear ambitions by peaceful means, including the economic boycott, some propose that they actually destroy its nuclear installations, just as Israel destroyed the Iraqi reactor during the Iraq-Iran War. This option's proponents suggest a joint direct American-Israeli operation, with logistical support from a number of states in the region, including allowing the two countries' military aircrafts to use the GCC's airspace, even if the air campaign involves thousands of sorties, last for weeks rather than days and destroys Iran's air defences before hitting the intended target. However, there is a lot of opposition to this scenario; while some doubt that it would achieve the intended results, others apprehend its potential repercussions. Most experts are certain that the country's widespread nuclear facilities, the fact that they are located deep underground and the West's limited information about the programme, mean that it is virtually impossible to destroy all the installations and that Iran will probably be able to rebuild them within four years, at the most. Over and above the failure to destroy the entire nuclear programme, some believe that by launching such an attack, the United States would automatically strengthen Iran's conservative government, and increase its support both internally and throughout the region. More ominous still would be Iran's subsequent efforts to thwart American policies in Iraq, Afghanistan and Palestine.[31]

Finally, the position of those who believe that the above option is unworkable is further strengthened by the fact that the programme rests on the skills and abilities of Iranian experts, who will no doubt escape the destruction and revive the programme using newly rebuilt facilities.[32] Moreover, several Israeli observers believe that even for Israel, likely to be the one to strike the reactor, the operation might seem like a miscalculated adventure with potentially disastrous repercussions, if it is not certain that Iran intends to use its nuclear weapons against it.[33] Even a pre-emptive strike by either the United States or Israel is not an act easy to consider because there is always the possibility that the other side will retaliate using what is left of its nuclear weapons, a lesson that the big powers' "mutually-assured destruction" strategy has taught us. In brief, therefore, those who propose deterring Iran from using its nuclear power rely on the latter realising that using these weapon, or helping others use them, will have dire consequences on the very survival of the Iranian state, provided, of course, it actually succeeds in developing such a weapon.[34]

Fourth: Recent developments in Iran's nuclear programme

The preceding paragraphs show that there are two choices, containment or elimination of the Iranian nuclear programme, and that each has its positive and negative aspects, without a clear preference outweighing either. As for recent developments in this area, in fact there is not any tangible progress that would make containment the preferred choice, although there are some indicators which make this more likely than the choice of elimination. According to researcher Suzanne Maloney, the American administrations which preceded Obama relied on the "stick" approach more than that of the "carrot" in their dealings with Iran and failed. Obama's administration imposed economic sanctions in 2012 and abandoned the policy of pressure and persuasion, instead following the path of regime change. This policy is worse than the previous policies since it does not afford the other side any incentive to change its behaviour and thus, does not help to defuse this confrontation.[35] The West has continued in its attempts to persuade Iran to discontinue the development of its nuclear programme for military purposes. Among the means of pressure against Iran is the economic boycott and the escalating tone of the discourse on nuclear terrorism and its link to attempts to develop nuclear weapons in the Middle East. The insinuation here by the West is that in the case of a nuclear weapon being developed, Iran could transfer it to terrorist organisations in the region.[36]

However, as Pollack states, the West is faced with the problem of information about what is happening in Iran, particularly as regards the directives of the political leadership and specifically Khamenei, the Supreme Leader of the Iranian Republic. This information is necessary to enable the West to crystallise a clear policy towards the Iranian nuclear programme. Despite the fact that many Western governments do not wish to rule out military action entirely, they are nevertheless inclined towards containment, primarily because of the potential cost, both human and material, of intervention. The costs can be further exasperated by failed military air strikes and the need to deploy ground troops to finish the mission, as was the case in Iraq.[37]

Since 2003, Iran has continued to develop its programme despite the embargo, ignoring the resolutions of the UN or the IAEA. This is a position Western observers regard as Iran's determination to achieve several aims, including independence, carrying out a regional role and spreading the ideas of the Iranian revolution. However, Iran sees the position of America, the UN and the IAEA as biased and undemocratic as well as showing double standards because all these agencies do not talk about Israel's nuclear weapons (estimated to be between 100 and 400 nuclear warheads), and this implies that they want Israeli dominance to continue in the region.[38] Hence, many observers confirm that Iran is aiming to shorten the period between creating the ability to produce a nuclear weapon and the actual production of this weapon before the world is able to stop that, even if the weapon has not been produced yet. The reports available indicate that Iran put an estimated 20 per cent ceiling on its enrichment of uranium, whereas the production of the weapon requires the enrichment of 90 per cent. Likewise, its reserve of nuclear fuel is 180kg less than the stock required to develop the weapon which is 240kg of the enriched uranium at 90 per cent. In addition, during their inspection of Iranian sites, the IAEA inspectors did not find any weapons programme.[39] It seems that the West did not object to allowing Iran some ability to enrich uranium without transferring to armament with more international supervision. Moreover, Iran had accepted a compromise to reduce its economic crisis resulting from the boycott and the freezing of its stocks.[40]

The desire of the two parties to come to a peaceful solution was confirmed by the agreement signed on 24 November 2013 in Geneva between Iran and the five countries who are permanent members of the Security Council (the United States, Britain, China, Russia, Germany). This agreement was based on the joint plan of action to "reach a mutually-agreed long-term comprehensive solution that would ensure Iran's nuclear programme will be exclusively peaceful." It is, of course, too early to know the outcomes of this solution.[41] Some sources point out that Iran has showed its good intentions towards a peaceful solution through its method of production which has kept the rate of enrichment at 20 per cent. Similarly, Iran has reduced its production of centrifuges such that since August 2013 it has only produced around four units while its production between May and August 2013 was around 1800 new units. If these figures are verified, there is no doubt that Iran will have started to reduce its method of developing its nuclear programme at the present time, whether out of fear of military strikes, or out of a desire to save itself from its economic crisis, or both.[42]

These policies may not be surprising if we remember the broad plans announced by President Hasan Rouhani after his election in June 2013 for his future policies. These appear pragmatic and not dogmatic like those of his predecessor Ahmedinejad and also confirm support from Iran's Supreme Leader for these policies. Among their aims is to hold serious negotiations with the US about the nuclear programme, reducing regional conflict and giving priority to the Iranian economy. After taking over the presidency, Rouhani sent several friendly messages to the US through his article in the *Washington Post* on 19 September 2013, a telephone conversation with Obama in September 2013, some interviews with American media and he did not forget to congratulate the world's Jews on the occasion of the Jewish new year.[43] Of course, we do not know whether Iran's wooing of the West and Israel will result in a rapprochement and lessening of the severity of the current confrontation surrounding the nuclear programme, or whether it will be no more than a summer cloud that will clear away as merely a memory for all parties that they are in a battle for control over the Middle East region, and especially the Arab nations. If so, Rouhani's fate will be the same as Khatemi when he cooperated with the Americans in Iraq and Afghanistan; then the West made his country part of the "axis of evil" and the Iranian political scene changed with the arrival of Ahmedinejad. The success of the diplomatic solution to this issue depends on the ability of both Obama and Rouhani to persuade the more emphatic partners in both their camps, and this is not an easy matter. The

Iranian government may be compelled to break up some of its nuclear structure and be completely transparent in the management of its nuclear programme to be free partly or completely from the economic boycott.[44]

Unfortunately, all this is happening at a time when the governments of the GCC states lack any coordination of what is taking place in their midst and leave the matter for the West to manage, especially the US. Meanwhile, the Arab regional system is not yet formed because of the suffocation it faces, particularly in Egypt, given that Iran's agreement with the US will be at the expense of the GCC states. They will be in the position of acknowledging the dominant role of Iran in the Arab Gulf region, especially as this will push these states to more military spending which is of no use to them except to support Western weapons factories.

PART V

Towards a Better Future

This book attempts to stress an unequivocal fact which is very difficult to discern through all the fog of publicity, despotism, oil wealth, fear and the global interest in the Arab world. This fact is that the oil-producing countries of the Gulf region whose oil wealth has, over the past thirty years, given them the opportunity to play a pivotal role in the Arab and Muslim worlds, have failed at the development and security levels not only locally and regionally, but within the wider Arab milieu as well. The first cause of this failure is the ruling families' narrow and short-term focus on personal interests, which made them marginalise the region's people, squander their resources and void their countries' institutions of their spirit and ability to perform. Addressing conditions in the Arab countries, a Western observer commented on this political conundrum saying, "Only by altering the political logic that sustains these regimes, moving from a base built on discretionary distribution of patronage to one grounded in the legitimacy that comes with procedural legality and political accountability, will political elites ever be persuaded to undertake economic reform."[1]

These countries' education systems produce large numbers of ill-equipped and unproductive graduates. This has led to large numbers of new graduates and soaring rates of unemployment in countries brimming with migrant workers. The judiciary has become the stick that these governments wield against their people and the means by which they tighten their grip on society and its future, while the media has become a tool that destroys values and morality and acts as propaganda for failing regimes, and the same could be said about all other institutions. These regimes failed because of their narrow perspective that fell short of forming a new generation loyal to its country, its Arab identity and Islam. They instilled in it the sense that if it does not pursue quick profit and those who can make it possible, they are doomed to be second-class citizens in their own homeland, and be overtaken by ignorant people, hypocrites, mercenaries, foreigners and those who turn in their orbit and curry favour with them. This, of course, cannot and will not create either a strong nation or a population that stands solidly behind its government, because internal solidarity requires freedom, participation, justice and sound criteria for choosing one's own leaders, and delineating the country's policies. These countries have therefore failed domestically, and their failure has spread to the wider Gulf and Arab regions. Naturally, however, the other face of this "profit at all cost" mentality is subservience to the outside world and adopting its agenda, even if it contradicts or conflicts with the people's agenda in the Gulf, and the Arab and Muslim worlds.

This is how these governments progressed from voicing empty slogans concerning development and liberation, to openly flaunting their subservience and their despotic rule. This is also how they became part of the siege on the Palestinian people who dared to rebel and take charge of their own destiny, armed only with their will, stones, blood and patience in the face of hunger, not to mention the unspeakable abuses that were, and are still, being inflicted on them today. Yet, despite the spirit that this valiant people has instilled in the hearts and minds of the Arab nation's population, the cost of despotism and the comfort it draws from foreign protection have kept escalating. In recent years, the region has witnessed an increase in the number of foreign bases on its soil, the occupation and destruction of Iraq, a drop in all Arab development indicators and the resurgence of Iran which seized the opportunity to become an influential player in the Arab region as a whole.[2] Iran's resurgence has attracted the attention of Jordan's King Abdullah who, while addressing a number of Western journalists, referred to the new Iranian zone of influence as "the Shi'a Crescent".[3] It would have been apt had the King of Jordan wondered who was to blame for Iran's infiltration into the Arab world; was it not the same Arab governments who allied themselves, unconditionally, with the United States, worked against the interests of their own people and forfeited the inalienable rights of Palestinian people? The region is still plagued by recurrent crises, and it seems that there will be no light at the end of the tunnel as long as these regimes remain in power. We still believe, however, that God has the power to change this nation's fate if it manages to change its own behaviour, positions and practices, in obedience to His words: "That is because God would never change a favour which He has conferred upon a people until they change their own condition, because God is All Hearing and Knowing."[4]

Perhaps the spirit infusing the current popular uprisings or intifadas taking place across the Arab world is a sign of such a change. These uprisings, though they might differ in character, without exception call for putting an end to autocracy, poverty, humiliation and foreign domination.[5] The revolutions and intifadas and the demands for reform that have taken place without foreign intervention since late 2010 are testament to the fact that the peoples of this region have the will and ability to change their circumstances. Moreover, it ought to be emphasised that the desired change in our region must be implemented using peaceful means and with the least human cost, no matter how much the autocratic regimes try to drag the region into civil wars. Consequently, it is inevitable that we should reconsider all three sides of the triangle, namely hereditary succession, oil and foreign powers, as they have brought neither sustainable development nor stability. Change requires a transformation in all three sides of the triangle, from heredity to participation, from dependence on oil to dependence on productive human beings, and from seeking dependence and refuge in foreign protection to Arab and Islamic integration. We wish to conclude this book with some of the key aspects of this subject and perhaps it may serve as a salutary lesson for those who wish to learn it.

Hence, for this change to take place, what is firstly required is that countries of the region, both the people and their leaders, grasp the most important lessons of the Arab Spring, the ripples of which are still being felt. Then they should work over the next few years on three main axes, axes that complement one another yet none can achieve the desired objective without help from the other two. These are: the axis of domestic reforms in each GCC and Arab country; the axis of integration at all levels, with GCC unity as the centre-point, followed by Arab unity ,and join Arab economic and security cooperation; and, finally, the axis of an active international role, mainly in international organisations where Arab and Muslim causes need defending, like other countries defend theirs. However, before entering into the various reforms required, we must examine the repercussions of the Arab Spring and how far it has changed the expectations and hopes of the Arab people, from the Gulf to the ocean, to see if the process of reform is consistent with the data emanating from this "Spring".

CHAPTER FIFTEEN

Repercussions of the Arab Spring

The youth uprisings that have erupted across the Arab world in recent years were set in motion after Mohamed Bouazizi's death in Tunisia in December 2010. Suddenly, the Bouazizi incident triggered what could be called an Arab political tsunami against the autocracy, corruption and injustice which had burdened the Arab world from the ocean to the Gulf. More than that was the revolutionary fever Bouazizi released from his small town of Sidi Bouzid which began to move from one Arab country to another, as if to affirm the extent to which Arabs could influence each other and the degree of their common suffering and hopes. Despite the fact that this wave of revolts has not yet ended and their results are unknown, we are certain that they express the feelings of millions of Arab people. That makes us optimistic that the final outcome will be positive even if this takes a while because these uprisings have broken the apathy forced by the autocratic regimes and started to move the silent, stagnant waters in which Arab citizens have been drowning for so long. These uprisings are distinct from past protests in the Arab world because they are popular and not monopolised by one strata of society at the expense of others, whether civilian or military. Thus, they have overcome the failures of previous revolts, which did not achieve the desired renaissance, and are close to declaring that the people's need for civilian or military guardians is over.[1]

Before we discuss the repercussions of the Arab Spring, and the demands for reform that accompanied them, we must first talk about the political and social roots of these uprisings. For the past decade, the Arab governments, be they hereditary regimes or republics, have wanted their relationship with their people to be one based on the seizure of political freedoms in exchange for providing some social justice through jobs and support for essential resources, like gas and fuel, as well as health and education services. Oil was the most important driver of this relationship whether directly, as is the case in the Gulf states, or indirectly in the form of worker remittances, tourism, loans and aid, as is the case in the non oil-producing Arab countries. Nevertheless, over time these governments were unable to adhere even to this "deficient social contract" since they failed to implement changes in their productive structures through serious development within the framework of Arab economic integration, in order to encompass the growing population numbers and raise their standard of living. Even the economic growth which these Arab countries were experiencing now and then as a result of the oil booms did not translate into an increase in jobs for their citizens, or help establish a productive middle class, as most of the jobs generated by this growth demanded low skills for low pay. This phenomenon, namely the concurrence of economic growth with high rates of unemployment, is not limited to the oil states. Indeed, it is also a widespread phenomenon in the other Arab countries. For example, in Jordan 63 per cent of new jobs in the first period of the twenty-first century were for foreign workers.[2] Certainly, this phenomenon has worsened in the non oil-producing Arab countries in recent years for two reasons. Firstly, Arab workers in the Gulf Arab countries have been replaced by foreign labour, especially those of Asian origin. Secondly, the negative effects which resulted from the global financial crisis made Western countries bring in fewer Arab workers, particularly those from North Africa. In addition to the above, the third oil boom has led to an increase in the costs of subsidisation and rates of inflation in the major Arab countries. These have caused a further decline in the living standards of Arab citizens.[3] If we add this development failure to the worsening size of corruption amongst the political leadership of the Arab countries in recent years, the absence of political freedom and the unwise application of the IMF policies which have aggravated economic and social problems, we should not be surprised by the eruption of protests seen across the Arab world since late 2010.[4]

For many reasons, which we will state in their natural context, not only have the repercussions of the Arab Spring varied but so too the responses by the region's countries, from one regime to another and from one state to another, even from one time period to another. Moreover, these repercussions have started to influence the balance of power in the region. Therefore, our analysis in this chapter will focus on the reverberations of the Arab Spring for all the Arab hereditary regimes and republics as well as on the balance of power in the region.

First: Hereditary governments

Until now, the hereditary governments have been able to temporarily contain the waves of the Arab Spring and avoid any fundamental improvements in their relationships with their peoples. The reason for that is not because Islam is opposed to democracy, nor is it because Arab culture and traditions have made them more accepting of autocratic rulers, as some Orientalists and others would claim. In fact, the majority of Muslims in the world, whether in Turkey, Indonesia, Albania, Senegal or India, live under systems of government that are elected and accountable to the people.[5] Moreover, a number of monarchies have fallen in the Arab world since the 1950s, for example, in Egypt in 1952, Iraq in 1958, Yemen 1962 and Libya in 1969.[6] Hence, there are other factors that have made the Arab hereditary regimes less susceptible to the Arab Spring than the republics and all of these factors are liable to change in the future. These include: the abundance or dearth of resources, external military or material interference or its absence, the size of the population and its influence on the formation of a narrow bloc demanding reforms and the size of the ruling family itself and its effect on curbing the decisions of the head of the state in the face of opposition. Another factor is the extent to which the sectarian dimension is prominent, as will be explained in the following section.[7]

1. Bahrain

The movement which began in the middle of February 2011 in Bahrain was the biggest in the history of the country. That may be due to the political congestion Bahrain was already suffering because of the restrictions imposed on electoral participation and the nature of its sectarian composition. The arrival of the Arab Spring uprisings ignited the feelings of all sides and raised the ceiling of opposition, especially among the Shi'a. A section of them established an alliance in March 2011 demanding a republic and the fall of the existing regime. However, the opposition, overstating their own strength, refused the negotiations suggested by Crown Prince Salman in March that included certain positive proposals. This may have lost Bahrain an historical opportunity at the time, even if the royal camp continued to face strong opposition from hardliners within the family.[8]

King Hamd Bin Isa Al Khalifa had justified his government's stance towards the demonstrations in a statement issued on 19 April 2011 in the *Washington Times*, saying, "Unfortunately, the legitimate demands of the opposition were hijacked by extremist elements with ties to foreign governments in the region."[9] Thus, the regime's fear of this opposition increased and it used excessive force as well as playing the sectarian card. The issue began to spill out from Bahrain to the rest of the Gulf region. When Iran began using threatening and provocative language against Bahrain, the other Gulf countries, particularly Saudi Arabia, the UAE and Kuwait, responded by sending the Peninsula Shield Force to secure Bahrain's internal front. The big powers, especially the United States, were not out of the picture altogether since they were conflicted between their interests and their public image in the Arab world. The news leaked out that early in the crisis the United States had asked the King of Bahrain to resort to a political solution, and this is what actually happened. However, Saudi Arabia then persuaded the Bahraini government to allow the entry of the Peninsula Force and promised to provide the country with financial aid. The reason for this may have been the Saudi government's lack of desire to move towards reform and especially the regime's fear that the contagion of the popular movement in Bahrain would spread to the Shi'a of Saudi Arabia. According to some sources, the Shi'a account for approximately 15 per cent of the population and are con-centrated in the eastern region of the kingdom where the oil fields are located. Therefore, the negotiations between the Bahraini government and the opposition were aborted, even though the contagion of the movement had in fact already reached the eastern region of Saudi Arabia.[10] Furthermore, the United States did not issue any statement opposing the Peninsula Force's deployment in Bahrain. This gave the impression that it supported this step because it feared Iran's role, or because, as the British Prime Minister David Cameron stated in a television interview on Western policy in the region, "Bahrain is not Syria."[11] In addition to the use of the security option of confronting demonstrations, the Bahraini government promised its people new residents and projects that would employ about 20,000 citizens in the interior ministry. Similarly, the governments of the GCC promised Bahrain aid estimated at $10 billion for the next ten years.[12]

Thus, the Arab Spring and the accompanying demonstrations, suppressions and obstruction of the political process put Bahrain into a vortex of tension which does not seem to be easily dealt with. This is the opinion of the former American ambassador to Bahrain, Ronald Neuman, who said: "Bahrain seems stuck in a vicious circle. The government and royal family will not fall, but nei-ther can they suppress the protests. Without reform, the economy stagnates. While Gulf Cooperation Council (GCC) aid will keep it afloat, the violence prevents foreign investment, and the economy is unable to generate the jobs needed to offer young Bahrain a better future. Massive mutual distrust between opposition and government, deepening communal divisions, and splits within both the royal family and the opposition that weaken leadership all combine to make compromise difficult."[13] In any case, we believe the future of Bahrain remains dependent on the ability of the Bahraini government to find a political solution that will tone down the sectarian discourse, avoid the internal strife that has befallen Lebanon and Iraq, restore the cycle of economic activity to what it was before this recent crisis and dispel the spectre of regional interventions. The starting point for this solution may be the reform initiative proposed by the crown prince during the first months of the crisis.[14]

2. Kuwait

In the context of our previous discussion on institutions, we emphasised the pioneering role of the Kuwaiti experiment and acknowledged its many flaws. We highlighted the fact that the way forward for this model should be a more corrective relationship with the ruling family that is to the benefit of the Kuwaiti people. The events of the Arab Spring confirmed the importance of this experiment and the role it has played in advancing the culture of Kuwaiti society and the people's awareness of their rights that they should insist on demanding. The Kuwaiti youth, together with the national opposition, were well aware, even prior to the Arab Spring, that their political experiment was largely failing as a result of the parliamentary bloc's inability to form political parties or governments and that these failures impacted on the development track in Kuwait. In the years 2005 and 2006, there was a youth movement that called for women's participation and lowering the number of electoral districts from twenty-five to five to reduce the chances of electoral fraud. The youth of this movement were able to make the government submit to their demands.

In November 2011, the youth and the opposition stormed the Kuwaiti National Assembly protesting against corruption and vote rigging. This forced the resignation of the prime minister, Shaikh Nasir al-Sabah.[15] The Assembly elections in 2012 brought in what the government had not wished for, namely a majority of victors from the Sunni Islamist current and with them the tribal youth. This group was able to form what they termed the "Majority Bloc" which numbered thirty-five MPs, and it seemed as if they could be a pressure group against the government and their supporters.[16] However, the Kuwaitis were surprised when 120 days after the election of this parliament, the constitutional court decided in its June 2012 ruling that the recent parliamentary elections had been unconstitutional. The court dissolved the parliament, and thereby its powerful opposition, returning matters to how they had been before.

The process of dissolving parliament in February 2012 was a new stage in the Arab Spring. Tens of thousands of Kuwaitis gathered at the Kuwaiti roundabout in front of the National Assembly which became the Tahrir Square for

Kuwaitis.[17] Since the old parliament that was reinstated by the decision of the constitutional court never held session, the Emir dissolved it in October of the same year and called for parliamentary elections at the start of December 2012.[18] The strikes continued and on 15 October there was a demonstration at the roundabout which security forces dispersed. Here appeared the symbol of the Arab Spring, Musallam al-Barrak, who had obtained the most votes for a single candidate in the parliamentary elections in February 2012. At this demonstration, he expressed the Kuwaitis' desire by telling the Emir of Kuwait: "We will not allow you, your highness, to take Kuwait into the abyss of autocracy ... We no longer fear your prisons and your riot batons."[19] The Emir of Kuwait replied to the protestors on 19 October 2012 with a speech, the most important part of which was as follows: "We will not accept the chaos on the streets and the mob riots that paralyse the movement of life and work in the country. We will not allow the seeds of discord in our good country. We will not accept the culture of violence and chaos to spread among our peaceful people. We will not accept our loyal youth to be misled by delusions and lies. We will not accept the will of the nation to be hijacked by hollow voices and false heroism."[20] Afterwards, the Emir of Kuwait issued a decision to change the election law to allow the voter to choose one candidate instead of four candidates, as was the case in the past.[21] This decision only further provoked the opposition since they announced their intention to boycott these elections in which tens of thousands of Kuwaitis were also participating.[22] Only the groups supporting the government participated in the elections including the Shi'a who obtained seventeen out of fifty seats, the largest share ever in their history. In the elections of February they had won only seven seats.[23]

After the elections the demonstrations continued and the government persisted in its use of the security forces. The opposition began to secretly organise themselves and in March 2013 they set up a new front for action called the "Popular Action Movement" in order to demand the formation of an elected government, a return to the former election law and formation of political parties.[24] From the above, it is clear that a large section of the people had decided to make the Kuwaiti Spring an opportunity to push the static parliamentary experiment forwards somewhat for the sake of Kuwait's future. Therefore, their slogan was "the generosity of the nation" and they were not fooled by the "carrot" used by the government at the start of the Arab Spring when the salaries of employees were raised by about 115 per cent, at an estimated cost of more than $1 billion, and monetary aid for the citizens reached around 5 billion Kuwaiti dinars, in addition to the promise to subsidise certain foods for free for roughly fourteen months.[25] There is no doubt that these opposition efforts will come to fruition in the coming years because governments come and go but the people remain. The sacrifices which the Kuwaiti people offered and still offer, as well as the government's insistence on using violence and continuing its autocracy, will make a growing number of Kuwaiti people stand by the opposition and thus change the balance of power between the two sides for the benefit of change.

3. Oman

The Oman Spring was the first to take place in the GCC states as the demonstrations began in January 2011 in the region of Sohar and during the same month spread to other regions, such as Muscat, Sur and even Dhofar. Sohar saw the largest number of demonstrations and strikes in which the Omanis protested against the projects that were concentrated in this region and were polluting the environment and depleting the groundwater as well as not providing jobs for the Omanis themselves. After two demonstrators were killed, the Sultan ordered that the demonstrations be left to gather wherever they wanted.[26] Sultan Qaboos' response was quicker than that of the other governments of the region since he dismissed around two-thirds of the ministers, ordered the minimum wage of 150 Omani riyals to be raised to 200 riyals a month and offered 150 riyals a month as compensation for the unemployed. The government also announced its intention to provide 50,000 new jobs.[27] In view of the insufficient resources in Oman, the rich states in the GCC announced their intention to offer aid worth $10 billion, similar to the amount they promised Bahrain.[28] With these steps, the Omani government was able to meet some of the demands of the workers who had the main role in the demonstrations. They returned to their homes, leaving a group of intellectuals alone to demand fundamental reforms. This weakened the power of the Omani Spring after that and gave the government an incentive to contain it. The situation worsened with the arrest of the intellectuals who had insisted on continuing to demand political reforms.[29]

4. Saudi Arabia

In Saudi Arabia, there were demonstrations in the eastern (Sharqiyah) region that coincided with the demonstrations in Bahrain while the rest of the kingdom made demands for reform. The most important of these demands were for the formation of an Islamic party, the establishment of a constitutional monarchy and elections for members of the Shura Council. However, all these demands were met with refusal or the imprisonment of the individuals who had made them.[30] The Saudi government has succeeded until now in circumventing any serious political reforms because they played several cards at a time when the opposition failed to create the participation for which it was aiming. The government pressured both Sunni and Shi'a religious scholars into condemning the demonstrations, even prohibiting them. The chief mufti of Saudi Arabia described the youth uprisings as sedition (*fitnah*) and their supporters as "corrupt" in addition to ruling that the demonstrations were prohibited. In the Sharqiyah region, some of the Shi'a religious scholars, including Hassan al-Saffar and Abdullah al-Khunaizi, demanded that the demonstrators end their protests.[31]

The government was also able to buy off some of the intellectuals who exaggerated the danger of the Arab Spring for the country, which in their minds is usually connected to the security of the regime, without any consideration for the rest of the population. The official media had a prominent role in misleading many sections of society into believing that the youth who were calling for a gathering on 11 March 2011, or what they called the "Day of Longing", were Shi'a and followers of Iran. This discouraged many Sunni youth in the kingdom from participating that day, and the only person who attended, Khalid al-Juhani, was arrested and sentenced the following year.[32] In addition to the use of the media, scholars and intellectuals, the government resorted to the security forces. This happened in Sharqiyah in the demonstrations which began on 17 February and continued to 14 March when the Peninsula Force entered Bahrain. The Shi'a demonstrated in solidarity with the Shi'a in Bahrain and demanded the release of prisoners. Some Western sources, relying it seems on the estimates of the Shi'a themselves, indicate that the number of demonstrators in the Shi'a regions in Sharqiyah reached 10,000 on the 18 and 19 March 2011.[33] The number of prisoners of conscience in Saudi Arabia continued to rise and the opposition estimates the number of prisoners to be around 30,000 at the present time, whereas the government says that the actual number is a third of this figure.[34] Whichever of the figures we take, this is a clear indicator of the crisis which the Saudi regime is undergoing and reveals its excessive dependence on the security option in confronting the reform demands which preceded the Arab uprisings and also accompanied them. In our opinion, this increasing number of prisoners of conscience is what pushed Abdul Aziz Fawzan, a member of the Human Rights Commission in the kingdom, to say that the issue of prisoners was a time-bomb that must be deactivated before it explodes.[35]

The campaign of arrests has continued in recent years and even targeted women in the city of Buraidah which is considered the heart of the Saudi state. On 5 January 2013, eleven women from Buraidah were arrested at a demonstration to demand the release of prisoners.[36] At the start of March, some men and women tried to assemble a kind of gathering in Buraidah again and around 161 of them were arrested.[37] The Saudi government has also used all forms of material incentives. In February and March 2011, it announced that it had allocated an amount estimated at $130 billion to be spent in the coming years in several ways including creating 60,000 positions in the interior ministry and building around 500,000 residential units, fixing the minimum wage at 3,000 Saudi riyals, offering bonuses to public sector workers, establishing a compensation system for the unemployed and increasing some of the budgets for social institutions, including religious institutions.[38]

5. UAE

In March 2011, 133 of the elite of Emirati society presented a petition to the president of the state Shaikh Khalifa bin Zayed al Nahyan. They demanded that all the members of the next Federal National Council should be elected and that it should have oversight and legislative powers instead of its current consultative role. Despite the fact that the demands in this petition did not go far, the government began an unjustified escalation and undertook a proactive campaign to discourage any sympathy for them.[39] The elected councils of teachers and lawyers were exchanged for new appointed ones, then the nationalities of some of those demanding reform were withdrawn and some activists on social media were arrested, including Dr Nasser bin Ghaith and Ahmad Mansur al-Shehhi.[40] Afterwards began a campaign of arrests among the members of the reform society which was established at the start of the 1970s. The number of prisoners from this society reached around ninety-four in April 2013 and their trial took place in July 2013. International observers were not permitted to attend the trials and while some of them were acquitted, sixty-nine of them were sentenced to prison for periods ranging between seven and fifteen years. Human Rights Watch condemned the accusations directed at those individuals and the manner in which the trials were carried out and demanded their release. Joe Stork, deputy director of Human Rights Watch's Middle East and North Africa division, said, "The conviction of 69 government critics is a low point for the UAE's worsening human rights record and its serious abuse of due process rights."[41] Human rights activists documented around thirty cases where the relatives of prisoners were prevented from travelling. During this time, an internet law issued in 2012 that prevented any discussion of the government was put into effect. As a result of this law, a nineteen-year-old youth, Muhammad al-Zumir, was sentenced to prison for three years and fined 500,000 dirhams because of his tweets on the social network Twitter in which he spoke about the conditions of the political prisoners. While global human rights organisations expressed their surprise and condemnation of these show trials, some local human rights advocates and others subservient to the prevailing culture in the UAE did not hesitate to defend these rulings, describing them as "transparent and clear" or "legal and not political". All that was, it seems, to the satisfaction of the government.[42] Like the rest of the GCC states at the start of the Arab Spring, the Emirati government announced an increase in wages by varying percentages which reached 70 per cent for military veterans and approximately 20 per cent for social security bonuses. Similarly it announced its allocation of around $2.7 billion to help the citizens who were unable to pay their debts.[43]

6. Qatar

There were no obvious manifestations of the Arab Spring in Qatar as there were in a number of the GCC states, with some exceptions. The first was represented by the case of the poet Muhammed Najib al-Ajami, known as Ibn al-Dib, was sentenced in November 2012 to fifteen years in prison. He had composed a poem called "Tunisian Jasmine" expressing his feelings towards the Arab Spring and implicitly criticising the Gulf rulers, and one verse read, "We are all Tunisia in the face of the repressive elites!"[44] The second exception was the publication of two books on the Arab Spring in 2012. The first, by a group of Qatari citizens led by the researcher and activist Dr Ali Khalifa al-Kawari, was published in Arabic in Beirut and proposed a broad agenda for reform.[45] The second book, published in English, was written by one of the members of the ruling family in Qatar, Muhammad al-Thani, a former minister for the economy and trade. In it, he called for gradual reforms to avoid unrest.[46] Some researchers attribute the Arab Spring's lack of influence on Qatar to a combination of relative security, caused by the presence of the American base, the abundance of oil and gas resources that enable the Qatari government to absorb any signs of dissent, and the country's social harmony which is devoid of any sectarian tension. Finally, there is a leadership whose vision is founded on a concern for Arab issues and moves with the trends of the Arab people, using the Al Jazeera channel to cover the most important events of the Arab Spring.[47]

7. Jordan

The Jordanian demonstrations began in December 2010, at the start of the Arab Spring. Like the other Arab peoples, the Jordanians called for political and social reforms and fighting against corruption. The demands came from all spectra of the previous opposition. They were joined by a new faction of Jordanian youth called "Al-Harak", most of which was made up of citizens from the east bank, usually considered loyal to the regime.[48] The regime found itself compelled to carry out some reforms to defuse the demonstrations and avoid their escalation to the level of an intifada or uprising, especially as it did not have huge resources to buy more loyalties. It made some changes to the constitution and in January 2013 there were parliamentary elections which were described as fair, contrary to the expectations of the Islamist opposition which boycotted them, and the participation by registered voters reached 56.5 per cent. For the first time, the king chose the prime minister and the formation of the government in consultation with members of parliament.[49] However, these fair elections are useless if the election law is unjust or if the elected parliament is without any worthwhile powers. The elections took place on the basis of the law of "one vote" whereby each voter votes for one of the candidates in his region. This is an election law intended to prevent any change in the current balance of power between the opposition and the regime. This election law has previously led to the rural areas outweighing the urban ones, and outweighing the voters in the east of Jordan at the expense of the Jordanians of Palestinian origin. Furthermore, the previous elections saw much fraud and produced weak parliaments that could not gain the respect and trust of the Jordanian electorate. Even if this election law had not existed, the current parliament is a kind of ineffective one as it is still under the control of the king. He appoints all the members of the House of Senate in accordance with Article 36 of the constitution and has the right to dissolve the House of Representatives in accordance with Article 34. Likewise, he appoints the prime minister and has the right to remove him.[50]

This unstable relationship between the Jordanian regime and its people is reflected in its foreign policy. Despite the fact that the regime has viewed the Syrian crisis as a refugee crisis on the Jordanian borders with over half a million refugees which constitutes an economic and security burden for its country, it is a crisis of Iranian extension in the region or what has been termed the "Shi'a crescent". However, the Jordanian government has not been able to extend to thinking about the possibility that the fall of al-Assad would lead to an Islamic regime allied with the Islamist opposition in Jordan and balanced against its rule.[51]

King Abdullah II has behaved towards the events in Egypt using the same logic. No sooner had the Egyptian army removed the elected government of Morsi and taken over power, than the king made a special visit to Egypt, followed by a visit to Jordan by the acting Egyptian president Adly Mansour in October 2013 during his visits to other Arab countries to gain support for the Egyptian coup.[52]

On the level of relations with the Gulf Arab countries, the Jordanian regime has not hesitated to accept the proposal put forward by the late Saudi king

Abdullah bin Abd al-Aziz in the midst of the events of the Arab Spring to include both Jordan and Morocco in the bloc of the GCC. In view of the fact that there is no consensus among the governments of the GCC on this idea, this explains why this has not yet been implemented. Of course, in principle there is no objection to this idea of a union, particularly given that the GCC states are connected in terms of their established economic and security relationships to the kingdoms of Jordan and Morocco and more gains may be achieved for both sides in the case of establishing a council of eight hereditary states. Nevertheless, the timing of this proposal indicates that considerations about the survival of the hereditary regimes and the maintenance of their current position is the primary motivation behind it. Thus, the danger of this plan is hidden from the view of the region's people.[53] For example, the Jordanian regime has been eager for "special" international relations with the United States and Europe which will serve mainly to deal with its people and are founded on trade, tourism and the so-called "war on terror", as well as the peace treaty with Israel, the exchange of information on regional issues and the acceptance of the IMF recipes. These have led to what seems like constant unrest, such as the riots in November 2012,[54] even given that Jordan is one of biggest recipients of American economic and military aid if measured per capita by country.[55]

8. Morocco

Morocco saw demonstrations in fifty-three cities beginning on 20 February 2011 under the slogan "down with despotism" and these were the biggest in the country's history. The demands focused on establishing a parliamentary monarchy and separating authority and accountability. However, these demonstrations only continued for a few months because of conflicts between the different currents and the proactive position taken by the Moroccan government. King Muhammad VI delivered a speech on television on 9 March 2011 which included a promise to carry out "comprehensive constitutional reforms" relating to the rule of law, an independent judiciary and an elected government that expressed the will of the Moroccan people. On 17 June, the king announced a draft of the new constitution and it was put to a referendum in July 2011. The percentage in agreement won with 98.5 per cent with the participation rate estimated at around 73 per cent. If these results are accurate, that is, if there was no fraud, this shows the popular belief that the new constitution was an important step towards democracy in Morocco. Parliamentary elections took place on the basis of this constitution in November 2011. The Justice and Development Party, which has Islamist leanings, won 27 per cent of the seats, or about double the percentage won by the Independence Party which had formed a government before the reforms of the Arab Spring.[56] Although the production of these reforms was outstanding in itself, there were those who remained sceptical about their seriousness because a careful reading of the articles of the constitution confirms that these are not real reforms. According to this reading, the prime minister who is appointed by the king according to the parliamentary majority may propose the appointment of ministers, as well as their removal, but the final decision remains with the king himself. Moreover, the king presides over the meeting of the Council of Ministers which is the very meeting where the key decisions are adopted according to Article 49. The right given by Article 104 to the prime minister to dissolve parliament is limited also by having to consult with the king who has the authority according to Article 51 to dissolve parliament, just as a decision like this can only be taken in a sitting of the council of ministers presided by the king himself.[57]

The articles of the constitution relating to the independence of the judiciary are in no better state than the articles for choosing the government. The most important reason for the protesters' demand for the independence of the judiciary stems from the fact that the Moroccan Minister of Justice also chairs the Council managing judicial affairs, whether that relates to the appointment, promotion, transfer, punishment or other issues. According to article 107 of the new constitution, the Ministry of Justice was separated from the institution that manages judicial affairs. However, this decision, in the opinion of some observers, is not enough to achieve the independence of the judiciary. This is for the simple reason that the Minister of Justice is the head of the institution of judicial affairs and manages its meetings in his status as the deputy of the king who is still president of this institution, meaning that it is still not independent.[58]

Yet, these drawbacks and others do not diminish the fact that the Moroccan experiment remains the best of the Arab experiments, even if it is still far from being a constitutional monarchy, one of the most important characteristics of which is the presence of an elected parliament that can form the government or bring it down. No doubt there are factors which have helped to create these incomplete reforms in addition to popular pressure, including the paucity of resources and the partial application of a taxation system as well as the freedom which the king has in decision-making given that the ruling family in Morocco is not large, so does not limit the king.[59] These reforms also contradict the advice offered by the French government during the height of the demonstrations to refrain from making reforms, as revealed by some sources, especially after France lost Ben Ali in Tunisia. We wish that all the Arab rulers would deafen their ears to the advice of Western governments and listen instead to the voices of their people.[60]

Second: Republics

The Arab republics were the actual arena for the events of the Arab Spring and were most affected by its events. The repercussions on these republics varied but included the rapid fall of the regime or its leader, plus either the relatively smooth transitional stage, as in Tunisia, or a difficult stage of change, as in Libya and Yemen, with signs of a breakthrough here and there, or the start of a transitional phase whose course was distorted, as in the case of Egypt. Finally, among these regimes there was one that directed its military arsenals towards its own people and changed the Spring into a catastrophic civil war, namely Syria. In the following section, we will examine the tracks of the Arab Spring in the Arab republics which witnessed significant events and the factors that led to these various tracks, foremost of which is the military's attitude toward the popular uprisings and the ability of the elites to compromise after the fall of the regime, in addition to the role of external financial and military factors.

1.   Tunisia

The first spark of the Tunisian revolt or the uprising was Mohamed Bouazizi, a man seeking a living. However, the regime regarded even this right as too much and prevented him from travelling with his cart to sell his goods to support his family. Thus, he felt his only choice was to immolate himself on 17 December 2010, and it was as if he had lit a fuse in the body of autocracy perched on the chests of the people of the entire Arab nation. Suddenly, the heirs to the revolutionary poet Abu al-Qassim al-Shabi[61] became dedicated to recovering their liberty. They knew that freedom needs a solid will to feed it. Hence, the uprising spread from the city of Sidi Bouzid in central Tunisia to Gafsa in the south, then to the north, and the sons of Tunisia were chanting the same slogan, "Yes to bread and water. No to Ben Ali."[62] These events were followed by the workers' announcement of a strike on 12 January 2011. The head of the regime tried to appease the people with empty promises that were not regarded as being genuine, while at the same time he ordered the army to intervene and fire on demonstrators after his security forces failed to contain the crowds. However, the army's chief of staff, General Rashid Ammar, was one of the makers of the revolution, although he did not know that yet. He not only refused to fire on the demonstrators but threatened to confront the security forces if they continued to kill the protesters. There was nothing left for Ben Ali except exile or prison, so he chose exile in Saudi Arabia. This moment provides a history lesson that the position of the army's leadership towards its people should be to protect them and return to their barracks.[63]

After these events came the transitional period with its complications. President Ben Ali was ousted on 27 February 2011 and his prime minister was replaced by Beji Caid Essebsi, who had not been part of Ben Ali's regime and was the former foreign minister under President Bourguiba. In October 2011, the council of deputies, or the legislative assembly, was elected. The majority of its parties were opposed to the former regime and the political game began between the civilians themselves, without the intervention of the army or security forces. Under these circumstances, the council formed the government and began to write the constitution. In spite of the slow pace that dominated the transition process, the disagreements which happened during it and the attempt by some groups to resort to violence, nonetheless the Tunisian elites, led by the Ennahda party, embarked boldly into the experiment of interaction and dialogue and mediation with the Workers Union within a religiously and culturally harmonious society.

A movement similar to the Egyptian Tamarod movement almost emerged in Tunisia to confront the Islamists with the army. However, seeing what the Egyptian army did in Rabaa Square convinced this group of the importance of excluding the military from politics, as was historically the case with the Tunisian army.[64] The result of these combined factors was parliament's approval of the constitution in January 2014 in the hope that the legislative elections would be held before the end of 2014. Therefore, Tunisia is at the forefront of the Arab Spring as well as achieving the transitional phase.[65] However, there are major economic and security challenges facing the new system that require persevering work, not only domestically, but also regionally and internationally.[66]

2. Egypt

There is no doubt that the military coup which took place in Egypt in July 2013 is a distortion of the aims of the revolution of 25 January 2011 and that it has put Egypt on an unknown track. We believe that there are three reasons that led to this deviation. The first is that the Egyptian elites who participated in the 2011 uprising failed to create the minimum agreement which would have put Egypt, together with the Arab nation, on the path to the desired renaissance, whatever the obstacles. The second reason lies in the army's insistence on preserving its historical legitimacy and interests at the expense of the Egyptian people and their revolutionary legitimacy embodied by 25 January. Lastly, the external factor represented by Gulf money and the West's silence over the coup played a major role in this departure from the aims of the youth's revolution.

A consideration of how these factors interacted explains how Egypt arrived at its present state. The beginnings of the Arab Spring materialised in Tahrir Square where the revolutionary youth from all sides flocked on 25 January, in addition of course to the gatherings that happened in Suez and other cities. The slogans for freedom and justice did not differ from those raised by the revolutionaries of Tunisia. As in Tunisia, when the security forces of Mubarak's regime failed to stop the demonstrations, the army refused to use their weapons. They forced Mubarak to step down on 11 February due to their reluctance at this stage to confront the protestors and also due to their wish to block Mubarak's instructions to hand over power to his son Gamal. As some believe, the army leadership feared Gamal's economic policies since these would compete with their own interests.[67]

However, the comparison between the tracks of the Tunisian and the Egyptian revolutions ends here since the Egyptian uprising entered a dark period thereafter as the army became an essential part of the political game. It pursued the "militarisation of politics" and prevented the Egyptian elites from creating participation through trial and error, even if this took a long time, and then reaching a similar compromise to the Tunisian one. It is worth mentioning that the meetings of the Tunisian elites had preceded the fall of Ben Ali's regime years in advance and this is what prevailed in creating participation and reassuring the elites that their cooperation together was better than cooperation with the regime or the army. However, the Egyptian elites lost this continuity and this enabled the army to perform the role of mediator in order to maintain authority.[68] Since 11 February 2011, the legislative and executive powers have been in the hands of the Supreme Council of the armed forces which only arrested Mubarak and removed the prime minister because of popular pressure. It supported Ahmad Shafiq in the presidential elections while he was part of the former regime. When Mohamed Morsi was elected as president, the military council continued to practise its independence, then responded to Morsi's opponents in 2013 by arresting the latter and taking over power in his place.

However, the origin of the problem is the elites who ignited the revolution and left the army to reap its fruits. The Muslim Brotherhood's limited political experience led them to confuse popularity and winning a majority of votes with the ability to rule. This demanded a process of building bridges with the other segments of society and finding a form of compromise to reassure the remaining members of society. This was especially in view of the fact that autocracy had taken root in the state including the army, media, security forces and judiciary and is what makes the intensification of mistakes and failures the prevailing issue. The Brotherhood's failure intensified the feeling of other segments of society that the Islamists were using the electoral process to impose their control and not to preserve the rights of all, or to create a rule of compromise, especially after the Brotherhood's coordination with the army in the absence of the other partners in the revolution. Similarly, the Brotherhood showed a lack of commitment to some political promises, such as not to put forward a candidate for the presidency.[69] As for the other parties, from the outset they had felt their opportunities for victory against the Islamic currents were limited. This drove these other parties to pursue the quickest and most futile ways towards the democratic process, namely the strengthening of the army and the remnants of the previous regime and practising the exclusion which they accused the Islamists of, even if that led to aborting the whole process of democratic change, as happened in July 2013. Therefore, they were unable to reach the satisfactory position of the liberals in Tunisia, since their dispute with the Islamists is ongoing but less harmful than their cooperation with the army.[70]

Perhaps Noam Chomsky gave the most accurate description of what occurred in July 2013 and its future ramifications. Despite being a friend of the liberals who supported the June 2013 uprising, he believes that they made a grave mistake by supporting the coup and the army's control of power. In an interview given in September 2013, he confirms that this decision would cause them harm because the army sought to maintain its economic empire and control over politics and would not hesitate to commit more atrocities and violence, especially as it feels that it has popular support. Chomsky ends his interview saying, "I think Egypt is entering into probably one of the darkest periods of its history ... Once you allow a military regime to take over, it's pretty hard to get out. It was hard enough to get rid of Mubarak. This may be harder."[71]

The external factor represented by the governments of the GCC states also had a role in changing the track of the Egyptian revolution. When Ben Ali fled, it seemed as if the Mubarak regime too was on the way to a resounding fall. The governments of the GCC sent many signals to Washington urging them not to abandon it or else they would jeopardise their interests in the oil-producing countries. The United States itself could do little faced with the peaceful youth revolutions that stunned the entire world. Thus, it has continued to pursue its pragmatic policies that rely on authoritarian regimes in the region while paying little attention to the domestic situation in these countries, solely to achieve American interests relating to oil, Israel and the so-called "war on terror". Whenever this colonial approach requires some cosmetic treatment, Western media issue statements on values and human rights but these statements remain worthless in reality and this fact has become etched in the memory of the Arab peoples for over sixty years.[72] The Gulf governments' attempts to contain the revolution continued, especially in Egypt even after Mubarak left the scene. Saudi Arabia offered $4 billion to the military council in Egypt, ostensibly as aid, but it was in fact an attempt to influence the council's decision on the fate of the members of the defunct regime and the future course of Egyptian society as well as its regional policy. However, events after Morsi's election became the most dangerous turn in the track of the Arab Spring. The efforts of the GCC governments, with the exception of Qatar and Oman to some extent, turned to the mobilisation for a counter revolt because some Gulf governments, especially those of Saudi Arabia and the UAE, found that the victory of the Brotherhood movement in Egypt meant the strengthening of Brotherhood Islamist groups in their own countries. Saudi Arabia, which feared the popular model in Iran, regarded the possible emergence of a Sunni Islamist model in Egypt as more dangerous in its significance than the Iranian model. This is particularly because this model was produced by a democratic process that would make the region's people view with suspicion the Saudis' own fragile model which they constantly claim is Islamic when in reality it is a model far from the fundamentals of Islam which emphasise freedom and justice, as we have explained in previous chapters.[73] The majority of Gulf governments were not content with preventing any aid to Morsi and began to incite the army and other forces in Egypt to stage a coup. After the campaign to slander Morsi's government and provoke the opposition in the streets, the defence minister Abdel Fattah al-Sisi, whom Morsi appointed after being elected president, was urged to oust the elected president. The amounts which Saudi Arabia and the UAE paid to help this coup were more than $12 billion.[74]

The events since the coup confirm Chomsky's statement. The army has struck all sectors of the opposition with unprecedented violence, though the lion's share was aimed at the Muslim Brotherhood due to their importance and status as the main competition for the army. Moreover, recent estimates show that there are currently more than 20,000 political prisoners in Egypt. However, if we examine the constitution of January 2014 that resulted from the coup in July 2013 it will confirm the future political track in Egypt. This constitution made the army and the security forces the guardians of Egyptian society instead of Egyptian society being represented by a parliament that questions and holds to account the army, security and other institutions of society, as usually happens in democratic systems. Article 201 of the constitution makes the minister of defence the commander in chief of the armed forces, not the president of the state. Article

203 states that the defence budget should be submitted to the National Defence Council; in other words it excludes the army from any popular oversight by the parliament. Even with respect to the National Defence Council, the budget is mentioned only once, without any details. Finally, Article 152 states the president of the state must not announce war or any military operations unless he consults with the National Defence Council.

Other countries have previously fallen into the trap of "military politics" through which Egypt is passing now, such as Turkey, Portugal, Chile and others. These countries paid a heavy price and lived under a relatively lengthy period of autocracy. However, more salient than that is the fact that there were factors available that helped them to escape military rule. Turkey and Portugal both benefitted from the promised membership of the European Community to reduce the role of the army of politics. Chile was burdened under Pinochet's rule for a long time, until the end of the Cold War became a favourable opportunity for the country's return to democracy. As for Egypt, which after the July 2013 coup became a "security state with a democratic face", its conditions do not resemble those countries that were able to break free of the army and return to democracy.[75] Egypt's return to the track of democracy demands another revolution, which will itself be long until it excludes the army from politics. This revolution will be costly if it occurs but it has become necessary because Egypt's track since the July 2013 coup will impact negatively on the size of the gains which the Arabs will realise from their Spring while striving to revive their renaissance project.

3. Yemen

The demonstrations in Yemen began in Sanaa on 15 January 2011 and then spread to other regions. Ali Abdullah Saleh had promised not to run for the presidency for another term but the Yemeni people, like other Arabs, had come to understand the methods of autocracy. Hence, they demanded Saleh's departure and around 20,000 demonstrators gathered on 3 February, or the "Day of Anger". However, the army continued to support Saleh since its leadership was composed of individuals from his family with the exception of the army general Muhsin al-Ahmar who was leader of a division. He had demanded Saleh's departure in March after the killing of some demonstrators. There is no doubt that his split with his forces created some deterrence in confronting Saleh's forces and prevented the latter from continuing to use violence against protesters. In June, Saleh faced an assassination attempt after which he went to Saudi Arabia for medical treatment. The United States during this time asked him to resign from his position and accept the Gulf initiative that would guarantee him immunity from any subsequent judicial prosecution. However, he initially refused that before agreeing to it on 23 November 2011. Afterwards, his deputy Hadi Mansur was elected as the new president by the agreement on 21 February 2012.[76]

Due to the Gulf initiative and the agreement following it in the transitional stage, Yemen avoided the possibility of entering a civil war. However, this initiative deprived the Yemeni people of the chance to get rid of many of the symbols of the former regime and left the leadership of the road to reform in the hands of the elites themselves. This was the cause of previous crises, whether political or economic. It does not seem that these elites will reach an agreement soon on the completion of the institutions necessary for the transition to a democratic state in the framework of what is called the National Dialogue Committee. The groups representing the south in the national dialogue are a minority that do not represent the south, most of which is not only content to demand reform but refuses the Gulf initiative and insists on separation because of the regime's previous failures to achieve participation and justice. In the north, the Houthis continued to achieve greater control over the areas of north Yemen by using both force and negotiations. They also reject the Gulf initiative and question the legitimacy of the transitional government because it squanders the goals of the revolution. As for the elites in Sanaa, they are still trying to correct the balance of power among themselves in the light of the new facts. Moreover, some of them are unenthusiastic about giving the south decentralisation that will lead to the division of Yemen once again.[77] Given the tug of war which Yemen is undergoing between the rest of its classes, and the economic, social and security problems the Yemenis inherited from Saleh's regime, is it possible for "Yemeni wisdom"[78] to get its people out of this deadlock? We hope so.

4. Libya

In Libya, the uprisings began in the western regions, particularly Benghazi where the oil wells are concentrated. Here too there were many complaints about the former Libyan regime. The unrest started in the shape of demonstrations against corruption and the lack of services, followed by the occupation of some public facilities and clashes with the security forces. Like Ben Ali in Tunisia, Gaddafi tried to contain the protests by offering more food subsidy and increasing wages along with other promises, but to no avail. On 15 February 2011, the situation was exacerbated by the arrest of Fathi Terbil, a lawyer and supporter of human rights, who was representing the families of relatives killed in the Abu Salim prison massacre of 1996. The demonstrators began occupying many state facilities and popular anger spread to Tripoli and Zintan. However, the regime used an unprecedented level of violence against the protestors and managed to regain its control over the oil facilities. The regime would have committed horrific massacres in Benghazi in order to destroy the revolt temporarily but for the shelling that the regime forces faced from the NATO alliance in mid-March. This foreign military intervention played a significant role in deciding the battle in favour of the rebels.[79] This intervention, in which Europe played a major role, though wrapped in humanitarian concerns, was nevertheless essentially to protect Western strategic interests in Libya. Around 97 per cent of Libyan exports, mostly consisting of premium grade oil, were sent to Europe at low cost because of the short distance between Libya and Europe. Libya was considered an important control point for illegal immigration from Africa to the European continent. At the outset of the revolt, Gaddafi had threatened the Europeans with the inundation of this migration if they cooperated with the opposition. Recently the Western countries had tried to avoid the spread of terrorism and all kinds of weapons in this area located south of the Mediterranean and neighbouring the European states.[80]

In the aftermath of NATO's intervention, the National Transitional Council, which had gained control over the eastern regions of Libya, was formed and the rebels continued their expansion. In August, they were able to regain the oil facilities and lift the siege on Misurata. On 22 August, the capital Tripoli was liberated and in October, Gaddafi's hometown of Sirt fell, then Gaddafi himself was killed. The Libyan people discovered how Libya had been reduced to his personality, family and popular committees and not allowed an institutional environment to exist or develop. Gaddafi utilised a policy of "divide and conquer" among the regions and tribes in order to preserve his regime and weaken the army, other than his protective teams. He also deepened the income gap with his preference for some regions that were loyal to him over others. Moreover, he created nominal institutions and incapacitated their work by the control of popular committees over them. He instituted a security regime that instilled fear in the Libyan people by carrying out televised executions. Thus, as soon as his regime fell, the people felt as if they had been born anew, assured of their desire to wipe away the experience of the last forty years or so from their memory. However, the fall of the previous regime put a difficult task before them in building a society out of nothing. This is a huge task, especially the transitional stage, which has not yet ended, having witnessed the emergence of many sides which are trying to fill the void left by the fall of the regime. These include armed groups attempting to maintain security and the gains of the revolution, groups of a regional tendency haggling for local gains or even separation, and groups practising all kinds of smuggling who want to exploit the absence of any centralised authority believing that they cannot respond to local needs. Some of these groups insist on excluding all those with ties to the old regime by ignoring their responsibilities in the past or the need for them to contribute to building the future Libya, and so forth. The majority of these fears are justified, nonetheless they must be dealt with through legitimate channels, not by occupying or destroying institutions, killing the workers in them, or taking over the oil facilities or airports or other practices that have hindered advancement, even if they have not stopped it completely.[81] Rather, there are those who believe that the lack of institutions in Libya is positive since this facilitates the building of a modern state without the need for uprooting or changing the institutions of the "deep state", represented by the army and security forces as well as the class of businessmen and corrupt administrative institutions (as in Egypt and Tunisia). The National Transitional Council of Libya began to pave the way for the transitional process after the killing of at least 15,000 Libyans and the destruction of a large part of the fundamental infrastructure.

On 3 August 2011, the council issued a constitutional declaration and became a provisional government in November. In July 2012, an election was held for the national committee which it was assumed would form the government and write the new constitution. However, objections to its role in writing the constitution forced the National Transitional Council to believe that writing the constitution should be left to an elected and independent body known after that as the Committee of Sixty. The government was formed by the General National Congress in November 2012 but the process for outlining the specifications for forming the committee charged with writing the constitution was sullied by the many disputes, which delayed the election of the members of the Committee of Sixty to February 2014. This is a positive step but the security and development challenges have forced the Libyans to strive from the start to avoid the trap of the rentier economy by building a private sector, training human resources, not allowing labour forces to accumulate in the public sector and passing laws that prevent the emergence of rentier behaviour. This behaviour was a reason for many of the failures of the oil states, as we confirmed in a previous chapter. Moreover, the people also wanted to maintain human rights and offer effective transitional justice and to realise the regional and ethnic balance. No doubt this overall picture of the Libyan track until now calls for cautious optimism because the road to building a free state of Libya is still a long one.[82]

5. Syria

In Syria, the peaceful and non-sectarian demonstrations began on 15 March 2011 but the regime's reaction was violent and five people were killed in the city of Daraa. It seems that was because the regime had already formed a committee in February 2011. This committee's advice was that the regimes of Tunisia and Egypt fell because they both had not used enough violence to suppress their protests.[83] Hence, the Syrian regime imposed the military siege on Daraa in April and its tanks were spread in a number of Syrian cities in later months, using all kinds of violence against the unarmed demonstrators. That occurred at the time in which opposition forces were still inside and outside Syria demanding political reforms and a way to remove Bashar al-Assad from power. The army leadership, especially the Republican Guard Division, the Third Corps, the Fourth Armoured Division and the intelligence forces, continued to support the regime, in contrast to what happened in Tunisia and Egypt, or to a lesser degree in Yemen, with minor splits which formed a core later known as the Syrian Free Army.[84] The regime used everything in its arsenal of weapons against the opposition including guns, tanks and aircraft, and turned to using chemical weapons on 21 August 2013 which killed between 300 and 1300 people, before using barrel bombs and explosives and poisonous gases.[85]

Whilst we strongly condemn any use of chemical weapons, we are surprised by some researchers, especially those in the West, who give partial and undocumented information accusing the opposition of using chemical weapons. They ignore the complete picture and the irrefutable facts that show it was the Syrian regime which began the violence against the protestors and which admitted the existence of these weapons in its stores. It showed its readiness to surrender them to the West to avoid a military strike, but it seems those researchers do not want to admit these facts because they already classified the resistance in Syria as a group of rebels, for reasons which cannot be explored in depth here.[86] The effects of this regime's war on its people began to extend to neighbouring countries, like Turkey, Lebanon and Jordan, because of the increasing number of displaced persons and likewise the increasing violence. The most recent reports show that the violence in Syria has reaped more than 100,000 victims and displaced millions, leaving at least 8 million Syrians in need of relief. Even the United Nations described the conditions of the Syrians as the biggest humanitarian catastrophe since the Rwanda crisis in 1994. The economic costs according to UN estimates are $84.4 billion from 2011-2013.[87]

This level of violence perpetrated by the Syrian regime after the beginning of the Arab Spring, in addition to destroying the city of Hama and killing at least 20,000 Syrians in the mid-1980s, should be a source of great anguish and soul-searching. From the Arab-Islamic viewpoint, we believe that our region is adequate for religious, ethnic and sectarian diversity. Rather, in that there is a reminder of a golden period in the history of our community. Consequently, if we want this region to return to forming a melting pot of cultures, we must accurately assess our circumstances in order to initiate a process of change towards a better future. Some of the minorities in the Arab world, like a large section of the Alawite sect during the mandate period in the 1940s, used to behave with the mentality of the minority and strengthened the French in order to repress the Arab liberation movement at the time by joining what was known as the "Special Forces of the East". Then this sect was preoccupied by the fronts of the Arab Ba'ath Party to which it turned, not for the sake of its nationalist vision but because of its socialism and likewise because of the party's secularism. The Alawites had always been members of a poor class and it also seems there was a state of enmity between them and the Arab Sunnis. The Alawites crowned their ascent with Hafiz al-Assad's takeover of the Syrian regime in the coup of November 1970. They became a minority that practised various forms of violence on others. There is not space here to explore the subject of the Alawite's takeover of the Ba'ath Party and the army, particularly by the al-Assad family; there are many documented sources on this subject that can be referred to.[88] Furthermore, the regime of Bashar al-Assad's call for the involvement of the forces of Hezbollah, the Iranian Revolutionary Guard and the Iraqi militias of al-Maliki not only made this conflict sectarian but also regional and international. Hence, other states stood beside al-Assad for reasons relating to their interests and expectations; as well as Iran, Hezbollah and the Iraqi militias, there was also Russia, diplomatically and militarily. Russia had several reasons which include maintaining its only naval facilities in the Middle East in the port of Tartus and its fear of an Islamist regime succeeding the current Syrian regime which would have consequences for Islamist extension in and around Russia.[89] There are those who think there is another reason for Russia's position, represented by Putin's desire to send a message to the leaders of Central Asia that Russia stands beside its friends in times of crisis. This position may prevent many of them from revolving in China's orbit.[90] In addition to Russia, Israel has continued to want the survival of the al-Assad regime because it guarantees the peace on the Golan front. Similarly, like Russia, it fears an Islamist regime will change Syria's relationship with Israel, or be more hostile towards it than the current regime.[91]

The opposition, under the pressure of the regime's violence, later turned into a resistance but continued to suffer fragmentation. The regime accused it of violence and the West hesitated to stand beside it. Even the support that the opposition obtained from the GCC states like Saudi Arabia and Qatar was not at the level that would influence the balance of power with the regime and their supporters. The rest of the Gulf avoided the Syrian sphere for different reasons, as an attempt to maintain relations with Iran, as was the case with Oman, or to avoid a greater attraction to sectarianism, as was the case with Bahrain.[92]

The future of the Syrian regime cannot be viewed in terms of the current balance of power between it and the opposition because there are several factors that will determine the survival of this regime or its departure.

Firstly, it is true that the opposition in view of the current data may not be able to win militarily but if its ranks are united and they prove to the world that they are striving for a civil state in which everyone is equal, they may obtain developed weapons. That will change the balance of power with the regime or weaken it to say the least. Secondly, the allies of the regime, like Iran, Russia and Hezbollah, may find with the passage of time that the costs of clinging to the al-Assad regime are greater than the gains they are trying to realise. Iran may abandon the al-Assad regime if an opportunity appears to create a solution for its nuclear programme and rebuild its economy. The economic boycott has exhausted the economy such that the inflation rate has reached 47 per cent and the unemployment rate is 18 per cent. The value of the Riyal has declined to approximately 80 per cent during 2012-2014 just as oil exports have decreased to 1.5 million barrels a day in the middle of 2013 from about 2.5 million barrels in 2011.[93] Rather, there are sources which show that there is a continuous dialogue between the United States and Iran around Syria. Moreover, Rouhani himself has stated that he will accept any president elected by the Syrian people. In other words, Iran is not sticking to the al-Assad regime, especially if it can find a place for itself in the negotiations of the transitional stage in Syria.[94] Even the Russians, who initially supported the al-Assad regime, showed in the statements of President Putin during his visit to Turkey on 3 December 2012 and also in the statements of his foreign minister in more than one platform that they do not defend al-Assad and do not intend to increase their technical and military aid for his regime. It seems as if they realise that there is an increasing possibility this regime will fall and they are trying to create a line of return in their relations with the Syrian people.[95] Furthermore, the Hamas movement has avoided the Syrian regime because of its killing of its own people. It is not unlikely that Hezbollah's support for the regime will decline if the shrapnel of the war in Syria reaches Lebanon and upsets the party's relationship to the other sectors of Lebanese society, or starts to threaten another civil war. Thirdly, the most important factor which makes it difficult for this regime to survive is its sectarian nature, because like the rest of the minority military and tribal regimes it can only continue by exercising autocracy and corruption together; in other words, political openness means its end. In fact, the hereditary systems are better able to adjust to freedom than this system because they can be turned into constitutional monarchies and the al-Assad regime cannot do that.[96] One Western researcher at the end of the 1980s spoke about the sectarian problem of this regime and what this means for its future: "It appears inevitable that the 'Alawis – still a small and despised minority, for all their present power – will eventually lose their control over Syria. When this happens, it is likely that conflicts along communal lines will bring them down, with the critical battle taking place between the 'Alawi rulers and the Sunni majority. In this sense, the 'Alawis' fall – be it through assassinations of top figures, a palace coup, or a regional revolt – is likely to resemble their rise."[97]

Now, if we suppose the al-Assad regime will go for military or political reasons, or a mixture of both, can Syrian society, engulfed by this civil war with all its various dimensions, agree to a democratic regime? In truth, it is not easy to answer this question because previous experiences are varied. Countries like Mozambique, Peru and Nicaragua were able to transition to democracy after their civil wars. In contrast, countries like Angola and Sri Lanka were not able to realise the same transition. Will Syria after al-Assad be in the first or second group? The answer depends on several variables which we cannot go into much detail here. However, it is sufficient to say that the most important of these variables is the manner in which the war ends, its human costs, and whether it had an ideological or ethnic character as well as the level of development and democracy in the country before the war and the presence of international peace forces. For example, many studies show that the war ending with the victory for the rebels is a better outcome for democracy than victory for the regime. Other studies, however, confirm that the opportunities for democracy are greater if the civil war ends with a political agreement that gives the broad outlines for establishing the next government based on a single citizenship. Moreover, the experiences of other countries demonstrate that whenever the human costs of the war are greater, the greater the opportunity is for democracy. Nevertheless, the opportunities for democratic change are less if the war is more ethnic and religious in its nature than being a political and ideological struggle. Unfortunately, this is the situation in Syria today.[98]

Third: Change in the balance of power

It is difficult to know definitively even now which states are the winners and losers of the Arab Spring. Nevertheless, we are certain that the Arab Spring will prompt changes in the local and regional balance of power, just as it has begun to bring about partial changes in the relationships between governments and their people. These changes may even go as far as redrawing the map of the Arab region in a way that will result in greater fragmentation or more unity. That will depend on the ability of the region's people and their elites to follow the path of consensus rather than discord and work towards participation instead of deepening differences. The following section presents an initial inventory of the trends concerning this change in the balance of power in the region.

There is no doubt that the fall of regimes loyal to the West resulting from the Arab Spring until now, like the regimes of Mubarak in Egypt, Ben Ali in Tunisia, Ali Saleh in Yemen and Qaddafi in Libya, has weakened the West's grip on the Arab region and paralysed its agenda there. The existence of governments that express the will of their people and make their decisions independently means that they are not going to accept a dependent or subordinate status. In this respect, the former ambassador of the United States to Saudi Arabia remarks, "The United States remains the most powerful external actor in the Middle East, but American primacy has been slain by the new assertiveness of the region's inhabitants. If we give others space to displace us, they will."[99]

However, the extent of this achievement will determine what happens in these countries in the future. If the countries of the Arab Spring succeed in the peaceful transition to societies where freedom, the rule of law and social justice prevail, and if they strive to cooperate with each other, then the balance of power with the Western countries will change for the benefit of the region. Moreover, there will be opportunities for the greatest renaissance of the Arabs. Whenever the desired process of transition is stalled by anti-revolutionary actions, or the lack of compromise between the reformist currents, and whenever the gains are delayed and the probability of regression is increased, opportunities arise for external penetration in the form of creative chaos and its sisters.[100]

As for Israel, it seemed as if it would have faced a significant loss had Morsi's government continued as it was in contact with Hamas and trying to strengthen its presence in the West Bank, as well as intimating that it would make changes to the clauses of the Camp David agreement. Nevertheless, the coup in Egypt stopped any progress on the Palestinian issue and the matter was linked to the position of the new regime. On the other hand, there are strategic gains for Israel if Syria's chemical weapons are destroyed as these represent some deterrence to Israel's nuclear weapons; hence, the destruction of these Syrian chemical weapons would make Israel the only state in the region that possess nuclear, chemical and biological weapons, and this would definitely weigh the balance in Israel's favour.[101]

The effects of the Arab Spring on Iran will be positive and negative, though we believe that the negative effects will supersede the positive over time and determine the issue of Syria. On the positive side, the American presence in the region is weakening due to the weakness of the Arabs in general, thereby allowing Iran to exert more influence in the Arab region, particularly in the Arab regional system's current transitional stage. The more the Arab world delays in repairing its condition, the more that helps Iran consolidate its position as an influential regional country, especially if Iran is able to develop its nuclear reactor. This has become a strong possibility now because the West's use of force against Iran is unlikely at present.[102] The negative effects of the Arab Spring, however, may not allow Iran to maximise its gains in the coming years due to the disputes in both Syria and Iraq as well as in Iran itself among the conservatives and reformists. At the start of the Arab Spring, Iran made gains with the fall of Mubarak, Ben Ali and Qaddafi, because these regimes were opposed to it for different reasons. Then when the Syrians demonstrated against the al-Assad regime, Iran stood by it and accused the Syrian demonstrators, who initially were demanding their rights peacefully, of being a group of foreign terrorists. Afterwards, Iran did not see any fault in sending its recruits to kill Syrian women and children with the deadliest weapons.[103]

Hezbollah, as we have previously explained, gained widespread support in the Arab world because of its resistance against Israel in 2006. However, it revealed its sectarian face and disgraceful political hypocrisy by siding with the al-Assad regime against the Syrian people. Here we need to measure the extent of the shift in support for Hezbollah in the Arab world since its intervention in Syria. Until then, it is sufficient for us to mention that in 2011 Hassan Nasrullah was reported as saying, "Yes, we did support the revolutionary movements in Tunisia, Libya and Egypt, but we leave each people to determine what's best for their countries ... and our position on Syria is based on our acknowledgement of all the things Hafez and Bashar al-Assad have done for Lebanon and for the resistance."[104] By this logic, which is irrational and unbefitting of someone in his position, Nasrullah wants to convince us that all peoples have the right to determine their fate except the Syrian people who must negotiate for their freedom with whatever their regime presents to Hezbollah. These contradictory positions of Iran and Hezbollah have led to a significant erosion in their credibility among the Arab people. If we bear in mind that the al-Assad regime has no hope of survival under any future settlement, whether political or military or both, that means Iran will not have any acceptance in the Arab world in the future because of its role in supporting al-Assad.[105] Likewise, Iran's influence in Iraq has begun to recede. The occupation of Iraq in 2003 enlarged America's role and made Iraq revolve in Iran's orbit after another sectarian regime had been in power there. Thus, the relative balance that prevailed between Iran, Iraq and the GCC states has ended. Iran with its Shi'a arm in Iraq has begun to exercise growing influence in the region at the expense of the GCC states, just as the United States has exploited this imbalance to establish its presence in the region. The previous balance may not return to the Gulf region in the near future without several dynamics that may weaken the Iranian side by diminishing its capacity to influence the course of affairs inside Iraq. These include the fact that Iraq's dependence on Iran since the fall of Saddam's regime is unacceptable to its Sunni Arabs and Kurds, even to the Shi'a Arabs themselves who represent the majority of Shi'a in Iraq. This is confirmed by the fact that the Shi'a Arabs defended Iraq in its war with Iran and their sectarian affiliation did not cause them to renounce their Iraqi nationality. Another factor is the independence of many Shi'a authorities in Iraq from those in Iran. For example, Ali Sistani is the Shi'a authority in Iraq and the Gulf and does not believe in the theory of *wilayat al-faqih* (guardianship of the jurists) on which the Iranian system of rule is based. Finally, Iran is unable to offer Iraqis a development model worthy of imitation, as the Iranian products cannot even compete with the Turkish ones in the Iraqi market.[106] In addition to the above factors, Iran's ability and desire for its presence in Iraq may be weakened by the domestic situation in Iran as a result of the conflict between the parties of the conservative current itself and the conflict between the conservative and the reformist currents over the nuclear programme and the economy. Furthermore, the Iraqis have realised that Iran is trying to dominate them rather than treat them as equals and this behaviour has aroused a nationalist reaction in Iraq.[107]

Turkey is another regional player that has begun to achieve a growing acceptance among most Arabs, even before the Arab Spring, and this feeling has deepened with the Arab Spring. It is truly unfortunate that some intellectuals in the Arab world are unable and unwilling to recognise this acceptance of the Turkish model among many sectors of the Arab world, particularly since the Justice and Development Party (AKP) took power in Turkey around ten years ago. This denial by some elites either goes back to reasons connected to the historical legacy of the relationship between the Arabs and Turks, and for which each party bears part of the responsibility, or for purely sectarian reasons. There is no doubt that we need field studies to resolve this issue and find out the actual feelings of the Arab people towards the Turks. Until that time, there are various reasons why many Arabs respect the current Turkish model. Before the arrival of the Justice and Development Party in 2002, Turkey's foreign policy wavered between standing by Western governments or adopting a neutral approach to issues in the Arab region. However, this later changed towards a greater rapprochement with the Arab sphere and its interests and was not only due to cultural and historical considerations, or considerations dictated by Turkish interests. Rather it was because the West, especially European countries like Germany and France, helped that situation as Turkey was not given full membership of the European Community for many reasons, foremost of which is its Islamic identity and its conflict with Greece over Cyprus.[108] Turkey stood with the people of Gaza when they faced Israel during the war known as "Operation Cast Lead" in 2008-09 which killed around 1400 Palestinians. The Turkish Prime Minister Erdogan did not hesitate to condemn this aggression, calling it "state terrorism" at a time when many Arab neighbours were silent.[109] At the height of the siege on Gaza, a Turkish ship called the *Mavi Marmara* carrying Turkish activists set out to break the siege. Israeli forces boarded the ship in international waters in May 2010 and killed nine Turkish civilians.[110] Turkey also extended its cooperation with the Arab countries, despite their autocratic regimes, and especially with Syria. In 2009, Turkey and Syria reached a strategic agreement for a visa exemption between the two countries. The agreement aimed at a type of economic integration, hoping to expand its circle to include Iraq and Iran, influenced by the union of the Schengen countries.

Since the beginning of the Arab Spring, Turkey has been eager to stand by the aspirations of the Arab people without confronting the Arab governments. In Libya, it hesitated to allow the entry of NATO troops but was forced to stand with the international community when it became increasingly likely that the Libyan people would face massacres. In Egypt, Turkey stood with the Egyptian people and was the first state to call what happened in Egypt in July 2013 a coup. In Syria, when the demonstrations began to spread in March 2011, the Turkish government advised al-Assad to carry out partial reforms. After his regime turned its weapons on its people, since June 2011 Turkey has stood with the Syrian opposition diplomatically and economically and taken in the largest share of Syrian refugees.[111] Therefore, it is unsurprising that many Iranian officials state that they do not face as much opposition to their presence in Syria from their traditional enemies, such as the United States and Israel, as they face from the competition from Saudi Arabia, and, to a lesser extent, from Turkey.[112] In addition to these positions in Turkish foreign policy towards the Arabs, since the arrival of the AKP in 2002 Turkey has achieved an unprecedented economic development according to the evidence of research centres that follow events in this country. In 2014 Turkey was named as one of six rising global economies to watch in future.[113] For these and other reasons, we believe that Turkey will have a pivotal role in the region and the countries of the Arab Spring can establish a strong relationship with Turkey in the coming years, whether on issues of security or development because that will provide many gains for both sides, such as the weakening of the Turkish-Israeli relationship.

With regard to the Russian position, this has been to support the al-Assad regime, although this has started to change somewhat recently. This position puts Russia in the list of losing states from the viewpoint of the region's people and the governments representing them, particularly in the short term. That may change in the long term though, for reasons decided by the interests of these people who are demanding the building of bridges with all the influential forces in the world today.[114]

Although the governments of the GCC states have not fallen and no partial reforms have occurred in their policies towards their policies until now, they lose from the Arab Spring in the long and short term as long as they stick to the security option and to buying loyalties. That is for the following reasons. Firstly, the Arab Spring led to a deepening of the historical conflicts between the governments of the regions. In March 2014, Saudi Arabia, the UAE and Bahrain jointly announced the withdrawal of their ambassadors from Qatar. This expressed their refusal of Qatar's position towards the Arab Spring in which it saw the early ideas that harmonised with the ambitions and aspirations of the region's peoples. However, this development and the polarisation that these countries are undergoing during this period is not a recent phenomenon but one with historical roots. It is a link in a series of developments, some related to the Arab world and some going back to historical conflicts between the Gulf states themselves. Previously, their governments differed over the former Emir of Qatar's coup against his father in 1995, and they also disagreed over the increase in the size of the Peninsula force, currency unification, border issues, foreign policies and other issues.[115] The hereditary regimes ruling the GCC states are by their nature unstable because of the disputes and mistrust between members of the ruling families themselves and between them and the rest of society. This conflict results in instability and declining prosperity and these characteristics are not suggested by us but confirmed in many recent studies about the region.[116] This absence of trust, which should be built on a legitimacy deriving from the will of the people, has made the region's governments more inclined to bilateral relations at the expense of the collective institutional work that gives rise to collective policies and leads to the advancement of these societies. Although they agree on general directions, their priorities differ, which is what creates much of the tension between them.[117] Secondly, these governments continue to offer donations and support whenever a political crisis happens and have been accustomed to doing so since the 1970s. This puts them in a vicious cycle of political crises accompanied by expectations of an increase in spending, given that raising people's expectations of more spending is a simple matter but lowering these expectations is much more difficult.[118] Moreover, if this was possible previously, it is no longer the case now. The increased population size in these countries as well as the increase in income have both resulted in a huge growth in the consumption of fuel, electricity and water which has to be obtained by desalinating sea water at a high cost and generating electricity, by either oil or gas. This means that the largest share of these state's production of oil and gas is consumed locally. This reflects negatively on exports and reduces oil revenues and investments for diversifying sources of income. For example, in 2011 it was reported that the refining capacity in Saudi Arabia was no longer meeting local demand for fuel and diesel. Subsequently, it will need to import refined products estimated at around $170 billion over ten years.[119] In May 2012, the IMF anticipated that if Kuwait continued its current way of spending it would not manage to provide any part of its oil revenues for future generations from early 2017; in other words, its spending will equal its oil revenues.[120] For the remaining GCC states, especially Oman and Bahrain, it is probable that a growing deficit in their public budgets will emerge starting from 2014 if oil prices fall which means they must review their rates of spending growth.[121]

Finally, even if these governments continue to use security options and manage to raise oil prices to about $100 per barrel (the break-even price, according to the estimates of international organisations, caused by the continuing rates of current spending) that will not stop demands for political reform. The Arab Spring confirmed that freedom is a demand in itself and that many of those who sacrificed their lives were from the middle class and did not rise up because they were suffering poverty. Rather, they rose up for the sake of dignity and the right to expression. Without doubt, the neglect of this fact by the region's governments will deepen the gap with their peoples over time, raise the costs of maintaining security and hinder the progress of development.[122]

CHAPTER SIXTEEN

Domestic Reform

In our opinion, domestic reform in every GCC and Arab county is the first step towards a genuine renaissance, and the ability to end the cycle of instability, to eliminate the sources of violence and deal with various ongoing regional and international challenges. These reforms to could also act as the catalyst for the GCC's and wider Arab integration, and for these countries' effective presence on the international scene. The Arab Spring in its various forms has confirmed the desire for change among the region's people. This is why in this chapter we will try to address the importance of reforms, their nature, the manner of their implementation, the potential obstacles that could impede them, and how best to deal with these obstacles. In particular, the fact is that the GCC states, even after the Arab Spring, still rely on the "carrot and stick" approach to maintaining current conditions instead of working towards reform, and this situation is no longer sustainable.

First: The inevitability of reform

Although the changes that affected various hereditary systems in the Gulf over the years have made them lose the flexibility enjoyed by tribal systems, they did not turn them into modern democratic or consultative systems either. Instead, they turned them into narrow family-based regimes akin to a caste system, a system that is neither in line with religious notions of freedom and justice, nor with modern democracy, a privilege that most of the world nations enjoy today, albeit at different levels. In its present form, therefore, the governance system that prevails in the Gulf can neither achieve genuine development nor ensure security, because it does not draw its legitimacy from the people; it survives thanks to the oil wealth, the loyalty it can buy and the foreign powers whose presence in the region gives these governments a false sense of security. Since we already documented this fact in the course of addressing development, security and the foreign factor, the question now is no longer whether these hereditary systems need to be changed or not, but rather how can we change them without exacerbating the internal violence that began to spread across the region, over ten years ago. Marina Ottaway, researcher at the American Carnegie Endowment says, in this context, that after 11 September 2001, the administration of George W. Bush reached the conclusion that, "The Saudi government was responsible for the rise of terrorist organizations in the Kingdom, not because it directly supported such groups, but because its authoritarianism and its poor economic policies were creating social conditions that favoured the growth of terrorism. Lack of democracy and economic opportunities among young Saudis caused frustration that manifested itself in the form of terrorist activities. Other Arab authoritarians were creating similar conditions in their countries. To contain terrorism the United States needed not only to rely on good intelligence and security measures but also to address the root causes of the problem by promoting democracy and economic reform. Thus was born the Bush administration's 'freedom agenda' for the Middle East."[1]

However, when Islamist currents performed well in elections held in some Arab countries, with Western encouragement, the West's enthusiasm for political reform waned. However, several Western observers stress the importance of reform even if it comes with certain constraints, as the only way out of the circle of violence and terror, and of the resulting instability whose far-reaching impact went well beyond the region, as evidenced by the experience of European, Latin American and East Asian countries. This was George W. Bush's foreign policy position which he later abandoned, and which, had he implemented, would have been a significant step forward from the platform that won him the presidency, and whose priorities did not include reform in the Arab countries. His administration even tried to avoid getting too close to various crises unfolding in this region, as US Secretary of State Condoleezza Rice says in an article in *Foreign Affairs* magazine.[2] This proves that the American government thought "friendly dictators were preferable to unfriendly democracies",[3] although several intellectuals and research institutions urged the American administration, after the liberation of Kuwait, to endorse reform in the Arab countries. Their reasoning was that both the Iraq War and the invasion of Kuwait were the outcome of crises festering in the Arab world, characterised primarily by a lack of democracy, and by simultaneous disparities in natural resource and population distribution, meaning that only reform could bring an end to the cycle of war, violence and instability in the region.[4]

In the same context, the 2003 United Nations Arab Development Report stressed the importance of political, economic and cultural reform as a prerequisite for raising the level of knowledge in the region, then putting it to good use in the development process.[5] Today, the conviction about the need to introduce change and reform is widespread even among members of the ruling families, especially in the wake of 11 September 2001, the violence in Saudi Arabia in 2003, and events in other parts of the region both before and after that date.[6] Even those in the West and the region who would rather do without reform have no alternative for protecting the interests of all involved, except continuing on the track that has allowed governments to implement unjust policies, a track which, according to Kenneth Pollack, has only led to more uprisings and revolutions in the region. It also led to unstable oil prices which, in turn, have affected the stability of the global economy, and dragged the United States into three wars, since 1987, each more costly than the preceding one, not to mention the increase in the number of terrorist acts against the United States that reached their zenith in September 2001.[7] Therefore, if the current situation is no longer acceptable to the world's nations and to some wise officials in the region's current administrations, then the people's rejection of the status quo, as proven by the events of the Arab Spring, and their attempts to change it are only natural, since they are the ones at the receiving end of it. There is no alternative, therefore, to changing the status quo, and this requires long-term reform policies implemented by governments that represent their people, laws that treat everybody equally, a dynamic and creative education system, and an economy based on close cooperation between the public and private sectors from which everyone can benefit. It also requires a social development process that is just and fair to present and future generations, even to various Arab countries; in other words, a development that crosses boundaries and generations. The widespread feeling among the region's people today is that they should brace themselves for more violence and instability, given the enormous failures of past years, meaning that a serious reform agenda would do much to alleviate current feelings of despair, and replace them with expectations for a better future, a feeling that will likely give reform a strong boost. This will initiate a new cycle of hope and hard work that will replace the current cycle of despair and destruction.[8] However, though it appears to be easy in theory, this reform process will no doubt encounter obstacles when the time comes to implement it. In view of that, we will begin by defining the nature of the reforms required, move on to the manner of their implementation and the problems they are likely to encounter, and end with suggestions as to how these problems could be overcome.

Second: Nature of the reforms required

The required reform process should be multi-dimensional; in the legal domain, the country's laws should treat people equally and act as a safety mechanism in which context problems could be resolved. If the legal system is not neutral and credible, conflicts will be resolved outside its framework, meaning that they would be resolved either in an illegal therefore corrupt manner, or through violence that only leads to chaos. When American laws discriminated against African Americans and British laws discriminated against the majority population in India, two local leaders, Martin Luther King in the USA and Mahatma Gandhi in India, resorted to civil disobedience to force a change in the status quo, a method both proven and legal. However, if changing the legal imbalance by force is not done correctly, as King and Ghandi did, it could lead to coups and rebellions seeking the regime's downfall as happened in Russia, Cuba and Iran, among other, a formula that often results in destruction and stalled development. Therefore, a flexible and fair legal system, i.e., one that can accommodate change, keep up with the pace and stage of the country's development and protect the people's rights, is an essential factor of stability and the cornerstone of any future cultural renaissance. Even if no revolutions or rebellions ensue, a legal system that lacks credibility will likely prevent the country from prospering by other means, including widespread corruption, establishment of tribunals specialised in various domains, illegal economic activities, tax evasion and increasing violence.[9]

In the political domain, the system should guarantee and protect the basic rights of individuals, including the freedom of expression and assembly without fear, and the government should be transparent and accountable to popularly elected bodies, that alone have the right to legislate and exercise oversight. Under such a system, instead of being the personal property of the ruling elite, as is mostly the case today, the country's assets would belong to society, which would then have the right to decide, through its representatives, how to make best use of them.

As for the education system, it should be radically reformed in a manner that would allow students to understand, analyse, critique, think and find solutions to different issues, and help train them in skills related to statistical analyses, quantum mathematics and the basic sciences that underlie key industries. Students should learn foreign languages in addition to the Arabic language, rather than in lieu of it, so that future generations would be in touch with the world while drawing all they can draw from their own Arab-Islamic culture, just as the world once did. We should expand the students' knowledge base instead of confining them to a narrow field of study that prevents them from seeing the bigger picture in which this narrow field of specialisation evolves. In the economic field, governments should provide the right conditions to help the private sector develop, in cooperation with the public sector, become the engine of sustainable development and provide employment for the growing number of new graduates in the region. In order for this to happen, these two sectors' activities should be subject to proper laws and various types of budgets should be made available to them, such as performance, programme and zero budgets. These help gauge the efficiency with which the country's resources are being used, steer unproductive consumer spending towards more worthy endeavours, reduce all types of waste, develop better water usages, and find efficient means of protecting the environment from the negative fallout of development projects.[10]

Finally, reforms should take place within the framework of Arab social values and tenets, because other countries' experiences show that development processes will not succeed or enjoy public support if they contradict societies' values and beliefs. We showed earlier how our cultural tenets could be the catalyst for, rather than the obstacle to, our future renaissance, especially if we succeed in separating these tenets from the values, customs and traditions that appended themselves to our original values during the period of despotism and repression.

Third: Reform-related issues

In order for the reform process in the GCC to succeed, a lot of wisdom is needed to tackle the wide range of obstacles that will no doubt impede its course. Here below are some of the main obstacles or issues that could arise once the process is underway.

1. Islam and democracy

Does it mean, when we talk about political reform and its economic and cultural aspects, that we need to adopt the Western democratic model? Does it also mean that we should take it as a package deal, including the West's traditions and values system, or does democracy have its own set of principles that one could apply in more than one context, and to more than one culture? In fact, opinions on the subject abound; however, the majority view, supported by a number of current democratic experiences, is that the developing countries do not have to adopt Western values in order for democracy to succeed. This means that the Gulf countries can adopt the basic principles of Western democracy, such as freedom of expression and assembly, accountability and transparency, elections, limits on the use of power and promoting the culture of advocacy in institutions, without adopting the entire Western value system and culture that sanctions abortion, homosexuality and other practices unacceptable to Arab societies. Many researchers in the West and the region have addressed this issue, and managed to delineate the relationship between Islam's tenets and the basic principles of democracy in a clear and satisfactory manner, although the effort still needs more work. It is perhaps worth quoting some of these opinions to dispel any misunderstanding that can potentially impede the course of reform. One of these opinions comes from Shaikh Yusuf al-Qardawi, one of the main *ulama* (religious scholars) of Islam today, stressing the fact that Islam is compatible with the spirit of democracy. He said, "We need to focus today on something we referred to earlier, namely that the core of democracy is, without doubt, compatible with the core of Islam. However, we must only go back to its very roots and draw it from its pure origins, the Qur'an, the *Sunnah* and the works of the rightly guided caliphs, and not from the history of the princes of injustice and kings of evildoing, or the *fatwas* of the doomed scholars of kings or the eager unwise ones who revolve in their orbit."[11]

We also have the Gulf-based researcher and coordinator of the Democratic Studies Project in the Arab Countries, Dr Ali al-Kawari, confirming that there is no preordained link between the practice of democracy and Western liberalism. He said, "This is why I say that democracy is not just a mechanism, but a method of defining options and making public decisions, a governance system founded on principles, institutions, mechanisms, limits and public guarantees common to all democratic governance systems regardless of the cultural context in which democracy is being practised. It is therefore clear that I neither view democracy as a particularly liberal mechanism, nor as specific to any other tenet, but rather as a governance system and a means of defining options and making public decisions that are, by necessity, influenced by the choices of the society in which democracy is being practised."[12]

Several other experts on the issue of Islam and democracy confirm al-Qardawi's and al-Kuwari's opinions, but there is unfortunately not enough space here to go into more detail about the subject.[13] Therefore, if we accept that Islam is compatible with the core of democracy, and that democracy can be separated from the liberal value system and attached to the Arab-Islamic value system, i.e., it can be applied to any cultural context a society chooses, then we would have taken a considerable step forward in resolving the issue of democracy and Islam. This brings us to the next step, which is the manner of applying the core of the democratic system to an Arab-Islamic cultural context. Although the issue requires further scrutiny by all involved, the debates that have already taken place and the actions following the Arab Spring have produced different opinions regarding the manner of applying democracy, while safeguarding the *Sharia*'s tenets. The first believes that the responsibility should be entrusted to a council of *ulama* whose job would be to guide the behaviour of Islamic states, including the way democracy is practised, in a manner to avoid a clash between the *shar'ia*'s tenets and democracy's practices. The second opinion says that there should be a constitutional provision stating that Islamic *sharia* is the main source of legislation, and leave the responsibility of ensuring that this happens to the constitutional court, while allowing the *ulama* to express their opinion as experts on the subject.[14] There is a third opinion set apart by the experience of Tunisia after the fall of the Ben Ali regime and his supporters. This states that the principles and values of Islam are not protected by constitutions, but by the believers' understanding, defence and practice of them, especially in an active civil society which does not exclude anyone. The insistence on making Islamic *sharia* the source of legislation at this stage, in which the Arab socie-ties, including Tunisia, are coming out of the stage of autocracy, may result in a group opposing the principles of religion and hindering society's progress. Consequently, the proponents of this opinion are satisfied for the constitutions to stipulate that the religion of the state is Islam, and this is a paragraph that exists originally in the Tunisian constitution of 1959. Therefore, the Ennahda party has withdrawn from issues that already appeared in its programme and are related to the role of the *sharia* in writing the constitution and women's issues, as well as subjects relating to the opposition to religious matters.[15] Regardless of whether we agree or disagree with the opinion of the Ennahda party, nevertheless by merely addressing the issue, the reform process will receive a strong boost, because it will bridge the gap between different parties calling for reform, and strengthen their position vis-à-vis their governments. Moreover, an agreement on the rules of the game that governs the reform process will reassure Western countries with strategic interests in the region and who, for several reasons, do not favour reform in this region. Among these reasons are the ongoing efforts by the region's governments to scare these countries by telling them that any change in the status quo would lead to chaos, uprisings and instability, and eventually hurt their interests in this vital region. However, now that violence has become endemic to the region due to stagnation and lack of change, the big powers could be more amenable to reform if it is properly managed, and relies on the cooperation among all those involved. The acceptance of change by the Western countries could also be the safety valve that prevents a possible counter-reaction against them, once change takes place, as happened in Iran against the United States in the wake of the Islamic Revolution.[16]

2. Do people in the Gulf want reform?

Another issue related to reform is the extent to which people in the Gulf want political reform, and are ready to sacrifice to make it happen. Many of these governments justify their reluctance to introduce reform by claiming, among other, that there is no popular demand for it in the region, either because the public do not understand it or because the reforms are incompatible with tribal social values. Are these claims justified? There are at least two opinions on the matter. Proponents of the first opinion say that if the people of the region are allowed to give their opinion on the matter without fear, they will choose political participation, and several surveys and field studies across the Middle East confirm this view.[17] Professor of political science, As'ad Abu Khalil, says that in the last ten years the majority of Arab men and women have clearly expressed the desire to see democracy in their countries.[18] Moreover, the results of a 2002 survey conducted by Zogby International in the UAE, Kuwait, Egypt and Lebanon, showed that 50-60 per cent of the region's people admire American democracy.[19] In the same vein, a report on democracy in the Kingdom of Bahrain concluded that the Bahraini people believe that the government thwarted the country's democratisation through measures aimed at containing the reform process.[20] We also have former Jordanian Foreign Minister, Marwan Muasher, saying as much in an article in the *New York Times*: "It is becoming clear that the Arab world needs to take the initiative in making its political and economic systems more democratic. The frustrations Arabs feel today – prompted by the slow pace of democratic reform, stagnant economies and political instability: all threaten the region's future. The moment has come for the Arab world to engage in a homegrown, evolutionary and orderly process of democratization--one that will respect Arab culture while at the same time giving citizens the power to be part of the political process."[21] There is no doubt that the developments which accompanied the Arab Spring confirm that the people of the Gulf do not only want but insist on obtaining these rights. There is not a single Gulf state, as we have explained in our discussion on the repercussions of the Arab Spring, which has not seen the expression of the desire for freedom, whether that is by demonstrations, as happened in Saudi Arabia, Oman, Bahrain and Kuwait, or by presenting petitions as in the UAE, or by publishing books and holding intellectual forums, as in Qatar.

Proponents of the second opinion, on the other hand, point to the people's negative attitude and their disinterest in both participation and the need to sacrifice for the sake of reform. According to Saudi researcher Madawi al-Rasheed, the Saudi government draws its legitimacy in the twenty-first century from economic prosperity and petrodollars, because it alone can define the relationship between ruler and subjects, which makes reformers akin to a general without soldiers. As proof, she points to the Saudi government's arrest of reformers, in recent years, without eliciting any public reaction or sympathy for those involved. She says in this context, "Reformers were taken out of their lecture halls, picked up at airports, or arrested in their offices without a word of protest from their own students, colleagues or acquaintances."[22]

Shaker Nabulsi conveys the same impression regarding the Saudi public's lack of interest in reform and its requirements, in the course of addressing the level of participation in the Saudi municipal elections held between November 2004 and February 2005, which did not exceed 10 per cent of the population of 20 million. The writer believes that the reason behind this negativity is the fact that "the elections were held during an economic boom due to rising oil prices. Such sudden booms in the Gulf usually serve to line pockets, silence voices, cleanse political sins and purify the hearts of reformists. Once stomachs are filled, taxes reduced and pockets inflated, people have little desire for democratic reform."[23]

We believe that the two above opinions confirm the link between the political and social dimensions of reform. The reason is that once reforms actually happen and people become free of these governments' extortion, which currently manifests itself in granting or withholding favours, we will see how public calls for participation, the willingness to be part of the process and readiness to sacrifice for it, will grow from where they are today. Today, the region's illegitimate governments are free to dispose of the country's oil wealth as they please, use it to extort the region's people and stifle the yearning within for liberation, self-esteem and dignity.

3. Role of local and foreign factors in reform

The third issue related to reform in the region has to do with the extent to which the proponents of reform in the GCC states and the Arab world are willing to accept outside support, if at all, especially after what took place in Iraq and Afghanistan. There is also the question as to whether countries like the United States and the European Union, as well as civil society and human rights organisations, are sincere in their call for political reform in the Arab world, as a whole, when they know well that reforms are likely to weaken their grip on the region. There is no single answer for all times and circumstances. However, the prevailing view so far, based on America's and the West's records in this region since the end of WWII, is that calls for reform in this region whether political or otherwise are unlikely to find an echo in the West, and that the latter applies double standards when democracy is involved. For while it calls for democracy in Eastern Europe, it closes its eyes to similar calls in the Arab world. The results of an opinion survey conducted by Zogby International in Jordan, Morocco, Saudi Arabia, Lebanon and the UAE, in 2006, confirm this fact and show that around 65 per cent of surveyed individuals did not believe that democracy was one of the United States' objectives in the Middle East.[24] Likewise, we have seen this two-faced attitude in the cases of Egypt and Ukraine where the West was silent about the military coup against the elected president in Egypt but stood with the Ukrainian people who revolted against their government and Russian interference.

This means that when they call for reform, the people of the region should rely on their fellow citizens, and strive to raise public awareness so that the calls for change and reform do not lead to more destruction and foreign intervention. This should not prevent the region's people from seeking the international community's support, like the attempts to break the siege on Gaza, as long as this support is unconditional and taps into the new attitude making its appearance in the West that now believes that change in the region is inevitable. This new attitude emanates from an awareness in the West that change is bound to be in its interest, since the alternative to reform is simply more violence and destruction in the world, not just the region. Today, some Westerners are even convinced that opposing these reforms would deal a heavy blow to the West and its credibility in the world, since it has raised the banner of freedom for so long, yet prevented others from enjoying it.[25] The foreign factor could play a determining role, especially when countries ruled by autocratic regimes, whether in the Gulf or elsewhere, express the desire to join international organisations and institutions. The Saudi government was forced to introduce a number of economic and legal reforms when it applied to join the World Trade Organisation (WTO), and to that end, it first had to develop the Kingdom's administration system in order to monitor the process, even if ultimate success of these reforms depends on their implementation and credibility among the public.[26] For example, although in 2004 the United Nations ranked Saudi Arabia, as far as the ability to attract foreign investments, at no. 31 among the world's nations, the actual amount of investments it attracted placed it at no. 138.[27] This means that rather than quantifying them by the numbers, reforms should be measured by their actual impact on the ground.

4. Dealing with regimes that reject reform

The fourth impediment that the reform process in the GCC and the Arab world is bound to encounter are the regimes' manoeuvrings to avoid reform, and the various means at their disposal to circumvent them using local support networks. As these networks' interests are intertwined with those of the regime, they are wary of any change that could strip them of their privileges. The amount of oil revenues under these governments' control has helped them avoid taxing the people and, in the process, avoid the public accountability that comes with that, a tactic they will no doubt continue to pursue to avoid introducing reforms.[28] They use this revenue to mitigate public anger, form alliances, weaken the voices calling for change and reform, and delay the development of an independent private sector or a vibrant civil society, manoeuvres easy to discern given the level of government interference in the economy, especially the amount of public sector jobs and different forms of support.[29] Finally, these governments have used the oil revenue to establish security agencies ready to be used against any opposition to them, and to shower their members with privileges to ensure that their loyalty is owed to them, first, ahead of the country and its future.[30] The proponents of reform should plan, above all, on dissociating these networks from their narrow short-term interests that are bound to conflict, down the road, with the country's path towards development and stability. They should convince the governments and their supporters that change has become a necessity and, as such, it is vital for them to cooperate with this effort to make change gradual rather than sudden, and thus avoid any radical changes that could prove costly to society and to them. This way, change will come as the result of an understanding round the need to readjust the balance of power, and this, in turn, would lead to the establishment of a better society without provoking costly eruptions. One of the ways this gradual process could come about is by transforming current governments in the GCC into genuine constitutional monarchies, a move that would, at the same time, preserve the symbolic status of the ruling families, and allow the implementation of necessary reforms.[31]

5. The priorities of reform

There is a fifth obstacle, yet, that has to do with which aspect of reform should be tackled first; should the process start with economic reforms then address political reforms, or perhaps the other way round, or should the two processes run in parallel? Those who believe that economic reforms should be tackled first give several reasons to justify their opinion. Some claim that introducing the kind of economic reforms that lead to economic prosperity, more jobs and higher standards of living in the region, is enough in itself, and justify this claim by saying that the region's people are not as interested in political reforms as they are in securing their daily livelihoods. Current regimes in the Gulf also uphold this view, which concurs with the big powers' own view that asking the GCC governments to introduce political reforms at this time might have negative repercussions on their interests.[32] However, even if we accept the premise that the Gulf citizens' priority is securing their daily livelihood, there are numerous counter-arguments to the claim that "economic reforms would be sufficient." We should remember that the present relationship between politicians, the business community, the administration and the army is such that economic reforms alone will lead to more instability. The reason is that the governments' attempts to liberalise the economy and increase competition will be met by staunch opposition from the powerful business class that benefits from a status quo, which guarantees it government support, bias in awarding contracts and other privileges that governments are willing to pay for in order to buy loyalty and acquiescence. The business class is not the only group that considers economic reforms as being harmful to its interests; members of the over-inflated administration systems, which governments use to mitigate society's anger and swell the number of their supporters, will not look favourably on efforts to reduce their numbers, privileges, revenue resources or advantages, all necessary steps in any reform process.

The third group to be hurt by economic reforms is the military, whose growing economic interests have made it part of the business class, not to mention the fact that the reforms will necessarily reduce the amount of funds usually allocated to them, and to the security services. As far as the military is concerned, this is not a welcome move. This is why current governments in the Gulf are unable to introduce significant reforms, given that they would weaken several sectors on which they depend in their effort to avoid taking any of the necessary steps likely to earn them genuine legitimacy, the kind that emanates from all sectors of society in the Gulf. All the above reasons together could explain why the region's governments are so loath to introducing serious economic reforms, and are content instead with a few pro-forma and publicity-oriented moves, that target the outside world. Some even say that despite their importance, the absence of economic reforms is not the only cause of instability in the region, as there are middle-class groups in the Gulf who do not support these regimes for various political, spiritual and social reasons, meaning that economic reforms alone would make no difference to them at all.[33]

Others believe that the introduction of economic reforms, and the advantages it would bring to institution building, the rule of law, the right to access information, transparency and the protection of individual rights, is a preliminary step towards political development. Farid Zakaria says in this context, "the process of economic development usually produces the two elements that are crucial to the success of liberal democracy. First, it allows key segments of society – most important, private businesses and the broader bourgeoisie – to gain power independent of the state. Second, in bargaining with these elements the state tends to become less rapacious and capricious and more rule-oriented and responsive to society's needs, or at least to the needs of the elite of that society. This process results in liberalization, often unintentionally."[34]

Those who advocate starting with economic reform point to the experience of East Asian countries like South Korea and Taiwan, that began by developing the private sector that eventually produced the middle class, and this class in turn propelled the political reform process forward, making it easier for the governance system to transition from autocracy to democracy. However, some doubt the ability of autocratic regimes to take the initiative and launch the transition process, for most Arab and GCC governments were unable to either ensure the rule of law or develop a transparent decision-making system because it is not in their interest to do so. Therefore, given the absence of the rule of law and a transparent decision-making system, there is no room for a competent private sector to grow and, according to these people, even if these two principles existed it does not mean that a private sector, that paves the way for democracy, will necessarily follow.[35] For example, despite Tunisia's considerable economic progress over the past few years, the benefits remained confined to a small circle of people, and instead of seeking some sort of equilibrium with the autocratic regime in power, the rich class kept asking for more privileges. The rich class in the Gulf seems to be going down that same path.[36] Furthermore, the potential for the development of a middle class that asks for its political rights is less probable when the central authority controls the oil revenue and uses it to buy loyalty, award contracts and silence alternative views.[37] Several experts on the region confirm this glaring absence, in several Arab countries, of any link between the initial economic reforms and the political development that follows them.[38]

Based on the above, we lean towards the opinion that places political reform at the forefront of change, because it can provide the right atmosphere to help economic reforms achieve their objectives, without impacting negatively on social justice. In other words, economic reforms would evolve in the right political environment instead of helping secure the interests of one group at the expense of another, as was the case during the privatisation process in Gulf and other Arab countries. However, this does not mean that economic reform should cease in order for political reforms to proceed; what is important is that these reforms take place within the framework of efficient, accountable and transparent legal and administrative institutions, to avoid potential negative repercussions. Nothing prevents these reforms from happening concurrently in a manner whereby each helps the other advance, i.e., certain political reforms could be the catalyst that stimulates economic performance, and a better economy could stimulate progress on the political front, and so on.[39]

6.   The case for gradual reform

The sixth issue has to do with the pace of reform; some call for a gradual process, which, while very sensible, could become an obstacle when used as a delaying tactic or a means of burying the process. The Arab and GCC's countries' experience is a case in point, and has been so for a long time. However, the governments' delaying tactics aside, calls for gradual reform come sometimes from the reformists themselves. The latter see the wisdom of first preparing the Gulf's citizens for what is to come, raise their awareness regarding the expected changes and ensure that they can perform the ensuing responsibilities with diligence. In their opinion, this would avoid deviating from the course of reform and prevent any setbacks that could turn the process into an arena of religious or ethnic conflict, a valid point of view that should not be ignored.[40] In order to prevent this gradual approach from becoming an obstacle or a means of voiding the process of meaning, social consensus should be built round the validity of the approach itself, and there should be a clear and well-defined agreement on its parameters and timeline. Moreover, a gradual process should not mean that some are given more opportunities than others are, as some in the West like to predict. Even Kenneth Pollack, the researcher at the Brookings Institution, does not hesitate to say, in the course of addressing reform in the region, that the advent of Islamists to power as the result of reform would pose a problem, and proposes a number of ways to deal with it, including a gradual approach.[41] The success of Islamist currents in certain Arab countries encouraged several researchers and decision-makers in the West to call for the establishment of civil society institutions, and not to rush to elections until someone more acceptable to the West,[42] and more steeped in Western liberal ideals, or so it seems, is ready in the wings.[43] Brent Scowcroft, Bush Senior's National Security Advisor, said in an interview with Jeffrey Goldberg of the *New Yorker* that the current situation in the Arab world was, and still is, the best scenario for the US because it gave it fifty years of stability, forgetting that it was also fifty years of theft and destruction in the Arab world. Scowcroft went on to say that since economic and social pressure on Arab kingdoms and dictatorships is likely to weaken them, rather than put pressure on them to transition to democracy, the United States should grant them technical and commercial assistance.

In a speech at Cairo University, on 20 June 2005, Condoleezza Rice, George W. Bush's National Security Advisor and later Secretary of State, repeated what Scowcroft had said, but arrived at a different conclusion that highlights the failure of US policy in the region. She said, "For 60 years, my country, the United States, pursued stability at the expense of democracy in this region, here in the Middle East – and we achieved neither. Now, we are taking a different course. We are supporting the democratic aspirations of all people."[44]

However, regardless of whether we are talking about those who, like Scowcroft, want to maintain the status quo in the region, or those who call for a gradual change in our value system to suit Western ideals, we believe that the objective is influencing the course and outcome of reform, a trap that Gulf and Arab countries should not fall into. Views like these also give governments in the region the opportunity to amend constitutions and election laws to prevent individuals, not to their or to the West's liking, from coming to the fore, usually free-minded Islamists or nationalists, after which the country will pay the same price that Algerian society did,[45] and Egyptian society is now paying after the July 2013 uprising.

We would like to attract the readers' attention to the fact that, today, many Western writers and researchers confirm that there is no big difference, in the Arab countries, between a liberal, a nationalist and an Islamist when American policies in the region are concerned, since most of these movements are against these policies.[46] This makes us happy, because it confirms that free-minded people in the Gulf and elsewhere in the Arab world, who put their nation's interests above all else, do not allow their differences to divide and weaken their nation vis-à-vis other nations. It is worth noting here that if reforms, including human rights and the right to elections and free assembly, are in their proper legal context people can only learn them through practice. Therefore, the fear by some that the lack of public political experience, or of the Islamists using the elections to come to power then blocking everyone else's access, is a mere illusion that should not delay the people's right to exercise their rights, since only through long experience can people adjust the course of reform. Civil society also has the right to assemble and demonstrate, a right sorely lacking in the Arab world, especially in the GCC states, and in the rare instances when they are allowed to do so, it is subject to the authorities' approval and control. In other words, just like the economy, civil society's development cannot take place in the shadow of an autocratic regime.[47]

7. Reform vs. security

The seventh issue related to reform is what we could call the strategy of "No sound is louder than the roar of battle," a slogan that governments in the region never tire of repeating when anyone talks about reform. They justify their position by saying that siding with the Palestinian people, or being prepared to counter any looming threat, are more important than reform, which means that these should wait until all outside threats are properly dealt with, an excuse often used to restrict local freedoms even further.[48] Those who ponder these authoritarian governments' records will realise that all their excuses about the country's security are flimsy at best, and that their domestic policies, that failed to win the people's support, have served to weaken their negotiating position with the outside world. Yet, here we have Israel swallowing almost the entire land of Palestine, and an Iran refusing to give back islands that belong to the UAE, and which it occupies, not to mention the overall deteriorating security conditions in the region. This is why excuses like these, solely designed to impede reform, should be rejected, since only reform can help the GCC and Arab countries strengthen their domestic front. Introducing such reforms could also make Israel feel that the balance of power is shifting in favour of the Arab countries, and make it more amenable to offering concessions at the peace table. They could also help the GCC governments develop a common security vision and, through this, become better able to deal with other countries' designs on the region, in particular Iran's, especially if they expand their security cooperation to include the wider Arab region, a subject we will return to in the course of addressing joint Arab action. In brief, what we are trying to say here is that reform would be a significant factor in bringing security to the region, and would give development a huge boost.

8. Migrant workers

As we have seen above, the GCC governments' distorted development policies have created a demographic problem, which, despite varying in intensity from country to country, points to only one direction, an increasing role for migrant workers in the GCC states. This is why addressing the issue of political and non-political reform requires that we first know the implications of these reforms gives the current demographic problem and then find a way of fulfilling the citizens' rights in participating in the decision-making process without infringing on the basic rights of migrant labourers as our religion and international laws requires us to do. Will the region's governments take advantage of this population imbalance to impede any reform process and tighten their grip on the region's population? Alternatively, will they try to find a balance and develop a strategy that reflects realities on the ground, even if implemented in incremental steps? We will know the answer to that in the next few years.[49]

CHAPTER SEVENTEEN

Gulf Unity

The previously mentioned local reforms are regarded as essential steps towards achieving security and development in the region. However, they are not sufficient on their own because the GCC states lack many of the essential elements of development in a world heavily reliant on competition and large regional blocs. This means that the GCC states should find a way to address these shortcomings through some form of integration with the wider Arab and Islamic region, since none of them is capable of ensuring its own security single-handedly given the many sources of instability in the region. It also means that they have to reconcile with their regional environment and find the right balance that guarantees them a maximum level of stability. This is in view of the fact that rather than bringing stability to the region, their dependence on foreign powers has exacerbated existing conflicts and increased chances for war, not to mention the exorbitant costs, an issue we addressed earlier in the book. This is why seizing all available opportunities for development and security in the region requires these countries to raise the level of cooperation among them, and to reduce chances for conflict and tension, both of which require efforts on more than one level. The first level is Gulf unity and a new kind of inter-Arab cooperation that includes expanding the free trade area between the Arab countries and developing a common Arab security strategy. What is certain, however, is that Gulf unity will not make significant progress unless they implement the reforms mentioned in the previous chapter; the main reason why these countries have so far not achieved integration, despite efforts in this regard since the establishment of the GCC in the early 1980s, is precisely the failure to implement these reforms. Therefore, although we have already mentioned the GCC's record in promoting integration, we will begin this chapter with a brief review of this record and examine how efforts towards integration could be improved in the next few years. To help us do that, we should learn from the experience of other blocs, especially the European Union, before weighing the costs and benefits of integration to the region as a whole.

First: History of integration in the Gulf

In 1981, six Gulf countries, Saudi Arabia, Kuwait, Oman, the UAE, Qatar and Bahrain, signed an agreement to establish what became known as the Gulf Cooperation Council (GCC). Although security considerations resulting from the Iranian Revolution and the Iran-Iraq War were the main reason behind the entity's creation, the new body had its own economic, cultural and political objectives. According to the GGCs' Unified Economic Agreement, the member countries intended to cooperate in various fields, including trade, the movement of factors of production, technology, transportation and communications, as well as fiscal and monetary policies. The Agreement also stated that member countries intended to work towards a gradual process of economic integration, starting with the establishment of a free trade area, followed three years later by a customs union, then a common Gulf market and, ultimately, total economic unity. However, as the next section will clearly show, when governments not accountable to their people are in power, decisions and implementation are not always one and the same.

1. The free trade area

In 1983, the GCC states decided to establish a free trade area, and in fact began dismantling customs barriers on trade in locally produced goods among member countries. However, since the free trade area does not oblige member countries to unify their customs duties with non-member countries, the process may lead to a phenomenon known as "trade deflection", which happens when goods are first shipped to a zone member with low customs duties before being forwarded to their intended destination. For example, a shipment from Germany is unloaded first at the port of Dubai because of its low tariffs, then forwarded on to a final destination that has a high tariff, like Saudi Arabia, to benefit from the difference between the two tariffs.[1] This problem is solved usually by applying the criteria of rules of origin, thereby confirming that the goods crossing the borders between member countries are locally produced, and therefore should be tax exempt, or else be taxed. Locally produced goods are, therefore, defined as those goods whose added value within the GCC area is no less than 40 per cent and the share of local ownership no less than 51 per cent. However, implementing these cross-border measures could be costly, since the European Union estimated its corresponding costs at 3 to 5 per cent of inter-European trade.[2] These measures also have a negative impact on trade between member countries. Some studies on the GCC's free trade experience show that trucks laden with goods, some perishable, waited sometimes up to two days at the borders because the relevant documents were either inaccurate or incomplete, or because customs officials at the border post were inadequately trained.[3] There are other obstacles, besides the rules of origin, impeding the cross-border transit of goods within the GCC states' free trade area, including a lack of agreement on product specifications, giving preferential treatment to locally produced goods, and various security considerations.[4] Thus, instead of establishing the Customs Union in 1983, according to which the GCC states were supposed to unify their customs duties with the rest of the world, these countries were content to set a fixed tariff of 4 to 20 per cent with the outside world. The decision was a compromise between Saudi Arabia's high tariffs that aim to protect the country's nascent industries, and the low tariff in Dubai, an important commercial regional centre that needs low tariffs to flourish.

It is worth mentioning that before reaching the agreement on the highest and lowest limits of customs duties, the GCC states' customs tariffs with the outside world were as follows: the UAE's was 4 per cent, Saudi Arabia's was 30 per cent, Bahrain's was 10 per cent, Oman's and Qatar's was 20 per cent and Kuwait's was 25 per cent.[5] The tariffs also differed from one country to the other, depending on the kind of product; in Saudi Arabia, for example, although tariffs on most goods ranged between 0 and 12 per cent, it was as high as 20 per cent for tobacco. In the UAE, tariffs on most products were in the range of 4 per cent, with a higher tariff on alcohol and tobacco. In Bahrain, tariffs on most products ranged between 5 and 10 per cent, with 20 per cent on cars and motor boats, up to 125 per cent on alcohol and, in 1997, tariffs on tobacco rose from 50 to 70 per cent. In Kuwait, tariffs ranged between 4 and 25 per cent, but remained relatively low on capital goods, food products and consumer goods. Finally, tariffs on most goods in Oman were around 5 per cent, with 100 per cent on alcohol and lemons, and an exemption for government imports.[6] The non-unified customs duties and similar economic infrastructures were not the only impediments to Gulf unity; non-customs related impediments were, and still are, another major obstacle to genuine economic integration in the Gulf.

Abdullah al-Quwaiz, former Undersecretary of the GCC for Economic Affairs, spoke about the above impediments, addressing first the difference between laws and legislation issued by the GCC's General Secretariat, and those issued by individual GCC states. The second impediment he addressed was the extremely slow process of unifying standards and measurements among Council members. This was so slow that more than ten years after the GCC's establishment only 107 of the criteria proposed by the Council's Secretariat had been approved. The third impediment was the member countries' inability to adopt a common position regarding the relationship between the public and private sectors as far as incentives and organisation were concerned. The fourth and final impediment was the high number of administrative obstacles impeding the cross-border transit of goods and individuals.[7] Therefore, the process of integration in the Gulf was slow from the outset because these countries' governments were not ready to give up any part of their sovereignty for the sake of a wider regional entity. Moreover, the lack of transparency and accountability made it such that no competent authority could monitor the implementation of the Council's decisions, not to mention the scarce human and material resources at the disposal of the GCC Secretariat. This naturally resulted in the development processes in these countries being characterised by waste due to duplicated projects that were unjustified economically and created wide disparities among different member countries. Border disputes among Council members added to the reigning tension and recurrent wars in the region only deepened the disagreements among these countries, with the fluctuating oil prices and revenues not helping much either.

2. The customs union

This stagnation, delay in establishing the customs union in the early part of the twenty-first century and the deepening economic crises could all explain why Saudi King Abdullah Bin Abdul-Aziz told the Muscat Summit Conference of 2001 that the Council will not achieve its stated objectives due to its slow procedures, and called on member countries to unify and speed up their efforts in the face of global challenges. The above statement by the Saudi King could also be the reason why the Muscat Summit came out with a new economic agreement, in lieu of the agreement of 1981, calling for the establishment of a customs union in January 2003, with a customs tariff of 5 per cent on foreign imports. The new agreement provided for the establishment of a monetary union among the GCC states, based on a single currency tied to the dollar, as of the beginning of 2010. However, this customs union would have had a certain negative fallout on these countries had they not succeeded in avoiding it, namely the "trade diversion" effect. This could have happened if, after the union's establishment, a commodity were imported from a member country at a higher price than it used to be imported from another country that was not a member of the new union. For example, Qatar used to import dates from Iraq prior to the customs union's establishment but when it became a union member alongside Saudi Arabia, the fact that the two countries shared a common customs tariff made the price of Saudi dates cheaper for the Qataris than Iraqi dates. This phenomenon means in effect that the purchasing power of these two countries' revenues dropped and could have led to lower levels of consumption in the union zone countries.[8] However, the GCC states avoided this negative impact by agreeing to a 5 per cent tariff which is more or less equivalent to the lowest customs tariff among union members under the free trade area; in other words, this helped avoid the potential impact of trade diversion.[9] Naturally, the establishment of the customs union in 2003 also meant the end of "trade deflection" and, with it, an end to the measures related to rules of origin. However, other problems remained due to the lack of accountability, transparency, data and statistics, and to the incompetence of the GCC's General Secretariat, or its lack of prerogatives.

Suffice it to say, that while it took the European Union three years to move from a free trade area to a customs union, the GCC states took over twenty years to do so. However, announcing the union's establishment does not necessarily mean, given the above-mentioned shortcomings, that the institutional environment is ready for closer integration. This is why it is not surprising to hear people in the region say that they do not feel this integration as being real; they still do not see the impact of the integration people talk about at summit conferences on their daily lives. Had this customs union been effective, it would have brought numerous benefits to the GCC states, including collective bargaining to establish free zones with other Arab countries, such as Yemen, which would have allowed them to import the workforce they need from that country. They would have also been able to establish free zones with the European Union and Asian countries to benefit from their markets and technology, instead of engaging in bilateral negotiations, as Bahrain and Oman did to establish free trade areas with the United States, when they knew that individual negotiations were at the expense of Gulf integration. When Bahrain establishes a free trade area with the United States while it is a member of a larger Gulf entity, it is in fact indirectly allowing American products to pass through it and then on to Saudi Arabia, which does not share a free trade area with the United States, and so on.[10] This regional entity could also help in the negotiations with the WTO aimed at abolishing the taxes imposed by consumer countries on crude oil, the main source of income for the region's countries.

3. The Gulf Common Market

Regardless of what these countries have managed to achieve during the customs union stage, given we have very little data available on that, at the twenty-eighth summit conference in Doha in December 2007, the GCC states announced the establishment of a Gulf Common Market, with a launch date of January 2008. The Common Market's creation presupposes the existence of a single economic citizenship, i.e., the equal treatment of all GCC citizens in matters related to the economy. These include the right to engage in economic activities, work in one's chosen profession, trade in stocks and shares, establish a company, seek employment in the public or private sector, benefit from a social and retirement insurance plan, real estate ownership, movement of capital, tax-related facilities, education and health services, and the rights of movement and residence.[11] Nevertheless, whilst all is well at the level of making decisions and issuing declarations, implementation of the Common Market is an entirely different matter. It is plagued by numerous problems, including the slow implementation of decisions, large number of exceptions and reservations, lack of commitment by some members to the programme's agenda which has created a large gap between resolutions, and practices, and the many obstacles that impeded earlier stages of integration.[12] On the other hand, the European Union only progressed from the customs union stage to the common market stage after eliminating all remaining non-tariff barriers, like border inspections, complex customs procedures, divergent criteria and control measures, contradictory labour laws and discrimination in government purchases. Eliminating these barriers led to the creation of the second largest economic bloc in the world, with an economy almost as large as that of the USA. This measured response and competent execution of the EU's decisions is, in our opinion, due to the presence of a political leadership that expresses the will of the people, and is accountable to them.[13]

4. The Monetary Union

Once the common market is established, the GCC states should expand their integration by exchanging their respective central banks for a single bank, and crown their integration with a so-called monetary union, followed by union at all levels, which is what the European Union did. The Maastricht Treaty, signed in 1991, announced that 2002 would be the year when the European Monetary Union would become a reality, and the Euro would become the Union's single currency. However, the European Monetary Union imposed a number of economic conditions on the European countries to make them eligible to join the

Union, the intention being to bring the member countries' economies closer to each other, in terms of growth rates, general budget, public debt size, monetary policies and the stability of their exchange rates.[14] By 1999, eleven of the fifteen EU countries had fulfilled these conditions and thus became founding members of the European Monetary Union, which continued to forge ahead towards its ultimate objective, political unity. In the GCC, as stated earlier, the decision to create a monetary union was adopted at the summit conference in 2001, and the establishment of a single currency was supposed to be announced in 2010, after tying the individual countries' currencies firmly to the dollar in 2007. The members agreed on a set of conditions necessary for launching the single currency, inspired by the EU's own conditions. The first condition is that the interest rate on short-term loans in each candidate country does not exceed 2 per cent above the average interest rates of the three countries with the lowest rates in the block. The second condition is that the rate of inflation in each country does not exceed 2 per cent above the average rate in the block, as a whole. The third condition is that in each candidate country the deficit rate in relation to the GDP does not exceed 3 per cent, under the present circumstances, and 5 per cent when there is a drop in oil prices. The fourth condition is that the public debts of individual countries should not exceed 60 per cent of their GDP and the fifth is that each country should maintain sufficient foreign reserves to cover at least four months' worth of imports.

The GCC states seemed to move forward towards the establishment of a single currency until decisions regarding the monetary union began to stall, as they had done before. Oman withdrew from the prospective union for unclear reasons, followed by the UAE after being refused from hosting the Union's central bank, which compelled the four remaining countries to announce the decision to forge ahead with their own plans to establish a monetary union. As usual, committees and experts were tasked with preparing the relevant documents, and it was announced that Saudi Arabia would host the union's central bank. We would be justified here in asking what benefits this integration stage, i.e., the monetary union, is likely to bring. There is no doubt that this union is an advanced step towards integration, in addition to several economic and political benefits,[15] because when several countries decide to unify their currencies, it benefits individuals, institutions and society as a whole. For example, if a single GCC currency were to exist, when a UAE citizen goes to Saudi Arabia on pilgrimage, he would not need to exchange his own currency for Saudi money, and would thus avoid paying the exchange fee. When we talk about currency exchanges by individuals and institutions, we are actually talking about large sums of money. Likewise, an Omani investor who wants to buy shares on the

Bahraini Stock Exchange would not have to worry about erratic exchange rates between different currencies. When several currencies are involved, the investor will not know for sure the value of his investments or the profit he stands to gain when he decides to take his investments back to Oman, a year or more later. The latter problem could be resolved, of course, by tying the GCC currencies to the dollar, for example, as was the case before. There is a growing tendency in recent years, however, towards relinquishing the dollar as the only peg currency, with Kuwait actually pegging its currency to a basket of currencies that includes the dollar, instead of only to the dollar. This trend seems to be gaining momentum, especially in light of the problems the American economy and the dollar are currently experiencing.

Naturally, the benefits of a single Gulf currency go well beyond simply reducing the cost of economic transactions and the level of investor uncertainty, and the resulting increase in the volume of trade and investment. A single currency will also allow the GCC states to embark on serious negotiations with other blocs in view of finding new forms of integration among them. A single Gulf currency will no doubt become one of the most important currencies in the world, especially if it becomes the currency of choice for crude oil sales to the rest of the world, or for part of these sales; it will encourage many investors to save it as insurance against the fluctuations of other currencies. It will also raise the value of shares traded on stock exchanges in the GCC, raise the level of transparency, develop the currently nonexistent database in the Gulf countries, and promote other integration-related benefits, which we will address later on.

Second: Promoting unity in the Gulf

It is clear from the above that Gulf integration still lacks the necessary political will and suffers from weak regional institutions, contradictory policies, scarce information and other impediments that only the above-mentioned comprehensive reforms can dispel. Therefore, the mechanisms necessary to promote economic integration in the Gulf, which we shall address in the following section, depend on the implementation of a number of reforms that foster the right atmosphere for these measures to achieve their objective. Among these measures are:

1. Eliminating non-tariff related barriers

Among the most important lessons learnt from experiences of regional integration around the world is that governments tend to replace obvious tariff barriers with non-tariff barriers that are difficult for people to detect, and governments in the Gulf are no different. The removal of tariff barriers is a necessary condition, but not enough on its own to increase the volume of trade among the GCC states, given the large number of non-tariff barriers that still exist. Governments should eliminate or suspend all obstructive measures, especially at this quite advanced stage of monetary integration. Among the non-tariff barriers we find the following:

a) Although at present the GCC states do not widely apply pre-emptive protectionist measures that prevent market dumping, counter other countries' export protectionist policies, or apply contingency protectionist measures that address the disequilibrium in the balance of payments, they still should first agree among themselves not to use them in the future, under any circumstance. Instead of resorting to such measures, they should agree to refer in the future all disagreements either to the GCC's conflict resolution committee, or to the WTO.

b) Border posts between different GCC states have numerous slow and often complex administrative procedures including forms that need to be filled, documents that need reverification, and various procedural delays that impede trade and raise its cost. These could be addressed by training the staff at the border posts, establishing a database, using generic forms and employing the most recent technology and customs clearing measures, used in the developed countries.[16]

c) The GCC states could streamline trade between them if they manage to reduce the differences between the standards, measurements and specifications of their products, including health, security and competition standards. These differences have been an impediment to the process of economic integration in the Gulf since the establishment of the GCC, in 1981. These could be reduced by either ratifying them or unifying many of them based on another country's standards, as Canada did when it used US standards to gauge the level of vehicle pollution in 1992, or when Switzerland used the EU's standards to manage its technologies and gauge industrial production standards. However, accepting the status quo means not preventing the circulation of a certain product in member countries, as long as one of them wants it, a system that could serve as an interim solution until the unification of standards and measurements for the long term.[17]

d) A practice that is widespread throughout the world, including the GCC states, is giving preferential treatment to local or national institutions when buying goods and services. This preferential or discriminatory policy comes in different shapes and forms including forcing foreign companies to use locally manufactured components in their products, i.e., using local labour and/or resources in their production process, or treating them preferentially in terms of price, or on condition that they be locally based. In Kuwait, for example, Kuwaiti products are treated preferentially in term of price, up to 5 per cent compared to the products of other GCC states, and up to 10 per cent compared to other countries' products. In Bahrain, government purchases give similar priority to local products. In Oman, the government subsidises loans to companies with local majority shares and whose products are earmarked for export.[18] Doing away with such forms of discrimination will, undoubtedly, increase competition among different Gulf-based companies, and make the use of local resources much more efficient. However, the experience of other regional blocs, like the EU, shows that it is difficult to eliminate this type of preferential treatment when there is no political will to do so, supported by highly efficient administrative institutions.

2. The balance sheet of costs and benefit

The establishment of a Gulf economic union will affect prices in respective member countries. Thus, while certain sectors will expand, others will narrow down and some industries will move from one member country to another, and while some government revenues will increase, others' will decrease. Moreover, because of their relative advantage and the establishment of large economic projects, economic integration among these countries could lead to either an increase or a decrease in the income gap between member countries, even within each country, although bridging the income gap between these countries would be a positive development. The fear, however, is that an increase in the income gap would provoke a drop in standards of living in certain member countries, and lead to a change of heart and less enthusiasm about Gulf integration. Other blocs' experience in this domain is varied and inconclusive. For example, while the European Union's experience shows that integration brought standards of living in member countries closer together, the experience of some developing countries shows the exact opposite, i.e., a wider gap in living standards among bloc members.[19] Nevertheless, despite the difficulty in gauging the impact this will have on each member country, most economists estimate that, on balance, the formation of regional blocs proved to be a positive experience. Though the benefits could seem quite small when we take into consideration the static effects of economic integration, i.e., generating trade and trade diversion in the early years after integration, these benefits could be much greater if they comprise the dynamic and long-term effects of integration. These effects include an increase in competition, benefits from the economies of scale and the ensuing drop in costs, the accumulation of capital, i.e., increase in productivity, technical advances, attraction of foreign investment, improved negotiating stances and other above-mentioned benefits.[20] Gulf integration will therefore have some positive and some negative effects, especially during the initial formation stage.

The experience of other regional blocs tells us that success and survival depend largely on the member countries' ability to distribute these costs and benefits fairly, and this in turn will strengthen the new entity itself. This is the reason why the GCC states should establish a body whose responsibility is to address the distributional effects, at every stage, using mechanisms that do not adversely affect the efficient use and distribution of resources. There are at least three different mechanisms to address the effects of distribution resulting from the unification of customs tariffs with the outside world. The first is compensating the member state for the revenue it loses by lowering its customs tariffs on foreign imports. The second is giving countries that incurred losses the right to decide where joint projects should be located, while ensuring that this distribution-oriented decision does not conflict with the efficient use of the new entity's resources. The third is leaving the door open for the possibility of exempting certain member states from the commitment to liberalise certain aspects of their economies, for a limited period only, provided these exemptions and their duration are clearly delineated so that they do not become permanent.[21]

3. Regulation and development of the financial sector

The importance of a well-developed financial sector to ensure the success of any development process is attributed to the writings of Joseph Schumpeter in the early 1930s.[22] Later on, both theoretical and practical studies have proved that financial development speeds up economic growth; in other words, the more advanced the financial sector is, the higher is the country's economic growth rate.[23] Financial development helps the economy grow in at least two ways: the first is through the presence of a highly efficient financial system, that makes risk management easier for savers and investors, and in turn helps steer more savings towards long-term and more productive investment assets.[24] The second way is by collecting and analysing data and, by doing this, steering investors towards worthwhile and profit-generating projects, taking advantage of economies of scale not available to individual investors. The reason is that while financial institutions reduce costs by collecting the relevant data for all their customers at the same time, individuals who do not enjoy this privilege have to pay more, since they have to do their own data collection and analysis. This means that in an advanced financial system, investors can obtain financial services at a lower cost, and this, in turn, reduces the cost of investment and increases the rate of economic growth.[25] Banks and financial markets are the main components of a financial system, and while banks play the main role early in the development process, once the economy becomes more developed and complex, the financial market assumes a more important role by cycling funds from the savers to the investors. Those who look closely at financial markets in the Gulf will realise that they are still at the embryonic stage, whether in terms of the amount of capital, liquidity, capital cycling, the number of companies listed on the stock markets, regulation, transparency or data available.[26] Therefore, to take better advantage of the available resources and successfully tackle the challenges that development brings in its wake in a global economy that is both wide open and largely reliant on competition, the GCC states should reform their financial systems by doing the following:

a) The GCC states should upgrade their financial sectors' performance with a social outlook that is transparent, accountable and allows for the establishment of private financial institutions compatible with the requirements of development. The latter should also be subject to oversight by the state to avoid the negative exploitation of public assets, and ensure that the private sector does not drag these countries' economies into financial crises that impede development and increase the debt burden. The presence of both public and private sector institutions, in the shadow of an efficient oversight system, is no doubt the best option. This requires, however, that the government sector be subject to public accountability, and that the private sector be national and productive rather than parasitic and overburdened by the urge to make a quick profit through speculations on local and global markets. The delineation of each of these two sectors' share of the market should not be arbitrarily decided, but should depend on the level of social development in the country. The more aligned the private sector is with society's development goals and the clearer and more efficient the oversight it is subjected to, the larger is the role it is able to play; and the reverse is also true.

b)   Since the financial sector in these countries is still at the formation level, and its size in terms of liquidity, capital and the capital cycle is still modest, it might as well leave the door open for foreign financial institutions in order to encourage competition. This would allow financial institutions to operate within a larger Gulf market and enable them to diversify their risks, take advantage of the economies of scale and learn from the foreign companies' administrative and technical skills within clear and targetted laws.[27]

c)   Finally, the experiences of other countries, whether industrialised or developing, show that the financial system's credibility and development rate depend largely on the judiciary's independence, the execution of contracts, transparency, overall economic stability and the political will to reform. It also shows that in order to reduce the risk of financial crises, a country needs to attract investments to productive long-term projects that are ready to shoulder their share of gains and losses, instead of attracting funds for speculation, which was and still is one of the reasons behind the recent series of financial crises. These crises have plagued the world for the past thirty years, the last being the American real estate crisis that soon became a global crisis, the dimensions of which are yet to be determined.[28]

Third: Costs and benefits of Gulf unity

If the GCC states succeed in turning their decisions into actual programmes, Gulf unity is likely to bring them numerous potential economic and non-economic benefits, in return for which they will have to pay a certain cost in the short term. People should be aware of these diverse benefits and the fact that they far outweigh the costs, so that all social strata in Gulf would have the will to forge ahead towards total unity, starting with the monetary union that has unfortunately stalled in recent years. We will therefore start by detailing the main benefits before addressing some of the costs, especially in the final stages of unity.

1.   Economic benefits of Gulf unity

Like all regional blocs, Gulf unity would bring a wide range of benefits to its member countries, some of which would be economic. The most important among these are:

a) Like other regional blocs, Gulf economic integration will probably favour trade liberalisation, one of the WTO's main objectives, as long as the customs tariffs do not lead to trade diversion, as we mentioned earlier in the context of addressing Gulf unity. This is tantamount to an admission that regional blocs can achieve a number of economic objectives for member countries that might not be that high on the WTO's deliberations or its agenda.[29]

b) Apart from being a framework within which issues that the WTO has no time for could be addressed and resolved, if this new entity manages to unify its ranks and behave as a bloc, instead of each GCC country negotiating separately with the club of big countries, not only would negotiations with the WTO be easier, they would reap more benefits. We shall return to this point when we address the GCC's active presence in international organisations.[30]

c) Economic integration will increase the volume of trade among member countries. The removal of tariffs and other barriers will help increase the volume of trade among these countries. There is no doubt that the more diverse these countries' economies are, the bigger the impact this would have, a fact confirmed by studies on various economic blocs. Unifying the bloc's currencies, and what it would mean in terms of reducing uncertainty and the cost of exchanging one currency for another, is also likely to increase the volume of trade among member countries. A recent study on the European Monetary Union's impact on trade among the Eurozone countries showed that the volume of trade went up by 4 per cent to 16 per cent, depending on the research method used, since Europe unified its currency.[31] Similar benefits are expected to accrue from an eventual union in the Gulf, even if these are likely to be more modest at the present stage due to the similarity of the countries' economic structures.

d) Economic integration will also help eliminate the obstacles that impede the movement of factors of production between member countries. This means that these would be able to move around under the single currency umbrella, making it easier to compare costs in the region. The fact that this would allow the factors of production to go where productivity is at its highest will improve the way member countries use their resources. This, in turn, will increase production and employment and bring economic prosperity to the region.[32]

e) One of the most important benefits from a deeper and more complete union in the Gulf is the potential increase in the size of the market. This increase will allow producers to start manufacturing commodities that the size of the market did not allow before integration. Once the size of the market is increased, producers will be able to benefit from the economies of scale, maintain competitive prices and start spreading their products, first in the local market then in world markets.[33] The experience of the European Union shows that many industries have benefitted from the creation of the European Common Market including aluminium, shoes, cars and refineries. For example, the EU's experience with manufacturing refrigerators is a good example of the dynamic impact that economic integration could have. Prior to integration, the countries that produced refrigerators, namely Italy, Germany and France, depended on factories that produced for the local market at a capacity of no more than 100,000 refrigerators per year, which entailed quite high costs. After integration, however, the market expanded and allowed the industry to use advanced technological tools it could not use before, due to the limited size of the market in each of these countries. Thus, in the late 1960s, an average refrigerator factory in Italy began producing 850,000 refrigerators per year, and in Germany and France, around 570,000 and 290,000 units respectively.[34] Over and above expanding the size of the market, integration fosters a climate of competition that in turn leads to creativity and inventiveness in the fields of manufacturing, management and technology, because each institution wants to dominate the market. An expanding market also attracts more foreign investments, which encourages people to make more skills, technology and capital available to the new market, in order to increase their profits from it.[35]

f) The creation of a Gulf entity, integrated economically and at all other levels, will help mitigate many of the current conflicts among the GCC members themselves, and reduce tensions between them and their neighbours. A typical example of that is the establishment of the European Coal and Steel Community in 1951 to mitigate disagreements between France and Germany at the time. Other examples of a regional bloc helping mitigate potential conflicts in a region are the agreements concluded between Argentina and Brazil,[36] and between Indonesia and Malaysia.[37] The reason integration reduces tensions among neighbouring countries in a given region is the role it plays in increasing interaction and trust among these nation's citizens, and in growing the network of mutual interests between countries and their respective populations, which makes conflicts more costly and less likely to happen.[38] Positive economic integration goes beyond that to also mitigating conflicts between the bloc's member states and their neighbours. Numerous studies indicate that one of the reasons behind the GCC's establishment in 1981 was the need to reduce potential threats from neighbouring countries like Iran and Iraq,[39] and one of the reason behind the creation of ASEAN, by a group of East Asian countries, was the need to contain the spread of communism.[40] Similarly, the Southern African Development Coordination Conference held in 1980 was aimed essentially at countering the apartheid regime in South Africa.[41] Therefore, we can say that if these countries manage to achieve integration and take significant steps towards other forms of integration with their neighbours, then many of the Gulf region's resources squandered on regional wars and conflicts over the past thirty years could be salvaged and redirected towards productive development projects. Over the past twenty years, the Arab countries' military expenses were estimated at 3000 billion dollars, i.e., $3 trillion.[42]

g) Gulf integration will improve the negotiating positions of the region's countries with the rest of the world because the benefits and costs that countries eventually reap are the outcome of the balance of power under which they negotiate with others. This means that the larger and stronger the bloc a country belongs to, the better it is able to protect its interests. We could use Europe again here as an example to clarify this particular impact of integration. The EU has succeeded in reaping considerable benefits in its trade and military negotiations, specifically because of its solidarity and the fact that it negotiates with others as a bloc. Before European unification, individual European countries entered into trade negotiations under the umbrella of the General Agreement on Tariffs and Trade (GATT), but after unification, they began negotiating as a single bloc.[43] Therefore, since the GCC states are well integrated in the world and depend on it for selling their oil and buying their other needs, unifying their negotiating positions will enable them to reap numerous benefits relevant to oil pricing, foreign investments, transfer of technology, purchasing consumer goods, and developing the production and marketing of their petrochemical industry. In other words, the conditions under which they interact with the world, whether commercially or otherwise, will improve significantly and open more avenues for development and stability.

Foreign investments, for example, bring with them advanced technologies and administrative skills from which they could benefit in developing their economies and raising their workers' productivity levels. There is also no doubt that foreign oil companies could play a major role in this development, as they did in Malaysia and other developing countries whose governments knew exactly what they wanted from these companies.[44]

h) Among the other benefits of a deeper integration to the GCC is their governments' commitment to introducing the series of reforms that this integration requires, whether internal or external, which would allow the country's interests to take precedence over the interests of local pressure groups. This will lend international credibility to the bloc's members, attract investments, deter enemies and provide more opportunities for development.[45]

i) Finally, one of the main features of this prospective Gulf union, expected to introduce the above-mentioned reforms, is the formation of a unified Gulf Army, and the first step towards this goal could be the reactivation of the Peninsula Shield Force. Though the formation of such an army is a necessary step to deter other countries' ambitions in the region, it is not sufficient on its own. It should be backed by an Arab regional order similar to the EU's or ASEAN's, or any other such formula, whose main axis will be formed by the Arab countries, coupled with a level of coordination and cooperation with neighbouring countries. The aim of this new order, the core of which could be formed initially by a number of Arab countries before the rest join, would be to fill the security vacuum left behind by Iraq's retreat from the scene, allay the GCC states' fears of Iran's increasing influence and relieve them from having to rely on foreigners for their protection. If its activation gradually reduces the foreign presence and acts as an effective deterrent to Iran's power in the region, this security order could ensure a measure of stability and build confidence. There is no doubt that the stronger this order becomes, once all the Arab countries have joined in and there is ongoing cooperation between them in various domains, particularly the economic domain, the more stability and prosperity it will help instil in the region. This will be the case especially if the Arabs succeed in rebuilding trust and eliminating residual feelings from the recent past, particularly feelings among Gulf citizens regarding Iraq's occupation of Kuwait, and the Iraqi people's feelings about attitudes in the Gulf vis-à-vis Iraq's occupation by the great powers. Such reconciliation is not a luxury but a necessity for the Arabs, who should choose between asserting their independence and their ability to make their potential renaissance a reality, or their downfall and remaining on the sidelines of history for a long time to come.[46]

2. Costs of Gulf unity

To enjoy the above benefits, the GCC states should pay a certain price while in transition from separate national entities, with their own institutions and policies, to a single entity that merges their institutions and policies to achieve the expected benefits. Here is a list of the most important costs they will have to shoulder, or, what we could call, the price of Gulf unity.

a) Once established, monetary union in the Gulf will mean that there is a single central bank and a single currency. It also means that monetary policies become the responsibility of the union's central bank, which in turn means that member countries will no longer be able to control either the interest rate or the amount of reserves available, as they did before, because these decisions are now subject to a collective vision that the central bank represents.[47] For example, if economic development in one of the GCC states were lagging behind, this country would want its interest rate to be low to help revive its economy, whereas a country suffering from inflation would want to raise the interest rate to control inflation. However, the presence of a unified central bank would mean that this bank would determine the interest rate for the union as a whole, a rate that might not be low enough to revive the economy of the first country, or high enough to reduce inflation in the latter. Therefore, a unified monetary policy might not be suitable for some members of this union.[48] However, even this temporary cost is hard to envisage by any of the GCC states, in the first few years, given the similarities between their economies, and their economic structures.

b) There is near consensus among economists that, in the short term, there will be an inverse relationship between inflation and unemployment. In other words, countries that want to fight unemployment will make larger cash amounts available to encourage economic growth and provide employment, even if this leads to an increase in the rate of inflation, while other countries may prefer to curb inflation even if it leads to an increase in the rate of unemployment. However, given that the central bank of an eventual Gulf Union would typically seek to institute a single rate of inflation, this rate might not be compatible with an unemployment rate acceptable to all member states.[49] Again, this particular price that some will have to pay should not be seen as an obstacle. The system of revenue and cost distribution, mentioned earlier in the context of addressing various means of deepening Gulf unity, could be a remedy to the problem in the short and middle terms, or until standards of living in the member states become closer to one another.

c) Gulf unity will no doubt bring numerous short-term and long-term benefits. However, these benefits might not be the same for all countries; they might differ from one group to another, one country to another and one time-period to another. In the beginning, we might find that certain countries have benefitted more than others did, and that some countries have lost to others better able to compete because either their workforce is more capable or their institutions more developed, and so on. This is only natural because unity means more openness to one another and more competition, and, as we saw earlier, this will help steer these countries' resources to where they would be used best in the bloc as a whole.[50] Thus, if the cost of restructuring the economies of member countries proves too high, they could apply various financial and monetary policies, even industrial policies, to address the issue, especially in the first years after unity. This would avoid a polarised development process, whereby one country in the union prospers while another suffers from abject poverty.

Chapter Eighteen

Joint Arab Action:
A Development and Security Necessity

We spoke about the developmental and security challenges that the GCC states continue to face, and highlighted the shortcomings that resulted from the developmental and security policies that these countries' governments have been pursuing over the past thirty years. This made it clear that what will determine these countries' future is their ability to take stock of their experience, and amend their path accordingly to ensure that their people will enjoy more stability and prosperity in the future. We underlined the need for these countries to overcome the division, dismemberment and dependency of previous years by laying the cornerstone of the right path to follow, which is the establishment of a Gulf union at the economic, security, political and other levels, the ultimate objective for whose sake the GCC was established. We indicated on several occasions in this book that efforts towards Gulf unity should not come at the expense of joint Arab action, but alongside it and in complement to it. For reasons that have to do with human and natural resources, the GCC states cannot achieve sustainable development, even with its huge oil reserves, without the support of their Arab hinterland; they cannot achieve stability without sheltering under the Arab security umbrella, and cannot be effective in international organisations except through joint Arab action. Yet, despite all these warnings and the past failures of joint Arab action at all levels, this option remains much better than the alternative. This alternative is for these countries to go on wasting their natural resources in the shadow of a foreign presence that manufactures war, increases dismemberment and fabricates crises in the region, without leading to any kind of development, as evidenced by these countries' experiences since the 1970s. Therefore, joint Arab action that goes hand in hand with efforts to deepen Gulf unity is the safety valve that will ensure that unity will bring development and stability, and the tool that will allow the GCC to play an effective Gulf role on the international stage. This is why we thought it necessary to shed light on the various dimensions of joint Arab action, and allow the reader to ascertain for himself the importance of the Arab dimension in ensuring the security and prosperity of the Gulf. To begin with, we must draw attention to two kinds of theses, one of which was circulated before the Arab Spring and the other at its start. The first argument is that the major states in the Arab region, like Egypt, Syria and Iraq, had their role marginalised and that the balance of power, especially the economic one, made the GCC states the pivotal countries in the region.[1] The second argument is that the uprisings of the Arab Spring had a nationalist character and aimed at political and economic reforms within each country, but were not concerned either with the dreams of Arab unity or the fight against colonialism.[2] We do not deny that key states in the Arab world, particularly Egypt, are in decline because of the failures of their successive governments in enabling them to undertake a leading role in the Arab world for certain internal and external reasons, nor that the Arab Spring uprisings focus on the issues of freedom and social justice. However, we do not want the members of Arab society to be deceived by these arguments that seek, intentionally or unintentionally, to ingrain the current conditions of the Arab world, including the division, backwardness, dependence and instability. The experience of the GCC, the development and security dimensions of which we have dealt with in previous chapters, confirms the importance of integrating the Arab world for development and security considerations. Those who propagate the economic power of the Gulf and attempt to mislead Gulf society into believing that it no longer needs its Arab brethren are the first to acknowledge the limited economic importance of these states. This does not extend beyond being an exhaustible oil source, oil surpluses and sovereign funds that are wasted on excessive consumer models and trade brands, turning them into resources committed to the successive financial crises which are afflicting Western economies. These facts are confirmed by one researcher who says: "As the West has been going through a period of profound financial distress and economic crisis since the late 2000s, the GCC states have been using their enhanced financial powers to buy up high-profile and iconic global brands (Harrods, Ferrari and Porsche), recapitalize otherwise depleted Western financial institutions (Merrill Lynch, Citigroup, and Barclays Bank), and carve out distinctive niches for themselves in global interest areas (mediation and renewable energy)."[3]

In terms of security, we know that the US has been dominating this region since the occupation of Iraq in 2003. This American domination has not achieved the minimum stability in the Gulf such that the region has continued to experience a state of instability or destructive wars, and that is attested to by Western sources themselves.[4] These wars have led to the depletion of the region's wealth and the biggest gainer of these by far is the US. According to a report issued by Congress in 2012, the GCC states are the biggest buyers of American arms inasmuch as their purchases between 2007 and 2010 were more than $26.7 billion, and this is the biggest arms deal in the history of the US.[5] The paradox hidden in the report's conclusion is that despite the amounts these countries invested in their armies, most of them "are not yet fully capable of independently sustaining significant tactical support to the United States in times of crisis".[6] We see no contradiction between the Arab uprisings' focus on freedom and social justice domestically and their hope for Arab unity and refusal of all forms of colonialism, and their desire for friendly and generous relations with all countries in the world, as long as they respect the rights of the Arab people. This aspect will be clarified in our discussion later.

First: Justifications

Those who ponder conditions in Arab world since the early 1970s, especially after the military defeat of June 1967, cannot deny the obvious downward trend it has experienced at all levels, despite its increasing oil wealth, a trend that has negatively affected all the Arab countries without exception. However, although it is important to understand the impact that this downward trend has had on each and every Arab country, we have only room here to look at some of its impact on the GCC states, to underline the fact that the Arab nation is like one body: when one organ suffers, all the others feel the pain. Thus, when Egypt was the leader of the Arab regional order, the Arab body was somewhat able to face its internal crises and external challenges; but when it no longer played that role, the entire order crumbled and the balance of power, as far as the Palestinian cause was concerned, began shifting gradually in favour of Israel. Whereas all the Arabs were once intent on liberating all of Palestine, the nation split into two camps after the peace treaties with Israel. The first camp lives in a dream world where peace is at hand; it places all its cards in the United States' hands, accepts the return of only lands occupied in 1967, as if it is an objective that might be on the verge of happening given the current balance of power, and garners all its energy to fight the second camp. The second camp, for its part, sees no use in holding negotiations when there is neither resistance nor a joint Arab position to back them up.

With the Arab countries becoming increasingly self-absorbed, the Palestinian cause risked becoming simply a refugee issue, were it not for operations here and there by a few pockets of resistance.[7] Soon, the situation deteriorated even further when the Arab order began to erode from within, as evidenced by Iraq's occupation of Kuwait, at a time when, as everyone remembers, even when the Arab order was at its lowest ebb Iraq played a role in containing the expanding influence of Iran. Finally, the Arab order reached the edge of the precipice, or was near collapse, when Iraq was itself occupied and Iran succeeded in infiltrating the Arab order, and the risk this poses to the GCC states' security in future years, especially in light of Iran's development of a nuclear weapon, as mentioned earlier.[8]

The second negative impact of the Arab regional order's decline on the GCC states is economic, manifested in the huge sums these countries have spent on development within the context of economic and population constraints that do not allow serious development to take place. The only way development could have taken place would be if these governments had eased these restrictions by establishing a large Arab market that brings more opportunities for growth than what we have today. Surpluses not squandered internally, but invested in international financial markets instead of spent on agricultural, industrial and commercial projects in the Arab world, were eroded by inflation, drops in the value of the dollar and successive financial crises, which proved the failure of single-country development, even in Dubai, the most successful model of all.[9] Of course, one should add to this the billions of dollars spent on war, reconstruction and assistance to refugees, which would not have been there at all had the Arab countries stayed on good terms and maintained cordial relations, making it difficult to drag them into destructive and losing wars. Another outcome of wasting oil revenues is increasing poverty and unemployment, a widening food gap and lower education levels in most Arab countries. These problems have together created an Arab crisis belt ready to ignite a variety of conflicts at any moment, a fact confirmed in recent years by events in Yemen, Somalia and elsewhere in the neighbourhood.[10] What further confirms the current stagnation in the Arab world, while the world around it is advancing, is that whereas in the 1950s the per capita income in Egypt was equal to that of South Korea, Egypt's per capita income at the beginning of the twenty-first century was less than 20 per cent of that in South Korea. Likewise, whereas in the 1950s, the per capita income in Morocco was equal to the per capita income in Malaysia, today it is only one third of that, and whereas, in that same period, the per capita in

Saudi Arabia was higher than that in Taiwan, in recent years it dropped down to half that figure.[11]

The third negative impact is socio-cultural. Today, most of these countries' citizens are minorities in their own countries, and threatened by absorption into the kaleidoscope of the foreign workers' cultures and values, simply because they abandoned their Arab heritage and believed that development could be imported, bought ready-made with oil revenues, intact with all its constituent elements. This is how the dreams of development have turned into apprehension, an apprehension that goes so far as doubting whether this region can preserve its Arab and Islamic identity in future years, since the ratio of locals to foreigners in some of these countries is currently less than 20 per cent.[12]

Finally, the fourth negative impact on the GCC states is a weaker negotiating stance, at all levels, vis-à-vis the outside world. We saw how the spirit of Arab solidarity in the 1950s, and the sense that there was a single nation with common hopes and pains, had borne fruit and led, among others, to the establishment of OPEC, nationalisation of the Suez Canal, construction of the High Aswan Dam and, later, stopping oil supplies after the October War. Today, if the GCC states try seriously to revive the Arab League and through it the Arab regional order, they can do a lot for the Arab nation's causes, for development and for the Palestinian cause. The reason is that interacting with the world within the context of an Arab collective would strengthen these countries' negotiating position, and bring in many of the benefits they have so far been unable to bring, due to weakness and dismemberment.

Second: Learning from the past

We underlined above the centrality of joint Arab action to the future development and security of the GCC states, and clearly saw the dear price that these countries have had to pay due to their failure to integrate their wider Arab milieu in a manner that would have brought them stability, economic prosperity and presence on the world stage. The European Union's experience proves that without unity, Europe would not have achieved the level of security and progress it enjoys today. It is worth mentioning here that Europe and the Arab world began working towards integration at the same time, some fifty years ago, and whereas European integration is now a fact, Arab integration is still no more than a pipedream.[13] What are then the reasons and obstacles that have so far prevented the Arabs from uniting?

The Arab Renaissance Project, drafted by the Centre for Arab Unity Studies with the participation of Arab intellectuals from different political currents, says that the Arab world has experienced two Arab renaissances so far. The first was initiated by people like Mohammad Ali Pasha in Egypt, Ahmad al-Bay in Tunisia, Mohammad IV and Hassan I in Morocco, and its political dimension centred round modernising the army, upgrading the infrastructure, fixing public finances, improving education, sending missions abroad and upgrading various administrative institutions. The movement had a fundamentalist religious dimension whose protagonists included al-Tahtawi, Khair Eddin al-Tunsi, Mohammad Abdo and al-Kawakibi.[14] The second renaissance, according to the Arab Renaissance Project, began with the 23 July 1952 Revolution in Egypt; it learned from those which preceded it and focussed on development, independence and unity. In Egypt, the second renaissance project was translated, among other things, into agricultural reforms, construction of the High Dam, industrial projects and oversight of financial institutions. In the wider Arab and Islamic worlds, the second Arab Renaissance Project was translated into anti-foreign pacts, giving priority to the Palestinian cause through the establishment of the Palestine Liberation Organisation, support for the Algerian revolution and the union between Egypt and Syria, for example.[15] However, though they contributed to founding a reservoir of practical and intellectual experience, the two renaissances were aborted and did not lead to a genuine renaissance.

The Arab Renaissance Project blames both failures on several factors. Firstly, the West deceived them by reneging on the promises made to Sherif Hussein: its division of the Arab region into small entities that are easy to manipulate and control, and the creation of Israel combined to dampen all hopes of unity, independence, and development in the region. The withdrawal and inactivity of the intellectual elite, coupled with the lack of modernisation at any level and the polarisation of reformist thought, compounded the weakness of the first renaissance project.[16] The second renaissance project, or the Nasserite Project, was also thwarted, this time by different methods, some of which were external, including the colonial powers' greed and ambitions in the region, supported and assisted by World Zionism and a number of hereditary authoritarian regimes that opposed change and wanted to maintain the status quo. There were also internal factors, including the failure of Nasser's regime to transform popularity into legitimacy, by establishing effective institutions capable of containing social conflicts and disagreements between different political currents, and steering them in the renaissance's direction. We should also remember that a project that depends on a single individual, no matter how influential he is, is doomed to fail once he passes on, which is precisely what happened to the Nasserite Revolution.[17]

Therefore, we could blame the demise of previous renaissances in the Arab world on two main factors: colonialism's ambition in all its shapes and forms and internal weaknesses. The latter are due to several reasons including authoritarianism, weakness of the institutional environment, misunderstanding of the culture, different forms of corruption, and the elite's inability to manage its disagreements, discriminate between what is important and what is not, and insistence on pursuing its narrow transient interests. Every day, the citizens of Gulf face these issues in their own countries, as they strive for unity in the Gulf, and they are likely to face them in their efforts to integrate the Arab nation. Yet, these are deserving efforts worth the price, since the aim is to break the vicious circle in which the GCC states and their Arab milieu find themselves today, a circle that includes foreign domination, local authoritarianism, regional wars, increasing poverty and destructive violence. This vicious circle will not be broken, however, until the above obstacles are surmounted, and Gulf unity becomes a reality supported by efforts to gradually integrate the region into the Arab world. As for other options, the region's citizens have already tried, tested and paid a very high price for them; they will continue to pay this high price until they wake up from their slumber, recognise where their priorities lie, and work diligently to make them happen. Is the Arab Spring the beginning of a new renaissance project? We hope that is the case.

Third: Future challenges

The kind of joint Arab action that the GCC states should promote and endorse is multidimensional; it has political, defence, educational and economic dimensions, all domains in which efforts are still, unfortunately, not up to par, a very costly reality especially in as far as security and development are concerned. However, given the GCC's oil wealth, the greed it attracts from all over the world and the level of development that this wealth could help achieve if the GCC states integrate the wider Arab region, these countries should seize the initiative to launch a process of joint Arab action at all levels, taking advantage of lessons learnt from previous attempts at unification. They are required to hasten the step towards more integration within their wider Arab milieu, which also happens to be what the region's people want. Yet, despite all the difficulties that Gulf and Arab citizens encountered during the oil-rich years, such as the attempt to detach them from their Arab identity and their loyalty to the Islamic nation, this observer feels that they still yearn to be closer to their brethren in language and religion. This yearning could be the outcome of their national governments' numerous failures, which obviously failed to reassure them about these governments' ability to achieve genuine development in a stable environment. In a recent study among a sample of Kuwait University students, the yearning for unity, in its Gulf, Arab and Islamic dimensions, was as high as 86.6 per cent, a very telling rate that deserves interpretation and analysis. From the above three options, the Islamic dimension scored the highest, with 93.2 per cent, while the Gulf and Arab dimensions scored 86.6 per cent and 85.9 per cent, respectively.[18] If we believe this sample to be representative, to a certain extent, of a widespread yearning for unity among GCC citizens, then not only is this a cause for optimism, it is also a negation of the theory which says that oil wealth has set Gulf citizens apart from the rest of the Arab and Islamic peoples. There remains, however, the greater challenge of transforming these sentiments into a tangible reality, whose fruits the Arab and Gulf citizens would be able to reap on both the security and development levels. In the next section, we will briefly address two possible avenues of joint Arab action, to underline the fact that it is entirely feasible, and warn about the challenges that lie in its path.

1. Economic integration

The best gradual approach to Arab unity could be the launch of an economic integration process, which, as everyone agrees, is sure to bring in numerous benefits. There are different views, however, as to how many benefits it will actually bring, and the manner of their distribution among various stakeholders, although this can be easily solved through the implementation of certain policies, some of which were mentioned earlier in the context of addressing Gulf unity. Moreover, the reason why today trade among the Arab countries does not exceed 10 per cent of the total amount of foreign trade,[19] is due to the many customs and other barriers that impede the cross-border transit of goods, services and factors of production. These barriers prevent the better exploitation of Arab resources in the implementation of highly productive projects, and limit the size of the market and the ability to benefit from the economies of scale. The first step towards integration should undoubtedly be to speed up the establishment of the Greater Arab Free Trade Area (GAFTA), on which work began in 1998, while making sure that all the Arab countries have a stake in it, and all the Agreement's provisions are implemented. According to the Arab Monetary Fund (AMF), as of the beginning of 2005, all trade in locally manufactured Arab industrial and agricultural products are exempt from customs duties, except the products of Algeria, Mauritania, Djibouti, Somalia and the Comoros Islands. AMF's report says that, as of 2003, eleven member countries embarked on a series of negotiations aimed at exempting their services sector from taxes, at a higher rate than their commitment to WTO members. If this actually happens, it would undoubtedly mean the expansion of the 1998 Agreement, according to which services, investments and even the establishment of regulatory institutions, were not tax exempted. There are issues on which there should be agreement if we want this integration to mark a significant step towards Arab economic unity.[20] However, since we have already mentioned, in the context of addressing Gulf unity, the mechanisms needed to ensure the success of the free trade area, we will not repeat them again here. Suffice it to say, if all the Arab countries join in and commit to the executive agenda agreed upon, and if all other sectors are liberalised gradually, the Arab region's benefits from trade, at this particular stage, will outweigh those of the GCC states, due to the difference in market size and variety of goods and services. Once the Greater Arab Free Trade Area stage is completed, the next stage would be the customs union, followed by all the other stages, with perhaps certain flexibility in the implementation of different stages, provided it does not impede the integration process per se.

In our opinion, the more the Arab integration process advances, the more we will see a gradual network of interests taking shape among the Arab countries; this will help reduce tensions among these countries, especially if decisions are made in an institutional environment and are subject to public oversight, and if liberalisation involves both tariff and non-tariff barriers. At the same time, one of the first noticeable impacts of this networking process will be an improvement in economic growth rates. An increase in the market size will also enable these countries to attract foreign investments and these, in turn, will bring advanced technology and better trading conditions with the outside world, due to these countries' strengthened negotiating position. Undoubtedly, the closer these countries come to integration, the closer they would be to total unity, and this requires training the necessary human resources who will assume the management of the new entity's institutions, be they legal, financial, political related to data-gathering. One of the lessons that Arab integration should learn from the European integration is the importance of having a political will with a capable administration system to back it up, and a dose of realism coupled with reasonable expectations. Finally, the countries involved should apply the right mechanisms to ensure that the costs and benefits of integration are fairly distributed. This will allow the process of integration to continue unabated, while avoiding disparities in income within each country, and between the member countries themselves.[21]

2. Arab security

In addressing Arab security policies, we said that the Arab regional order no longer exists, and that the bitter reality is that the Arab world is still divided into regions under the influence of big powers, mainly the United States of America, at the onset of the twenty-first century. Sharing the competition for influence are Israel and Iran, as well as a number of emerging Asian countries, like China and India, who are attempting to secure a foothold in the region to satisfy their growing need for energy.[22] What makes matters worse is that attempts to revive the Arab security order, manifested in the Arab Joint Defence Agreement, will not be easy for four different reasons. The first is because of the peace treaties that Jordan and Egypt have signed with Israel, and the treaty between Israel and the Palestinian leadership in Ramallah. The second reason is the diminishing trust between the Arab countries and their unpreparedness for joint action or because, as former Kuwaiti Foreign Minister and current Emir said, "Arab security is contingent on restoring trust among the Arab countries."[23] Third is the fall of Iraq under Iranian influence, even if temporarily. The fourth is the fact that the GCC states still revolve in the big powers' orbit, especially that of the United States. Despite all that, the region's leaders and people should be aware that correcting this imbalance vis-à-vis the big and smaller regional powers is a vital necessity, since it means that the Arabs will be able to regain their occupied lands, control their resources, rid the area of foreign presence and establish cooperation and an equal relationship with their neighbours.[24] To make this possible, however, a number of reforms should be introduced, including political reforms that reconcile Arab governments with their people and with each other, because legitimacy fosters trust and leads to more cooperation; otherwise, the region's security will remain hostage to intermediaries and agents, especially foreign ones. It is true that these political reforms, especially if they are genuine rather than mere window dressing, will not please the big powers that are used to applying double standards when their interests are at stake. We believe, however, that both Western and Arab governments will come to accept this political game, and what it means in terms of benefits for the region's people, once they realise that the alternative is simply more violence that will turn the equation into a zero-sum game, one in which they would both ultimately be the losers.[25] Naturally, forces within Arab society should not wait until the region turns to rubble, but continue to apply pressure by any means possible to expand the margin of freedoms and make this much hoped for reconciliation a reality. The pace of economic integration should be stepped up in tandem with these political reforms until a day comes when economic unity is a done deal. This is because economic integration forges common interests, raises the cost of conflict and makes the common people realise that development means stability; they will also understand why they need to cooperate with others and accept certain temporary sacrifices to maximise their future benefits. These and other reforms are important because they embody the comprehensive nature of security, rather than focus on its military dimension alone; however, in order to implement the above security objectives, the Arab countries should have the ability to defend themselves against any threat, ensure the security of their citizens and protect their natural resources. This makes it imperative that they work dynamically and flexibly on several dimensions, because the main objective is not to maintain the status quo, which means weakness and fragility, but change it for the better by strengthening each and every constituent element of the Arab regional order. The first dimension that needs to be worked on to strengthen the Arab regional order is upgrading the Gulf countries' ability to defend themselves, which could be achieved through the activation of the Peninsula Shield Force, which despite its formation is yet to achieve its objectives. The presence of a common defence system is no doubt important for the GCC states, not simply because it builds trust among member countries, but also because it is a prelude to their eventual integration into the Arab defence umbrella. The second dimension is the creation of a well-trained and equipped Arab force, along the lines of the Rapid Deployment Force, made up of all the Arab states, including the GCC states; it would have the ability to deploy anywhere in the Arab region, and enjoy all the logistical support it needs, including airports, bases, weapons depots, etc. What would be a positive development is if Saudi Arabia and Egypt together took the first step in this direction, with the expectation that this will encourage all the other Arab countries to join. The US will see this step as a mixed bag of reduced military commitments, yet no increased threat to its interests in the region, especially considering the difficulties it is facing in Iraq and Afghanistan. The third dimension likely to breathe life into Arab joint security is increasing Arab support for the resistance in Palestine which would enable it to continue resisting Israeli expansionism and secure better political advantages at the peace negotiations. Such a step will not only benefit the Palestinians; given what Palestine means to all the Arabs, it will be a common avenue of cooperation and interest among them and the Islamic world that surrounds them, i.e., it will be a wake-up call for those still in deep slumber. Here, Arab elites should assume the reins of leadership, raise the people's awareness about the issue and keep the Palestinian cause alive in their hearts and minds. The fourth dimension is being well prepared to repel anyone who dares transgress against this nation's rights. We are a people whom God Almighty has cautioned us against attacking those who have not attacked us, colonised our land or exploited our wealth; he ordered us instead to do good unto them and to be just towards them. He said, "God does not forbid you respecting those who have not made war against you on account of (your) religion, and have not driven you forth from your homes, that you show them kindness and deal with them justly; surely God loves the doers of justice."[26]

On the other hand, God ordered us to defend ourselves when others attack us. He said: "God only forbids you respecting those who made war upon you on account of (your) religion, and drove you forth from your homes and backed up (others) in your expulsion, that you make friends with them, and whoever makes friends with them, these are the unjust."[27] We live in an unjust and belligerent world; the United States dropped nuclear bombs on Hiroshima and Nagasaki, and the impact of their crime on the citizens of these cities is still clear for all to see. As for Britain and France, their behaviour during the Opium Wars was depicted by Joseph Stieglitz, winner of the Nobel Prize for economics in 2001, who said, "The West had little of value to sell to China other than drugs, which it had been dumping into Chinese markets, with the collateral effect of causing widespread addiction. It was an early attempt by the West to correct a balance-of-payments problem."[28] This is why the Arabs should use all possible means to strengthen themselves, including the development of a peaceful nuclear programme ready, if need be, to convert into a military programme, to act as a deterrent against any nuclear threat to the Arab countries. They should keep other options on the table as well, like boycotts and using oil as a weapon, to a certain extent, in order to raise the people's standards and deter their enemies as they diligently work towards their nation's renaissance. In other words, these measures and others are necessary in order to protect, sustain and ensure the success of efforts to revive the Arab regional order. Finally, the West is trying to institute some sort of discussion mechanism, akin to debating platforms, where countries engage in a give and take to mitigate tensions between them, control the spread of weapons and build trust among the parties concerned. Western Europe used a similar system in Eastern Europe after the Cold War, and some in the West suggest that the same be done among the Arab countries and others in the neighbourhood.[29] However, although such a platform could be acceptable as a forum for discussing security issues in the Gulf and the Arab world, we should be conscious of two relevant points. The first is the need to reject Israel's involvement under any circumstance, and the second is not to depend on this venue to change the balance of power because such meetings usually aim at preserving the status quo, not change it, and this is not in line with the Arab security strategy addressed earlier.

Therefore, it is clear from the above that joint Arab action, whether in the abovementioned contexts or otherwise, is a necessity, regardless of the obstacles and time required. Even if we revive and protect one part or one sector of the Arab world at a time, each of these steps is a building block, and the blocks will eventually accumulate and revive the Arab order, and the Islamic world that surrounds it. It will reconcile the GCC states with each other, and reconcile them with their Arab and Islamic milieus. Not only will reconciliation reduce the foreign presence and build free and productive human beings, it will reassure others that the region can protect themselves, achieve progress and deal with others within the framework of globalisation, based on equality and mutual respect between nations, by applying the golden rule "do unto others as you would have them do unto you."

There is no doubt that the events of the Arab Spring have made this dream possible since the Arab governments, especially in the Gulf countries, have realised that the current conditions cannot continue and that they must move forwards with a new vision and agendas. The factors which could facilitate the two security and development tracks in the Arab sphere include the following. First, the GCC states should gradually integrate Yemen into the organisation of the GCC in order to utilise its human resources and prevent it from turning into a centre of violence that will unbalance the stability of the whole region. Second, any conflict with the countries of the Arab uprisings should be avoided so that the Arab world does not revert to a Cold War situation like that of the 1950s and 1960s which disrupted the Arab countries, squandered their resources and hindered their progress. Third, the efforts of the GCC states together with the other Arab countries must intensify in order to stabilise Iraq and Syria and not abandon them to revolve in the orbit of Iran, or in an arena of regional and international wars. This is because the exclusion of Syria or Iraq from the Arab sphere weakens the Arab nation and upsets the balance of power with both Israel and the other regional countries. Moreover, continuing the current conflict in Syria might lead to its break-up into small states including a statelet of Alawites in Latakia, another of Druze in the south, and a third of Kurds in the north-east of Syria.[30]

CHAPTER NINETEEN

Effective Participation in International Organisations

The Arabs have paid a high price for failing to realise the important role that international organisations have played throughout the years, and for not leaving their mark on them. The Security Council, the International Monetary Fund and the World Trade Organisation are platforms where the mighty decide the fate of the world in a manner that serves their interests. History attests to that fact, ever since the establishment of these organisations after WWII, whether in terms of the resolutions concerning the Palestinian issue, the occupations of Iraq and Afghanistan, policies regarding loans granted to developing countries, the successive financial crises or laws that govern international trade. It is also regrettable that these organisations still reflect the same balance of power that followed WWII. Moreover, the industrialised nations insist on maintaining the rules of the game as they were sixty years ago, although many developing countries have since gained independence and today account for much greater numbers of the world's population than do the industrial countries and despite the negative impact that the obvious deficiencies in these organisations' structures and performance have had on the developing world's prosperity and stability, including the GCC's. Kishore Mahbubani's, Singapore's former representative to the United Nations and Dean of the Lee Kuan Yew School of Public Policy at the National University of Singapore, described the West's unjust control of international organisations in a way that was absolutely right. He said, "The great paradox of the twenty-first century is that this undemocratic world order is sustained by the world's most democratic nation-states, the Western nations. At home, they would never allow a minority of the population to make manda-tory decisions over the majority. Globally, this is exactly what the West does.

The 900 million people who live in Western countries elect governments that in turn control a world order determining the fate of the remaining 5.6 million people on the planet. Effectively, 12 per cent of the world's population controls global decision making."[1]

This is why the GCC states should try to remedy the situation in the future, availing themselves of the Arab world's support, the influence it enjoys thanks to its oil wealth and the cooperation of Islamic and developing countries. The following brief overview pinpoints the deficiencies in the international organisations' performance, their impact, and the dire need for restructuring them in the coming years. In our opinion, this should include the management, reformulation and fair implementation of their agendas and policies.

First: Management and Agenda

The Security Council is a key organisation when issues of war and peace in the world are at stake; however, the member countries with veto power, namely the United States, Britain, France, Russia and China, are those that emerged victorious from WWII. Thus, despite the appearance of new powers on the world stage, these countries have not allowed them to take their rightful place on the Security Council.[2] Likewise, although the World Bank, in theory, belongs to its 184 members, its actual policies reflect the industrialised countries' domination over it, in particular the United States of America. Of its twenty-four executive directors, five represent the countries with the largest number of shares in the Bank, i.e., the United Kingdom, United States, France, Germany and Japan; Saudi Arabia, China and Russia have a director each, and the other sixteen directors represent the remaining 176 countries. China, which accounts for around 13 per cent of the world's production, India, which accounts for 6 per cent of the world's production and Saudi Arabia which accounts for 0.6 per cent of world production, have an equal number of votes in the Bank, i.e., 2.8 per cent of the vote each. In the IMF, the voting process clearly favours the industrialised countries, whereby a country like Belgium with a population of 10 million, has 2.13 per cent of the vote, while China, with a population of over 1.3 billion, has only 2.94 per cent of the vote.[3] There is also an unwritten agreement whereby the World Bank's presidency goes to the United States, and the executive directorship of the IMF – the World Bank's sister organisation that attends to monetary affairs and balances of payments – goes to a European country, although this custom has begun to change in recent years out of embarrassment, not conviction.[4] According to the current system, therefore, since the United States has over 15 per cent of the Bank's total votes, it has the right to veto any decision, meaning it can force the Bank to give loans to countries that support it and deny them to those that disagree with it. The United States used its power to do so on several occasions throughout the Bank's history, notably when it withdrew the Bank's commitment to finance Egypt's High Dam project in 1956, under the late President Nasser, and again when it prevented the Bank from providing loans to Saddam Hussein's regime after 1990.[5] Likewise, while from 1997 to 2004 Haiti could not obtain a loan from the Bank due to political disagreements between Aristide, the country's elected president, and the American administration, both Egypt and Jordan, who are less poor and enjoyed less political freedom than Haiti, received loans from the Bank in return for going along with the American peace plan.[6] Furthermore, when the Palestinian people elected Hamas, they were denied all kinds of international assistance because Hamas' agenda is not in line with the Oslo Agreement, which the United States and other industrial nations support, along with President Mahmoud Abbas.

For its part, the WTO is just as much under the control of the industrialised countries as are the other organisations. In 1999, member countries were looking for a new secretary general to serve a four-year term and there were two candidates to choose from, Supachai Panitchpakdi from Thailand, who enjoyed the support of most third world countries, and Mike Moore from New Zealand, who enjoyed the support of the industrialised countries, particularly the United States and the European Union. Although it was natural and logical to choose the former, sources confirm that Madeleine Albright, Secretary of State under the Clinton administration, called Thailand's Foreign Minister in June 1999, and told him that the American President was worried about conditions at the WTO and was offering Supachai another post, that of chief liaison between the WTO, World Bank and IMF. In other words, the latter was being asked to withdraw his candidacy as secretary general. After a heated telephone discussion, the Thai Foreign Minister proposed that the secretary general's term be reduced to three years, with the first three going to Moore and the second three to Supachai, and this is what actually happened. We chose to give this example to show that what happens in the corridors of power is different from what appears in official newspapers.[7] Moreover, if we look closely at the WTO's administration system, we will see clearly that while the developing countries account for 80 per cent of its members, 80 per cent of its main agencies' employees are citizens of industrialised countries. In 2001, 410 of the general secretariat's employees were citizens of industrialised countries, and ninety-four were citizens of developing countries.[8] Likewise, if we closely examine the organisation's agenda we would find that the industrialised nations' priorities take precedence over all other priorities. The Uruguay Round Agreement, which paved the way for the WTO's establishment to succeed GATT as a trade liberalising mechanism, began by liberalising the sectors that the industrialised countries considered a priority. The decision to liberalise the services sector, taken at that round, was at the insistence of the industrialised countries because their share of global exports was over 70 per cent. In 2001, the volume of service exports by the United States alone amounted to US$263 billion, while Britain's exports amounted to $108 billion and this sector's exports, that same year, amounted to 7.3 per cent of the EU's GDP.[9]

However, the agenda of the Uruguay Round did not include workforce related movements and services, one of the priorities of developing countries that allows their workforce to migrate to industrialised countries and send remittances back home. At the same time, the industrialised countries managed to put the issue of intellectual copyright on the agenda because it was in their interest to do so. Prior to the Uruguay Round Agreement, scientific progress in many countries, including the United States, Japan, South Korea, Germany and recently China, depended on imitating other countries' products and technology, before adding their own creativity and improvements to the product. However, the WTO's current provisions no longer allow this to happen because the original holders of the patent have exclusive ownership of this knowledge, and can sell it as licences to their agents in other countries, for local production only. Such provisions naturally help maintain the industrialised countries' exclusive control over technological progress and its use, especially in medical breakthroughs and the information technology domain. One of the most ardent supporters of free international trade, Jagdish Bhagwati, believes that it is a mistake to give the industrialised countries this right, since it is akin to taxing the use of knowledge by the developing world.[10] Moreover, these provisions took effect at a time when American drug manufacturers reaped $37 billion in profit in 2001, $7 billion of which were sales to the developing countries, i.e., 39 per cent annual rate of return.[11]

The above problems and others resulting from the developing world not playing an effective role in the management of international organisations have led to discrimination, carelessness and a lack of understanding of the developing world's problems and needs. It is impossible for these organisations to play an effective role in ensuring financial stability, development and environmental protection in the future if they do not grant the developing countries, including the GCC and Arab countries, a prominent managerial role. Not only would this turn them into genuine international organisations, they would also be able to manage globalisation with more efficiency and fairness. Joseph Stiglitz said as much in a report he co-authored with a group of international experts, upon a request from the UN's Secretary General, on how to deal with the recent financial crisis. He states, "The participation of developing countries is essential if there is to be an adequate provision of global and regional public goods, such as climate protection and financial stability. Accordingly, these agendas can only be successfully realized if the developing country perspective is appropriately reflected in global decision making."[12]

Second: Policies

The above-mentioned organisations base their assumptions on the new classical theory, which has many names. This theory insists on the fact that the market system knows how best resources could be used and can extricate itself, by itself, from economic crises like stagnation, unemployment and inflation. This explains why these international organisations have tried hard to minimise state interventions in the market system, although the last thirty years, which witnessed the highest levels of trade liberalisation under their wing, were catastrophic for the development and stability of the global economic market, the recent financial crisis being the most recent example. Thus, despite assurances to the Third World regarding the new economic system's ability to address poverty, improve standards of living and ensure development, the reality has never caught up with the dream, since, according to Stiglitz, the number of poor people in Africa increased by around 100 million people between 1990-1998.[13] Jeffrey Sachs, former Professor of Economics at Harvard University and consultant to a number of developing countries, says that these organisations' policies have little scientific merit and are ineffective, and points out their impact on Africa. He says in this context, "By the start of the twenty-first century Africa was poorer than during the late 1960s, when the IMF and World Bank had arrived on the African scene, with disease, population growth, and environmental degradation spiralling out of control."[14]

Elsewhere, Sachs points out to the lack of coordination between these two organisations and institutions of the United Nations specialising in the developing countries, which limits their knowledge about these countries. This shortcoming in the two organisations' understanding of conditions in the developing countries explains, in his opinion, the failure of their development policies. He explains the industrialised world's preference for the World Bank and IMF rather than the United Nations, saying, "As the old advice puts it, Follow the money. The rich countries hold sway in the IMF and the World Bank much more than in the UN agencies. Unlike the UN General Assembly, and most of the boards of the specialized agencies, where it's 'one country, one vote,' in the IMF and the World Bank, it's 'one dollar, one vote.'"[15]

The two international organisations' record on economic and financial stability is no different from their record on development. Again, Stiglitz says that he felt embarrassed, as head of President Clinton's Council of Economic Advisors, whenever the industrialised countries asked poor countries to eliminate any customs barriers on trade with the outside world, while they themselves had similar barriers on sugar, textiles and agricultural imports from the developing world that badly impacted their economic performance.[16] Thus, just as the industrialised countries used the liberalisation of the trade in goods to their economic advantage, liberalising the movement of capital led to similar, if not worse, results for the economies of developing countries. For although, until the 1970s, the industrialised countries forbade the movement of capital, and even established advanced financial institutions and a series of safety measures to address various crises, they forced the developing countries, through the IMF and World Bank, to liberalise the movement of capital when their institutional ability did not allow them to do so, especially speculation money. As a result, conditions in the developing countries have become, according to Stiglitz, like "small boats. Rapid capital market liberalization, in the manner pushed by the IMF, amounted to setting them off on a voyage on a rough sea, before the holes in their hulls have been repaired, before the captain has received training, before life vests have been put on board. Even in the best of circumstances, there was a high likelihood that they would be overturned when they were hit broadside by a big wave."[17]

This is exactly what actually befell the developing countries as the result of the movement of speculative money, especially in light of the successive financial crises, the last of which is the current one that led to a slow-down in economic growth, rising rates of unemployment and an increase in the developing countries' debt burden. Even the boom of 2010 is still under threat because the conditions imposed on the developing world were simply wrong, as indicated earlier.[18] There is a massive failure in how these international organisations evaluate the performance in developing countries. Seven months before the fall of Mubarak a report by the IMF was painting a rosy picture of the Egyptian economy, confirming that the policies it had adopted since 2004 had led to a decrease in financial, monetary and external imbalances and that they offered an suitable environment for investments, just as they helped to cushion the effects of the financial crisis.[19]

Third: The Tools

Earlier in this book, we mentioned, in the context of reforms relevant to maintaining security in the Gulf, that strengthening and unifying the domestic front and establishing a unified GCC army would put these countries on the right security track. However, real security will only happen when the Gulf countries integrate the wider Arab region within the context of the joint Arab defence umbrella, or any other arrangement the Arabs will agree on. This arrangement should ensure comprehensive Arab security, revive the Arab regional order as a single entity capable of deterring any attack against one of its members, and dispel the tenuous internal rifts that have already lasted far too long. Furthermore, ensuring sustainable development is no different from ensuring security. Thus, although Gulf unity will make resources available and allow the implementation of certain development projects, this development will remain hostage to a series of demographic factors and the scarcity of resources other than oil, making it imperative for these countries to hasten their economic integration with the Arab world, and learn from experience to avoid earlier mistakes. The first step could be to ensure the success of the Greater Arab Free Trade Area (GAFTA), to which some Arab countries have committed themselves, while others have not. In addition to GAFTA, the GCC states could also embark on a gradual integration process into the wider Arab region by launching a number of joint projects in the agricultural, petroleum, communications and services domains. This gradual integration process, coupled with the revival of the Arab joint defence agreement, would activate the role of Arab regional institutions, embodied by the Arab League, which, given their oil wealth, strategic location and rich human resources, would have a tangible impact on all issues that link these countries to the rest of the world. This means that the GCC states should revive their links with the wider Gulf and Arab regions so as to speak to the world with one voice and engage it with a common vision and shared capabilities. We will see then how, just as chances for development and security have improved, the opportunity to engage in negotiation with others and reap more benefits from them will improve as well.

Conclusion

In this book, we have addressed numerous issues relating to development and security in the GCC states and the wider Arab region, and the Arab Spring provides further confirmation of the centrality of many of these issues. Again, we reiterate that the main aim of this book is still to motivate all of Arab society, from the Gulf to the ocean. That is by highlighting the security and development challenges which this society is facing in the world today. Some will say that we have done this with unusual candour, even after the Arab Spring created an awareness of our reality and emboldened sectors of society into criticising the present situation. Therefore, we decided to turn this conclusion into a message of affection and friendship and an invitation to our readers to understand and sympathise with our views. It is our feeling that these countries have already suffered enough from restrictions that have lasted far too long, wrought untold miseries and negatively affected progress on many levels. The fact that this has also affected their security, as well as that of the Arab world around them and of future of generations to come, made it necessary for us to be candid and honest. We believe that these societies will do well, one way or another, as long as people continue to talk openly and frankly among themselves while keeping their debates within the confines of minor intellectual skirmishes. The alternative which we fear for these societies is that the current restrictions will make some despair that anything good could ever come out of governments in power, or that they, or other strata of society, will ever be able develop themselves before developing their own countries, at which point everything becomes possible. The region's history, both modern and ancient, is rife with such examples, particularly the events which occurred in the countries of the Arab Spring.

Therefore, our hope is that those who disagree with some of the ideas in this book and find them incompatible with their own short-term interests will try to see the forest from the trees. The reforms we are calling for will bring numerous benefits not only to them personally, but to their children, grandchildren and the Arab nation as a whole, for many years to come. We are certain that they care as much as we do about future generations and the place their nation occupies in the world, and hope for their sakes that our expectations of them are in the right place. We say to those who did not fully grasp our ideas to, at least, be patient with us and not expect us to think and operate solely within the confines of their own thoughts and circle of activities. The effort of trying to come to terms with these ideas could be the key that opens new horizons they did not even know existed and that activates their potential, thereby adjusting their course. They say, after all, that man is the enemy of ignorance. We should also remember that life is a school and that we continue to learn from the cradle to the grave, as long as we are prepared to listen to each other and not reject someone's opinion simply because we deem it strange, incomprehensible or out of the ordinary. George Bernard Shaw is quoted as saying that, "The reasonable man adapts himself to the world. The unreasonable one persists in trying to adapt the world to himself. All progress, therefore, depends on the unreasonable man."[1] Although we do claim neither to have special talents nor to be geniuses, we still believe in the spirit of Shaw's statement. We therefore ask our readers to allow us a small margin of Shaw's unreasonableness, with the hope that it will ultimately be to our society's benefit.

There are those who raise the white flag of surrender and say, "There is no hope for change" or "We cannot improve on what exists now" whenever someone calls for reform or positive change. To them we say that we must ensure, as must other members of society in the region, that our governments turn their backs on autocracy, and embrace freedom. We should make sure that our intellectuals light the path of future generations, instead of being opportunists and sycophants, and that our business people are pioneers in the fields of trade, industry and scientific breakthroughs, and build their wealth in a worthy and honest manner instead of acting as agents of foreign companies or tools of autocratic regimes.

Finally, we call on the Arab people to be aware and active, to earn their livelihood by the sweat of their brows and demand their full and inalienable rights, instead of expecting gifts and donations, or living in misery and humiliation while others in the world carry on the fruitful effort and honourable struggle for the sake of their legitimate rights. The Arab Spring confirms that these people really do exist in society and some of them have demanded their rights and made sacrifices during the years of the Arab Spring, even if there is a silent majority who have decided on marginalisation for themselves even until now. Had they adopted a positive position, one group would have outweighed the other and the track of the Arab Spring would have been less costly. However, these are the years on earth which test humanity, its values and behaviour. As the Qur'an says, "no change will you find in God's way (Sunnah)".[2]

No one should ever believe that what we said about various sectors of Gulf and Arab society means that we are at odds with them, but quite the contrary. We strongly believe that we should stand together, hand in hand, as one family, and that despite our legitimate differences of opinion, attitudes and practices we never doubted the loyalty of the overwhelming majority of them. This kind of advocacy is what saves society from destruction and disintegration, and ultimately guides it towards stability and prosperity.

Notes

INTRODUCTION

1. Robin Wright, *Dreams and Shadows: The Future of the Middle East,* (New York: Penguin Press, 2008), pp. 17-18.
2. Yusuf Khalifah al-Yusuf " 'Indama tusbih al-sultah ghanimah: halat majlis al-ta'awun al-khaliji", Al-Mustaqbal al-'Arabi, vol. 31, no. 351, May 2008, pp. 70-87. Translated as "When rulership becomes privileged booty (*ghanimah*): the condition of the Gulf Cooperation Council", Contemporary Arab Affairs, vol. 1, no. 4, 2008, pp. 631-648.

PART I

CHAPTER ONE

1. These countries are Saudi Arabia, the United Arab Emirates (UAE), Kuwait, the Sultanate of Oman, Qatar and Bahrain.
2. For example, Article 4 of Part I of the Kuwaiti Constitution states that, "Kuwait is a hereditary Emirate, the succession to which shall be in the descendants of the late Mubarak al-Sabah." The Bahraini Constitution states in Article One, Part One, B, "Rule, in Bahrain, being hereditary, shall pass from his Highness Sheikh Isa Bin Salman al-Khalifa to his eldest son and from him to eldest son again and so forth generation after generation." In Oman, Article 5 of Part One of the Basic Law states, "The system of government is a hereditary Sultanate in which succession passes to a male descendant of Sayyid Turki bin Sa'id bin Sultan," Article 8 the Qatari Constitution states that, "The rule of the State is hereditary in the family of al-Thani and in the line of the male descendants of Hamad bin Khalifa bin Hamad bin Abdullah bin Jassim," while in the United Arab Emirates the constitution states that the highest authority in the Union is vested in the Higher Council comprising the rulers of the seven emirates.
3. *Dustur Kuwayt* [The Constitution of Kuwait], (Kuwait: Dar Qartas li-l-nashr, 1999), pp. 7-8.
4. Qur'an, *Al-Qasas*, 28:26
5. Ibid., *Al Imran* 3:159
6. Ibid., *Al-Shura* 42:38
7. Muhammad bin Ahmad al-Qurtubi, *Tafsir al-Qurtubi: Al-Jami' li-ahkam al-Qur'an* [Commentary of the Holy Qur'an: Compendium of Legal Rulings of the Qur'an], (Beirut: Dar Al-Kitab al-Arabi, n.d.), p.251.

8.   Muhammad Abu Zahrah, *Tarikh al-Madhahib al-Islamiyyah* [History of the Islamic Sects], 2 vols, (Cairo: Dar Al-Fikr al-Arabi, 1996), p. 25

9.   Narrated by Abu-Dawud and Al-Tirmidhi. This is a sound and good hadith.

10.   Quran, *Al Imran* 3:159.

11.   Yusuf al-Qardawi, "*Al-Siyyasah al-shar'iyyah fi daw' nusus al-shar'iyyiah wa maqasidaha,* [Legal Policies in Light of the Shari'a's Text and Intention], (Cairo: Maktabah Wahbah, 1998), p. 115.

12.   Sayyid Qutb, *Al-'Adalah al-ijtima'iyyah fi al-Islam* [Social Justice in Islam], 15th ed., (Cairo: Dar El Shorouk, 2002), pp. 146-165.

13.   Bernard Lewis, "Freedom and Justice in the Modern Middle East", *Foreign Affairs* (May-June 2005), vol. 84, no. 3, pp. 36-51. Reprinted in Bernard Lewis, *Faith and Power: religion and politics in the Middle East,* (Oxford: Oxford University Press, 2010), p. 194

14.   Bernard Lewis, *Faith and Power: religion and politics in the Middle East* (Oxford: Oxford University Press, 2010), p. 192.

15.   Ibid.

16.   Ibid., pp. 136-137.

17.   Muhammad 'Abid al-Jabri, *Al-'Aql al-akhlaqi al-'arabi: dirasah tahliliyyah naqdiyyah li nudhum al-qiyam fi al-thaqafah al-'arabyyiah; Naqd al-'aql al-'arabi* [The Arab Moral Mind: An Analytical Critical Study of Value Systems in Arab Culture; Critique of the Arab Mind, 4], (Beirut: Centre for Arab Unity Studies, 2001), pp. 225-231.

18.   Mustafa al-Siba'i, "*Islamuna: ta'rif mujaz* [Our Islam: a brief introduction], (Beirut: Dar Al-wuraq li-l-nasr wa al-tawzi', 2001), pp. 29-30.

19.   'Ali Khalifah al-Kawari, ed., *Al-Khalij al-'arabi wa al-dimuqratiyyah: nahwa ru'yah mustaqbaliyyah li-ta'ziz al-masa'i al-dimuqratiyyah* [The Arabian Gulf and Democracy: Towards a Future Vision to Promote Efforts towards Democracy], (Beirut: Centre for Arab Unity Studies. 2002), p. 55.

20.   Paul Salem, "Kuwait: Politics in a participatory Emirate" in: Marina Ottaway and Julia Choucaire-Vizoso, eds., *Beyond the Façade: Political Reform in the Arab World,* (Washington, DC: Carnegie Endowment for International Peace, 2008), pp. 212-213.

21.   Muhammad al-Rumaihi, "Harakat 1938 al-Islahiyyah fi al-Kuwait wa al-Bahrain wa Dubai" [The 1938 Reform Movement in Kuwait, Bahrain and Dubai], *Majallat dirasat al-khalij wa al-jazirah al-'arabiyyah,* vol. 1, 1975, pp. 29-68.

22.   Y. S. F. al-Sabah, *The Oil Economy of Kuwait,* (London: Kegan Paul International, 1980), p. 3.

23.   Jill Crystal, *Oil and Politics in the Gulf: Rulers and Merchants in Kuwait and Qatar,* (Cambridge: Cambridge University Press, 1995), p. 47.

24.   Al-Sabah, op. cit., p. 48.

25.   Crystal, op. cit., p. 51.

26.   Ibid., p. 52

27.   Ibid., pp. 63-64

28.   Nicolas Gavrielides, "Tribal Democracy: the Anatomy of Parliamentary Elections in Kuwait" in: Linda Layne, ed., *Elections in the Middle East: Implications of Recent Trends,* (Boulder, Colo.: Westview Press, 1987), p. 161.

29.   Crystal, op. cit., p.73.

30.   Ibid., pp. 81-83.

31.   Ibid., pp. 89-94.

32.   Ibid., pp. 110-111.

33.   Christopher M. Davidson, *Dubai: The Vulnerability of Success,* (New York: Columbia University Press, 2008), p. 32.

34.   Ibid., p. 33

35.   Ibid., pp. 32-34

36. Ibid., pp. 36-37

37. Ibid., p. 53

38. Frank Stoakes, "Social and Political Change in the Third World: Some Peculiarities of Oil-Producing Principalities of the Persian Gulf," in: Derek Hopwood, ed., *The Arabian Peninsula: Society and Politics, Studies on Modern Asia and Africa,* no. 8, (London: Allen and Unwin, 1972), pp.189-215, p. 197.

39. Crystal, *Oil and Politics in the Gulf: Rulers and Merchants in Kuwait and Qatar,* pp. 153-154.

40. Madawi al-Rasheed, "Bin Laden's Puritans Keep Saudis in Thrall to Rebellious Cycle" in: Joshua Craze and Mark Huband, eds., *The Kingdom: Saudi Arabia and the Challenges of the 21ˢᵗ Century,* (London: C. Hurst and Company, 2009), pp.40-49, p. 43.

41. Ibid., p. 44

42. Joseph K. Kechichian, "The Role of the Ulama in the Politics of an Islamic State: The Case of Saudi Arabia", *International Journal of Middle East Studies,* vol. 18, no. 1, 1986, pp. 53-71, p.62.

43. Daryl Champion, *The Paradoxical Kingdom: Saudi Arabia and the Momentum of Reform,* (New York: Columbia University Press, 2003) p. 63.

44. Mahan Abedin, "Saudi Dissent More than Just Jihadis" in: Craze and Huband, eds., *The Kingdom: Saudi Arabia and the Challenges of the 21ˢᵗ Century,* pp. 35-40.

45. Michael Herb, *All in the Family: Absolutism, Revolution and Democracy in the Middle Eastern Monarchies,* (New York: State of New York Press, 1999), p. 172.

46. Al-Rasheed, "Bin Laden's Puritans Keep Saudis in Thrall to Rebellious Cycle," op. cit., pp. 41-42.

47. Ibid., pp. 44-45

48. J.B. Kelly, *Arabia, the Gulf and the West: A Critical View of the Arabs and their Oil Policy* (New York: Basic Books, 1980), pp. 182-183.

49. Fred Halliday, *Arabia without Sultans,* (London: Saqi Books, 2002), pp. 440-46.

50. Herb, *All in the Family: Absolutism, Revolution and Democracy in the Middle Eastern Monarchies,* pp. 175-176.

51. Ibid., pp. 314-364

52. Interview with the Shah in *Newsweek,* 21 May 1973, pp.40-44.

53. Herb, op. cit., pp. 17-19.

54. Al-Kawari, ed. *Al-Khalij al-'arabi wa al-dimuqratiyyah: nahwa ru'yah mustaqbaliyyah li-ta'ziz al-masa'i al-dimuqratiyyah,* p. 56.

55. See the commentary by Said Hareb in: op. cit., p. 153.

56. Quran, *Al-Nahl* 16:90

57. 'Abd al-Rahman al-Kawakibi, *"Tabai' al-istibdad wa masari' al-isti'bad"* [The Characteristics of Despotism and Deaths of Enslavement] in: *Al-A'mal al-kamilah li-l-kawakibi* [The Complete Works of al-Kawakibi], ed., Muhammad Jamal Tahhan, (Beirut: Centre for Arab Unity Studies, 1995), p. 447.

CHAPTER TWO

1.   Fadwa Ahmad Mahmud Nusairat, "Al-Masihiyyun al-'arab wa fikrat al-qawmiyyah al-'arabiyyah fi bilad al-sham wa misr, 1840-1918" [Arab Christians and the Concept of Arab Nationalism in Greater Syria and Egypt], *Al-Mustaqbal al-'Arabi,* Year 32, No. 368, October 2009, pp. 25-27.

2.   Samuel Huntington, *Who Are We: The Challenges to America's National Identity,* (New York: Simon and Schuster, 2004), p. 30.

3.   Francis Fukuyama, *Trust: The Social Virtues and the Creation of Prosperity,* (London: Penguin Books, 1995), p. 5.

4. Natan Sharansky, *Defending Identity: Its Indispensable Role in Protecting Democracy*, (New York: PublicAffairs, 2008), p. x.

5. Ibid., p. 2

6. Lawrence Harrison, *The Central Liberal Truth*, (Oxford: Oxford University Press, 2006), pp. 87-119.

7. Bernard Lewis, *What Went Wrong? The Clash between Islam and Modernity in the Middle East*, (London: Weidenfeld Nicolson, 2002), p. 156.

8. Will Durant. *The Age of Faith. The Story of Civilization, Volume IV: A history of medieval civilization—Christian, Islamic, and Judaic—from Constantine to Dante: A.D. 325-1300.* (Simon and Schuster: New York, 1950)..

9. David Landes, *The Wealth and Poverty of Nations*, (New York: Norton and Company, 1999), p. 54.

10. Ibid., p. 64, fn.

11. Speech delivered by Prince Charles at the Foreign Office's Conference Centre in 1996. Reported in *Asharq al-Awsat*, 15 December 1996.

12. 'Abd al-ilah Balqaziz, *Al-Islam wa al-siyyasah: dawr al-haraka al-islamiyyah fi sawgh al-majal al-siyyasi* [Islam and Politics: the Role of Islamic Movements in Defining the Political Arena], (Beirut: Al-Markaz al-'arabi al-thaqafi, 2001), p. 17.

13. Harrison, *The Central Liberal Truth*, p. 18.

14. Quran, *Hud*, 11:61.

15. Muhammad Abu Zahrah, *Tarikh al-Madhahib al-Islamiyya*h,pp. 23-24.

16. Muhammad Asad, *The Principles of State and Government in Islam* (Gibraltar: Dar al-Andalus, 1980), p. 28.

17. Fahmi Huwaidi, "Al-Islam wa al-dimuqratiyyah" [Islam and democracy] in: Majdi Hammad et al, *Al-Harakat al-Islamiyyah wa al-dimuqratiyyah: dirasat fi al-fikr wa al-mumarasah* [Islamic Movements and Democracy: Studies in Thought and Practice], (Beirut: Centre for Arab Unity Studies, 1999), p. 46.

18. 'Ali Khalifah al-Kawari, "Jawhar al-dimuqratiyyah la yata'aradu ma'a jawhar al-Islam" [The Core of Democracy Does not Conflict with the Core of Islam], *Al-Mustaqbal al-'arabi*, Year 32, No. 374, April 2010, p. 131.

19. See Ismail al-Shatti's commentary in: 'Ali Khalifah al-Kawari, ed., *Al-Khalij al-'arabi wa al-dimuqratiyyah*, p. 133.

CHAPTER THREE

1. Donald Hawly, *The Trucial States*, (London: Allen and Unwin, 1970), p. 195.

2. Ibid., p. 196

3. Rosemarie Said Zahlan, *The Origins of the United Arab Emirates*, (London: Macmillan Press Ltd, 1978), p. 7.

4. Frauke Heard-Bey, *From Trucial States to United Arab Emirates*, (London: Longman, 1982), pp. 192-193.

5. John G. Lorimer, *Gazetteer of the Persian Gulf, Oman and Central Arabia*, 19 vols. (Calcutta: Superintendent Government Printing, 1915), vol. 2, p. 409

6. Zahlan, *The Origins of the United Arab Emirates*, pp. 56-57.

7. Crystal, *Oil and Politics in the Gulf: Rulers and Merchants in Kuwait and Qatar*, p. 4.

8. Madawi Al-Rasheed, *A History of Saudi Arabia*, (Cambridge, MA: Cambridge University Press, 2002),pp. 86-91.

9. Herb, *All in the Family: Absolutism, Revolution and Democracy in the Middle Eastern Monarchies*, p. 127.

10. Christopher M. Davidson, *The United Arab Emirates: A Study in Survival*, (Boulder CO: Lynne Rienner Publishers, 2005), p. 8.

11. Al-Rasheed, *A History of Saudi Arabia*, pp. 49-58.

12. Ibid., pp. 59-68

13. Crystal, *Oil and Politics in the Gulf: Rulers and Merchants in Kuwait and Qatar*, pp. 6-9.

14. Herb, *All in the Family: Absolutism, Revolution and Democracy in the Middle Eastern Monarchies*, p. 50.

15. Jill Crystal, "Civil Society in the Arabian Gulf," in: Augustus Richard Norton, ed., *Civil Society in the Middle East*, (Leiden: Brill, 2001), vol. 2, pp. 259-286.

16. Champion, *The Paradoxical Kingdom: Saudi Arabia and the Momentum of Reform*, p. 101.

17. Crystal, op. cit., p. 261.

18. Ibid., p. 262

19. Economic Commission for Africa, *African Governance Report II*, (Oxford: Oxford University Press: Oxford. 2009), pp. 102-104.

20. Steffen Hertog, *Princes, Brokers and Bureaucrats: Oil and the State in Saudi Arabia*, (Ithaca and London: Cornell University Press, 2010), pp. 11-35.

21. Madawi al-Rasheed, *Contesting the Saudi State: Islamic Voices from a New Generation*, (Cambridge, MA: Cambridge University Press, 2007), p. 74.

22. Champion, *The Paradoxical Kingdom: Saudi Arabia and the Momentum of Reform*, p. 59.

23. Crystal, *Oil and Politics in the Gulf: Rulers and Merchants in Kuwait and Qatar*, pp. 10-11.

24. Baqir Salman al-Najjar, *Al-Dimuqratiyyah al-'asiyyah fi al-khalij al-'arabi*, [The Intractable Democracy in the Arabian Gulf], (Beirut: Dar al-Saqi, 2008), p. 79.

25. Ibid., pp. 203-204

26. See: *Al-'Amal al-khairi* [Charitable Activity], Arabic television programme aired on Al Jazeera as part of the series "In Depth" on 30 August 2010.

27. Daniel L. Byman and Jerrold D. Green, "The Enigma of Political Stability in the Persian Gulf Monarchies", *Middle East Review of International Affairs*, vol. 3, no. 3, (September 1999), p. 28.

28. Anthony H. Cordesman, *Bahrain, Oman, Qatar and the UAE: Challenges of Security*, CSIS Middle East Dynamic Net Assessment, (Boulder, CO: West View Press, 1997), p. 137.

29. Madawi al-Rasheed, "*Mashru' tahdith al-hukm al-sa'udi: waraqat al-'amal al-muqadamah lil-halqah al-niqashiyyah: al-sa'udiyyah ila 'ayna?*" [Project to reform the Saudi governance system: working paper presented at the discussion group meeting 'Saudi Arabia, where to?'], *Al-Mustaqbal al-'arabi*, year 32, no. 368 (October 2009), p. 121.

30. Usama 'Abd al-Rahman, *Shazaya fi al-fikr wa al-tanmiyah wa al-watan* [Fragments on thought, development and the nation], (Sharjah: Kitab Al-Khalij, 2002), pp. 35-36.

31. 'Abd al-Ilah Balqaziz, ed., *Al-Mu'aradah wa al-sultah fi al-watan al-'arabi: azmat al-mu'aradah al-siyasiyyah al-'arabiyyah* [Opposition and power in the Arab world: the Arab political opposition crisis], Beirut: Centre for Arab Unity Studies, 2001), p. 11.

32. Al-Rasheed, *Contesting the Saudi State: Islamic Voices from a New Generation*, p. 57

33. See: Ismail al-Shatti's debate in: Balqaziz, op. cit., p. 149.

34. Muhammad Bin Sunitan, *Al-Nukhab al-sa'udiyyah: dirasah fi al-tahawwulat wa al-Ikhfaqat*, [The Saudi Elites: A Study of Transformations and Failures], Doctoral theses series 48, (Beirut: Centre for Arab Unity Studies, 2004), pp. 130-131.

35. Usama 'Abd al-Rahman, *Shazaya fi al- fikr wa al-tanmiyah wa al-watan*, p. 52.

36. Quran *Fatir* 35:28.

37. Al-Rasheed, *Contesting the Saudi State: Islamic Voices from a New Generation*, p. 81.

38. Ibn Sunitan, *Al-Nukhab al-sa'udiyyah: dirasah fi al-tahawwulat wa al-ikhfaqat*, p. 111.

39. Balqaziz, ed., *Al-Mu'aradah wa al-sultah fi al-watan al-'arabi: azmat al-mu'aradah al-siyasiyyah al-'arabiyyah*, p. 21.

40. See: Munir Shafiq's commentary on 'Abd al-Ilah Balqaziz's paper *Azmat al-Mu'aradah al-Siyasiyyah fi al-watan al-Arabi* [The Arab Political Opposition Crisis] in: ibid, p. 83.

41. See: Fawwaz Gerges, "*Tahaffuzat 'arabiyyah' ala al-dimuqratiyyah*" [Arab Reservations about Democracy], in: 'Ali Khalifah al-Kawari, ed., *Azmat al-dimuqratiyyah fi al-buldan al-'arabiyyah: i'tiradat wa tahaffuzat 'ala al-dimuqratiyyah fi al- 'alam al-'arabi* [Crisis of Democracy in the Arab World: Objections and Reservations Concerning Democracy in the Arab World] (Beirut: Dar al-Saqi, 2004), p. 20.

42. See: Khaled Hroub, in: ibid, pp. 187-188.

43. See: Abd al-Wahab al-Afandi, in: ibid, pp. 195-196.

44. Khair al-Din Hasib, "Iftitahiyyat al-'adad: Al-Tayyaran al-qawmi al-'arabi wa al-islami: janahan la yuhaliqan illa ma'an," (Editorial: The Nationalist and Islamic Currents: Two wings that Can Only Fly Together), *Al-Mustaqbal al-'arabi*, year 26, no. 295 (September 2003), p. 7.

45. Halim Barakat, *Al-Mujtama' al-'arabi al-mu'asir: bahth istitla'i ijtima'i* [Contemporary Arab society: a sociological overview],10 ed. (Beirut: Centre for Arab Unity Studies, 2008), p. 551.

CHAPTER FOUR

1. *World Development Report 2003: Dynamic Development in a Sustainable World* (New York: World Bank, 2003), p. 37.

2. Narrated by al-Hakim.

3. *World Development Report 2002, Building Institutions for Markets* (New York: World Bank, 2002), pp. 5-10.

4. Nancy Birdsall and Arvind Subramanian, "Saving Iraq from its Oil", *Foreign Affairs* vol. 83, no. 4 (July-August 2004), pp. 77-89.

5. Byman and Green, "The Enigma of Political Stability in the Persian Gulf Monarchies", p. 22.

6. Herb, *All in the Family: Absolutism, Revolution and Democracy in the Middle Eastern Monarchies*, p. 60.

7. Ibn Sunitan, *Al-Nukhab al-sa'udiyyah: dirasah fi al-tahawwulat wa al-ikhfaqat*, p. 61.

8. Ibid., p. 62

9. Ibid., p. 64

10. Herb, op. cit., p. 34

11. Ibn Sunitan, op. cit., p. 67

12. Ibid., pp. 74-75

13. See: Monty G. Marshall, "Polity IV Project: Political Regime Characteristics and Transitions, 1800-2009," Centre for Systemic Peace and Colorado State University, http://www.systemicpeace.org/polity/polity4.htm

14. Economic Commission for Africa, *African Governance Report II*, (Oxford: Oxford University Press: Oxford, 2009), pp. 1-3.

15. Ghanim al-Najjar, *Madkhal lil-tatawwur al-siyasi fi al-kuwait* [Introduction to political development in Kuwait], 2 vols, (Kuwait: Dar Qartas, 1966), pp. 13-70.

16. Yusuf al-Jassim, "*Munaqashat muntada al-tanmiyah*" [Discussions of the development seminar], in: al-Kawari, ed., *Al-Khalij al-'arabi wa al-dimuqratiyyah*, p. 247.

17. Salem, "Kuwait: Politics in a Participatory Emirate", p. 211.

18. Nathan J. Brown, "Moving Out of Kuwait's Political Impasse," Carnegie Endowment (25 June 2007), http://carnegieendowment.org/publications/index.cfm?fa=view&id=23320&prog=zg

19. Ahmad Al-Khatib, *Al-Kuwait min al- Imarah ila al-dawla: dhikrayat al-'amal al-watani wa al-qawmi*, [Kuwait from emirate to state: memories of national and nationalist activism), supervised by Ghanim Najjar, (Casablanca: Arab Cultural Centre, 2007), pp. 207-210.

20. Ahmad 'Ali al-Dayyin, *Wiladat dustur al-kuwait* [Birth of the Kuwaiti Constitution], (Kuwait: Dar Al-Qartas, 1999), pp. 8-54.

21. Al-Kawari, ed., *Al-Khalij al-'arabi wa al-dimuqratiyyah*, p. 59.

22. Ahmad 'Ali Al-Dayyin, "*Al-Dimuqratyyiah wa al-intikhabat fi al–Kuwait* [Democracy and Elections in Kuwait], in: 'Ali Khalifah al-Kawari, ed., *Al-Intikhabat al-Dimuqratiyyah wa waqi' al-intikhabat fi al-aqtar al-'arabiyya*h [Democratic elections and the status of elections in the Arab world], Democratic Studies Programme in the Arab Countries, (Beirut: Centre for Arab Unity Studies and the Democratic Studies Programme in the Arab Countries, 2008), p.126.

23. See Ismail al-Shatti's follow-up, in: Al-Kawari, ed., *Al-Khalij al-'arabi wa al-dimuqratiyyah*, p. 140.

24. Salem, "Kuwait: Politics in a Participatory Emirate" p. 224.

25. Ibid., pp. 226-227.

26. Michael Herb, "Kuwait: The Obstacle of Parliamentary Politics," in: Joshua Teitelbaum, ed., *Political Liberalization in the Persian Gulf* (New York: Columbia University Press, 2009), pp. 134-135.

27. Robert Dahl, *Polyarchy: Participation and Opposition*, (New Haven, CT: Yale University Press, 1972).

28. Herb, "Kuwait: The Obstacle of Parliamentary Politics", pp. 154-155.

29. Amr Hamzawi, "The Saudi Labyrinth: Is there a Political Opening?" in: Choucaire-Vizoso, eds., *Beyond the Façade: Political Reform in the Arab World*, pp. 198-200.

30. Ibid., p. 204.

31. David Gardner, *Last Chance: The Middle East in the Balance*, (London: I.B. Tauris, 2009), p. 112.

32. Al-Rasheed, *Mashru' tahdith al-hukm al-sa'udi*, pp. 101-154.

33. Hamzawi, "The Saudi Labyrinth: Is there a Political Opening?", p. 205.

34. J. E. Peterson, "Bahrain: Reform – Promise and Reality," in: Teitelbaum, ed., *Political Liberalization in the Persian Gulf*, pp. 157-158.

35. Herb, "Kuwait: The Obstacle of Parliamentary Politics", pp. 174-175.

36. Ibid., p. 175

37. Adeed Dawisha, *Saudi Arabia's Search for Security*, Adelphi Papers; no. 158, (London: International Institute for Strategic Studies, 1979), p. 20.

38. Peterson, "Bahrain: Reform – Promise and Reality," pp. 160-161.

39. Ibid., p. 162

40. Ibid., pp. 163-164

41. Ibid., pp. 166-167

42. Ibid., pp. 167-168

43. BBC News, "Bahrain Profile", http://www.bbc.com/news/world-middle-east-14541322

44. Elisheva Rosman-Stollman, "Qatar: Liberalization as Foreign Policy," in: Teitelbaum, ed., *Political Liberalization in the Persian Gulf*, p. 190.

45. *The Peninsula Qatar* (5 October 2002).

46. *The Peninsula Qatar* (1 June 2003).

47. Rosman-Stollman, op. cit., p. 191.

48. Ibid., p. 192

49. Qatari Ministry for Foreign Affairs http://www.mofa.gov.qa

50. Ibid.

51. Qatar News Agency (30 April 2003)

52. Mehran Kamrava, *Qatar: Small State, Big Politics*, (Ithaca, CA; London: Cornell University Press, 2013), pp. 65-68.

53. Kelly, *Arabia, the Gulf and the West*, pp. 141-142.

54. Uzi Rabi, "Oman: Say Yes to Oman, Say No to the Tribe," in: Teitelbaum, ed., *Political Liberalization in the Persian Gulf*, pp. 211-212.

55. *Al-Usbu' al-'arabi* (26 September 2000).

56. *Times of Oman* (3 October 2003).

57. *Al-Watan* (Sultanate of Oman), 4 October 2003.

58. Rabi, "Oman: Say Yes to Oman, Say No to the Tribe" , pp. 217-218.

59. Wright, *Dreams and Shadows: The Future of the Middle East*, p. 9.

60. Michael Herb, "A nation of Bureaucrats: Political Participation and Economic Diversification in Kuwait and the United Arab Emirates", *International Journal of Middle East Studies*, vol. 41, no. 3 (2009), p. 379.

61. *The Washington Post*, April 27, 2007.

62. Freedom House, "The Worst of the Worst: The World's Most Repressive Societies", (Washington, DC: Freedom House, 2007).

63. Davidson, *The United Arab Emirates: A Study in Survival*, pp. 34-37.

64. Christopher M. Davidson, "The United Arab Emirates: Economy First Politics Second" in: Teitelbaum, ed., *Political Liberalization in the Persian Gulf*, pp. 245-248.

65. Ibid., p. 239

66. Al-Yusuf, *Al-Imarat al-'arabiyyah al-muttahidah 'ala muftaraq turuq* [The United Arab Emirates at the crossroads], (Beirut: Centre for Arab Unity Studies, 2013), pp. 130-132.

67. *World Development Report 2002: Building Institutions for Markets* (New York: World Bank, 2002), pp. 181-182.

68. McKinsey and Company, "Public Service Broadcasting around the World: A McKinsey Report for the BBC" (January 1999).

69. William Rugh, *The Arab Press: News Media and Political Process in the Arab World* (Syracuse, NY: Syracuse University Press, 1979).

70. Freedom House, *Freedom of the Press 2013: Middle East Volatility Amid Global Decline. Selected Data from Freedom House's Annual Press Freedom Index* (New York: Freedom House, 2013).

71. Ibrahim al-Ba'iz, "Al-I'lam fi duwal al-khalij: qira'ah naqdiyyah" [Media in the Gulf Countries: A Critique], in: Ibrahim al-Ba'iz et al, *Al-I'lam fi duwal al-khalij: dawruhu al-tanmawi wa masaruhu al-mustaqbali* [Media in the Gulf Countries: Its Role in Development and Future Course], (Dubai: Dar Qortas Publishing House, 2007), pp. 14-15.

72. Ibid., p. 16

73. Ibid., p. 29

74. Ibid., p. 138

75. Hamad 'Abd al-'Aziz al-Kawari, "Al-I'lam al-khaliji ila ayna?" [Media in the Gulf, Where to?], in: *Al-I'lam fi duwal al-khalij*, pp. 54-55.

76. Ibid., p. 55

77. Nahawand al-Kadri Issa, *Qira'ah fi thaqafat al-fada'iyyat al-'arabiyyah: al Wuquf 'ala tukhum al-tafkik*, [A Review of Arab Satellite Culture: Standing at the Threshold of Dismantlement], (Beirut: Centre for Arab Unity Studies, 2008), pp. 29-30.

78. Usama 'Abd al-Rahman, *Al-Islam wa al-tanmiyah* [Islam and Development], (Beirut: Centre for Arabic Unity Studies, 2000), p. 72.

79. Kenneth M. Pollack, *A Path Out of the Desert: A Grand Strategy for America in the Middle East*, (New York: Random House, 2008), p. 111.

80. *Arab Human Development Report 2003: Building a Knowledge Society*, (New York: United Nations Publications, 2003), p. 81.

81. Champion, *The Paradoxical Kingdom: Saudi Arabia and the Momentum of Reform*, pp. 265-266.

82. Ibid., p. 262.

83. Ibid., p. 263.

84. Nora Boustany, "Traditional Saudis Take Dim View of Attempts to Modernize Islam," *Washington Post*, 24 August 1994, p. 22.

85. Champion, op. cit., p. 272.

86. *World Development Report 2002: Building Institutions for Markets*, (New York: World Bank, 2002), p. 117.

87. Kenneth W. Dam, *The Law-Growth Nexus: The Rule of Law and Economic Development*, (Washington, DC: Brookings Institution Press, 2006), p. 87.

88. Edward Glaeser et al., "Coase Versus the Coasians," *Quarterly Journal of Economics*, vol. 116, no. 3 (2001), pp. 855-856.

89. Rafael La Porta et al., "Related Lending," *Quarterly Journal of Economics*, vol. 118, no. 1 (2003), pp. 231-268.

90. *World Development Report 2002: Building Institutions for Markets*, pp. 130-131.

91. *Doing Business 2013* (Washington, DC: World Bank, 2013), p. 90.

92. Jamel Zarrouk, "A Survey of Barriers to Trade and Investment in Arab Countries," in: Ahmed Galal and Bernard Hoekman, eds., *Arab Economic Integration: Between Hope and Reality* (Cairo: Egyptian Center for Economic Studies; Washington, DC: Brookings Press, 2003).

93. Marcus Noland and Howard Pack, *The Arab Economies in a Changing World*, (Washington, DC: Peterson Institute for International Economics, 2007), p. 145.

94. Zogby International, *Six Arab Nations Survey Report*, Submitted to the World Economic Forum's Arab Business Council (November 2005)

95. William Clatanoff et al., "Saudi Arabia's Accession to the WTO: Is a Revolution Brewing?", *Middle East Policy* vol. 13, no. 1 (2006), pp. 1-23.

PART II

1. Leonardo Maugeri, *The Age of Oil: The Mythology, History and Future of the World's Most Controversial Resource*, (London: Praeger, 2006), pp. 44-45.

2. United States Senate, *The International Petroleum Cartel. Staff Report to [i.e. of] the Federal Trade Commission Submitted to the Subcommittee on Monopoly of the Select Committee on Small Business: Congress* (Washington, DC: US Govt., 1952), p. 114.

3. Anthony Sampson, *The Seven Sisters: The Great Oil Companies and the World they Shaped*, (New York: Viking Press, 1975), p. 106.

CHAPTER FIVE

1. Franklin Tugwell, *The Politics of Oil in Venezuela*, (Stanford, CT: Stanford University Press, 1975), p. 7.

2. Maugeri, *The Age of Oil: The Mythology, History and Future of the World's Most Controversial Resource*, p. 24.

3. Tugwell, op. cit., p. 147.

4. Paul Collier, *The Plundered Planet*, (Oxford: Oxford University Press, 2010), p. 70.

5. Tugwell, op. cit., p. 147.

6. Robert Vitalis, *America's Kingdom: Mythmaking on the Saudi Oil Frontier*, (London: Verso, 2009), pp. 39-44.

7. Collier, *The Plundered Planet*, p. 70

8. Muhammad Bin 'Abd Allah al-Saif, *'Abd Allah al-Tariki: sukhur al-naft wa rimal al-siyyasah,*[Abdullah Al-Tariki: Oil Rocks and Policy Sands], (Beirut: Riyad al-Rayyis li-l-kutub wa al-nashr, 2007), p. 106.

9. Ibid., p. 108

10. Ibid, p. 112

11.   Vitalis, *America's Kingdom: Mythmaking on the Saudi Oil Frontier*, p. 210.

12.   Maugeri, *The Age of Oil: The Mythology, History and Future of the World's Most Controversial Resource*, p. 65.

13.   Stephen Kinzer, *All the Shah's Men: An American Coup and the Roots of Middle East Terror* (Hoboken, NJ: J. Wiley and Sons, 2003), pp. 1-16.

14.   On the role of non-governmental organizations in unveiling information, see: http://www.publishwhatyoupay.org/

15.   Tugwell, *The Politics of Oil in Venezuela*, pp. 57-58.

16.   Al-Khatib, *Al-Kuwait min al- Imarah ila al-dawla: dhikrayat al-'amal al-watani wa al-qawmi*, pp. 278.

17.   Ibid., p. 275

18.   Ibid., p. 280

19.   Hussain 'Abd Allah, *Mustaqbal al-Naft al-Arabi* [The Future of Arab Oil], 2nd edition, edited and updated (Beirut: Centre for Arab Unity Studies, 2006), pp. 64-65.

20.   Vitalis, *America's Kingdom: Mythmaking on the Saudi Oil Frontier*, p. 130.

21.   Ibid., p. 134

22.   *Al-Nadwa* (Riyadh), 31 July 1960.

23.   Daniel Yergin, *The Prize: Epic Quest for Oil, Money and Power*, (New York: Simon and Schuster, 1991), p. 514.

24.   Ibid., pp. 522-523

25.   Vitalis, *America's Kingdom: Mythmaking on the Saudi Oil Frontier*, pp. 270-271.

26.   Ibid., pp. 233-234.

27.   Maugeri, *The Age of Oil: The Mythology, History and Future of the World's Most Controversial Resource*, pp. 85-86.

28.   George W. Stocking, *Middle East Oil: A Study in Political and Economic Controversy*, (Knoxville TN: Vanderbilt University Press, 1970), pp. 214-225.

29.   Ibid., pp. 247-253

30.   'Atif Sulaiman, *Al-Tharwah al-naftiyyah wa dawruha al-'arabi: al-dawr al-siyyasi wa al-iqtisadi li-l-naft al-'arabi* [Oil Wealth and its Arab Role: The Political and Economic Role of Arab Oil], (Beirut: Centre for Arab Unity Studies, 2009), p. 132.

31.   Maugeri, *The Age of Oil: The Mythology, History and Future of the World's Most Controversial Resource*, p. 69.

32.   Tugwell, *The Politics of Oil in Venezuela*, p. 82.

33.   Al-Saif, *'Abd Allah al-Tariki: sukhur al-naft wa rimal al-siyyasah*, pp. 58-161.

34.   'Abd Allah, *Mustaqbal al-Naft al-Arabi*, pp. 231-234.

35.   Vitalis, *America's Kingdom: Mythmaking on the Saudi Oil Frontier*, pp. 88-95.

36.   Ibid., p. 136

37.   Ibid., pp. 96-98

38.   Wanda Jablonski, "Interview with Tariki," *Petroleum Week*, February 22, 1957, pp. 22-23.

39.   Vitalis, *America's Kingdom: Mythmaking on the Saudi Oil Frontier*, pp. 135-136, and notes 22-23, p. 304.

40.   Al-Khatib, *Al-Kuwait min al-Imarah ila al-dawla*, pp. 158-164.

41.   Vitalis, op. cit., pp. 111-112.

42.   Ibid., pp. 140, 154

43.   Al-Khatib, op. cit., p. 158.

44.   Maugeri, *The Age of Oil: The Mythology, History and Future of the World's Most Controversial Resource*, pp. 235-236.

45.   British Petroleum, *BP Statistical Review of World Energy*, (London: BP, 2013), p. 16. http://www.bp.com/content/dam/bp/pdf/statistical-review/statistical_review_of_world_energy_2013.pdf

46. Ibid., p. 8.

47. 'Abd Allah, *Mustaqbal al-Naft al-Arabi*, pp. 266-268.

48. Ibid., p. 269

49. Maugeri, *The Age of Oil: The Mythology, History and Future of the World's Most Controversial Resource*, pp. 78-79.

50. 'Abd Allah, op. cit., pp. 272-274.

51. League of Arab States, *Al-Taqrir al-iqtisadi al-'arabi al-muwahhad* 2012 [Unified Arab Economic Report], (Abu Dhabi, Cairo: Arab Monetary Fund, Arab Fund for Economic and Social Development, League of Arab States and Organisation of Arab Petroleum Exporting Countries), p.81

CHAPTER SIX

1. Jahangir Amuzegar, *Managing the Oil Wealth*, (London: I.B. Tauris, 2001), pp. 23-31.

2. Maugeri, *The Age of Oil: The Mythology, History and Future of the World's Most Controversial Resource*, p. 80.

3. Morris A. Adelman, *The Genie Out of the Bottle: World Oil since 1970*, Cambridge, MA: MIT Press, 1995), p. 96.

4. Maugeri, op. cit., p. 81.

5. 'Abd Allah, *Mustaqbal al-Naft al-Arabi*, p. 231.

6. Maugeri, *The Age of Oil: The Mythology, History and Future of the World's Most Controversial Resource*, p.114.

7. Ibid., p. 122

8. Ibid., pp. 129-130

9. Ibid., pp. 135-136

10. Robert Mabro, ed., *OPEC and the World Oil Market: The Genesis of the 1986 Price Crisis*, (Oxford: Oxford University Press-Oxford Institute for Energy Studies, 1986), p. 166.

11. Maugeri, *The Age of Oil: The Mythology, History and Future of the World's Most Controversial Resource*, p. 139.

12. Francisco Parra, *Oil Politics: A Modern History of Oil*, (London: I.B. Tauris 2004), p. 287.

13. Maugeri, op. cit., p. 145.

14. Paul Stevens, "Co-operation between Producers and Consumers", in: Robert E. Looney, ed., *Handbook of Oil Politics* (London: Routledge; Taylor and Francis Group, 2012), pp. 85-86.

15. Yusuf Khalifah al-Yusuf, "'Ajz al-muwazanah al-'ammah fi dawlat al-imarat al-'arabiyyah al-muttahidah" [Deficit in the United Arab Emirates' Budget], *Gulf and Arabian Peninsula Studies Magazine*, no. 70 (July 1993), pp. 97-105.

16. Amuzegar, *Managing the Oil Wealth*, pp. 41-42.

17. Joseph Stanislaw and Daniel Yergin, "Oil: Reopening the Door", *Foreign Affairs* (September-October 1993), p. 89.

18. Maugeri, *The Age of Oil: The Mythology, History and Future of the World's Most Controversial Resource*, pp. 248-249.

19. Nicholas Cacchione, *Is Gasoline still a Great Bargain?* (Norwalk, CT: John S. Herold, 2005).

20. Naim A. Sherbiny, "Arab Oil Production in the Context of International Conflicts" in: Naim A. Sherbiny and Mark A. Tessler, eds., *Arab Oil: Impact on the Arab Countries and Global Implications*, Praeger Special Studies in International Business, Finance and Trade (New York: Praeger, 1976), p.44.

21. Pollack, *A Path Out of the Desert*, p. 316.

22. William B. Quandt, *Saudi Arabia in the 1980s: Foreign Policy, Security, and Oil*, (Washington, DC: The Brookings Institution, 1981), p. 123.

23. Kelly, *Arabia, the Gulf and the West*, pp. 263-264.

24.　Quandt, op. cit., p.131.

25.　Ibid., p. 132

26.　"The Bush-Saudi Axis", *Time* (15 September 2003).

27.　*The New York Times*, 3 April 1986, p. 1.

28.　Crystal, *Oil and Politics in the Gulf: Rulers and Merchants in Kuwait and Qatar*, p. 105.

29.　Phoebe Marr, *The Modern History of Iraq*, 2nd ed. (Boulder, CO: West View Press, 2004), p. 220.

30.　Ibid., p. 221

31.　Craig Unger, *House of Bush, House of Saud: The Secret Relationship between the World's Two Most Powerful Dynasties*, (New York: Scribner, 2004), p.11.

32.　Bob Woodward, *Plan of Attack*, (New York: Simon and Schuster, 2004), p. 324.

33.　Said K. Aburish, *The Rise, Corruption and Coming Fall of the House of Saud*, (London: Bloomsbury Publishing Ltd., 1994), p. 283..

34.　Ibid.

35.　Amuzegar, *Managing the Oil Wealth*, p. 25.

36.　'Abd Allah, *Mustaqbal al-Naft al-Arabi*, p. 14.

37.　Bob Woodward, *State of Denial*, (New York: Simon and Schuster, 2006), p. 287.

PART III

1.　Richard M. Auty, *Sustaining Development in Mineral Economics: The Resource Curse Thesis*, (London: Routledge, 1993), pp. 241-258.

2.　Michael Roemer, *Fishing for Growth: Export-Led Development in Peru, 1950-1967*, (Cambridge MA: Harvard University Press, 1970).

3.　Hazem Beblawi, "The Rentier State in the Arab World" in: Hazem Beblawi and Giacomo Liciani, eds., *The Rentier State, Nation, State and Integration in the Arab World*, vol. 2 (London: Croom Helm, 1987).

4.　Tim Niblock and Monica Malik, *The Political Economy of Saudi Arabia*, (London: Routledge, 2007), pp. 14-18.

CHAPTER SEVEN

1.　Amuzegar, *Managing the Oil Wealth*, (London: I.B. Tauris, 2001), pp. 16-20.

2.　International Monetary Fund (IMF), *Regional Economic Outlook: Middle East and Central Asia* (Washington, DC: International Monetary Fund, 2010), pp. 19-24.

3.　Yusuf Khalifah al-Yusuf, " 'Ajz al-muwazanah al-'ammah fi dawlat al-imarat al-'arabiyyah al-muttahidah", pp. 75-82.

4.　T. Stauffer, "Income Measurement in Arab States" in: Beblawi and Liciani, eds. *The Rentier State in the Arab World*, pp. 22-48.

5.　Partha Dasgupta, "Valuing Objects and Evaluating Policies in Imperfect Economies", *Economic Journal*, vol. 111, no. 471 (April 2001), pp. 1-29.

6.　Jahangir Amuzegar, "Oil Wealth: A Very Mixed Blessing", *Foreign Affairs* (Spring 1982), pp. 814-835.

7.　Hossein Askari, *Middle East Oil Exporters: What Happened to Economic Development?* (London: Edward Elgar, 2006), p. 88.

8.　Ibid., p. 89.

9.　International Monetary Fund (IMF), *World Economic Outlook 1998*, (Washington, DC: International Monetary Fund, 1998), p. 21.

10.　Daniel Yergin, "Insuring Energy Security", vol. 85, no. 2 *Foreign Affairs* (March-April 2006), pp. 71-75.

11. These include Egypt, Morocco, Tunisia, Jordan, Lebanon and Pakistan.

12. Askari, *Middle East Oil Exporters: What Happened to Economic Development?*, pp. 88-92.

13. Michael T. Klare, *Blood and Oil*, (New York: Metropolitan Books, Henry Holt and Company 2004), p. 87.

14. Marie-Claire Aoun, "Oil and Gas Resources of the Middle East and North Africa: A Curse or Blessing?", in: Jean-Marie Chevalier and Patrice Geoffron, eds., *The New Energy Crisis: Climate, Economics, and Geopolitics*, 2nd ed. (London: Palgrave and MacMillan, 2013), pp. 141-142.

15. CBS News (25 June 2000)

16. League of Arab States, *Al-Taqrir al-iqtisadi al-'arabi al-muwahhad 2012*, p. 380.

17. Ibid., Appendix 2/6, p. 384.

18. Non-petroleum imports include taxes on income and profit, taxes on goods and services, custom duties on foreign trade, grants and income from investments.

19. William Ascher, *Why Governments Waste Natural Resource: Policy Failures in Developing Countries*, (Baltimore; Johns Hopkins University Press, 1999).

20. Hossein Askari, *Collaborative Colonialism: The Political Economy of Oil in the Persian Gulf* (New York: Palgrave MacMillan, 2013), p. 143.

21. Stephen S. Cohen and J. Bradford De Long, *The End of Influence: What Happens When Other Countries Have the Money*, (New York: Basic Books, 2010), pp. 72-73.

22. Robert B. Stucliffe, *Industry and Underdevelopment*, (London: Addison-Wesley Publishing Company, 1971), pp. 198-242.

23. League of Arab States, *Al-Taqrir al-iqtisadi al-'arabi al-muwahhad 2012*, Appendix 3/4, p. 359.

24. *BP Statistical Review of World Energy*, p. 16.

25. League of Arab States, op. cit., p. 81.

26. Jaap Kalkman and Alexander Keller, *Global Petrochemicals: Who is Really Benefiting from the Growth in the New World?*, Roland Berger Strategy Consultants (November 2012), http://www.rolandberger.com/media/publications/2012-11-11-rbsc-pub-Global_Petrochemicals.html

27. Unified Arab Report 2012, Appendix 17/2, p. 340.

28. World Bank, *World Development Indicators 2010* (Washington, DC: World Bank, 2010), p. 375.

29. League of Arab States, *Al-Taqrir al-iqtisadi al-'arabi al-muwahhad 2012*, Table 5, p. 76.

CHAPTER EIGHT

1. Lorimer, *Gazetteer of the Persian Gulf, Oman and Central Arabia*, pp. 1450-1451.

2. Davidson, *Dubai: The Vulnerability of Success*, p. 24.

3. Ibid., p. 51

4. Ibid., p. 51

5. Ibid., pp. 19-21

6. Ibid., p. 53

7. Donald Hawley, *The Emirates: Witness to a Metamorphosis*, (Norwich: Michael Russell, 2007), p. 295.

8. Easa Saleh al-Gurg, *The Wells of Memory: An Autobiography*, (London: John Murray, 1998), pp. 89 and 121

9. Crystal, *Oil and Politics in the Gulf: Rulers and Merchants in Kuwait and Qatar*, pp. 126-127.

10. Rupert Hay, *The Persian Gulf States*, (Washington, DC: Middle East Institute, 1959), p. 110.

11. Al-Khatib, *Al-Kuwait min al- Imarah ila al-dawla: dhikrayat al-'amal al-watani wa al-qawmi*, pp. 204-206.

12. Davidson, *Dubai: The Vulnerability of Success*, p. 52.

13.   Estimates indicate that in 2009, the GCC states' population was 39.6 million, the highest number being in Saudi Arabia, and the lowest in Bahrain.

14.   Onn Winckler, "Labor and Liberalization: The Decline of the GCC Rentier System," in: Teitelbaum, ed., *Political Liberalization in the Persian Gulf*, p. 67.

15.   Ibid., p. 67-71

16.   Ibid., p. 73-79

17.   Martin Baldwin-Edward, "Labour Immigration and Labour Markets in the GCC states: National Patterns and Trends", LSE Kuwait Programme research paper no. 15 (March 2011), p. 11, http://www.lse.ac.uk/middleEastCentre/kuwait/research/papers/labourimmigration. aspx.

18.   Ibid., p. 20

19.   League of Arab States, *Al-Taqrir al-iqtisadi al-'arabi al-muwahhad 2012*, p. 341.

20.   Some statistics indicate that 70 per cent of all degrees granted by Saudi universities were in human sciences and Islamic studies.

21.   UN, *Human Development Report 2007-2008: Fighting Climate Change: Human Solidarity in a Divided World*, (New York: United Nations Development Report, 2008).

22.   Cohen and De Long, *The End of Influence: What Happens When Other Countries Have the Money*, p. 78.

23.   See for example, Nader Farajani, ed., *Al-'Amalah al-ajnabiyyah fi aqtar al-khalij al-'arabi* [Foreign Labour in the GCC states], (Beirut: Centre for Arab Unity Studies, 1983). Also see Yusuf Khalifah al-Yusuf, "Al-Bu'd al-sukkani li-l-tanmiyah fi al-dawlat al-imarat al-'arabiyyah al-muttahidah" [The Population Dimension in the United Arab Emirates], *Al-Ta'awun* (magazine of the GCC General Secretariat), no. 29, (March 1993), pp. 98-126.

24.   Juhaina Sultan Saif al-Issa, "Al-Ta'thirat al-ijtima'iyyah li-l-murabbiyah al-ajnabiyyah 'ala al-usra" [The Social Impact of Foreign Nannies on the Family], in Nader Farajani, ed., op. cit., pp. 169-181.

25.   'Abd al-Razzaq al-Faris, "Dawr al-qita' al-khass fi intishar al-'amalah al-ajnabiyyah" [The Private Sector's Role in the Spread of Foreign Labour], in Nader Farajani, ed., op. cit., pp. 151-156.

26.   Haidar Ibrahim, "Athar al-'amalah al-ajnabiyyah 'ala al-thaqafa al-'arabiyyah" [Impact of Foreign Labour on Arab Culture], in Nader Farajani, ed., op. cit., pp. 251-270.

27.   'Ali As'ad Watfah, "Al-'Amalah al-wafidah wa tahaddiyyat al-huwiyyah al-thaqafiyyah fi duwal al-khalij al-'arabi" [Foreign Labour and the Challenges of Cultural Identity in the Arab Gulf Countries], *Al-Mustaqbal al-'arabi*, year 30, no. 344 (October 2007), p. 78

28.   Ibid., p. 79

29.   See 'Abd 'Allah Fahmi al-Nafisi's commentary on 'Abd al-Malik Khalaf al-Tamimi's paper, "Al-Athar al-siyasiyyah li-l-hijra al-ajnabiyyah" [Political Implications of Foreign Migration], in: Nader Farajani, ed., op. cit., pp. 309-312.

30.   Paul Rivlin, *Arab Economies in the Twenty-First Century*, (Cambridge, MA: Cambridge University Press, 2009), p. 221.

31.   Watfah, "Al-'Amalah al-wafidah wa tahaddiyyat al-huwiyyah al-thaqafiyyah fi duwal al-khalij al-'arabi", pp. 76-78

32.   Steffen Hertog, *Princes, Brokers and Bureaucrats: Oil and the State in Saudi Arabia*, p. 199.

33.   Ibid., footnote 81, p. 198

34.   Ibid., footnote 87, p. 199

35.   *Arab News* (29 April 2004).

36.   *Saudi Gazette* (23 August 2004).

37.   *Arab News* (6 July 2004).

38.   *Saudi Gazette* (21 May 2008).

39.   Hertog, *Princes, Brokers and Bureaucrats: Oil and the State in Saudi Arabia*, p. 219.

40. Michael Sturn et al., "The Gulf Cooperation Council Countries: Economic Structure, Recent Developments, and the Role in the Global Economy", *Occasional Paper Series*, no. 92, (European Central Bank: 2008), p. 17.

41. Winckler, "Labor and Liberalization: The Decline of the GCC Rentier System", pp. 63-64.

42. Thomas L. Friedman, *The World is Flat: A Brief History of the Twenty-First Century*, (New York: Farrar, Straus and Giroux, 2005), pp. 460-463.

43. Paul Rivlin, *Arab Economies in the Twenty-First Century*, footnote no. 11, p. 225.

44. Alan Richards, "Economic Reform in the Middle East: the Challenge to Governance" in: Nora Bensahel and Daniel Byman, eds., *The Future Security Environment in the Middle East* (Santa Monica, CA: Projects Air Force, 2004), p. 112.

CHAPTER NINE

1. Daniel L. Byman and Jerrold D. Green, *Political Violence and Stability in the States of the Northern Persian Gulf*, (Santa Monica, CA: RAND, 1999).

2. Monica Malik, "The Role of the Private Sector," in: Rodney Wilson et al., *Economic Development in Saudi Arabia* (London: Routledge Curzon, 2004), pp. 128-129.

3. Yusuf Khalifah al-Yusuf, "*Tarshid al-dawr al-tanmawi li-l-qita' al-'amm fi duwal majlis al-ta'awun al-khaliji*" [Rationalising the Public Sector's Role in the GCC states' Development], *Majallah al-'ulum al-'ijtima'iyyah*, year 27, no. 3 (1999), pp. 45-54.

4. Mahmoud Abdel-Fadil, "The Macro-Behaviour of Oil-Rentier States in the Arab Region" in: Hazem Beblawi and Giacomo Liciani, eds., *The Rentier State, Nation, State and Integration in the Arab World*, p. 83.

5. Peter Evans, "The State as Problem and Solution: Predation, Embedded Autonomy, and Structural Change" in: Stephen Haggard and Robert Kaufman, eds., *The Political Economy of Adjustment* (Princeton, NJ: Princeton University Press, 1992), p.164.

6. Nazih N. Ayubi, "Political Correlates of Privatization Programs in the Middle East", *Arab Studies Quarterly*, vol. nos. 2-3 (1992), pp. 51-52.

7. Theda Skocpol, "Bringing the State Back In: Strategies of Analysis in Current Research" in: Peter Evans, Dietrich Rueschemeyer and Theda Skocpol, eds., *Bringing the State Back In* (Cambridge: Cambridge University Press, 1985), p.9.

8. Peter B. Evans, *Embedded Autonomy: State and Industrial Transformation*, Princeton Paperbacks (Princeton, NJ: Princeton University Press, 1995), pp. 43-45.

9. James M. Cypher and James L. Dietz, *The Process of Economic Development*, (London: Routledge, 1997), p. 226.

10. Steffen Hertog, "The Private Sector and Reform in the Gulf Cooperation Council", LSE Kuwait Programme research paper no. 30 (July 2013), pp. 34-35.

11. World Bank, *From Privilege to Competition: Unlocking Private-Led Growth in the Middle East and North Africa*, (Washington, DC: World Bank, 2009), p. 51.

12. Ibid., footnote 4, p. 67

13. Ibid., p. 52

14. Ibid., footnote 6, p. 67

15. Ibid., pp. 54-55

16. Ibid., pp. 56-57

17. Ibid., pp. 58-59

18. League of Arab States, *Al-Taqrir al-iqtisadi al-'arabi al-muwahhad 2012*, p.86.

19. World Bank, *From Privilege to Competition: Unlocking Private-Led Growth in the Middle East and North Africa*, p. 60

20. Ibid., Figure no. (2-12), p. 62.

21. Andrezej Kapiszewski, "Arabs Versus Asian Migrant Workers in the GCC states", United

Nations Expert Group Meeting on International Migration and Development in the Arab Region,(Beirut 2006), pp. 6-10, http://www.un.org/esa/population/meetings/EGM_Ittmig_Arab/P02_Kapiszewski.pdf

22.   Ibid., p. 27

23.   Hertog , "The Private Sector and Reform in the Gulf Cooperation Council", pp. 50-52.

24.   Commission on Growth and Development, *The Growth Report: Strategies for Sustained Growth and Inclusive Development*, (Washington, DC: World Bank, 2008).

25.   David Dollar and Aart Kraay, "Trade, Growth and Poverty", Policy Research Working Paper 2615 (Washington, DC: World Bank, 2001).

26.   Joseph E. Stiglitz, *Freefall: America, Free Markets and the Sinking of the World Economy*, New York: W.W. Norton, 2010), pp.196-209.

27.   World Bank, *From Privilege to Competition: Unlocking Private-Led Growth in the Middle East and North Africa*, pp. 72-73.

28.   Thomas W. Lippman, *Inside the Mirage: America's Fragile Partnership with Saudi Arabia*, (Boulder, CO: West View, 2004), pp. 241-242.

29.   World Bank, op. cit., pp. 28-29.

30.   Soraya Altorki and Donald P. Cole, *Arabian Oasis City: The Transformation of 'Unayzah*, (Austin: University of Texas, 1989), pp. 112-113.

31.   Steffen Herzog, *Princes, Brokers and Bureaucrats: Oil and the State in Saudi Arabia*, pp. 110-114.

32.   Marcus Noland and Howard Pack, *The Arab Economies in a Changing World*, (Washington, DC: Peterson Institute for International Economics, 2007), pp. 200-201.

33.   Ibid., p. 8

34.   F. Gregory Gause III, *Oil Monarchies: Domestic and Security Challenges in the Arab Gulf States*, (New York: Council on Foreign Relations Press, 1994), p. 58.

35.   Noland and Pack, op. cit., p. 238.

36.   Malik, "The Role of the Private Sector," pp. 126-138.

37.   Ibid., p. 133

38.   Ibid., p. 131

39.   Ibid., p. 132

40.   Ibid., pp. 134-135.

41.   Ibid., p. 136

42.   Yusuf Khalifah al-Yusuf, "Al-'Awlamah wa iqtisadat duwal majlis al-ta'awun al-khaliji" [Globalisation and the economies of the countries of the Gulf Cooperation Council] in Samir Amin, ed., *Al-Mujtama' wa al-iqtisad amama al-'awlamah* [Society and Economy in the face of Globalisation], Al-Mustaqbal al-'Arabi series no. 33, (Beirut: Centre for Arab Unity Studies), pp. 70-98.

43.   World Bank, *From Privilege to Competition: Unlocking Private-Led Growth in the Middle East and North Africa*, pp. 173-174.

44.   Hertog, "The Private Sector and Reform in the Gulf Cooperation Council", p. 32.

45.   Lippman, *Inside the Mirage: America's Fragile Partnership with Saudi Arabia*, p. 235.

46.   Qur'an, *Al-Baqarah*, 1:251

47.   Lee Kuan Yew, *From the Third World to the First*, (New York: Harper Collins Publishers, 2000), p. 136.

48.   Kishore Mahbubani, *The New Asian Hemisphere: The Irresistible Shift of Global Power to the East*, (New York: Public Affairs, 2008), p. 73.

49.   World Bank, *From Privilege to Competition: Unlocking Private-Led Growth in the Middle East and North Africa*, p. 177.

50.   Ibid., pp. 177-178

51.   Beng-Huat Chua, "Values and Development in Singapore," in: Lawrence E. Harrison and

Peter L. Berger, eds., *Developing Cultures: Case Studies* (London: Routledge, 2006), pp. 101-105.

52. Al-Yusuf, "Tarshid al-dawr al-tanmawi li-l-qita' al-'amm fi duwal majlis al-ta'awun al-khaliji", pp. 45-101.

53. Ezra F. Vogel, *The Four Little Dragons: The Spread of Industrialization in East Asia*, (Cambridge, MA: Cambridge University Press, 1991), pp. 14-15.

54. Ibid., pp. 20-21

55. Ibid., p. 17

56. Chien-Kuo Pang, *The State and Economic Transformation: The Taiwan Case*. Developing Economies of the Third World (New York: Garland Pub., 1992), p. 76.

57. Vogel, *The Four Little Dragons: The Spread of Industrialization in East Asia* , pp. 30-31.

58. Ibid., p. 34

59. S. Ho, "South Korea and Taiwan," *Asian Survey* (December 21, 1981), p. 196.

60. Robert Wade, *Governing the Market: Economic Theory and the Role of Government in East Asian Industrialization*, (Princeton, NJ: Princeton University Press, 1990), pp. 306-325.

61. World Bank. *World Development Report 1997: The State in a Changing World*, (New York: World Bank, 1997), p. III.

62. John M. Page, "The East Asian Miracle: An Introduction," *World Development*, vol. 22, no. 4 (April 1994), pp. 615-625.

63. Paul Streeten, "Governance" in: M.G. Quibria and J. Malcolm Dowling, eds., *Current Issues in Economic Development: An Asian Perspective* (Oxford: Oxford University Press, 1996), pp. 45-46.

64. *Financial Times*, 7 October 1991.

65. Stiglitz, *Freefall: America, Free Markets and the Sinking of the World Economy*, p. 199.

CHAPTER TEN

1. International Monetary Fund, *Regional Economic Outlook: Middle East and Central Asia* (Washington, DC: International Monetary Fund, 2008), pp. 35-36.

2. Aoun, "Oil and Gas Resources of the Middle East and North Africa: A Curse or a Blessing?", Table 5.4 , p.153.

3. The phenomenon was first observed in the Dutch gas sector, which is why it is called the Dutch Disease. In brief, the Dutch Disease is a concept that explains the relationship between the increasing exploitation of natural resources coupled with a decline in the manufacturing sector. It claims that an increase in revenues from natural resources will make a given nation's currency stronger compared to that of other nations (manifest in an exchange rate), resulting in the nation's other exports becoming more expensive for other countries to buy, making the manufacturing sector less competitive.

4. Crystal, *Oil and Politics in the Gulf: Rulers and Merchants in Kuwait and Qatar*, p. 104.

5. "Falling Dollar Puts Pressure on OPEC", *Financial Times*, 23 July 2007.

6. International Monetary Fund. *Regional Economic Outlook: Middle East and Central Asia* (Washington, DC: International Monetary Fund, 2000), p. 11.

7. Zeinab Karake-Shalhuob, "GCC Sovereign Wealth Funds and Islamic Finance: Financial Foundations for the Post-Oil Gulf" in: Nabil A. Sultan, David Weir and Zeinab Karake-Shalhoub, eds., *The New Post Oil Arab Gulf* (London: Saqi Books, 2011), p.68.

8. *Financial Times*, 13 March 2009.

9. *Al-Taqrir al-istratiji al-'arabi 1988* [Arab Strategic Report], (Cairo: Al-Ahram Centre for Political and Strategic Studies, 1988), p. 403.

10. *Al-Hayat*, 4 July 1992, p. 9.

11. Dean Baker, *Plunder and Blunder: The Rise and Fall of the Bubble Economy*, (Sausalito, CA: Poli Point Press, 2009), p. 104.

12. Maugeri, *The Age of Oil: The Mythology, History and Future of the World's Most Controversial Resource*, (London: Praeger, 2006), p. 141.

13. David Charter, "Sarkozy Calls for Halt to Foreign Ownership", *The Times*, 21/10/2008.

14. Crystal, *Oil and Politics in the Gulf: Rulers and Merchants in Kuwait and Qatar*, pp. 96-97.

15. Macartan Humphreys and Martin E. Sandbu, "The Political Economy of Natural Resources" in: Macartan Humphreys, Jeffrey D. Sachs and Joseph E. Stiglitz, eds., *Escaping the Resource Curse, Initiative for Policy Dialogue at Columbia* (New York: Columbia University Press, 2007), pp. 194-197.

16. Cohen and De Long, *The End of Influence: What Happens When Other Countries Have the Money*, pp. 79-80.

17. Al-Yusuf, " 'Ajz al-muwazanah al-'ammah fi dawlat al-imarat al-'arabiyyah al-muttahidah", pp. 96.

18. World Bank. *Arab Development Assistance: Four Decades of Cooperation*, (Washington, DC: World Bank, 2010), p. 5.

19. Ibid., pp. 6-7

20. Ibid., pp. 8-9

21. Espen Villanger, "Arab Foreign Aid: Disbursement Patterns, Aid Policies and Motives," CMI Report R 2007: 2 (Chr. Michelsen Institute, 2007), http://www.cmi.no/publications/publication/?2615=arab-foreign-aid-disbursement-pattern.

22. World Bank. *Arab Development Aid: Four Decades of Cooperation*, pp. 13-14.

23. Ibid., pp. 13-14

24. Villanger, op.cit., pp. 17-22.

25. Ibid., p. 17

26. League of Arab States, *Al-Taqrir al-iqtisadi al-'arabi al-muwahhad 2009* [Unified Arab Economic Report], (Abu Dhabi, Cairo: Arab Monetary Fund, Arab Fund for Economic and Social Development, League of Arab States and Organisation of Arab Petroleum Exporting Countries, 2009), pp. 25-26.

27. Villanger, op.cit., pp. 12-13.

28. Jagdish Bhagwati, "The Problem with Foreign Aid," *Foreign Affairs* (January-February 2010), pp. 125-130.

CHAPTER ELEVEN

1. Ivar Kolstad and Tina Soeide, "Corruption in Natural Resource Management: Implications for Policy Makers", *Resources Policy*, vol. 34 no. 4, (December 2009), pp. 214-226.

2. Nicholas Shaxson, *Poisoned Wells: The Dirty Politics of African Oil* (New York: Palgrave MacMillan, 2007), p. 215.

3. Halvor Mehlum, Karl Moene and Ragnar Torvik, "Institutions and the Resource Curse", *The Economic Journal*, vol. 116, no. 508 (January 2006), pp. 1-20.

4. Richard Damania and Erwin Bulte, *Resources for Sale: Corruption, Democracy, and the Natural Resource Curse*, Discussion Paper no. 0320, (Center for International Economic Studies, University of Adelaide, 2003).

5. Richard M. Auty, "Elites, Rent-Cycling and Development: Adjustment to Land Scarcity in Mauritius, Kenya and Cote d'Ivoir", *Development Policy Review*, vol. 28, no. 4 (2010), pp. 411-433.

6. Shaomin Li, Shuhe Li and W. Zhang, "The Road to Capitalism: Competition and Institutional Change in China", *Journal of Comparative Economics*, vol. 28, no.2 (2001), pp. 269-292.

7. Deepak Lal, "Why Growth Rates Differ: The Political Economy of Social Capability in 21 Developing Countries", in: Bon Ho Koo and Dwight H. Perkins, eds., *Social Capability and Long-Run Economic Growth* (Basingstoke: MacMillan, 1995).

8. Ivar Kolstad and Arne Wiig, "Is Transparency the Key to Reducing Corruption in Resource Rich Countries?", *World Development*, vol. 37, no. 3 (March 2009), pp. 521-532.

9. Lippman, *Inside the Mirage: America's Fragile Partnership with Saudi Arabia*, pp. 143-144.

10. Pollack, *A Path Out of the Desert*, p. 102.

11. Gause, *Oil Monarchies: Domestic and Security Challenges in the Arab Gulf States*, p. 43.

12. Amuzegar, *Managing the Oil Wealth*, pp. 170-171.

13. Pollack, *A Path Out of the Desert*, pp. 102-106.

14. Hertog, *Princes, Brokers and Bureaucrats: Oil and the State in Saudi Arabia*, p. 74.

15. Pollack, op. cit., p. 107.

16. Ibid., p. 108.

17. Hertog, op.cit., pp. 16-18.

18. Paul Salem, "Kuwait: Politics in a participatory Emirate", p. 220.

19. Ali Khalifa al-Kawari, *Oil Revenues in the Gulf Emirates: Patterns of Allocation and Impact on Economic Development*, (Epping, UK: Bowker in Association with the Centre for Middle Eastern and Islamic Studies of the University of Durham, 1974).

20. Lippman, *Inside the Mirage: America's Fragile Partnership with Saudi Arabia*, p. 105.

21. Herb, *All in the Family: Absolutism, Revolution and Democracy in the Middle Eastern Monarchies*, p. 31.

22. Peter W. Wilson and Douglas F. Graham, *Saudi Arabia: the Coming Storm*, (New York: M.E. Sharpe, 1994), p. 20.

23. Aburish, *The Rise, Corruption and Coming Fall of the House of Saud*, p. 68.

24. Byman and Green, *Political Violence and Stability in the States of the Northern Persian Gulf*, p. 16.

25. Alain Gresh, "The World Invades Saudi Arabia", *Le Monde Diplomatique and Guardian Weekly*, pp. 4-5.

26. 'Ali Khalifah al-Kawari, "Al-Tafrah al-naftiyyah al-thalithah: qira'ah awwaliyyah fi dawa'i al-tafrah wa hajmiha: halat aqtar majlis al-ta'awun" [The Third Oil Boom: Preliminary Review of the Boom's Impact and its Size: the Case of the GCC states], *Al-Mustaqbal al-'arabi*, Year 31, no. 362 (April 2009), pp. 37-40.

27. Gause, *Oil Monarchies: Domestic and Security Challenges in the Arab Gulf States*, pp. 74-75.

28. Ibn Sa'ad, *Al-Tabaqat al-kubra*, vol. 3, p. 137. Narrated with a sound isnad from Hamid Bin Hilal.

29. Ibid.p. 143. This is a sound narration according to al-Bukhari and Muslim.

30. Al-Tabari, Abu Ja'far Muhammad Ibn Jarir, *Ta'rikh al-rusul wa al-muluk*, vol. 2, p. 452. Narrated by the historian Saif Bin Omar, on the authority of Muhammad Bin Ishaq, with a sound isnad according to al-Bukhari and Muslim.

31. Narrated by Ahmad, vol. 1, p. 42. Ahmad Shakir said it is a sound isnad, as did Abu Da'ud, hadith no. 2950.

32. Ibn Sa'ad, *Al-Tabaqat al-kubra*, vol. 2, p. 209. Narrated with a sound isnad; Ibn Sallam, Abu 'Ubayd al-Qasim, *Al-Amwal*, p. 281.

33. Al-Tabari, op. cit., vol. 2, p. 651.

34. Ibid., p. 697.

35. Ibn Sallam, op. cit., p. 265

36. Ahmad Yusuf Ahmad and Nevine Mas'ad, eds., *Hal al-ummah al-'arabiyyah, 2007-2008: thuna'iyyah al-taftit wa al-ihtiraq* [State of the Arab World 2007-2008: Duality of Fragmentation and Penetration], (Beirut: Centre for Arab Unity Studies, 2008), p. 113.

37. Hertog, *Princes, Brokers and Bureaucrats: Oil and the State in Saudi Arabia*, pp. 86-90.

38. David Holden and Richard Johns, *The House of Saud: The Rise and Rule of the Most Powerful Dynasty in the Arab World*, (London: Pan Books, 1982), p. 324.

39. United States Senate, *The Gulf Security Architecture: Partnership with the Gulf Cooperation Council*, United States Senate Committee on Foreign Relations, Majority Staff Report (19 June 2012), p. 2.

40. See: Al-Jazeera documentary "Ma Wara' al-Khabar," [What Lies behind the News], on 14 September 2010.

41. Askari, *Middle East Oil Exports: What Happened to Economic Development?*, p. 263.

PART IV

1. *BP Statistical Review of World Energy*, p. 6.
2. Ibid., p.8.
3. Ibid., p.20.
4. Kenneth M. Pollack, "Securing the Gulf", *Foreign Affairs* (July-August 2003), pp. 3-4.
5. Michael T. Klare, *Blood and Oil: The Dangers and Consequences of America's Growing Petroleum Dependency*, (New York: Metropolitan Books, 2004), pp. 26-27.
6. Ibid., p. 37
7. Pollack, *A Path Out of the Desert*, pp. 21-22.

CHAPTER TWELVE

1. Gause, *Oil Monarchies: Domestic and Security Challenges in the Arab Gulf States*, p. 176.
2. Ibid., pp. 180-182
3. Maugeri, *The Age of Oil: The Mythology, History and Future of the World's Most Controversial Resource*, pp. 63-75.
4. David E. Long, *The United States and Saudi Arabia*, (Boulder, CO: West View Press, 1985), pp. 51-53.
5. Klare, *Blood and Oil: The Dangers and Consequences of America's Growing Petroleum Dependency*, pp. 37-38.
6. *The New York Times*, 10 October 1981.
7. Friedman, *The World is Flat: A Brief History of the Twenty-First Century*, p. 411.
8. Elaine Sciolino, "Ally's Future: US Pondering Saudi Vulnerability," *New York Times*, 11 November 2001.
9. Gause, *Oil Monarchies: Domestic and Security Challenges in the Arab Gulf States*, p. 68.
10. Michael A. Palmer, *Guardians of the Gulf*, (New York: Simon and Schuster, 1992), pp. 29-35.
11. Chester J. Patch, *Arming the Free World: The Origins of the United States Military Assistance Program, 1945-1950*, (Chapel Hill, NC: University of North Carolina Press, 1991), pp. 88-129.

CHAPTER THIRTEEN

1. Pollack, "Securing the Gulf", p. 4.
2. Kinzer, *All the Shah's Men: An American Coup and the Roots of Middle East Terror*.
3. Kelly, *Arabia, the Gulf and the West*, pp. 47-48.
4. Ibid., p. 50
5. Ibid., p. 51
6. Ronald E. Neuman, "Bahrain: A Very Complicated Little Island", *Middle East Policy*, 20:4 (Winter 2013), p. 46.
7. John Duke Anthony, *Arab States of the Lower Gulf: People, Politics, Petroleum* (Washington, DC: The Middle East Institute, 1975), pp.148-149.
8. Ibid., p. 210

9. James Onley, "Britain's Informal Empire in the Gulf: 1820-1971", *Journal of Social Affairs* (American University of Sharjah), 22:87 (2005), pp. 29-45.

10. Michael T. Klare, *Rising Powers, Shrinking Powers: The New Geopolitics of Energy*, (New York: Metropolitan Books, Henry Hold and Company, 2008), p. 185.

11. R. K. Ramazani, "Security in the Persian Gulf", *Foreign Affairs*, vol. 4 (1979), p. 1.

12. Klare, *Blood and Oil: The Dangers and Consequences of America's Growing Petroleum Dependency*, p. 43

13. House Committee on International Relations (HCIR), *United States Arms Policies in the Persian Gulf and Red Sea Areas*, Report of a staff survey mission to Ethiopia, Iran and the Arabian Peninsula, 95th Congress, (Washington, D.C.: HCIR, 1977), p. 11.

14. George Ball, "What Brought the Shah Down", *Washington Star* (14 March 1979).

15. Parsi, *Treacherous Alliance: The Secret Dealings of Israel, Iran and the U.S.*, p. 21.

16. Ibid., pp. 23-24

17. Ibid., pp. 34-45.

18. Michael A. Palmer, *Guardians of the Gulf*, (New York: Simon and Schuster, 1992), pp. 106-111.

19. Barry Rosen, *Iran Since the Revolution*, (New York: Columbia University Press, 1985), pp. 56-59.

20. Parsi, *Treacherous Alliance: The Secret Dealings of Israel, Iran and the U.S.*, p. 113.

21. Joyce Battle, ed., *Iraqgate: Saddam Hussein, US Policy and Prelude to the Persian Gulf War*, (Washington, DC: National Security Archive, 1995).

22. Parsi, op. cit., pp. 117-126.

23. Scott Armstrong, Malcolm Byrne and Tom Blanton, *The Chronology: The Documented Day-by-Day Account of the Secret Military Assistance to Iran and the Contras*, (New York: Warner Books, 1987), p. 444.

24. Jacob Goldberg, "Saudi Arabia and the Iranian Revolution: the Religious Dimension," in: David Menashri, ed., *The Iranian Revolution and the Muslim World* (Boulder, CO: West View Press, 1990), p. 158.

25. Ray Takeyh, *Hidden Iran: Paradox and Power in the Islamic Republic*, (Washington, DC: Times Books, 2006), p. 65.

26. Ibid., p. 65

27. John Calabrese, *Revolutionary Horizons: Regional Foreign Policy in Post-Khomeini Iran*, (New York: St. Martin's Press, 1994), pp. 45-73.

28. Yahya Sadowski, *Scuds or Butter?: The Political Economy of Arms Control in the Middle East*, (Washington, DC: Brookings Institution, 1993), p. 63.

29. Giandomenico Picco, *Man Without a Gun: One Diplomat's Secret Struggle to Free the Hostages, Fight Terrorism and End a War*, (New York: Random House, 1999), pp. 113-114.

30. Anoushiravan Ehteshami, *After Khomeini: The Iranian Second Republic*, (London: Routledge, 1995), p. 142.

31. Parsi, *Treacherous Alliance: The Secret Dealings of Israel, Iran and the U.S.*, p. 133.

32. Ibid., p. 134

33. Peter Galbraith, *The End of Iraq*, (New York: Simon and Schuster, 2006), p. 37.

34. Lawrence Freedman and Efraim Karsh, *The Gulf Conflict, 1990-1991: Diplomacy and War in the New World Order* (Princeton, NJ: Princeton University Press, 1995), pp. 47-48.

35. Galbraith, op. cit. pp. 37-38

36. Ibid., p. 39

37. *The New York Times*, 9 August 1990.

38. Senate Armed Services Committee (SASC), *Crisis in the Persian Gulf Region: U.S. Policy Options and Implications*, Hearings 101st Congress, (Washington, D.C., U.S. Government printing Office, 1990), p. 11.

39. Klare, *Blood and Oil: The Dangers and Consequences of America's Growing Petroleum Dependency*, p. 50.

40. Bob Woodward, *The Commanders*, (New York: Simon and Schuster, 1991), pp. 225-226 and 236-237.

41. Ibid., pp. 263-273

42. Ahmad Rashid, *Taliban: The Power of Militant Islam in Afghanistan and Beyond*, revised ed., (London: I. B. Tauris, 2008), p. 133.

43. Freedman and Karsh, *The Gulf Conflict, 1990-1991: Diplomacy and War in the New World Order*, pp. 299-409.

44. Klare, *Blood and Oil: The Dangers and Consequences of America's Growing Petroleum Dependency*, p. 53.

45. Ibid., p.54

46. Samuel Huntington, "The Clash of Civilizations," *Foreign Affairs*, vol. 72, no. 1 (Summer 1993), pp. 22-49.

47. Klare, op. cit., p.55.

48. Parsi, *Treacherous Alliance: The Secret Dealings of Israel, Iran and the U.S.*, p. 140.

49. Ibid., p. 99

50. Shireen T. Hunter, *Iran after Khomeini*, Washington Papers, Book 156 (New York: Praeger, 1992), p. 126.

51. Davide Kimche, *The Last Option: after Nasser, Arafat and Saddam Hussein: The Quest for Peace in the Middle East*, (New York: Maxwell Macmillan International, 1991), p. 233.

52. Hooshang Amirahmadi, "The Spiraling Gulf Arms Race", *Middle East Insight*, vol. 2 (1994), p. 48.

53. John L. Esposito and R. K. Ramazani, *Iran at the Crossroads*, (New York: Palgrave, 2001), p. 220.

54. R. K. Ramazani, "Move Iran Outside the Axis," *Christian Science Monitor*, 19 August 2002.

55. Paul J. White and William S. Logan, eds, *Remaking the Middle East*, (Nationalism and Internationalism), (New York: Berg, 1997), p. 204.

56. Parsi, *Treacherous Alliance: The Secret Dealings of Israel, Iran and the U.S.*, p. 153.

57. R. K. Ramazani, "Review of Mahmoud Sariolgjalam's: The Foreign Policy of the Islamic Republic," *Discourse: An Iranian Quarterly*, vol. 2 (2001), p. 216.

58. Takeyh, *Hidden Iran: Paradox and Power in the Islamic Republic*, p. 67.

59. Ibid., p. 68

60. Ibid., p. 68

61. R. K. Ramazani, "The Emerging Arab-Indian Rapprochement: Towards an Integrated US Policy in the Middle East", *Middle East Policy* (June 1998).

62. Shimon Peres and Arye Naor, *The New Middle East*, (New York: Henry Hold, 1993), p. 146.

63. Ibid., p. 19

64. Ibid., pp. 33-34

65. Parsi, *Treacherous Alliance: The Secret Dealings of Israel, Iran and the U.S.*, p. 161.

66. Ibid., pp. 165-170

67. Emma Murphy, "The Impact of the Arab-Israeli Peace Process on the International Security and Economic Relations in the Persian Gulf," *Iranian Journal of International Affairs*, vol. 2 (Summer 1996), pp. 428 and 432-433.

68. F. Gregory Gause III, "The Illogic of Dual Containment," *Foreign Affairs*, March-April 1994.

69. Kenneth M. Pollack, *The Persian Puzzle: The Conflict between Iran and America*, (New York: Random House, 2004), p. 363.

70. Fred Kaplan, *Daydream Believers: How a Few Grand Ideas Wrecked American Power*, (New Jersey: John Wiley and Sons, 2008), pp. 124-125.

71. Gardner, *Last Chance: The Middle East in the Balance*, p. 74.

72. Neil Mackay, "Bush Planned Iraq 'Regime Change' before Becoming President," *Sunday Herald*, 15 June 2002.

73. Project for the New American Century, *Rebuilding America's Defenses: Strategy, Forces and Resources for a New Century*, A Report of the Project for the New American Century (September 2000).

74. Kaplan, *Daydream Believers: How a Few Grand Ideas Wrecked American Power*, p. 126.

75. Bob Woodward, *State of Denial*, (New York: Simon and Schuster, 2006), p. 408.

76. Philippe Sands, *Lawless World: America and the Making and Breaking of Global Rules from FDR's Atlantic Charter to George Bush's Illegal War*, (New York: Viking, 2005), pp. 174-204.

77. Vanity Fair and Pentagon Transcripts of Wolfowitz Interview from Gardner, *Last Chance: The Middle East in the Balance*, p. 212.

78. Gardner, *Last Chance: The Middle East in the Balance*, p. 77.

79. Ibid, p. 76

80. Bob Woodward, *Plan of Attack*, pp. 228-231.

81. David Ottaway, "The King and Us: US-Saudi Relations in the Wake of 9/11", *Foreign Affairs* (May-June 2009), p. 123.

82. Bob Woodward, *The War Within: A Secret White House History*, (New York: Simon and Schuster, 2004), p. 347.

83. Ibid., p. 248

84. Gardner, *Last Chance: The Middle East in the Balance*, p. 81.

85. Parsi, *Treacherous Alliance: The Secret Dealings of Israel, Iran and the U.S.*, p. 143.

86. Takeyh, *Hidden Iran: Paradox and Power in the Islamic Republic*, pp. 178-179.

87. Charles Kurzman, "Pro-US Fatwa", *Middle East Policy*, vol. 10, no. 3 (Fall 2003), pp. 155-166.

88. Vali Nasr, *The Shi'a Revival: How Conflicts within Islam will Shape the Future*, (New York: W. W. Norton: New York, 2006), p. 170.

89. Takeyh, *Hidden Iran: Paradox and Power in the Islamic Republic*, p. 177.

90. Gardner, *Last Chance: The Middle East in the Balance*, p. 83.

91. Gregory Beals, "A Missed Opportunity with Iran", *Newsday*, 2 February 2006.

92. Parsi, *Treacherous Alliance: The Secret Dealings of Israel, Iran and the U.S.*, p. 244.

93. Ibid., pp. 245-247

94. International Crisis Group, *Iran in Iraq: How Much Influence?*, Middle East Report, no. 38 (21 March 2005), p.1.

95. Saud al-Faisal, "The Fight Against Extremism and the Search for Peace", address to the Council on Foreign Relations, 20 September 2005. http://www.cfr.org/radicalization-and-extremism/fight-against-extremism-search-peace-rush-transcript-federal-news-service-inc/p8908

96. Nasr, *The Shi'a Revival: How Conflicts within Islam will Shape the Future*, p. 184.

97. Takeyh, *Hidden Iran: Paradox and Power in the Islamic Republic*, p. 71.

98. Shireen T. Hunter, "Iran and Syria: From Hostility to Limited Alliance," in: Hooshang Amirahmadi and Nader Entessar, eds., *Iran and the Arab World* (New York: Palgrave Macmillan, 1990).

99. Takeyh, op. cit., pp. 71-72.

100. Matthew Kalman, "Israel Set War Plan More than a Year Ago", *San Francisco Chronicle*, 21 July 2006.

101. Parsi, *Treacherous Alliance: The Secret Dealings of Israel, Iran and the U.S.*, pp. 274-275.

102. Hassan M. Fattah, "Fearful of Iran, Arab Leaders Criticise Militants", *New York Times*, 17 July 2006.

103. Gardner, *Last Chance: The Middle East in the Balance*, p. 29.

104. Max Blumenthal, "Birth Pangs of a New Christian Zionism", *The Nation*, 8 August 2006.

105. Parsi, *Treacherous Alliance: The Secret Dealings of Israel, Iran and the U.S.*, p. 275.

106. Ibid., p. 276

107. Ibid., p. 277

108. Khalid al-Dakhil, "Regional Power in an Area of Turmoil" in: Joshua Craze and Mark Huband, ed., *The Kingdom: Saudi Arabia and the Challenges of the 21ˢᵗ Century* (London: Hurst and Company, 2009), p. 96.

109. Gause, "The Illogic of Dual Containment," pp. 193-194.

110. *The New York Times*, 11 May 1993, p. 11

111. Jim Krane, *City of Gold: Dubai and the Dream of Capitalism*, (New York: St. Martin's Press, 2009), pp. 167-176.

112. Henry Kissinger, *Diplomacy*, (New York: Simon and Schuster, 1994), pp. 29-55.

113. Jimmy Carter, *Our Endangered Values: America's Moral Crisis*, (New York: Simon and Schuster, 2005), pp. 97-98.

114. Henry Kissinger, *The Autonomy of Two Major Crises*, (New York: Simon and Schuster, 2004), pp. 7-13.

115. David Frum and Richard Perle, *An End to Evil: How to Win the War on Terror*, (New York: Random House, 2003), pp. 180-191.

116. Zbigniew Brzezinski and Brent Scowcroft, "A "Road Map for Israeli-Palestinian Amity", *Wall Street Journal*, 13 December 2003.

117. Glenn E, Robinson, "Being Yasir Arafat: A Portrait of Palestine's President," *Foreign Affairs*, 82:6 (November-December 2003), pp. 137-138.

118. Michael Herzog, "Can Hamas be Tamed?", *Foreign Affairs* (March-April 2006), pp. 83-94.

119. Daniel Byman, "Do Targeted Killings Work?", *Foreign Affairs* (March-April 2006), pp. 95-111.

120. Gardner, *Last Chance: The Middle East in the Balance*, p. 29.

121. Walter Russell Mead, "The New Israel and the Old: Why Gentile Americans Back the Jewish State", *Foreign Affairs* vol. 87, no. 4 (July-August 2008), pp. 28-46.

122. Ahmad and Mas'ad, eds., *Hal al-ummah al-'arabiyyah, 2007-2008: thuna'iyyah al-taftit wa al-ihtiraq*, p. 118.

123. David Rose, "The Gaza Bombshell", *Vanity Fair* (April 2008).

124. Ahmad and Mas'ad, op. cit., pp. 118-119.

125. Ibid., pp. 120-125

126. Chas W. Freeman, Jr., "Coping with Kaleidoscopic Change in the Middle East", *Middle East Policy*, 20: 4 (Winter 2013), p. 31

CHAPTER FOURTEEN

1. *Wall Street Journal*, 25 June 2004.

2. Takeyh, *Hidden Iran: Paradox and Power in the Islamic Republic*, pp. 136-137.

3. Ibid., p. 138

4. Ibid., p. 139

5. Islamic Republic News Agency (IRNA), 25 May 2004.

6. Agence France-Presse (AFP) 25 May 2004.

7. Takeyh, *Hidden Iran: Paradox and Power in the Islamic Republic*, p. 139.

8. Ian O. Lesser, "Weapons of Mass Destruction in the Middle East: Proliferation Dynamics and Strategic Consequences," in: Bensahel and Byman, eds., *The Future Security Environment in the Middle East*, pp. 268-277.

9. Dore Gold, "Middle East Proliferation, Israeli Missile Defense and the ABM Treaty Debate," *Jerusalem Letter*, no. 430 (15 May 2000), pp. 5-6.

10. Nasr, *The Shia Revival: How Conflicts within Islam will Shape the Future*, p. 223.

11. Takeyh, *Hidden Iran: Paradox and Power in the Islamic Republic*, p. 143.

12. Nasir, op. cit., p. 223

13. Takeyh, op. cit., p. 141.

14. "Iran Looms as a Growing Strategic Threat for Israel", *Jerusalem Post* (21 November 1991).

15. Kinzer, *All the Shah's Men: An American Coup and the Roots of Middle East Terror*, pp. 17-29.

16. Nasr, *The Shia Revival: How Conflicts within Islam will Shape the Future*, p. 222.

17. Takeyh, *Hidden Iran: Paradox and Power in the Islamic Republic*, pp. 76-82.

18. Ibid., pp. 140-146

19. Patrick J. Garrity, *Why the Gulf War Still Matters: Foreign Perspectives on the War and the Future of International Security*, (Los Alamos, NM: Center for National Security Studies, 1993).

20. Lesser, "Weapons of Mass Destruction in the Middle East: Proliferation Dynamics and Strategic Consequences", pp. 270-271.

21. Pollack, *A Path Out of the Desert*, p. 363.

22. Takeyh, *Hidden Iran: Paradox and Power in the Islamic Republic*, pp. 146-149.

23. Ibid., p. 150

24. Ibid., pp. 151-152.

25. Parsi, *Treacherous Alliance: The Secret Dealings of Israel, Iran and the U.S.*, pp. 279-284.

26. James M. Lindsay and Ray Takeyh, "After Iran Gets the Bomb", *Foreign Affairs,* vol. 89, no. 2 (March-April 2010).

27. Barry R. Posen et al., "The Containment Conundrum: How Dangerous is a Nuclear Iran?", *Foreign Affairs* (July-August 2010), pp. 160-162.

28. Barry Rubin, "The Containment Conundrum: The Right Kind of Containment", *Foreign Affairs*, vol. 89, no. 4 (July-August 2010), pp. 163-164.

29. Lindsay and Takeyh, "After Iran Gets the Bomb".

30. Rubin, op. cit., p. 165

31. Pollack, *A Path Out of the Desert*, pp. 371-372.

32. Parsi, *Treacherous Alliance: The Secret Dealings of Israel, Iran and the U.S.*, pp. 278-279.

33. Barry Rubin, "Why Israel Shouldn't Attack Iranian Nuclear Installations Unless it Has to Do So", Rubin Center for Research in International Affairs (14 July 2010). http://www.rubincenter.org/2010/07/why-israel-shouldnt-attack-iranian-nuclear-installations/

34. Posen et al., "The Containment Conundrum: How Dangerous is a Nuclear Iran?", p. 163.

35. Suzanne Maloney, "Obama's Counter Productive New Iran Sanctions: How Washington Is Sliding Toward Regime Change", *Foreign Affairs* (5 January 2012).

36. Kayhan Barzegar, "Nuclear Terrorism: An Iranian Perspective", *Middle East Policy*, 21:1 (Spring 2014), pp. 32-33.

37. John Waterbury, "Unthinkable: Iran, the Bomb, and American Strategy by Kenneth M. Pollack (Review)", *Foreign Affairs* (January-February 2014), p. 203.

38. Chuck Freilich, "Decision Time in Jerusalem", *Journal of International Security Affairs*, no. 18 (Spring 2010), p. 55.

39. William Luers, Thomas R. Pickering and Jim Walsh, "For a New Approach to Iran", *New York Review Books* (15 August 2013),.

40. Olli Heinonen, "Unthinkable: Iran, the Bomb, and American Strategy by Kenneth M. Pollack (Review)", *Middle East Journal*, 68:1 (Winter 2014), pp. 156-158.

41. European External Action Service. *Joint Plan of Action*, Geneva, 24 November 2013. http://eeas.europa.eu/statements/docs/2013/131124_03_en.pdf

42. Mahmood Monshipouri and Manochehr Dorraj, "Iran's Foreign Policy: A Shifting Strategic Landscape", *Middle East Policy*, 20:4 (Winter 2013), p. 139.

43. Ibid., pp. 133-147.

44. David E. Singer, "Big Challenges Remain Despite Progress on Iran", *The New York Times*, 29 September 2013.

PART V

1. Eva Bellin, "The Political-Economic Conundrum," in: Thomas Carothers and Marina Ottaway, eds., *Uncharted Journey: Promoting Democracy in the Middle East*, Global Policy Books (Washington, DC: Carnegie Endowment for International Peace, 2006), pp. 137-138.
2. Takeyh, *Hidden Iran: Paradox and Power in the Islamic Republic*, pp. 161-187.
3. Robin Wright and Peter Baker, "Iraq, Jordan See Threat to Election from Iran; Leaders Warn Against Forming Religious States", *Washington Post*, August 12, 2004.
4. Qur'an, Al-Anfal 8:53
5. In reference to the popular uprising in Tunisia that brought down the country's autocratic regime without foreign intervention, signalling the onset of a movement for change.

CHAPTER FIFTEEN

1. Michael Scott Doran, "The Heirs of Nasser", *Foreign Affairs*, vol. 90, no.3 (May-June 2011), pp.17-19.
2. World Bank, "Hashemite Kingdom of Jordan: Resolving Jordan's Labor Market Paradox of Concurrent Economic Growth and Unemployment", World Bank Report no. 39201-JO (Washington, D.C.: World Bank, 23 December 2008), p. i. http://datatopics.worldbank.org/hnp/files/edstats/JORpub08.pdf
3. Onn Winckler, "The 'Arab Spring': Socioeconomic Aspects", *Middle Policy*, vol. 20, no. 4 (Winter 2013), pp. 72-73.
4. Yusuf Khalifah al-Yusuf, "Dirasat halat al-imarat" [Study on the state of the Emirates], in: Isma'il Shatti, ed., *Al-Fasad wa-al-⊠ukm al-⊠ali⊠ fi al-bilad al-'Arabiyah: buhuth wa-munaqashat al-nadwah al-fikriyyah allati nazzamaha markaz dirasat al-Wahdah al-'Arabiyyah bi-l-ta'awun ma'a al-ma'had al-swidi bil-Iskandariyyah* [Corruption and good governance in the Arab countries: proceedings of the symposium organised by the Centre for Arab Unity Studies in cooperation with the Swedish Institute Alexandria] (Beirut: Centre for Arab Unity Studies, 2004), pp. 577-600.
5. Alfred Stepan, Juan J. Linz and Juli F. Minoves, "Democratic Parliamentary Monarchies", *Journal of Democracy*, vol. 25, no. 2 (April 2014), p. 41.
6. Sean L. Yom and F. Gregory Gause III, "Resilient Royals: How Arab Monarchies Hang On", *Journal of Democracy*, vol. 23, no. 4 (October 2012), p. 77.
7. Stepan, Linz and Minoves, Ibid., pp. 38-39.
8. Ronald E. Neumann, "Bahrain A Very Small Complicated Little Island", *Middle East Policy*, vol. 20, no. 4 (Winter 2013), p. 49.
9. King Hamad Bin Isa Al-Khalifa, "Stability is Prerequisite for Progress", *Washington Times*, 19 April 2011.
10. "Bahrain: America's Big Paradox", Press TV (17 March 2011), http://edition.presstv.ir/detail/170463.html
11. "David Cameron on GP: 'Bahrain Is not Syria'", BBC News (20 April 2012), http://www.bbc.co.uk/news/uk-17789082
12. Steffen Hertog, "The Cost of Counter -revolution in the GCC", *Foreign Policy* (3 June 2011), p. 1.
13. Neuman, "Bahrain: A Very Complicated Little Island", pp. 45-58.
14. International Crisis Group, *Popular Protest in North Africa and the Middle East (VIII): Bahrain's Rocky Road to Reform*, Middle East Report no. 111 (28 July 2011), pp. 9-14. http://www.crisisgroup.org/en/regions/middle-east-north-africa/iraq-iran-gulf/bahrain/111-popular-protest-in-north-africa-and-the-middle-east-viii-bahrains-rocky-road-to-reform.aspx
15. "Kuwait's Prime Minister Resigns After Protests", BBC News (28 November 2011). http://www.bbc.co.uk/news/world-middle-east-15931526

16. Gwenn Okruhlik, "The Identity Politics of Kuwait's Election", *Foreign Policy* (8 February 2012). http://foreignpolicy.com/2012/02/08/the-identity-politics-of-kuwaits-election/

17. "Kuwait Protest at Court at Court Ruling Dissolving Parliament", BBC News (27 June 2012). http://www.bbc.co.uk/news/world-middle-east-18606540

18. "In Bid to End Crisis, Kuwait's Parliament Is Dissolved", *The New York Times*, 7 October 2012. http://www.nytimes.com/2012/10/08/world/middleeast/in-bid-to-end-crisis-kuwaits-parliament-is-dissolved.html?_r=0

19. Toby Matthiesen, *Sectarian Gulf* (Stanford, CA: Stanford Briefs, 2013), pp. 104-105.

20. Emir Shaikh Sabah al-Ahmad al-Jabir al-Sabah, Speech delivered on 19 October 2012. http://www.da.gov.kw/ara/speeches/amir_speeches_2012.php?p=19102012

21. Kristin Smith Diwan, "Kuwait's Balancing Act", *Foreign Policy* (23 October 2012). http://foreignpolicy.com/2012/10/23/kuwaits-balancing-act/

22. "Kuwait Election: Thousands Join Anti-Government Protest", BBC News (30 November 2012). http://www.bbc.co.uk/news/world-middle-east-20558819

23. Matthiesen, *Sectarian Gulf*, p. 105.

24. Ibid., p. 105.

25. "Inside the Coddled Kingdom", *The Toronto Star* (17 February 2011), p. 10.

26. Matthiesen, op. cit., pp. 112-113.

27. Sara Hamdan, "Oman Offers Some Lessons to a Region Embroiled in Protest", *The New York Times*, 4 April 2011.

28. "Gulf Cooperation Council Sets Up 20 bn-dollar Fund for Bahrain: Oman Projects", Saudi Press Agency (11 March 2011).

29. Matthiesen, *Sectarian Gulf*, p. 115.

30. "Saudi authorities detain founders of new party", AFP (19 February 2011).

31. Stephane Lacroix, "Comparing the Arab Revolts: Is Saudi Arabia Immune?", *Journal of Democracy*, vol. 22, no. 4 (October 2011), p. 56.

32. Matthiesen, *Sectarian Gulf*, p. 29.

33. Lacroix, op. cit.., pp. 52-53.

34. Sue Lloyd Roberts, "Saudi Arabia Show of Force Stifles 'Day of Rage' Protests", BBC Newsnight (11 March 2011). http://news.bbc.co.uk/1/hi/programmes/newsnight/9422550.stm

35. Al-Ahram (27 March 2011) http://gate.ahram.org.eg/UI/Front/Inner.aspx?NewsContentID=54154

36. "Saudi Arabia: 11 Women Still Held after Protest", Amnesty International (8 January 2013).

37. "161 Arrested in Buraidah", Arab News (2 March 2013). http://www.arabnews.com/saudi-arabia/161-arrested-buraidah

38. Neil MacFarquhar, "Saudi Cash is Key to Quiet in the Kingdom", *The International Herald Tribune* (10 June 2011), p. 4.

39. Yusuf Khalifah al-Yusuf, *Al-Imarat al-'arabiyyah al-muttahidah 'ala muftaraq turuq* [The United Arab Emirates at the crossroads], (Beirut: Centre for Arab Unity Studies, 2013), pp. 28-30.

40. Anna Louie Sussman, "Repression in the United Arab Emirates", *The Nation* (1 June 2011). http://www.thenation.com/article/161058/repression-united-arab-emirates

41. "UAE: Unfair Trial, Unjust Sentences", International Federation for Human Rights (FIDH), (3 July 2013). https://www.fidh.org/International-Federation-for-Human-Rights/north-africa-middle-east/united-arab-emirates/uae-unfair-trial-unjust-sentences-13590

42. Rori Donaghy, "UAE's political show trials", Open Democracy (29 January 2014). http://www.opendemocracy.net/arab-awakening/rori-donaghy/uaes-political-show-trials

43. *The National* (1 December 2011).

44. Al Wafd Gate http://www.alwafd.org

45. 'Ali Khalifah al-Kawari.,ed., *Al-Sha'b yurid al-islah fi qatar... aydan* [The People Want Reform... In Qatar, Too], (Beirut: Al-Maaref Forum, 2012)

46. Mohamed A. J. Althani, *The Arab Spring and the Gulf States: Time to Embrace Change*, (London: Profile Books, 2012).

47. Kamrava, *Qatar: Small State, Big Politics*, pp. 41-45.

48. Sean L. Yom and Wael al-Khatib, "Jordan's New Politics of Tribal Dissent", *Foreign Policy* (7 August 2012). http://foreignpolicy.com/2012/08/07/jordans-new-politics-of-tribal-dissent/

49. Curtis R. Ryan, "Jordan's Unfinished Journey: Parliamentary Elections and the State of Reform", POMED, Policy Brief (March 2013), pp. 1-4.

50. Stepan, Linz and Minoves, "Democratic Parliamentary Monarchies", p. 49.

51. Curtis R. Ryan, "Jordanian Policy and the Arab Spring", *Middle East Policy*, vol. 21, no. 1 (Spring 2014), p. 149.

52. Ibid., p. 151.

53. Ibid., p. 148.

54. Ryan, "Jordan's Unfinished Journey: Parliamentary Elections and the State of Reform", p. 2.

55. Yom and Gause, "Resilient Royals: How Arab Monarchies Hang On", p. 85.

56. Stepan, Linz and Minoves, "Democratic Parliamentary Monarchies", pp. 42-43.

57. Ahmed Benchemsi, "Morocco: Outfoxing the Opposition", *Journal of Democracy*, vol. 23, no. 1 (January 2012), p. 64.

58. Ibid., p. 65.

59. Stepan, Linz and Minoves, "Democratic Parliamentary Monarchies", p. 37 and p. 44.

60. Yom and Gause, "Resilient Royals: How Arab Monarchies Hang On", p. 84.

61. During the Arab uprisings, the Tunisian poet Abu Qassim al-Shabi (1909-1934) was widely quoted in chants and slogans, particularly his poems "The Will to Live" and "To the Tyrants of the world."

62. "In the Heart of Tunisia. Thala: The Occupied Police Station", Anarkismo (24 April 2011). http://www.anarkismo.net/article/19380?userlanguage=ca&save_prefs=true

63. Ann M. Lesch, "Troubled Political Transitions: Tunisia, Egypt, and Libya", *Middle East Policy*, vol. 21, no. 1 (Spring 2014), pp. 62-63.

64. Mohamed Kerrou, "Tunisia's Historic Step Toward Democracy", Carnegie (17 April 2014). http://carnegie-mec.org/2014/04/22/tunisia-s-historic-step-toward-democracy/hd9t

65. Lesch, "Troubled Political Transitions: Tunisia, Egypt, and Libya", p. 68.

66. Daniel Brumberg, "Transforming the Arab World's Protection-Racket Politics", *Journal of Democracy*, vol. 24, no. 3 (July 2013), pp. 95-102.

67. Alfred Stepan and Juan J. Linz, "Democratization Theory and the 'Arab Spring'", *Journal of Democracy*, vol. 24, no. 2 (April 2013), p. 28.

68. Ibid., pp. 23-24.

69. Muqtedar Khan, "Islam, Democracy and Islamism after the Counterrevolution in Egypt", *Middle East Policy*, vol. 21, no. 1 (Spring 2014), p. 78.

70. David M. Faris, "Deep State, Deep Crisis: Egypt and American Policy", *Middle East Policy*, vol. 20, no. 4 (Winter 2013), pp. 100-103.

71. Sarah Harvard, "Noam Chomsky on Crisis in Egypt: "It's Pretty Hard to Get Out"", *DL Magazine* (2 September 2013), http://dlmagazine.org/2013/09/exclusive-interview-noam-chomsky-crisis-egypt-its-pretty-hard-out/

72. Aaron David Miller, "Cairo Wasn't Obama's to Lose", in Mark Lynch, Susan B. Glasser, and Blake Hounshell, eds., *Revolution in the Arab World: Tunisia, Egypt and the unmaking of an era*, A Special Report from Foreign Policy, (Washington, D.C.: Slate Group, 2011), pp. 194-197.

73. Neil MacFarquhar, "Saudi Scramble in Bid to Contain Regional Unrest", *New York Times*, 28 May 2011, p. 1.

74. "Riyadh Rushes to Support Egypt's New Military Rulers", Al Monitor (11 July 2012). http://www.al-monitor.com/pulse/politics/2013/07/relationship-saudi-arabia-cairo-following-morsi-ouster.html

75. Nathan J. Brown, "Egypt's Constitutional Cul-De-Sac", Carnegie Endowment (31 March 2014). http://carnegieendowment.org/2014/03/31/egypt-s-constitutional-cul-de-sac

76. Jason Brownlee, Tarek Masoud and Andrew Reynolds, "Why the Modest Harvest?", *Journal of Democracy*, vol. 24, no. 4 (October 2013), p. 39.

77. April Longley Alley, "Yemen Changes Everything and Nothing", *Journal of Democracy*, vol. 24, no. 4 (October 2013), pp. 79-81.

78. The expression derives from a saying (hadith) of the Prophet: "Faith is Yemeni, wisdom is Yemeni", as related in Bukhari's hadith collection.

79. Lesch, "Troubled Political Transitions: Tunisia, Egypt, and Libya", p. 63.

80. Charles Dunne, Stephen McInerney and Karim Mezran, "Libya Needs the U.S for Its Transition to Democracy", *Washington Post*, 4 May 2013.

81. Mieczystaw P. Boduszynski and Duncan Pickard, "Libya Starts from Scratch", *Journal of Democracy*, vol. 24, no. 4 (October 2013), pp. 86-88.

82. Dirk Vandewalle, "After Qaddafi", *Foreign Affairs*, vol. 91, no. 6 (November-December 2012), pp. 8-15.

83. Steven Heydemann, "Syria and the Future of Authoritarianism", *Journal of Democracy*, vol. 24, no. 4 (October 2013), p. 62.

84. Brownlee, Masoud and Reynolds, "Why the Modest Harvest?", p. 40.

85. Philippe Droz-Vincent, "State of Barbary (Take Two): From the Arab Spring to the Return of Violence in Syria", *Middle East Journal*, vol. 68, no. 1 (Winter 2014), pp. 33-58.

86. Seymour Hersh, "The Red Line and the Rat Line. Seymour M. Hersh on Obama, Erdoğan and the Syrian rebels", *London Review of Books*, vol. 36, no. 8 (17 April 2014), pp. 21-24. http://www.lrb.co.uk/v36/n08/seymour-m-hersh/the-red-line-and-the-rat-line

87. Yezid Sayigh, "The Assad Regime: Winning on Points", Carnegie Endowment for International Peace (10 April 2014). http://carnegie-mec.org/2014/04/10/assad-regime-winning-on-points/h7vJ

88. Daniel Pipes, "The Alawi Capture of Power in Syria", *Middle Eastern Studies*, vol. 25, no. 4 (October 1989), pp. 429-450; and Ayse Tekdal Fildis, "Roots of Alwaite-Sunni Rivalry in Syria", *Middle East Policy*, vol. 19, no. 2 (Summer 2012), pp. 148-156.

89. Ivan Konstantinov, "Genie of Islamism Comes out of the Bottle", *Nezavisimaia Gazeta* (13 March 2012).

90. David Albright et al., "The United States, Its Middle East Allies and Iran: What is the Way Forward?", *Middle East Policy*, vol. 21, no. 1 (Spring 2014), pp. 25-26.

91. Josef Olmert, "Israel and Alawite Syria: The Odd Couple of the Middle East?", *Israel Journal of Foreign Affairs*, vol. 7, no. 1 (2013), pp. 17-25.

92. Amal A. Kandeel, "Regional Upheaval: The Stakes for the GCC", *Middle East Policy*, vol. 20, no. 4 (Winter 2013), pp. 59-61.

93. Monshipouri and Dorraj, "Iran's Foreign Policy: A Shifting Strategic Landscape", p. 135.

94. Michael Jansen, "Will Diplomacy Get a Chance?", *Panorama: Gulf Today* (20 September 2013), pp. 40-41.

95. Mark N. Katz, "Russia and the Conflict in Syria: Four Myths", *Middle East Policy*, vol. 20, no. 2 (Summer 2013), pp. 38-39.

96. Stepan and Linz, "Democratization Theory and the 'Arab Spring'", p. 28.

97. Pipes, "The Alawi Capture of Power in Syria", pp. 429-450; and Fildis "Roots of Alwaite-Sunni Rivalry in Syria", p. 446.

98. Virginia Page Fortna and Reyko Huang, "Democratization After Civil War: A Brush-Clearing Exercise", *International Studies Quarterly*, vol. 56, no.4 (December 2102), pp. 801-808.

99. Freeman Jr., "Coping with Kaleidoscopic Change in the Middle East", p. 36.

100. Helen Cooper and Robert Worth, "In Arab Spring, Obama Finds a Sharp Test", *The New York Times*, 24 September 2012. http://www.nytimes.com/2012/09/25/us/politics/arab-spring-proves-a-harsh-test-for-obamas-diplomatic-skill.html?_r=0

101. Freeman Jr., "Coping with Kaleidoscopic Change in the Middle East", p. 33.

102. Albright et al., "The United States, Its Middle East Allies and Iran: What is the Way Forward?", pp. 1-28.

103. Al-Arabiya News Online (21 September 2012).

104. Nabeel A. Khoury, "The Arab Cold War Revisited: The Regional Impact of the Arab Spring", *Middle East Policy*, vol. 20, no. 2 (Summer 2013), p. 87, footnote 19.

105. Reza Ekhtiari Amiri, Mohammad Agus Yusoff and Fakhreddin Soltani, "Arab Spring: Geopolitical Implications for Iran", *International Journal of Asian Social Science*, vol. 2, no. 9 (2012), pp. 1533-1547.

106. Henner Furtig, "Conflict and Cooperation in the Persian Gulf: The Interregional Order and the U.S Policy", *Middle East Journal*, vol. 61, no. 4 (Fall 2007), p. 636

107. Babak Rahimi, "Iran's Declining Influence in Iraq", *Washington Quarterly* (Winter 2012), pp. 25-40.

108. Birgul Demirtas, "Turkish-Syrian Relations: From Friend 'Esad' to Enemy 'Esed'", *Middle East Policy*, vol. 20, no. 1 (Spring 2013), pp. 116-117.

109. Ibid., p.115.

110. Banu Eligur, "Crisis in Turkish-Israeli Relations (December 2008-June 2011): From Partnership to Enmity", *Middle Eastern Studies*, vol. 48 (2012), pp. 429-459.

111. Demirtas, op. cit., p. 116.

112. Albright et al., "The United States, Its Middle East Allies and Iran: What is the Way Forward?", p. 7.

113. Daniel Dumbey, "Six Markets to Watch: Turkey. How Erdogan Did It and Could Blow It", *Foreign Affairs* (January-February 2014), pp. 29-34.

114. Katz, "Russia and the Conflict in Syria: Four Myths", pp. 43-44.

115. Al-Yusuf, *Al-Imarat al-'arabiyyah al-muttahidah 'ala muftaraq turuq*, pp. 323-241.

116. Kristian Coates Ulrichsen, *Insecure Gulf: The End of Certainty and the Transition to the Post-Oil Era*, (New York: Columbia University Press, 2011), p. 25.

117. Joseph Kostiner, "GCC Perceptions of Collective Security in the Post-Saddam Era", in: Mehran Kamrava, ed., *International Politics of the Persian Gulf*, (New York: Syracuse, 2011), p. 117.

118. Hertog, "The Cost of Counter-revolution in the GCC".

119. Kevin Baxter, "Riyadh's Rising Fuel Subsidy Bill", *Middle East Economic Digest*, vol. 55, no. 37 (16 September 2011), pp. 22-23.

120. "IMF Tells Kuwait to Cut Spending or Risk Running Out of Oil Money", *The National* (17 May 2012).

121. "Gulf Arab States Should Cut State Spending Growth: IMF", *Reuters* (29 October 2012).

122. Matthiesen, *Sectarian Gulf*, pp. 129-130.

CHAPTER SIXTEEN

1. Marina Ottaway, "Evaluating Middle East Reform", in: Marina Ottaway and Julia Choucaire-Vizoso, eds., *Beyond the Façade: Political Reform in the Arab World*, (Washington, DC: Carnegie Endowment for International Peace, 2008), p. 2.

2. Condoleezza Rice, "Campaign 2000: Promoting the National Interest", *Foreign Affairs*, vol. 79, no. 1 (January-February 2000).

3. Pollack, *A Path Out of the Desert*, p. 227.

4. Muhammad Muslih and Augustus Richard Norton, "The Need for Arab Democracy", *Foreign Policy*, no. 83 (Summer 1991), p. 3.

5. United Nations Development Programme, *Arab Human Development Report 2003: Building a Knowledge Society*, (New York: United Nations Publications, 2003), pp. 151-157.

6. Patrick E. Tyler, "Saudis Plan to End US Presence", *The New York Times*, 9 February, 2003.

7. Pollack, *A Path Out of the Desert*, pp. 102-110.

8. Ibid., 219-220

9. Ashraf Ghani and Clare Lockhart, *Fixing Failed States: A Framework for Rebuilding a Fractured World*, (New York: Oxford University Press, 2009), pp. 124-127.

10. Adam Przeworski, *Democracy and the Market: Political and Economic Reforms in Eastern Europe and Latin America*, Studies in Rationality and Social Change (New York: Cambridge University Press, 1991), p. 144.

11. Yusuf al-Qardawi, *Min fiqh al-dawlah fi al-Islam* [Statecraft in Islam], 6th edn, (Cairo: Dar El Shorouk, 2009), p. 139; Fahmi Huwaidi, "Al-Islam wa al-dimuqratiyyah" [Islam and Democracy]," *Al-Mustaqbal al-'arabi*, year 15, no. 166 (December 1992), pp. 4-37; Muhammad 'Abd al-Malik al-Mutawakkil, "Al-Islam wa huquq al-insan" [Islam and human rights], *Al-Mustaqbal al-'arabi*, year 19, no. 216 (February 1997), pp. 1-34.

12. Ali Khalifa Al-Kawari, "Jawhar al-dimuqratiyyah la yata'aradu ma'a jawhar al-Islam", p. 135.

13. John L. Esposito and James P. Piscatori, "Democratisation and Islam", *Middle East Journal*, vol. 45, no. 3 (Summer 1991), pp. 427-440.

14. Ali Khalifa Al-Kawari, "La taqumu al-dimuqratiyyah fi zill hukumah diniyyah: munaqasha li-rai al-ustadh rashid al-ghannushi" [Democracy Cannot Be Implemented under a Religious System: A Discussion of Dr. Rachid al-Ghannouchi's Opinion], *Al-Mustaqbal al-'Arabi*, Year 31, No. 362 (April 2009), pp. 148-150.

15. Interview with Rachid al-Ghannouchi, leader of the Tunisian Ennahda party, with Ahmad Mansur on the Al Jazeera programme "Bila hudud" [Without limits], 19 February 2014.

16. Pollack, *A Path Out of the Desert East*, pp. 282-286.

17. Ibid., p. 239

18. As'ad Abu Khalil, "A Viable Partnership: Islam, Democracy and the Arab World", *Harvard International Review*, vol. 15, no. 2 (Winter 1992-1993), p. 23.

19. Pollack, op. cit., p. 239.

20. Thomas O. Melia, *The People of Bahrain Want to Participate in the King's Political Reform Project: A Report on Focus Groups Conducted in the Kingdom of Bahrain*, (Washington: National Democratic Institute, July 2002), p. 1.

21. Marwan Muasher, "A Path to Democracy", *New York Times*, 4 June 2003.

22. Madawi Al-Rasheed, "Money Replaces Ideas as Petitioners' Silence Leaves Saudi Reform at an Imams", in: Craze and Huband, eds., *The Kingdom: Saudi Arabia and the Challenges of the 21ˢᵗ Century*, pp. 22-24.

23. Shaker Nabulsi, "Modernity Vies with Tradition as Saudi Debate the Future", in: Craze and Huband, eds., *The Kingdom: Saudi Arabia and the Challenges of the 21ˢᵗ Century*, p. 25.

24. Shibley Telhami, "2006 Annual Arab Public Opinion Survey", Brookings Institute, (February 8, 2007), p. 15.

25. Noah Feldman, *After Jihad: America and the Struggle for Islamic Democracy*, (New York: Farrar, Straus and Giroux, 2004), p. 14.

26. Monica Malik and Tim Niblock, "Saudi Arabia's Economy: The Challenge of Reform", in: Paul Aarts and Gerd Nonneman, eds., *Saudi Arabia in the Balance: Political Economy, Society, Foreign Affairs* (New York: New York University Press, 2005), pp. 85-87.

27. United Nations Conference on Trade and Development (UNCTAD), *World Investment Report 2004* (Geneva: UNCTAD, 2004), Annex, Tables A. 1.5 and A. 1.7.

28. Michael L. Ross, "Does Oil Hinder Democracy?", *World Politics*, vol. 53 (April 2001), pp. 325-361.

29. Lisa Anderson, "Arab Democracy: Dismal Prospects", *World Policy Journal* (Fall 2001), pp. 53-60.

30. Marcus Noland and Howard Pack, *The Arab Economies in a Changing World*, (Washington, DC: Peterson Institute for International Economics, 2007), p. 31.

31. International Crisis Group, *Can Saudi Arabia Reform Itself?*, Middle East Report no. 28 (14 July 2004), pp. 20-26.

32. Fareed Zakaria, *The Future of Freedom: Illiberal Democracy at Home and Abroad*, (New York: W. W. Norton and Company, 2003), p. 69.

33. Tamara Cofman Wittes, *Freedom's Unsteady March: America's Role in Building Arab Democracy*, (Washington, DC: Brookings Institution, 2008), pp. 59-62.

34. Zakaria, op. cit., p. 72.

35. Thomas Carothers, "How Democracies Emerge: The 'Sequencing' Fallacy", *Journal of Democracy*, vol. 18, no. 1 (2007), pp. 15-16.

36. Eva Bellin, *Stalled Democracy: Capital, Labor and the Paradox of State-Sponsored Development*, (Cornell: Cornell University Press, 2002), pp. 3-5.

37. Wittes, *Freedom's Unsteady March: America's Role in Building Arab Democracy*, pp. 63-64.

38. Tarik M. Yousef, "Development, Growth and Policy Reforms in the Middle East and North Africa since 1950", *Journal of Economic Perspectives*, vol. 18, no. 3 (2004), pp. 91-116.

39. Pollack, *A Path Out of the Desert*, p. 263.

40. International Crisis Group, *Can Saudi Arabia Reform Itself?*, pp. 19-20

41. Pollack, op. cit., pp. 267-273.

42. Jeffrey Goldberg, "Breaking Ranks: What Turned Brent Scowcroft against the Bush Administration", *The New Yorker*, 31 October 2005, p. 60.

43. James Glanz, "A Little Democracy or A Genie Unbolted", *The New York Times*, 29 January 2006.

44. Condoleezza Rice, Remarks at the American University in Cairo (20 June 2005), http://2001-2009.state.gov/secretary/rm/2005/48328.htm

45. John Esposito and Dalia Mogahed, *Who Speaks for Islam?: What a Billion Muslims Really Think*, (Washington, DC: Gallup Press, 2008), p. 44.

46. Robert Malley and Peter Harling, "Beyond Moderates and Militants", *Foreign Affairs* (September-October 2010), pp. 18-29.

47. Kareem Elbayar, "NGO Laws in Selected Arab States", *International Journal of Not-for-Profit Law*, vol. 7, no. 4 (2005), pp. 3-27.

48. Pollack, *A Path Out of the Desert*, p. 305.

49. Joshua Teitelbaum, "Understanding Political Liberalization in the Gulf: An Introduction," in: Joshua Teitelbaum, ed., *Political Liberalization in the Persian Gulf*, p. 18

CHAPTER SEVENTEEN

1. Maurice Schiff and L. Alan Winters, *Regional Integration and Development*, (Washington, DC: International Bank for Reconstruction and Development/The World Bank, 2003), pp. 79-80.

2. Jan Herin, "Rules of Origin and Differences between Tariff Levels in EFTA and in the EC", Occasional Paper no. 13, (Geneva: European Free Trade Association (EFTA), February 1986).

3. 'Abd Allah 'Abd al-Rahman al-Sunaidi, *"Al-Naql al-barri bayna duwal majlis al-ta'awun li-duwal al-khalij al-'arabi: al-waqi' wa al-afaq"* [Land Transport between the Gulf Cooperation Council Countries: Realities and Horizons], *Al-Ta'awun*, year 8, no. 34 (June 1994).

4. 'Abd Allah al-Quwaiz, "*Al-Suq al-khalijiyyah al-mushtarakah: al-imkanat wa al-injazat* [The Gulf Common Market: Possibilities and Achievements], *Al-Ta'awun*, no. 55 (1993), pp. 31-56.

5. Jamal Zarrouk, "Intra-Arab Countries Trade", in: Said El-Naggar, ed., *The Determinants of Intra-Regional and Extra-Regional Trade in the Arab Countries* (Abu-Dhabi: Arab Monetary Fund, 1991).

6. International Monetary Fund, *Annual Report on Exchange Arrangements and Exchange Restrictions 1998*, (Washington, DC: International Monetary Fund, 1998).

7. Al-Quwaiz, "*Al-Suq al-khalijiyyah al-mushtarakah: al-imkanat wa al-injazat*", pp. 31-56.

8. Michael P. Todaro and Stephen C. Smith, *Economic Development*, The Addison-Wesley Series in Economics (New York: Addison-Wesley, 2003), p. 580.

9. Thomas F. Rutherford and Josephina Martinez, "Welfare Effects of Regional Trade Integration of Central America and Caribbean Nations with NAFTA and MERCOSUR", *World Economy*, vol. 23 (2003), pp. 799-825.

10. Steffen Hertog, "The GCC and Arab Economic Integration: A New Paradigm", *Middle East Policy*, vol. 14, no. 1 (2007), pp. 52-68.

11. See the Doha Declaration on the establishment of the Gulf Common Market at the Gulf Cooperation Council's twenty-eighth summit conference, 4 December 2007.

12. 'Abd al-Mun'im Sayyid 'Ali, *Al-Ittihad al-naqdi al-khaliji wa al-'umlah al-khalijiyyah al-mushtarakah* [The Gulf Monetary Union and Common Gulf Currency], (Centre for Arab Unity Studies, 2008), p. 147.

13. Robert J. Carbaugh, *International Economics*, 10th ed. (Mason-Ohio: South Western, 2004), p. 272.

14. Ibid., p. 273.

15. Michele Chang, *Monetary Integration in the European Union*, European Union Series (Palgrave Macmillan Firm), (New York: Palgrave Macmillan, 2009), pp. 63-65.

16. Brian R. Staples, "Trade Facilitation", Draft paper prepared for the WTO 2000 Conference, Geneva, (Washington D.C.: World Bank, 1998).

17. World Bank, *Trade Blocs*, A World Bank Policy Research Report (Oxford: Oxford University Press, 2000).

18. International Monetary Fund, *Annual Report on Exchange Arrangements and Exchange Restrictions 1998*.

19. World Bank, *Trade Blocs*.

20. Joseph F. Francois and Clinton R. Shields, *Modeling Trade Policy: Applied General Equilibrium Assessments of North American Free Trade*, (Cambridge MA: Cambridge University Press, 1994).

21. Peter Robson, *The Economics of International Integration*, 3rd ed., (London: Allen and Unwin, 1987).

22. Joseph A. Schumpeter, "The Theory of Economic Development: An Enquiry into Profits, Capital, Credit, Interest and the Business Cycle", *Harvard Economic Studies*, vol. XLVI (Cambridge MA: Harvard University Press, 1932).

23. Ross Levine, "Financial Development and Economic Growth: Views and Agenda", *Journal of Economic Literature*, vol. 35, no. 2 (1997), pp. 688-726.

24. Valerie R. Bencivenga and Bruce D. Smith, "Financial Intermediation and Endogenous Growth", *Review of Economic Studies*, vol. 58 (1991), pp. 195-209.

25. R. G. King and R. Levine, "Financial Intermediation and Economic Development", in: Colin Mayer and Xavier Vives, eds., *Capital Markets and Financial and Financial Intermediation* (Cambridge, MA: Cambridge University Press, 1993).

26. World Bank, *World Development Indicators 2010* (Washington, DC: World Bank, 2010), pp. 305-306.

27. World Bank, *Can Africa Claim the 21st Century?*, (Washington, DC: World Bank, 2000).

28. Paul Krugman, *The Return of Depression Economics and the Crisis of 2008*, (New York: W. W. Norton and Company (1997), pp. 239-252.

29. Michelle A. Sager, "Regional Trade Agreements: Their Role and the Economic Impact on Trade Flows", *The World Economy*, vol. 20 (1997), pp. 239-252.

30. Miles Kahler, "International Institutions and the Political Economy of Integration", *Integrating National Economies*, (Washington, DC: Brookings Institution, 1995).

31. Alejandro Micco, Ernesto H. Stein and Guillermo Luis Ordonez, "The Currency Union Effects on Trade: Early Evidence on EMU", *Economic Policy*, vol. 18, no. 37 (2003), pp. 315-356.

32. Keith Pilbeam, *International Finance*, 3rd ed. (New York: Palgrave Macmillan, 2006), p. 426.

33. The industries that are characterised by economies of scale have high static costs and variable low costs. This means that the more these industries are able to produce, the more they are able to distribute their static costs among a larger number of consumers, which means lower costs and higher production. This reduction in costs coupled with an increase in production, i.e., a market expansion, also means lower prices because the cost determines the price. Thus the more the market expands the lower the costs will be, and the lower the costs the lower the prices. This reduction in prices in turn improves these products' ability to compete. It is worth mentioning that there are other examples of industries of scale, including electricity, communications, etc.

34. Nicholas Owen, *Economies of Scale, Competitiveness and Trade Patterns Within the European Community*, (New York: Oxford University Press, 1983), pp. 119-139.

35. Carbaugh, *International Economics*, pp. 270-271.

36. Rubens Ricupero, "What Policy Makers Should Know About Regionalism", keynote address presented at World Bank Conference on What Policy Makers Should Know About Regionalism, Geneva, May 1998.

37. Dean A. De Rosa, "Regional Trading Arrangements among Developing Countries: The ASEAN Example", Research Report 103, (Washington DC: International Food Policy Research Institute, 1995).

38. Maurice Schiff, and L. Alan Winters, "Regional Integration, Security and Welfare", in: *Regionalism and Development: Report of the European Commission and World Bank Seminar*, Brussels 2 June 1997, Studies Series (European Commission); no. 1 (Luxembourg: Office for Official Publications of the European Communities; Lanham, MD: Berman Associates [Distributor], 1998).

39. Joseph Kechichian, "The Gulf Cooperation Council: The Search for Security", *Third World Quarterly*, vol. 7, no. 4 (1985), pp. 853-881.

40. World Bank, *Can Africa Claim the 21st Century?*

41. Faezeh Foiroutan, "Regional Integration in Sub-Saharan Africa: Past Experience and Future Prospects", in: Jaime De Melo and Arvind Panagarya, eds., *New Dimensions in Regional Integration* (London: Center for Economic Policy Research, 1993).

42. See: television programme aired on Al Jazeera Channel in the series *Ma Wara' Al-khabar* [What lies behind the news], on Tuesday 14 September 2010.

43. Andre Sapir, "The European Community: A Case of Successful Integration? A comment", in: De Melo and Panagarya, op. cit.

44. Todaro and Smith, *Economic Development*, p. 581.

45. Richard E. Baldwin, Rikard Forslid and Jan Haaland, "Investment Creations and Investment Diversion: A Simulation Study of the EU's Single Market Program", World Economy, vol. 19 (1996), pp. 635-659.

46. Pollack, "Securing the Gulf", pp.2-16.

47. Chang, *Monetary Integration in the European Union*, pp. 117-122.

48. Pilbeam, *International Finance*, p. 427.

49. Ibid., p. 428

50. Ibid., p. 42

CHAPTER EIGHTEEN

1. Raymond Hinnebusch, "The Middle East Regional System", in: Raymond Hinnebusch and Anoushirvan Ehteshami, eds., *The Foreign Policies of Middle East States* (Boulder, CO: Lynne Rienner, 2002), p. 50.
2. Fouad Ajami, "The Arab Spring at One", *Foreign Affairs*, vol. 91, no. 2 (March-April 2012), pp. 56-65.
3. Kamrava, *Qatar: Small State, Big Politics*, p. 25.
4. Ulrichsen, *Insecure Gulf: The End of Certainty and the Transition to the Post-Oil Era*, p. 26.
5. United States Senate Committee on Foreign Relations, *The Gulf Security Architecture: Partnership with the Gulf Cooperation Council*, Majority Staff Report (19 June 2012), p. 2.
6. Ibid., p. 4.
7. Yusuf Khalifah al-Yusuf, "Ab'ad al-hisar 'ala al-sha'ab al-filastinini" [Impact of the Siege on the Palestinian People], *Al-Mustaqbal al-'Arabi*, year 29, no. 331 (September 2006), pp. 101-112.
8. *Al-Mashru' al-nahdawi al-'arabi* [The Arab Renaissance Project], (Beirut: Center for Arab Unity Studies, 2010), p. 15.
9. Ahmad Yusuf Ahmad and Nevine Mas'ad, eds., *Hal al-ummah al-'arabiyyah, 2009-2010: al-nahdah aw al-suqut* [State of the Arab World 2009-2010: Renaissance or Downfall], (Beirut: Centre for Arab Unity Studies, 2010), pp. 304-306.
10. *Al-Mashru' al-nahdawi al-'arabi*, pp. 17-18.
11. Ahmed Galal and Bernard Hoekman, "Overview", in: Ahmed Galal and Bernard Hoekman, eds., *Arab Economic Integration: between Hope and Reality*, (Cairo: Egyptian Center for Economic Studies; Washington, DC: Brookings Institution Press, 2003), p. 2.
12. *Al-Mashru' al-nahdawi al-'arabi*, p. 116.
13. Galal and Hoekman, op. cit., p. 1.
14. *Al-Mashru' al-nahdawi al-'arabi*, pp. 32-33.
15. Ibid., pp. 34-35
16. Ibid., pp. 36-38
17. Ibid., pp. 38-40
18. 'Ali As'ad Watfah, "Hal taraju'u al-shu'ur al-qawmi al-'arabi? qira'ah susiyulujiyyah fi ara' tullab jami'at al-Kuwait" [Is there a Decline in Arab Nationalist Sentiment? A Sociological Assessment of student views at Kuwait University], *Al-Mustaqbal al-'arabi*, year 33, no. 378 (August 2010), p. 17.
19. League of Arab States, *Al-Taqrir al-iqtisadi al-'arabi al-muwahhad 2009*, Appendix (4/9), p. 352.
20. Ibid., p. 213
21. L. Alan Winters, "What Can the Arab Countries Learn from Europe?", in: Ahmed Galal and Bernard Hoekman, eds., *Arab Economic Integration: Between Hope and Reality*, pp. 159-160.
22. Michael T. Klare, *Rising Powers, Shrinking Powers: The New Geopolitics of Energy*, (New York: Metropolitan Books, Henry Holt and Company, 2008), pp. 194-205.
23. *Al-Ahram*, 2 August 1993.
24. *Al-Mashru' al-nahdawi al-'arabi*, pp. 108-113.
25. Nora Bensahel, "Political Reform in the Middle East", in: Bensahel and Byman, eds., *The Future Security Environment in the Middle East*, pp. 52-56.
26. Qur'an, Al-Mumtahanah 60:8.
27. Qur'an, Al-Mumtahanah 60:9
28. Joseph E. Stiglitz, *Freefall: America, Free Markets and the Sinking of the World Economy*, New York: W.W. Norton, 2010), pp. 219-220.

29. Pollack, *A Path Out of the Desert*, pp. 410-412.

30. Al-Yusuf, *Al-Imarat al-'arabiyyah al-muttahidah 'ala muftaraq turuq*,p. 347.

CHAPTER NINETEEN

1. Kishore Mahbubani, *The New Asian Hemisphere: The Irresistible Shift of Global Power to the East*, (New York: Public Affairs, 2008), p. 104.

2. Ibid., pp. 103-104

3. Mohammad El-Erian, *When Markets Collide: Investment Strategies for the Age of Global Economic Change*, (New York: McGraw-Hill, 2008), pp. 42-45.

4. Thomas Oatley and Jason Yackeel, "American Interests and IMF Lending", *International Politics*, vol. 41, no. 3 (2004), pp. 415-429.

5. Jean-Germain Gros and Olga Prokopovych, *When Reality Contradicts Rhetoric: World Bank Lending Practices in Developing Countries in Historical, Theoretical and Empirical Perspectives*, Monograph Series (Dakar: CODESRIA, 2005), p. 8.

6. Ibid., pp. 51-52

7. Surin Pitsuwan, "Dr. Supachai's Long and Winding Road to Geneva", *Bangkok Post*, 8 August 2002.

8. Fatoumata Jawara and Aileen Kwa, *Behind the Scenes at the WTO*, (London: Zed Books, 2004), p. 200.

9. World Trade Organization, *International Trade Statistics 2002*, (Geneva: WTO, 2002).

10. Sarah Sexton, "Trading Health Care Away? GATS, Public Service and Privatization", *South Bulletin*, vol. 15 (July 2001).

11. Brook K. Baker, "Pharma's Relentless Drive for Profits Explains US Trade Negotiations", Global Policy Forum (December 10, 2002).

12. Joseph E. Stiglitz et al., *The Stiglitz Report: Reforming the International Monetary and Financial Systems in the Wake of the Global Crisis*, (New York: New Press, 2010), p. 132.

13. Joseph E. Stiglitz, *Globalization and its Discontents*, (New York: W. W. Norton and Company, 2002), p. 5.

14. Jeffrey Sachs, *The End of Poverty: Economic Possibilities for Our Time*, (New York: Penguin Press, 2005), p. 189.

15. Ibid., pp. 285-287

16. Stiglitz, *Globalization and its Discontents*, pp. 6-7

17. Ibid., p. 17

18. Yusuf Khalifah al-Yusuf, "Ittijahat tatawwur al-azma al-maliyyah al-dawliyyah: al-mu'ashshirat wa al-dalalat 'am 2010" [Trends in the Development of the Global Financial Crisis: Indicators and Signs for 2010], *Dirasat sharq awsatiyyah*, year 14, no. 52 (Summer 2010), pp. 107-120.

19. International Monetary Fund (IMF), *Arab Republic of Egypt: 2010 Article IV Consultation-Staff Report*, IMF Country Report no. 10/94 (April 2010), p. 3.

CONCLUSION

1. Donald R. Keough, *The Ten Commandments for Business Failure*, (New York: Portfolio, 2008), p. 184.

2. Qur'an, al-Ahzab 33:62; Fatir 35:43; al-Fath 48:23.

Bibliography

Arabic sources

'Abd Allah, Hussain. *Mustaqbal al-Naft al-Arabi* [The Future of Arab Oil], 2nd edition, edited and updated (Beirut: Centre for Arab Unity Studies, 2006)

'Abd al-Rahman, Usama. *Shazaya fi al-fikr wa al-tanmiyah wa al-watan* [Fragments on thought, development and the nation], (Sharjah: Kitab Al-Khalij, 2002)

'Abd al-Rahman, Usama. *Al-Islam wa al-tanmiyah* [Islam and Development], (Beirut: Centre for Arabic Unity Studies, 2000)

Abu Zahrah, Muhammad. *Tarikh al-Madhahib al-Islamiyyah* [History of the Islamic Sects], 2 vols, (Cairo: Dar Al-Fikr al-Arabi, 1996)

Al-Ahram, 27 March 2011 http://gate.ahram.org.eg/UI/Front/Inner.aspx?NewsContentID=54154

Al-Ahram, 2 August 1993

Al-Arabiya News Online, 21 September 2012

Al-Ba'iz, Ibrahim. "Al-I'lam fi duwal al-khalij: qira'ah naqdiyyah" [Media in the Gulf Countries: A Critique], in: *Al-I'lam fi duwal al-khalij: dawruhu al-tanmawi wa masaruhu al-mustaqbali* [Media in the Gulf Countries: Its Role in Development and Future Course], Ibrahim al-Ba'iz et al, (Dubai: Dar Qortas Publishing House, 2007)

Al-Dayyin, Ahmad 'Ali. *Wiladat dustur al-kuwait* [Birth of the Kuwaiti Constitution], (Kuwait: Dar Al-Qartas, 1999)

Al-Dayyin, Ahmad 'Ali. "*Al-Dimuqratyyiah wa al-intikhabat fi al–Kuwait* [Democracy and Elections in Kuwait], in: 'Ali Khalifah al-Kawari, ed., *Al-intikhabat al-dimuqratiyyah wa waqi' al-intikhabat fi al-aqtar al-'arabiyya*h [Democratic elections and the status of elections in the Arab world], Democratic Studies Programme in the Arab Countries, (Beirut: Centre for Arab Unity Studies and the Democratic Studies Programme in the Arab Countries, 2008)

Ahmad, Ahmad Yusuf and Nevine Mas'ad, eds., *Hal al-ummah al-'arabiyyah, 2007-2008: thuna'iyyah al-taftit wa al-ihtiraq* [State of the Arab World 2007-2008: Duality of Fragmentation and Penetration], (Beirut: Centre for Arab Unity Studies, 2008)

Ahmad, Ahmad Yusuf and Nevine Mas'ad, eds., *Hal al-ummah al-'arabiyyah, 2009-2010: al-nahdah aw al-suqut* [State of the Arab World 2009-2010: Renaissance or Downfall], (Beirut: Centre for Arab Unity Studies, 2010)

Al-Faris, 'Abd al-Razzaq. "Dawr al-qita' al-khass fi intishar al-'amalah al-ajnabiyyah" [The Private Sector's Role in the Spread of Foreign Labour], in: *Al-'Amalah al-ajnabiyyah fi aqtar al-khalij al-'arabi*, ed. Nader Farajani (1983)

Al-Hayat, 4 July 1992

'Ali, 'Abd al-Mun'im Sayyid. *Al-Ittihad al-naqdi al-khaliji wa al-'umlah al-khalijiyyah al-musht-arakah* [The Gulf Monetary Union and Common Gulf Currency], (Centre for Arab Unity Studies, 2008)

Al-Issa, Juhaina Sultan Saif. "Al-Ta'thirat al-ijtima'iyyah li-l-murabbiyah al-ajnabiyyah 'ala al-usra" [The Social Impact of Foreign Nannies on the Family], in: *Al-'Amalah al-ajnabiyyah fi aqtar al-khalij al-'arabi*, ed. Nader Farajani (1983)

Al-Jabri, Muhammad 'Abid. *Al-'Aql al-akhlaqi al-'arabi: dirasah tahliliyyah naqdiyyah li nudhum al-qiyam fi al-thaqafah al-'arabyyiah; Naqd al-'aql al-'arabi* [The Arab Moral Mind: An Analytical Critical Study of Value Systems in Arab Culture; Critique of the Arab Mind, 4], (Beirut: Centre for Arab Unity Studies, 2001)

Al-Jassim, Yusuf. "Munaqashat muntada al-tanmiyah" [Discussions of the development seminar], in: 'Ali Khalifah al-Kawari, ed., *Al-Khalij al-'arabi wa al-dimuqratiyyah: nahwa ru'yah mustaqbaliyyah li-ta'ziz al-masa'i al-dimuqratiyyah* (2002)

Al Jazeera programme "Bila hudud" [Without limits]. Interview with Rachid al-Ghannouchi, leader of the Tunisian Ennahda party, with Ahmad Mansur, (19 February 2014)

Al Jazeera series "Ma Wara' Al-khabar" [What lies behind the news], (14 September 2010)

Al-Kawakibi, 'Abd al-Rahman. "Tabai' al-istibdad wa masari' al-isti'bad" [The Characteristics of Despotism and Deaths of Enslavement] in: *Al-A'mal al-kamilah li-l-kawakibi* [The Complete Works of al-Kawakibi], ed., Muhammad Jamal Tahhan, (Beirut: Centre for Arab Unity Studies, 1995)

Al-Kawari, 'Ali Khalifah, ed. *Al-Sha'b yurid al-islah fi qatar... aydan* [The People Want Reform... In Qatar, Too], (Beirut: Al-Maaref Forum, 2012)

Al-Kuwari, 'Ali Khalifah. "Jawhar al-dimuqratiyyah la yata'aradu ma'a jawhar al-Islam" [The Core of Democracy Does not Conflict with the Core of Islam], *Al-Mustaqbal al-'arabi*, Year 32, No. 374, April 2010

Al-Kawari, 'Ali Khalifah. "La taqumu al-dimuqratiyyah fi zill hukumah diniyyah: munaqasha li-rai al-ustadh rashid al-ghannushi" [Democracy Cannot Be Implemented under a Religious System: A Discussion of Dr. Rachid al-Ghannouchi's Opinion], *Al-Mustaqbal al-'Arabi*, Year 31, No. 362 (April 2009), pp. 148-150

Al-Kawari, 'Ali Khalifah. "Al-Tafrah al-naftiyyah al-thalithah: qira'ah awwaliyyah fi dawa'i al-tafrah wa hajmiha: halat aqtar majlis al-ta'awun" [The Third Oil Boom: Preliminary Review of the Boom's Impact and its Size: the Case of the GCC states], *Al-Mustaqbal al-'arabi*, Year 31, no. 362 (April 2009)

Al-Kawari, 'Ali Khalifah, ed. *Al-Khalij al-'arabi wa al-dimuqratiyyah: nahwa ru'yah mustaqbali-yyah li-ta'ziz al-masa'i al-dimuqratiyyah* [The Arabian Gulf and Democracy: Towards a Future Vision to Promote Efforts towards Democracy], (Beirut: Centre for Arab Unity Studies. 2002)

Al-Kawari, Hamad 'Abd al-'Aziz. "Al-I'lam al-khaliji ila ayna?" [Media in the Gulf, Where to?], in: *Al-I'lam fi duwal al-khalij: dawruhu al-tanmawi wa masaruhu al-mustaqbali*, Ibrahim al-Ba'iz et al, (2007)

Al-Khatib, Ahmad. *Al-Kuwait min al- Imarah ila al-dawla: dhikrayat al-'amal al-watani wa al-qawmi*, [Kuwait from emirate to state: memories of national and nationalist activism), supervised by Ghanim Najjar, (Casablanca: Arab Cultural Centre, 2007)

Al-Mashru' al-nahdawi al-'arabi [The Arab Renaissance Project], (Beirut: Center for Arab Unity Studies, 2010)

Al-Mutawakkil, Muhammad 'Abd al-Malik. "Al-Islam wa huquq al-insan" [Islam and human rights], *Al-Mustaqbal al-'arabi*, year 19, no. 216 (February 1997)

Al-Nafisi, 'Abd 'Allah Fahmi. Commentary on 'Abd al-Malik Khalaf al-Tamimi's paper, "Al-Athar al-siyasiyyah li-l-hijra al-ajnabiyyah" [Political Implications of Foreign Migration], in: *Al-'Amalah al-ajnabiyyah fi aqtar al-khalij al-'arabi*, ed. Nader Farajani (1983)

Al-Nadwa (Riyadh), 31 July 1960

Al-Najjar, Baqir Salman. *Al-Dimuqratiyyah al-'asiyyah fi al-khalij al-'arabi*, [The Intractable Democracy in the Arabian Gulf], (Beirut: Dar al-Saqi, 2008)

Al-Najjar, Ghanim. *Madkhal lil-tatawwur al-siyyasi fi al-kuwait* [Introduction to political development in Kuwait], 2 vols, (Kuwait: Dar Qartas, 1966)

Al-Qardawi, Yusuf. "*Al-Siyyasah al-shar'iyyah fi daw' nusus al-shar'iyyiah wa maqasidaha*, [Legal Policies in Light of the Shari'a's Text and Intention], (Cairo: Maktabah Wahbah, 1998)

Al-Qardawi, Yusuf. Min fiqh al-dawlah fi al-Islam [Statecraft in Islam], 6th edn, (Cairo: Dar El Shorouk, 2009)

Al-Qurtubi, Muhammad bin Ahmad. *Tafsir al-Qurtubi: Al-Jami' li-ahkam al-Qur'an* [Commentary of the Holy Qur'an: Compendium of Legal Rulings of the Qur'an], (Beirut: Dar Al-Kitab al-Arabi, n.d.)

Al-Quwaiz, 'Abd Allah. "*Al-Suq al-khalijiyyah al-mushtarakah: al-imkanat wa al-injazat* [The Gulf Common Market: Possibilities and Achievements], *Al-Ta'awun*, no. 55 (1993)

Al-Rasheed, Madawi. "*Mashru' tahdith al-hukm al-sa'udi: warayat al-'amal al-muqadamah lil-halqah al-niqashiyyah: al-sa'udiyyah ila 'ayna?*" [Project to reform the Saudi governance system: working paper presented at the discussion group meeting 'Saudi Arabia, where to?'], *Al-Mustaqbal al-'arabi*, year 32, no. 368 (October 2009), p. 102-133

Al-Rumaihi, Muhammad. "Harakat 1938 al-Islahiyyah fi al-Kuwait wa al-Bahrain wa Dubai" [The 1938 Reform Movement in Kuwait, Bahrain and Dubai], *Majallat dirasat al-khalij wa al-jazirah al-'arabiyyah*, vol. 1, (1975)

Al-Sabah, Shaikh Sabah al-Ahmad al-Jabir. Speech delivered on 19 October 2012. http://www.da.gov.kw/ara/speeches/amir_speeches_2012.php?p=19102012

Al-Saif, Muhammad Bin 'Abd Allah. '*Abd Allah al-Tariki: sukhur al-naft wa rimal al-siyyasah*," (Abdullah Al-Tariki: Oil Rocks and Policy Sands), (Beirut: Riyad al-Rayyis li-l-kutub wa al-nashr, 2007)

Al-Shatti, Ismail. 'Ali Khalifah al-Kawari, ed., *Al-Khalij al-'arabi wa al-dimuqratiyyah*, p. 133.

Al-Siba'i, Mustafa. *Islamuna: ta'rif mujaz* [Our Islam: a brief introduction], (Beirut: Dar Al-wuraq li-l-nasr wa al-tawzi', 2001)

Al-Sunaidi, 'Abd Allah 'Abd al-Rahman. "Al-Naql al-barri bayna duwal majlis al-ta'awun li-duwal al-khalij al-'arabi: al-waqi' wa al-afaq" [Land Transport between the Gulf Cooperation Council Countries: Realities and Horizons], *Al-Ta'awun*, year 8, no. 34 (June 1994)

Al-Tabari, Abu Ja'far Muhammad Ibn Jarir, *Ta'rikh al-rusul wa al-muluk*

Al-Taqrir al-istratiji al-'arabi 1988 [Arab Strategic Report], (Cairo: Al-Ahram Centre for Political and Strategic Studies, 1988)

Al-Usbu' al-'arabi, 26 September 2000

Al Wafd Gate http://www.alwafd.org

Al-Watan (Sultanate of Oman), 4 October, 2003

Al-Yusuf, Yusuf Khalifah. *Al-Imarat al-'arabiyyah al-muttahidah 'ala muftaraq turuq* [The United Arab Emirates at the crossroads], (Beirut: Centre for Arab Unity Studies, 2013)

Al-Yusuf, Yusuf Khalifah. "Ittijahat tatawwur al-azma al-maliyyah al-dawliyyah: al-mu'ashshirat wa al-dalalat 'am 2010" [Trends in the Development of the Global Financial Crisis: Indicators and Signs for 2010], *Dirasat sharq awsatiyyah*, year 14, no. 52 (Summer 2010), pp. 107-120

Al-Yusuf, Yusuf Khalifah. " 'Indama tusbih al-sultah ghanimah: halat majlis al-ta'awun al-khaliji", Al-Mustaqbal al-'Arabi, vol. 31, no. 351, (May 2008), pp. 70-87

Al-Yusuf, Yusuf Khalifah. "Ab'ad al-hisar 'ala al-sha'ab al-filastinini" [Impact of the Siege on the Palestinian People], *Al-Mustaqbal al-'Arabi*, year 29, no. 331 (September 2006), pp. 101-112

Al-Yusuf, Yusuf Khalifah. "Dirasat halat al-imarat" [Study on the state of the Emirates], in: Isma'il Shatti, ed., *Al-Fasad wa-al-'ukm al-'ali fi al-bilad al-'Arabiyah: buhuth wa-munaqashat al-nadwah al-fikriyyah allati nazzamaha markaz dirasat al-Wahdah al-'Arabiyyah bi-l-ta'awun ma'a al-ma'had al-swidi bil-Iskandariyyah* [Corruption and good governance in the Arab countries: proceedings of the symposium organised by the Centre for Arab Unity Studies in cooperation with the Swedish Institute Alexandria] (Beirut: Centre for Arab Unity Studies, 2004), pp. 577-600

Al-Yusuf, Yusuf Khalifah. "Al-Bu'd al-sukkani li-l-tanmiyah fi al-dawlat al-imarat al-'arabiyyah al-muttahidah" [The Population Dimension in the United Arab Emirates], *Al-Ta'awun* (magazine of the GCC General Secretariat), no. 29, (March 1993)

Al-Yusuf, Yusuf Khalifah. " 'Ajz al-muwazanah al-'ammah fi dawlat al-imarat al-'arabiyyah al-muttahidah" [Deficit in the United Arab Emirates' Budget], *Gulf and Arabian Peninsula Studies Magazine*, no. 70 (July 1993)

Al-Yusuf, Yusuf Khalifah. "Tarshid al-dawr al-tanmawi li-l-qita' al-'amm fi duwal majlis al-ta'awun al-khaliji" [Rationalising the Public Sector's Role in the GCC states' Development], *Majallah al-'ulum al-'ijtima'iyyah*, year 27, no. 3 (1999)

Al-Yusuf, Yusuf Khalifah. "Al-'Awlamah wa iqtisadat duwal majlis al-ta'awun al-khaliji" [Globalisation and the economies of the countries of the Gulf Cooperation Council] in: *Al-Mujtama' wa al-iqtisad amama al-'awlamah* [Society and Economy in the face of Globalisation]. ed., Samir Amin. Al-Mustaqbal al-'Arabi series no. 33, (Beirut: Centre for Arab Unity Studies)

Al-Yusuf, Yusuf Khalifah. "Ittijahat tatawwur al-azma al-maliyyah al-dawliyyah: al-mu'ashshirat wa al-dalalat 'am 2010" [Trends in the Development of the Global Financial Crisis: Indicators and Signs for 2010], *Dirasat sharq awsatiyyah*, year 14, no. 52 (Summer 2010)

Arab Monetary Fund. *Al-Hisabat al-qawmiyyah li-l-duwal al-'arabiyyah 1978-2011* [National statistics of Arab States 1978-2011] (Abu Dhabi: Arab Monetary Fund, 2012)

Asad, Muhammad. *The Principles of State and Government in Islam* (Gibraltar: Dar al-Andalus, 1980)

Balqaziz, 'Abd al-ilah. *Al-Islam wa al-siyyasah: dawr al-haraka al-islamiyyah fi sawgh al-majal al-siyyasi* [Islam and Politics: the Role of Islamic Movements in Defining the Political Arena], (Beirut: Al-Markaz al-'arabi al-thaqafi, 2001)

Balqaziz, 'Abd al-ilah, ed. *Al-Mu'aradah wa al-sultah fi al-watan al-'arabi: azmat al-mu'aradah al-siyasiyyah al-'arabiyyah* [Opposition and power in the Arab world: the Arab political opposition crisis], Beirut: Centre for Arab Unity Studies, 2001)

Barakat, Halim. *Al-Mujtama' al-'arabi al-mu'asir: bahth istitla'i ijtima'i* [Contemporary Arab society: a sociological overview],10 ed. (Beirut: Centre for Arab Unity Studies, 2008)

Dustur Kuwayt [The Constitution of Kuwait], (Kuwait: Dar Qartas li-l-nashr, 1999)

Farajani, Nader, ed., *Al-'Amalah al-ajnabiyyah fi aqtar al-khalij al-'arabi* [Foreign Labour in the GCC states], Research and Discussions of the Intellectual Seminar organised by the Centre for Arab Unity Studies, in cooperation with the Arab Planning Institute (Beirut: Centre for Arab Unity Studies, 1983)

Gerges, Fawwaz. "Tahaffuzat 'arabiyyah' ala al-dimuqratiyyah" [Arab Reservations about Democracy], in: *Azmat al-dimuqratiyyah fi al-buldan al-'arabiyyah: i'tiradat wa tahaffuzat 'ala al-dimuqratiyyah fi al- 'alam al-'arabi* [Crisis of Democracy in the Arab World: Objections and Reservations Concerning Democracy in the Arab World], ed., 'Ali Khalifah al-Kawari, (Beirut: Dar al-Saqi, 2004)

Harrison, Lawrence *The Central Liberal Truth*, (Oxford: Oxford University Press, 2006)

Hasib, Khair al-Din. "Iftitahiyyat al-'Adad: Al-Tayyaran al-Qawmi al-'Arabi wa al-Islami: Janahan la Yuhaliqan illa Ma'an," (Editorial: The Nationalist and Islamic Currents: Two wings that Can Only Fly Together), *Al-Mustaqbal al-'arabi*, year 26, no. 295 (September 2003)

Huwaidi, Fahmi. "Al-Islam wa al-dimuqratiyyah" [Islam and democracy] in: *Al-Harakat al-Islamiyyah wa al-dimuqratiyyah: dirasat fi al-fikr wa al-mumarasah* [Islamic Movements and Democracy: Studies in Thought and Practice], Majdi Hammad et al, (Beirut: Centre for Arab Unity Studies, 1999)

Huwaidi, Fahmi. "Al-Islam wa al-dimuqratiyyah" [Islam and Democracy]," *Al-Mustaqbal al-'arabi*, year 15, no. 166 (December 1992)

Ibn Sa'ad, Muhammad. *Al-Tabaqat al-kubra*

Ibn Sallam, Abu 'Ubayd al-Qasim. *Al-Amwal*

Ibn Sunitan, Muhammad. *Al-Nukhab al-sa'udiyyah: dirasah fi al-tahawwulat wa al-Ikhfaqat*, [The Saudi Elites: A Study of Transformations and Failures], Doctoral theses series 48, (Beirut: Centre for Arab Unity Studies, 2004)

Ibrahim, Haidar. "Athar al-'amalah al-ajnabiyyah 'ala al-thaqafa al-'arabiyyah" [Impact of Foreign Labour on Arab Culture], in: *Al-'Amalah al-ajnabiyyah fi aqtar al-khalij al-'arabi*, ed. Nader Farajani (1983)

Issa, Nahawand al-Kadri. *Qira'ah fi thaqafat al-fada'iyyat al-'arabiyyah: al Wuquf 'ala tukhum al-tafkik*, [A Review of Arab Satellite Culture: Standing at the Threshold of Dismantlement], (Beirut: Centre for Arab Unity Studies, 2008)

League of Arab States et al, *Al-Taqrir al-iqtisadi al-'arabi al-muwahhad* 2012 [Unified Arab Economic Report], (Abu Dhabi, Cairo: Arab Monetary Fund, Arab Fund for Economic and Social Development, League of Arab States and Organisation of Arab Petroleum Exporting Countries, 2012)

League of Arab States et al, *Al-Taqrir al-iqtisadi al-'arabi al-muwahhad* 2009 [Unified Arab Economic Report], (Abu Dhabi, Cairo: Arab Monetary Fund, Arab Fund for Economic and Social Development, League of Arab States and Organisation of Arab Petroleum Exporting Countries, 2009)

Nusairat, Fadwa Ahmad Mahmud. "Al-Masihiyyun al-'arab wa fikrat al-qawmiyyah al-'arabiyyah fi bilad al-Sham wa Misr, 1840-1918" [Arab Christians and the Concept of Arab Nationalism in Greater Syria and Egypt], *Al-Mustaqbal al-'Arabi*, Year 32, No. 368, October 2009, pp. 25-27

Qatar Ministry for Foreign Affairs http://www.mofa.gov.qa

Qatar News Agency, 30 April 2003

Qutb, Sayyid. *Al-'Adalah al-ijtima'iyyah fi al-Islam* [Social Justice in Islam], 15th ed., (Cairo: Dar El Shorouk, 2002)

Sulaiman, 'Atif. *Al-Tharwah al-naftiyyah wa dawruha al-'arabi: al-dawr al-siyyasi wa al-iqtisadi li-l-naft al-'arabi* [Oil Wealth and its Arab Role: The Political and Economic Role of Arab Oil], (Beirut: Centre for Arab Unity Studies, 2009)

Watfah, 'Ali As'ad. "Hal taraju'u al-shu'ur al-qawmi al-'arabi? qira'ah susiyulujiyyah fi ara' tullab jami'at al-Kuwait" [Is there a Decline in Arab Nationalist Sentiment? A Sociological Assessment of student views at Kuwait University], *Al-Mustaqbal al-'arabi*, year 33, no. 378 (August 2010)

Watfah, 'Ali As'ad. "Al-'Amalah al-wafidah wa tahaddiyyat al-huwiyyah al-thaqafiyyah fi duwal al-khalij al-'arabi" [Foreign Labour and the Challenges of Cultural Identity in the Arab Gulf Countries], *Al-Mustaqbal al-'arabi*, year 30, no. 344 (October 2007)

English sources

Aarts, Paul and Gerd Nonneman (eds). Saudi Arabia in the Balance: Political Economy, Society, Foreign Affairs (New York: New York University Press, 2005)

Abdel-Fadil, Mahmoud. "The Macro-Behaviour of Oil-Rentier States in the Arab Region" in: *The Rentier State, Nation, State and Integration in the Arab World* eds., Hazem Beblawi and Giacomo Liciani, (1987)

Abedin, Mahan. "Saudi Dissent More than Just Jihadis" in: *The Kingdom: Saudi Arabia and the Challenges of the 21st Century,* eds., Joshua Craze and Mark Huband, (2009)

Abu Khalil, As'ad. "A Viable Partnership: Islam, Democracy and the Arab World", *Harvard International Review*, vol. 15, no. 2 (Winter 1992-1993)

Aburish, Said K. *The Rise, Corruption, and Coming Fall of the House of Saud*. London: Bloomsbury Publishing Ltd., 1994

Adelman, Morris A. *The Genie Out of the Bottle: World Oil Since 1970*. Cambridge, MA: MIT Press, 1995

Agence France-Presse (AFP). "Saudi authorities detain founders of new party", 19 February 2011

Agence France-Presse (AFP), 25 May 2004

Ajami, Fouad. "The Arab Spring at One", *Foreign Affairs*, vol. 91, no. 2 (March-April 2012), pp. 56-65

Albright, David et al., "The United States, Its Middle East Allies and Iran: What is the Way Forward?", *Middle East Policy*, vol. 21, no. 1 (Spring 2014), pp.1-28

Al-Dakhil, Khalid. "Regional Power in an Area of Turmoil" in: *The Kingdom: Saudi Arabia and the Challenges of the 21ˢᵗ Century*, eds., Joshua Craze and Mark Huband, (2009)

Al-Faisal, Saud. "The Fight Against Extremism and the Search for Peace", address to the Council on Foreign Relations, 20 September 2005. http://www.cfr.org/radicalization-and-extremism/ fight-against-extremism-search-peace-rush-transcript-federal-news-service-inc/p8908

Al-Gurg, Easa Saleh. *The Wells of Memory: An Autobiography*. (London: John Murray, 1998)

Al-Kawari, Ali Khalifa. *Oil Revenues in the Gulf Emirates: Patterns of Allocation and Impact on Economic Development*. (Epping, UK: Bowker in Association with the Centre for Middle Eastern and Islamic Studies of the University of Durham, 1974)

Al-Khalifa, King Hamad Bin Isa, "Stability is Prerequisite for Progress", *Washington Times*, 19 April 2011

Alley, April Longley. "Yemen Changes Everything and Nothing", *Journal of Democracy*, vol. 24, no. 4 (October 2013), pp. 79-81

Al Monitor. "Riyadh Rushes to Support Egypt's New Military Rulers", 11 July 2012. http://www.al-monitor.com/pulse/politics/2013/07/relationship-saudi-arabia-cairo-following-morsi-ouster.html

Al-Rasheed, Madawi. *A History of Saudi Arabia*. (Cambridge, MA: Cambridge University Press, 2002)

Al-Rasheed, Madawi. *Contesting the Saudi State: Islamic Voices from a New Generation*. (Cambridge, MA: Cambridge University Press, 2007)

Al-Rasheed, Madawi. "Bin Laden's Puritans Keep Saudis in Thrall to Rebellious Cycle" in: Joshua Craze and Mark Huband, eds., *The Kingdom: Saudi Arabia and the Challenges of the 21ˢᵗ Century* (2009)

Al-Rasheed, Madawi. "Money Replaces Ideas as Petitioners' Silence Leaves Saudi Reform at an Imams", in: *The Kingdom: Saudi Arabia and the Challenges of the 21ˢᵗ Century*, eds., Joshua Craze and Mark Huband, (2009)

Al-Sabah, Y. S. F. *The Oil Economy of Kuwait*, (London: Kegan Paul International, 1980)

Althani, Mohamed A. J. *The Arab Spring and the Gulf States: Time to Embrace Change*, (London: Profile Books, 2012)

Altorki, Soraya and Donald P. Cole. *Arabian Oasis City: The Transformation of 'Unayzah*. (Austin: University of Texas, 1989)

Al-Yusuf, Yusuf Khalifah. "When rulership becomes privileged booty (ghanimah): the condition of the Gulf Cooperation Council", *Contemporary Arab Affairs*, 1:4, 2008, pp. 631-648

Amirahmadi, Hooshang. "The Spiraling Gulf Arms Race", *Middle East Insight*, vol. 2 (1994), pp. 45-49

Amiri, Reza Ekhtiari, Mohammad Agus Yusoff and Fakhreddin Soltani, "Arab Spring: Geopolitical Implications for Iran", *International Journal of Asian Social Science*, vol. 2, no. 9 (2012), pp. 1533-1547

Amnesty International. "Saudi Arabia: 11 Women Still Held after Protest", 8 January 2013

Amuzegar, Jahangir. "Oil Wealth: A Very Mixed Blessing", *Foreign Affairs* (Spring 1982), pp. 814-835

Amuzegar, Jahangir. *Managing the Oil Wealth: OPEC's Windfalls and Pitfalls*. (London: I.B. Tauris, 2001)

Anarkismo. "In the Heart of Tunisia. Thala: The Occupied Police Station", 24 April 2011. http://www.anarkismo.net/article/19380?userlanguage=ca&save_prefs=true

Anderson, Lisa. "Arab Democracy: Dismal Prospects", *World Policy Journal* (Fall 2001), pp. 53-60

Anthony, John Duke. *Arab States of the Lower Gulf: People, Politics, Petroleum.* (Washington, DC: The Middle East Institute, 1975)

Aoun, Marie-Claire. "Oil and Gas Resources of the Middle East and North Africa: A Curse or Blessing?", in: *The New Energy Crisis: Climate, Economics, and Geopolitics* , eds. Jean-Marie Chevalier and Patrice Geoffron. 2nd ed. (London: Palgrave and MacMillan, 2013)

Arab News. "161 Arrested in Buraidah", 2 March 2013. http://www.arabnews.com/saudi-arabia/161-arrested-buraidah

Arab News, 29 April 2004

Arab News, 6 July 2004

Armstrong, Scott, Malcolm Byrne and Tom Blanton. *The Chronology: The Documented Day-by-Day Account of the Secret Military Assistance to Iran and the Contras.* (New York: Warner Books, 1987)

Asad, Muhammad. *The Principles of State and Government in Islam.* (Gibraltar, UK: Dar Al-Andalus, 1980)

Ascher, William. *Why Governments Waste Natural Resources Policy Failures in Developing Countries.* (Baltimore, MD; London: John Hopkins University Press, 1999)

Asharq al-Awsat, 15 December 1996

Askari, Hossein. *Collaborative Colonialism: The Political Economy of Oil in the Persian Gulf.* (New York: Palgrave MacMillan, 2013)

Askari, Hossein. *Middle East Oil Exporters: What Happened to Economic Development?* (London: Edward Elgar, 2006)

Auty, Richard M. *Sustaining Development in Mineral Economies: The Resource Curse Thesis.* (London: Routledge, 1993)

Auty, Richard M. "Elites, Rent-Cycling and Development: Adjustment to Land Scarcity in Mauritius, Kenya and Cote d'Ivoir". *Development Policy Review*: vol. 28, no. 4, (2010), pp.411-433

Ayubi, Nazih N. "Political Correlates of Privatization Programs in the Middle East". *Arab Studies Quarterly* vol. 14, nos. 2-3, (1992), pp.47-54

Baker, Brook K. "Pharma's Relentless Drive for Profits Explains US Trade Negotiations", *Global Policy Forum* (December 10, 2002)

Baker, Dean. *Plunder and Blunder: The Rise and Fall of the Bubble Economy.* (Sausalito, CA: Poli Point Press, 2009)

Baldwin, Richard E., Rikard Forslid and Jan Haaland, "Investment Creations and Investment Diversion: A Simulation Study of the EU's Single Market Program", *World Economy*, vol. 19 (1996), pp. 635-659

Baldwin-Edward, Martin. "Labour Immigration and Labour Markets in the GCC states: National Patterns and Trends," LSE Kuwait Programme research paper no. 15 (March 2011), http://www.lse.ac.uk/middleEastCentre/kuwait/research/papers/labourimmigration.aspx

Ball, George. "What Brought the Shah Down", *Washington Star,* 14 March 1979

Barzegar, Kayhan. "Nuclear Terrorism: An Iranian Perspective", *Middle East Policy*, 21:1 (Spring 2014), pp.29-40

Battle, Joyce (ed.). *Iraqgate: Saddam Hussein, U. S Policy, and Prelude to the Persian Gulf War.* (Washington, DC: National Security Archive, 1995)

Baxter, Kevin. "Riyadh's Rising Fuel Subsidy Bill", *Middle East Economic Digest*, vol. 55, no. 37 (16 September 2011)

BBC News. "Bahrain Profile", http://www.bbc.com/news/world-middle-east-14541322

BBC News. "Kuwait Election: Thousands Join Anti-Government Protest",30 November 2012. http://www.bbc.co.uk/news/world-middle-east-20558819

BBC News. "David Cameron on GP: 'Bahrain Is not Syria'", 20 April 2012, http://www.bbc.co.uk/news/uk-17789082

BBC News. "Kuwait Protest at Court at Court Ruling Dissolving Parliament", 27 June 2012. http://www.bbc.co.uk/news/world-middle-east-18606540

BBC News. "Kuwait's Prime Minister Resigns After Protests", 28 November 2011. http://www.bbc.co.uk/news/world-middle-east-15931526

Beals, Gregory. "A Missed Opportunity with Iran", *Newsday*, 2 February 2006

Beblawi, Hazem. "The Rentier State in the Arab World", in: *The Rentier State. Nation, State, and Integration in the Arab World*, eds., Hazem Beblawi and Giacomo Luciani (1987)

Beblawi, Hazem and Giacomo Liciani, eds., *The Rentier State, Nation, State and Integration in the Arab World*; v. 2. (1987)

Bellin, Eva. "The Political-Economic Conundrum," in: *Uncharted Journey: Promoting Democracy in the Middle East*, Global Policy Books, eds., Thomas Carothers and Marina Ottaway (Washington, DC: Carnegie Endowment for International Peace, 2006).

Bellin, Eva. *Stalled Democracy: Capital, Labor, and the Paradox of State-Sponsored Development* (Cornell: Cornell University Press, 2002)

Benchemsi, Ahmed. "Morocco: Outfoxing the Opposition", *Journal of Democracy*, vol. 23, no. 1 (January 2012), pp.57-69

Bencivenga, Valerie R. and Bruce D. Smith, "Financial Intermediation and Endogenous Growth", *Review of Economic Studies*, vol. 58 (1991), pp. 195-209

Bensahel, Nora. "Political Reform in the Middle East", in: *The Future Security Environment in the Middle East*, eds., Nora Bensahel and Daniel Byman (2004), pp. 52-56

Bensahel, Nora and Daniel Byman. *The Future Security Environment in the Middle East* (Santa Monica, CA: Projects Air Force, 2004)

Bhagwati, Jagdish. "The Problem with Foreign Aid". *Foreign Affairs* (January-February 2010)

Birdsall, Nancy and Arvind Subramanian. "Saving Iraq from its Oil", *Foreign Affairs* 83, no. 4 (July-August 2004), pp. 77-89

Blumenthal, Max. "Birth Pangs of a New Christian Zionism", *The Nation*, (8 August 2006)

Boduszynski, Mieczystaw P. and Duncan Pickard. "Libya Starts from Scratch", *Journal of Democracy*, vol. 24, no. 4 (October 2013), pp.86-96

Boustany, Nora. "Traditional Saudis Take Dim View of Attempts to Modernize Islam," *Washington Post*, 24 August 1994

British Petroleum (BP). *BP Statistical Review of World Energy* (London: BP, 2013)

British Petroleum (BP). *BP Statistical Review of World Energy*. (London: BP, 2007)

Brown, Nathan J. "Egypt's Constitutional Cul-De-Sac", Carnegie Endowment, 31 March 2014. http://carnegieendowment.org/2014/03/31/egypt-s-constitutional-cul-de-sac

Brown, Nathan J. "Moving Out of Kuwait's Political Impasse," Carnegie Endowment, 25 June 2007, http://carnegieendowment.org/publications/index.cfm?fa=view&id=23320&prog=zg

Brownlee, Jason, Tarek Masoud and Andrew Reynolds, "Why the Modest Harvest?", *Journal of Democracy*, vol. 24, no. 4 (October 2013), pp.29-44

Brumberg, Daniel. "Transforming the Arab World's Protection-Racket Politics", *Journal of Democracy*, vol. 24, no. 3 (July 2013), pp. 95-102

Brzezinski, Zbigniew and Brent Scowcroft, "A "Road Map for Israeli-Palestinian Amity", Wall Street Journal, 13 December 2003

Byman, Daniel. "Do Targeted Killings Work?", Foreign Affairs (March-April 2006), pp. 95-111

Byman, Daniel L. and Jerrold D. Green. *Political Violence and Stability in the States of the Northern Persian Gulf*. (Santa Monica, CA: RAND, 1999)

Byman, Daniel L. and Jerrold D. Green, "The Enigma of Political Stability in the Persian Gulf Monarchies", *Middle East Review of International Affairs*, 3:3, (September 1999)

Cacchione, Nicholas. *Is Gasoline Still a Great Bargain?* (Norwalk, CT: John S. Herold, 2005)

Calabrese, John. *Revolutionary Horizons: Regional Foreign Policy in Post-Khomeini Iran.* (New York: St. Martin's Press, 1994)

Carbaugh, Robert J. *International Economics.* 10th ed. (Mason-Ohio: South-Western, 2004)

Carothers, Thomas. "How Democracies Emerge: The 'Sequencing Fallacy', *Journal of Democracy,* vol. 18, no. 1 (2007), pp. 12-27

Carter, Jimmy. *Our Endangered Values: America's Moral Crisis.* (New York: Simon and Schuster, 2005)

CBS News, 25 June 2000

Champion, Daryl. *The Paradoxical Kingdom: Saudi Arabia and the Momentum of Reform.* (New York: Columbia University Press, 2003)

Chang, Michele. *Monetary Integration in the European Union.* (New York: Palgrave Macmillan, 2009)

Charter, David. "Sarkozy Calls for Halt to Foreign Ownership". The Times, 21 October 2008

Chua, Beng-Huat. "Values and Development in Singapore," in: *Developing Cultures: Case Studies,* eds., Harrison, Lawrence and Peter L. Berger. (London: Routledge, 2006)

Clatanoff, William et al., "Saudi Arabia's Accession to the WTO: Is a Revolution Brewing?", *Middle East Policy* 13: 1 (2006), pp.1-23

Cohen, Stephen S. and J. Bradford De Long. *The End of Influence: What Happens When other Countries Have the Money.* (New York: Basic Books, 2010)

Collier, Paul. *The Plundered Planet.* (Oxford: Oxford University Press, 2010)

Commission on Growth and Development. *The Growth Report: Strategies for Sustained Growth and Inclusive Development.* (Washington, DC: World Bank, 2008)

Cooper, Helen and Robert Worth. "In Arab Spring, Obama Finds a Sharp Test", *The New York Times,* 24 September 2012. http://www.nytimes.com/2012/09/25/us/politics/arab-spring-proves-a-harsh-test-for-obamas-diplomatic-skill.html?_r=0

Cordesman, Anthony H. *Bahrain, Oman, Qatar, and The UAE: Challenges Of Security. CSIS Middle East Dynamic Net Assessment.* (Boulder, CO: West View Press, 1997)

Craze, Joshua and Mark Huband, ed., *The Kingdom: Saudi Arabia and the Challenges of the 21st Century* (London: Hurst and Company, 2009)

Crystal, Jill. *Oil and Politics in the Gulf: Rulers and Merchants in Kuwait and Qatar.* Cambridge Middle East Library; 24. (London: Cambridge University Press, 1995)

Crystal, Jill. "Civil Society in the Arabian Gulf," in: Augustus Richard Norton, ed., *Civil Society in the Middle East,* vol. 2 (Boston: Brill, 2001), pp. 266-267

Cypher, James M. and James L. Dietz. *The Process of Economic Development.* (London: Routledge, 1997)

Dahl, Robert. *Polyarchy: Participation and Opposition.* (New Haven, CT: Yale University Press, 1972)

Dam, Kenneth W. *The Law-Growth Nexus: The Rule of Law and Economic Development.* (Washington, DC: Brookings Institution Press, 2006)

Damania, Richard and Erwin Bulte. "Resources for Sale: Corruption, Democracy, and the Natural Resource Curse". Discussion Paper no. 0320, (Centre for International Economic Studies, University of Adelaide: 2003)

Dasgupta, Partha. "Valuing Objects and Evaluating Policies in Imperfect Economies", *Economic Journal,* 111: 471 (April 2001), pp. 1-29

Davidson, Christopher M. "The United Arab Emirates: Economy First Politics Second," in: *Political Liberalization in the Persian Gulf,* ed., Joshua Teitelbaum, (2009)

Davidson, Christopher M. *Dubai: The Vulnerability of Success.* (New York: Columbia University Press, 2008)

Davidson, Christopher M. *The United Arab Emirates: A Study in Survival.* (Boulder CO: Lynne Rienner Publishers, 2005)

Dawisha, Adeed. "Saudi Arabia's Search for Security". *Adelphi Papers*; no.158. (London: International Institute for Strategic Studies, 1979)

De Melo, Jaime and Arvind Panagarya, (eds.). *New Dimensions in Regional Integration*. (London: Centre for Economic Policy Research, 1993)

Demirtas, Birgul. "Turkish-Syrian Relations: From Friend 'Esad' to Enemy 'Esed'", *Middle East Policy*, vol. 20, no. 1 (Spring 2013), pp. 111-120

De Rosa, Dean A. "Regional Trading Arrangements among Developing Countries: The ASEAN Example". Research Report; 103. (Washington, DC: International Food Policy Research Institute, 1995)

Diwan, Kristin Smith. "Kuwait's Balancing Act", *Foreign Policy* (23 October 2012). http://foreignpolicy.com/2012/10/23/kuwaits-balancing-act/

Dollar, David and Aart Kraay. "Trade, Growth, and Poverty". Policy Research Working Paper; 2615. (Washington, DC: World Bank, 2001)

Donaghy, Rori, "UAE's political show trials", *Open Democracy*, 29 January 2014. http://www.opendemocracy.net/arab-awakening/rori-donaghy/uaes-political-show-trials

Doran, Michael Scott. "The Heirs of Nasser", *Foreign Affairs*, vol. 90, no. 3 (May-June 2011)

Droz-Vincent, Philippe. "State of Barbary (Take Two): From the Arab Spring to the Return of Violence in Syria", *Middle East Journal*, vol. 68, no. 1 (Winter 2014), pp. 33-58

Dumbey, Daniel. "Six Markets to Watch: Turkey. How Erdogan Did It and Could Blow It", *Foreign Affairs* (January-February 2014), pp. 29-34

Dunne, Charles, Stephen McInerney and Karim Mezran, "Libya Needs the U.S. for Its Transition to Democracy", *Washington Post*, 4 May 2013

Durant, Will. *The Age of Faith. The Story of Civilization, Volume IV: A history of medieval civilization—Christian, Islamic, and Judaic—from Constantine to Dante: A.D. 325-1300*. (Simon and Schuster: New York, 1950)

Economic Commission for Africa. *African Governance Report II*. (Oxford: Oxford University Press, 2009)

Ehteshami, Anoushiravan. *After Khomeini: The Iranian Second Republic*. (London: Routledge, 1995)

Elbayar, Kareem. "NGO Laws in Selected Arab States", *International Journal of Not-for-Profit Law*, vol. 7, no. 4 (2005), pp. 3-27

El-Erian, Mohamed A. *When Markets Collide: Investment Strategies for the Age of Global Economic Change*. (New York: McGraw-Hill, 2008)

Eligur, Banu. "Crisis in Turkish-Israeli Relations (December 2008-June 2011): From Partnership to Enmity", *Middle Eastern Studies*, vol. 48 (2012), pp. 429-459

El-Naggar, Said (ed.). *The Determinants of Intra-Regional and Extra-Regional Trade in the Arab Countries*. (Abu-Dhabi: Arab Monetary Fund, 1991)

Esposito, John L. and Dalia Mogahed. *Who Speaks for Islam?: What a Billion Muslims Really Think*. (Washington, DC: Gallup Press, 2008)

Esposito, John L. and James P. Piscatori, "Democratisation and Islam", *Middle East Journal*, vol. 45, no. 3 (Summer 1991), pp. 427-440

Esposito, John L. and R. K. Ramazani. *Iran at the Crossroads*. (New York: Palgrave, 2001)

European External Action Service. *Joint Plan of Action*, Geneva, 24 November 2013. http://eeas.europa.eu/statements/docs/2013/131124_03_en.pdf

Evans, Peter. "The State as Problem and Solution: Predation, Embedded Autonomy, and Structural Change" in: Stephen Haggard and Robert Kaufman (eds.) *The Political Economy of Adjustment*. (Princeton, NJ: Princeton University Press, 1992)

Evans, Peter B. *Embedded Autonomy: State and Industrial Transformation*. (Princeton, NJ: Princeton University Press, 1995)

Faris, David M. "Deep State, Deep Crisis: Egypt and American Policy", *Middle East Policy*, vol. 20, no. 4 (Winter 2013), pp.

Fattah, Hassan M. "Fearful of Iran, Arab Leaders Criticise Militants", *New York Times*, 17 July 2006

Feldman, Noah. *After Jihad: America and the Struggle for Islamic Democracy*. (New York: Farrar, Straus, and Giroux, 2004)

Financial Times. 13 March 2009

Financial Times. "Falling Dollars Puts Pressure on OPEC", 23 July 2007

Financial Times, 7 October 1991

Fildis, Ayse Tekdal. "Roots of Alwaite-Sunni Rivalry in Syria", *Middle East Policy*, vol. 19, no. 2 (Summer 2012), pp. 148-156

Foiroutan, Faezeh. "Regional Integration in Sub-Saharan Africa: Past Experience and Future Prospects", in: *New Dimensions in Regional Integration*, eds., Jaime De Melo and Arvind Panagarya, (1993)

Fortna, Virginia Page and Reyko Huang, "Democratization After Civil War: A Brush-Clearing Exercise", *International Studies Quarterly*, vol. 56, no.4 (December 2102), pp. 801-808

François, Joseph F. and Clinton R. Shiells. *Modeling Trade Policy: Applied General Equilibrium Assessments of North American Free Trade*. (Cambridge, MA: Cambridge University Press, 1994)

Freedman, Lawrence and Efraim Karsh. *The Gulf Conflict, 1990-1991: Diplomacy and War in the New World Order*. (Princeton, NJ: Princeton University Press, 1995)

Freedom House. *Freedom of the Press 2013: Middle East Volatility Amid Global Decline. Selected Data from Freedom House's Annual Press Freedom Index*. (New York: Freedom House, 2013)

Freedom House. *The Worst of the Worst: The World's Most Repressive Societies*. (Washington, DC: Freedom House, 2007)

Freeman, Jr., Chas W. "Coping with Kaleidoscopic Change in the Middle East", *Middle East Policy*, 20: 4 (Winter 2013), pp.29-36

Freilich, Chuck. "Decision Time in Jerusalem", *Journal of International Security Affairs*, no. 18 (Spring 2010), pp.55-64

Friedman, Thomas L. *The World is Flat: A Brief History of the Twenty-First Century*. (New York: Farrar, Straus and Giroux, 2005)

Frum, David and Richard Perle. *An End to Evil: How to Win the War on Terror*. (New York: Random House, 2003)

Fukuyama, Francis. *Trust: The Social Virtues and the Creation of Prosperity*. (London: Penguin Books, 1995)

Furtig, Henner. "Conflict and Cooperation in the Persian Gulf: The Interregional Order and the U.S Policy", *Middle East Journal*, vol. 61, no. 4 (Fall 2007), pp.627-640

Galal, Ahmed and Bernard Hoekman, eds., *Arab Economic Integration: between Hope and Reality*, (Cairo: Egyptian Center for Economic Studies; Washington, DC: Brookings Institution Press, 2003)

Galal, Ahmed and Bernard Hoekman. "Overview", in: Ahmed Galal and Bernard Hoekman, eds., *Arab Economic Integration: between Hope and Reality*, (2003)

Galbraith, Peter W. *The End of Iraq*. (New York: Simon and Schuster, 2006)

Gardner, David. *Last Chance: The Middle East in the Balance*. (London: I.B. Tauris, 2009)

Garrity, Patrick J. *Why the Gulf War Still Matters: Foreign Perspectives on the War and the Future of International Security*. (Los Alamos, NM: Centre for National Security Studies, 1993)

Gause III, F. Gregory. *Oil Monarchies: Domestic and Security Challenges in the Arab Gulf States*. (New York: Council on Foreign Relations Press, 1994)

Gause III, F. Gregory. "The Illogic of Dual Containment," *Foreign Affairs*, (March-April 1994)

Gavrielides, Nicolas. "Tribal Democracy: the Anatomy of Parliamentary Elections in Kuwait" in: Linda Layne, ed., *Elections in the Middle East: Implications of Recent Trends*, (Boulder, Colo.: Westview Press, 1987)

Ghani, Ashraf and Clare Lockhart. *Fixing Failed States: A Framework for Rebuilding a Fractured World*. (New York: Oxford University Press, 2009)

Glaeser, Edward et al. "Coase Versus the Coasians," *Quarterly Journal of Economics*, vol. 116, no. 3 (2001), pp.853-899

Glanz, James. "A Little Democracy or A Genie Unbolted", *The New York Times*, 29 January 2006

Gold, Dore. "Middle East Proliferation, Israeli Missile Defense and the ABM Treaty Debate," *Jerusalem Letter*, no. 430 (15 May 2000), pp. 5-6.

Goldberg, Jacob. "Saudi Arabia and the Iranian Revolution: the Religious Dimension," in: David Menashri, ed., *The Iranian Revolution and the Muslim World* (Boulder, CO: West View Press, 1990), pp.

Goldberg, Jeffrey. "Breaking Ranks: What Turned Brent Scowcroft against the Bush Administration", *The New Yorker*, (31 October 2005)

Gresh, Alain. "The World Invades Saudi Arabia". *Le Monde diplomatique*, and *Guardian Weekly*, October 2013

Gros, Jean-Germain and Olga Prokopovych, *When Reality Contradicts Rhetoric: World Bank Lending Practices in Developing Countries in Historical, Theoretical and Empirical Perspectives*, Monograph Series (Dakar: CODESRIA, 2005)

Halliday, Fred. *Arabia Without Sultans*. (London: Saqi Books, 2002)

Hamdan, Sara. "Oman Offers Some Lessons to a Region Embroiled in Protest", *The New York Times*, (6 April 2011)

Hamzawi, Amr. "The Saudi Labyrinth: Is there a Political Opening?" in: Choucaire-Vizoso, eds., *Beyond the Façade: Political Reform in the Arab World*

Hanieh, Adam. *Capitalism and Class in the Arab Gulf States*. (New York: Palgrave MacMillan, 2011)

Harrison, Lawrence. *The Central Liberal Truth*. (Oxford: Oxford University Press, 2006)

Harvard, Sarah. "Noam Chomsky on Crisis in Egypt: "It's Pretty Hard to Get Out"", DL Magazine (2 September 2013), http://dlmagazine.org/2013/09/exclusive-interview-noam-chomsky-crisis-egypt-its-pretty-hard-out/

Hawley, Donald. *The Emirates: Witness to a Metamorphosis*. (Norwich: Michael Russell, 2007)

Hawley, Donald. *The Trucial States*. (London: Allen and Unwin, 1970)

Hay, Rupert. *The Persian Gulf States*. (Washington, DC: Middle East Institute, 1959)

Heard-Bey, Frauke. *From Trucial States to United Arab Emirates*. (London: Longman, 1982)

Heinonen, Olli. "Unthinkable: Iran, the Bomb, and American Strategy by Kenneth M. Pollack (Review)", *Middle East Journal*, 68:1 (Winter 2014)

Herb, Michael. *All in the Family: Absolutism, Revolution, and Democracy in the Middle Eastern Monarchies*. SUNY Series in Middle Eastern Studies. (New York: State University of New York Press, 1999)

Herb, Michael. "Kuwait: The Obstacle of Parliamentary Politics," in: *Political Liberalization in the Persian Gulf*, ed., Joshua Teitelbaum, (2009)

Herb, Michael. "A nation of Bureaucrats: Political Participation and Economic Diversification in Kuwait and the United Arab Emirates", *International Journal of Middle East Studies*, 41:3 (2009), pp. 375-395

Herin, Jan."Rules of Origin and Differences between Tariff Levels in EFTA and in the EC", Occasional Paper no. 13, (Geneva: European Free Trade Association (EFTA), February 1986)

Hersh, Seymour. "The Red Line and the Rat Line. Seymour M. Hersh on Obama, Erdoğan and the Syrian rebels", *London Review of Books*, vol. 36, no. 8 (17 April 2014), pp. 21-24. http://www.lrb.co.uk/v36/n08/seymour-m-hersh/the-red-line-and-the-rat-line

Hertog, Steffen. "The Private Sector and Reform in the Gulf Cooperation Council", LSE Kuwait Programme research paper no. 30 (July 2013)

Hertog, Steffen. "The Cost of Counter -revolution in the GCC", *Foreign Policy* (3 June 2011)

Hertog, Steffen. *Princes, Brokers, and Bureaucrats: Oil and the State in Saudi Arabia*. (Ithaca, CA; London: Cornell University Press, 2010)

Hertog, Steffen. "The GCC and Arab Economic Integration: A New Paradigm", *Middle East Policy*, vol. 14, no. 1 (2007), pp. 52-68

Herzog, Michael. "Can Hamas be Tamed?", *Foreign Affairs* (March-April 2006), pp. 83-94

Heydemann, Steven. "Syria and the Future of Authoritarianism", *Journal of Democracy*, vol. 24, no. 4 (October 2013), p.

Hinnebusch, Raymond and Anoushirvan Ehteshami (eds.). *The Foreign Policies of Middle East States*. (Boulder, CO: Lynne Rienner, 2002)

Hinnebusch, Raymond. "The Middle East Regional System", in: Raymond Hinnebusch and Anoushirvan Ehteshami (eds.), *The Foreign Policies of Middle East States* (2002), p. 50

Ho, S. "South Korea and Taiwan". Asian Survey (21 December 1981)

Holden, David and Richard Johns. *The House of Saud: The Rise and Rule of the Most Powerful Dynasty in the Arab World*. (London: Pan Books, 1982)

House Committee on International Relations (HCIR). *United States Arms Policies in the Persian Gulf and Red Sea Areas*. Report of a staff survey mission to Ethiopia, Iran and the Arabian Peninsula, 95th Congress, (Washington, DC: HCIR, 1977)

Humphreys, Macartan and Martin E. Sandbu, "The Political Economy of Natural Resources" in: Macartan Humphreys, Jeffrey D. Sachs and Joseph E. Stiglitz (eds.). *Escaping the Resource Curse. Initiative for Policy Dialogue at Columbia*. (New York: Columbia University Press, 2007)

Hunter, Shireen T. *Iran after Khomeini*. (New York: Preager, 1992)

Hunter, Shireen T. "Iran and Syria: From Hostility to Limited Alliance," in: Hooshang Amirahmadi and Nader Entessar (eds.). *Iran and the Arab World*. (New York: Palgrave Macmillan, 1990)

Huntington, Samuel. *Who Are We: The Challenges to America National Identity*. (New York: Simon and Schuster, 2004)

Huntington, Samuel. "The Clash of Civilizations," *Foreign Affairs*, vol. 72, no. 1 (Summer 1993), pp. 22-49

International Crisis Group. *Popular Protest in North Africa and the Middle East (VIII): Bahrain's Rocky Road to Reform*, Middle East Report no. 111 (28 July 2011), pp. 9-14. http://www.crisisgroup.org/en/regions/middle-east-north-africa/iraq-iran-gulf/bahrain/111-popular-protest-in-north-africa-and-the-middle-east-viii-bahrains-rocky-road-to-reform.aspx

International Crisis Group. *Iran in Iraq: How Much Influence?*, Middle East Report, no. 38 (21 March 2005)

International Crisis Group. *Can Saudi Arabia Reform Itself?*, Middle East Report no. 28 (14 July 2004)

International Federation for Human Rights (FIDH). "UAE: Unfair Trial, Unjust Sentences", 3 July 2013. https://www.fidh.org/International-Federation-for-Human-Rights/north-africa-middle-east/united-arab-emirates/uae-unfair-trial-unjust-sentences-13590

International Monetary Fund. *Regional Economic Outlook: Middle East and Central Asia*. (Washington, DC: International Monetary Fund, 2010)

International Monetary Fund (IMF), *Arab Republic of Egypt: 2010 Article IV Consultation- Staff Report*. IMF Country Report no. 10/94 (April 2010)

International Monetary Fund. *Regional Economic Outlook: Middle East and Central Asia*. (Washington, DC: International Monetary Fund, 2008)

International Monetary Fund. *Regional Economic Outlook: Middle East and Central Asia*. (Washington, DC: International Monetary Fund, 2000)

International Monetary Fund. *World Economic Outlook 1998*. (Washington, DC: International Monetary Fund, 1998)

International Monetary Fund. *Annual Report on Exchange Arrangements and Exchange Restrictions*. (Washington, DC: International Monetary Fund, 1998)

Islamic Republic News Agency (IRNA), 25 May 2004

Jablonski, Wanda. "Interview with Tariki," *Petroleum Week*, (22 February 1957)

Jansen, Michael. "Will Diplomacy Get a Chance?", *Panorama: Gulf Today* (20 September 2013), pp. 40-41

Jawara, Fatoumata and Aileen Kwa. *Behind the Scenes at the WTO*. (London: Zed Books, 2004)

Jerusalem Post. "Iran Looms as a Growing Strategic Threat for Israel", 21 November 1991

Kahler, Miles. *International Institutions and the Political Economy of Integration. Integrating National Economies*. (Washington, DC: Brookings Institution, 1995)

Kalkman, Jaap and Alexander Keller. "Global Petrochemicals: Who is Really Benefiting from the Growth in the New World?", (Roland Berger Strategy Consultants: November 2012), http://www.rolandberger.com/media/publications/2012-11-11-rbsc-pub Global_Petrochemicals.html

Kalman, Matthew. "Israel Set War Plan More than a Year Ago", *San Francisco Chronicle*, 21 July 2006

Kamrava, Mehran. *Qatar: Small State, Big Politics*. (Ithaca, CA; London: Cornell University Press, 2013)

Kandeel, Amal A. "Regional Upheaval: The Stakes for the GCC", *Middle East Policy*, vol. 20, no. 4 (Winter 2013), pp. 59-61

Kapiszewski, Andrezej. "Arabs Versus Asian Migrant Workers in the GCC states". (United Nations Expert Group Meeting on International Migration and Development in the Arab Region: Beirut, 2006) http://www.un.org/esa/population/meetings/EGM_Ittmig_Arab/P02_Kapiszewski.pdf

Kaplan, Fred. *Daydream Believers: How a Few Grand Ideas Wrecked American Power*. (New Jersey: John Wiley and Sons, 2008)

Karake-Shalhuob, Zeinab. "GCC Sovereign Wealth Funds and Islamic Finance: Financial Foundations for the Post-Oil Gulf" in: *The New Post Oil Arab Gulf*, eds., Nabil A. Sultan, David Weir and Zeinab Karake-Shalhoub. (London: Saqi Books, 2011)

Katz, Mark N. "Russia and the Conflict in Syria: Four Myths", *Middle East Policy*, vol. 20, no. 2 (Summer 2013), pp.

Kechichian, Joseph K. "The Role of the Ulama in the Politics of an Islamic State: The Case of Saudi Arabia", *International Journal of Middle East Studies*, vol. 18, 1986, pp.53-71

Kechichian, Joseph K. "The Gulf Cooperation Council: The Search for Security", *Third World Quarterly*, vol. 7, no. 4 (1985), pp. 853-881

Kelly, J. B. *Arabia, the Gulf, and the West: A Critical View of the Arabs and their Oil Policy*. (New York: Basic Books, 1980)

Keough, Donald R. *The Ten Commandments for Business Failure*. (New York: Portfolio, 2008)

Kerrou, Mohamed. "Tunisia's Historic Step Toward Democracy", Carnegie (17 April 2014). http://carnegie-mec.org/2014/04/22/tunisia-s-historic-step-toward-democracy/hd9t

Khan, Muqtedar. "Islam, Democracy and Islamism after the Counterrevolution in Egypt", *Middle East Policy*, vol. 21, no. 1 (Spring 2014), pp.75-86

Khoury, Nabeel A. "The Arab Cold War Revisited: The Regional Impact of the Arab Spring", *Middle East Policy*, vol. 20, no. 2 (Summer 2013)

Kimche, Davide. *The Last Option: After Nasser, Arafat, and Saddam Hussein: The Quest for Peace in the Middle East*. (New York: Maxwell Macmillan International, 1991)

King R. G. and R. Levine, "Financial Intermediation and Economic Development", in: *Capital Markets and Financial Intermediation*, eds. Colin Mayer and Xavier Vives. (Cambridge, MA: Cambridge University Press, 1993)

King R. G. and R. Levine, "Financial Intermediation and Economic Development", in: *Capital Markets and Financial Intermediation*, eds. Colin Mayer and Xavier Vives. (Cambridge, MA: Cambridge University Press, 1993)

Kinzer, Stephen. *All the Shah's Men: An American Coup and the Roots of Middle East Terror*. (Hoboken, NJ: J. Wiley and Sons, 2003)

Kissinger, Henry. *The Autonomy of Two Major Crises*. (New York: Simon and Schuster, 2004)

Kissinger, Henry. *Diplomacy*. (New York: Simon and Schuster, 1994)

Klare, Michael T. *Blood and Oil: The Dangers and Consequences of America's Growing Petroleum Dependency*. (New York: Metropolitan Books, 2004)

Klare, Michael T. *Rising Powers, Shrinking Powers: The New Geopolitics of Energy*. (New York: Metropolitan Books, Henry Holt and Company, 2008)

Kolstad, Ivar and Tina Soeide. "Corruption in Natural Resource Management: Implications for Policy Makers." *Resources Policy*: 34: 4, 2009. pp. 214-226

Kolstad, Ivar and Arne Wiig. "Is Transparency the Key to Reducing Corruption in Resource Rich Countries?". *World Development*: vol. 37, no. 3, 2009 pp. 521-532

Konstantinov, Ivan. "Genie of Islamism Comes out of the Bottle", *Nezavisimaia Gazeta*, 13 March 2012

Kostiner, Joseph. "GCC Perceptions of Collective Security in the Post-Saddam Era", in: *International Politics of the Persian Gulf*, ed., Mehran Kamrava (New York: Syracuse, 2011)

Krane, Jim. *City of Gold: Dubai and the Dream of Capitalism*. (New York: St. Martin's Press, 2009)

Krugman, Paul. *The Return of Depression Economics and the Crisis of 2008*. (New York: W.W. Norton and Company, 2009)

Kurzman, Charles. "Pro-US Fatwa", *Middle East Policy*, vol. 10, no. 3 (Fall 2003), pp. 155-166

Lacroix, Stephane. "Comparing the Arab Revolts: Is Saudi Arabia Immune?", *Journal of Democracy*, vol. 22, no. 4 (October 2011), pp.48-59

Lal, Deepak. "Why Growth Rates Differ: The Political Economy of Social Capability in 21 Developing Countries", in: *Social Capability and Long-Run Economic Growth*, eds., Bon Ho Koo and Dwight H. Perkins. (Basingstoke: MacMillan, 1995)

Landes, David. *The Wealth and Poverty of Nations*. (New York: Norton and Company, 1999)

La Porta, Rafael et al., "Related Lending," *Quarterly Journal of Economics*, 118: 1 (2003), pp

Lesch, Ann M. "Troubled Political Transitions: Tunisia, Egypt, and Libya", *Middle East Policy*, vol. 21, no. 1 (Spring 2014), pp. 62-74

Lesser, Ian O. "Weapons of Mass Destruction in the Middle East: Proliferation Dynamics and Strategic Consequences," in: *The Future Security Environment in the Middle East*, eds., Nora Bensahel and Daniel Byman (2004)

Levine, Ross. "Financial Development and Economic Growth: Views and Agenda", *Journal of Economic Literature*, vol. 35, no. 2 (1997), pp. 688-726

Lewis, Bernard. *Faith and Power*. (Oxford: Oxford University Press, 2010)

Lewis, Bernard. "Freedom and Justice in the Modern Middle East", *Foreign Affairs* vol. 84, no. 3, (May-June 2005), pp. 36-51

Lewis, Bernard. *What Went Wrong? The Clash between Islam and Modernity in the Middle East*. (London: Weidenfeld Nicolson, 2002)

Li, Shaomin, Shuhe Li and W. Zhang. "The Road to Capitalism: Competition and Institutional Change in China". *Journal of Comparative Economics*: vol. 28, no. 2, 2001.

Lindsay, James M. and Ray Takeyh, "After Iran Gets the Bomb", *Foreign Affairs,* vol. 89, no. 2 (March-April 2010)

Lippman, Thomas W. *Inside the Mirage: America's Fragile Partnership with Saudi Arabia*. (Boulder, CO: West View Press, 2004)

Long, David E. *The United States and Saudi Arabia*. (Boulder, CO: West View Press, 1985)

Lorimer, John G. *Gazetteer of the Persian Gulf, Oman and Central Arabia*. 19 vols. (Calcutta: Superintendent Government Printing, 1915)

Luers, William, Thomas R. Pickering and Jim Walsh, "For a New Approach to Iran", *New York Review Books* (15 August 2013)

Mabro, Robert. (ed.). *OPEC and the World Oil Market: The Genesis of the 1986 Price Crisis*. (Oxford, UK: Oxford University Press-Oxford Institute for Energy Studies, 1986)

MacFarquhar, Neil. "Saudi Cash is Key to Quiet in the Kingdom", *The International Herald Tribune*, 10 June 2011, p. 4

MacFarquhar, Neil. "Saudi Scramble in Bid to Contain Regional Unrest", *New York Times*, 28 May 2011, p. 1

Mackay, Neil. "Bush Planned Iraq 'Regime Change' before Becoming President," *Sunday Herald*, 15 June 2002

Mahbubani, Kishore. *The New Asian Hemisphere: The Irresistible Shift of Global Power to the East.* (New York: Public Affairs, 2008)

Malik, Monica. "The Role of the Private Sector," in: *Economic Development in Saudi Arabia*, eds., Rodney Wilson et al. (London: Routledge Curzon, 2004)

Malik, Monica and Tim Niblock, "Saudi Arabia's Economy: The Challenge of Reform", in: *Saudi Arabia in the Balance: Political Economy, Society, Foreign Affairs*, eds., Paul Aarts and Gerd Nonneman (New York: New York University Press, 2005), pp. 128-138

Malley, Robert and Peter Harling, "Beyond Moderates and Militants", *Foreign Affairs* (September-October 2010), pp. 18-29

Maloney, Suzanne. "Obama's Counter Productive New Iran Sanctions: How Washington Is Sliding Toward Regime Change", *Foreign Affairs* (5 January 2012)

Marr, Phoebe. *The Modern History of Iraq.* 2nd ed. (Boulder, CO: West View Press, 2004)

Marshall, Monty G. "Polity IV Project: Political Regime Characteristics and Transitions, 1800-2009," Centre for Systemic Peace and Colorado State University, http://www.systemicpeace.org/polity/polity4.htm

Matthiesen, Toby. *Sectarian Gulf.* (Stanford, CA: Stanford Briefs, 2013)

Maugeri, Leonardo. *The Age of Oil: The Mythology, History, and Future of the World's Most Controversial Resource.* (London: Praeger, 2006)

McKinsey and Company, "Public Service Broadcasting around the World: A McKinsey Report for the BBC" (January 1999)

Mead, Walter Russell. "The New Israel and the Old: Why Gentile Americans Back the Jewish State", *Foreign Affairs* vol. 87, no. 4 (July-August 2008), pp. 28-46

Mehlum, Halvor, Karl Moene and Ragnar Torvik. "Institutions and the Resource Curse", *The Economic Journal*, 116:508, (January 2006) pp. 1-20

Melia, Thomas O. *The People of Bahrain Want to Participate in the King's Political Reform Project: A Report on Focus Groups Conducted in the Kingdom of Bahrain*, (Washington: National Democratic Institute, July 2002)

Micco, Alejandro, Ernesto H. Stein and Guillermo Luis Ordonez, "The Currency Union Effects on Trade: Early Evidence on EMU", *Economic Policy*, vol. 18, no. 37 (2003), pp. 315-356

Miller, Aaron David. "Cairo Wasn't Obama's to Lose", in Mark Lynch, Susan B. Glasser, and Blake Hounshell, eds., *Revolution in the Arab World: Tunisia, Egypt and the unmaking of an era.* A Special Report from Foreign Policy, (Washington, D.C.: Slate Group, 2011)

Monshipouri, Mahmood and Manochehr Dorraj, "Iran's Foreign Policy: A Shifting Strategic Landscape", *Middle East Policy*, 20:4 (Winter 2013)

Muasher, Marwan. "A Path to Democracy", *New York Times*, 4 June 2003

Murphy, Emma. "The Impact of the Arab-Israeli Peace Process on the International Security and Economic Relations in the Persian Gulf," *Iranian Journal of International Affairs*, vol. 2 (Summer 1996)

Muslih, Muhammad and Augustus Richard Norton, "The Need for Arab Democracy", *Foreign Policy*, no. 83 (Summer 1991)

Nabulsi, Shaker. "Modernity Vies with Tradition as Saudi Debate the Future", in: *The Kingdom: Saudi Arabia and the Challenges of the 21st Century*, eds., Joshua Craze and Mark Huband, (2009)

Nasr, Vali. *The Shi'a Revival: How Conflicts within Islam will Shape the Future.* (New York: W.W. Norton, 2006)

Neuman, Ronald E. "Bahrain: A Very Complicated Little Island", *Middle East Policy*, 20:4 (Winter 2013), pp.

Newsweek, 21 May 1973, pp. 40-44

Niblock, Tim and Monica Malik. *The Political Economy of Saudi Arabia*. (London: Routledge, 2007)

Noland, Marcus and Howard Pack. *The Arab Economies in a Changing World*. (Washington, DC: Peterson Institute for International Economics, 2007)

Oatley, Thomas and Jason Yackeel. "American Interests and IMF Lending", *International Politics*, vol. 41, no. 3 (2004), pp. 415-429

Okruhlik, Gwenn. "The Identity Politics of Kuwait's Election", *Foreign Policy* (8 February 2012). http://foreignpolicy.com/2012/02/08/the-identity-politics-of-kuwaits-election/

Olmert, Josef. "Israel and Alawite Syria: The Odd Couple of the Middle East?", *Israel Journal of Foreign Affairs*, vol. 7, no. 1 (2013), pp. 17-25

Onley, James. "Britain's Informal Empire in the Gulf: 1820-1971". *Journal of Social Affairs* (American University of Sharjah): vol. 22, no. 87, (2005)

Ottaway, David. "The King and Us: US-Saudi Relations in the Wake of 9/11", *Foreign Affairs* (May-June 2009), p. 123.

Ottaway, Marina. "Evaluating Middle East Reform", in: Marina Ottaway and Julia Choucaire-Vizoso, eds., *Beyond the Façade: Political Reform in the Arab World*, (2008)

Ottaway, Marina and Julia Choucaire-Vizoso, eds., *Beyond the Façade: Political Reform in the Arab World*, (Washington, DC: Carnegie Endowment for International Peace, 2008)

Owen, Nicholas. *Economies of Scale, Competitiveness, and Trade Patterns Within the European Community*. (New York: Oxford University Press, 1983)

Page, John M. "The East Asian Miracle: An Introduction". World Development: vol. 22, no. 4, April 1994

Palmer, Michael A. *Guardians of the Gulf*. (New York: Simon and Schuster, 1992)

Pang, Chien-Kuo. *The State and Economic Transformation: The Taiwan Case. Developing Economies of the Third World*. (New York: Garland Pub., 1992)

Parra, Francisco. *Oil Politics: A Modern History of Oil*. (London: I.B. Tauris, 2004)

Parsi, Trita. *Treacherous Alliance: The Secret Dealings of Israel, Iran, and the U. S.* (New Haven, CT: Yale University Press, 2007)

Patch, Chester J. (Jr.). *Arming the Free World: The Origins of the United States Military Assistance Program, 1945-1950*. (Chapel Hill, NC: University of North Carolina Press, 1991)

Peres, Shimon and Arye Naor. *The New Middle East*. (New York: Henry Holt, 1993)

Peterson, J. E. "Bahrain: Reform – Promise and Reality," in: *Political Liberalization in the Persian Gulf*, ed., Joshua Teitelbaum, (2009)

Picco, Giandomenico. *Man Without a Gun: One Diplomat's Secret Struggle to Free the Hostages, Fight Terrorism, and End a War*. (New York: Random House, 1999)

Pilbeam, Keith. *International Finance*. 3rd ed. (New York: Palgrave Macmillan, 2006)

Pipes, Daniel. "The Alawi Capture of Power in Syria", *Middle Eastern Studies*, vol. 25, no. 4 (October 1989), pp. 429-450

Pitsuwan, Surin. "Dr. Supachai's Long and Winding Road to Geneva", *Bangkok Post*, 8 August 2002

Pollack, Kenneth M. *A Path Out of the Desert: A Grand Strategy for America in the Middle East*. (New York: Random House, 2008)

Pollack, Kenneth M. *The Persian Puzzle: The Conflict between Iran and America*. (New York: Random House, 2004)

Pollack, Kenneth. "Securing the Gulf". *Foreign Affairs*, vol. 82, no. 4, (July-August 2003)

Posen, Barry R. et al., "The Containment Conundrum: How Dangerous is a Nuclear Iran?", *Foreign Affairs* (July-August 2010)

Press TV. "Bahrain: America's Big Paradox", 17 March 2011, http://edition.presstv.ir/detail/170463.html

Project for the New American Century, *Rebuilding America's Defenses: Strategy, Forces and Resources for a New Century*, A Report of the Project for the New American Century, (September 2000)

Publish What You Pay (PWYP). http://www.publishwhatyoupay.org/

Przeworski, Adam. *Democracy and the Market: Political and Economic Reforms in Eastern Europe and Latin America. Studies in Rationality and Social Change.* (New York: Cambridge University Press, 1991)

Quandt, William B. *Saudi Arabia in the 1980s: Foreign Policy, Security, and Oil.* (Washington, DC: The Brooking Institutions, 1981)

Rabi, Uzi. "Oman: Say Yes to Oman, Say No to the Tribe," in: *Political Liberalization in the Persian Gulf*, ed., Joshua Teitelbaum, (2009)

Rahimi, Babak. "Iran's Declining Influence in Iraq", *Washington Quarterly* (Winter 2012), pp. 25-40

Ramazani, R. K. "Move Iran Outside the Axis," *Christian Science Monitor*, 19 August 2002

Ramazani, R. K. "Review of Mahmoud Sariolgjalam's: The Foreign Policy of the Islamic Republic," *Discourse: An Iranian Quarterly*, vol. 2 (2001)

Ramazani, R. K. "The Emerging Arab-Indian Rapprochement: Towards an Integrated US Policy in the Middle East", *Middle East Policy* (June 1998)

Ramazani, R. K. "Security in the Persian Gulf", *Foreign Affairs*, vol. 4 (1979)

Rashid, Ahmed. *Taliban: The Power of Militant Islam in Afghanistan and Beyond*, revised ed., (London: I. B. Tauris, 2008)

Reuters. "Gulf Arab States Should Cut State Spending Growth: IMF", (29 October 2012)

Rice, Condoleezza. Remarks at the American University in Cairo (20 June 2005). http://2001-2009.state.gov/secretary/rm/2005/48328.htm

Rice, Condoleezza. "Campaign 2000: Promoting the National Interest", *Foreign Affairs*, vol. 79, no. 1 (January-February 2000)

Richards, Alan. "Economic Reform in the Middle East: the Challenge to Governance" in: *The Future Security Environment in the Middle East*, eds., Nora Bensahel and Daniel Byman (2004)

Ricupero, Rubens. "What Policy Makers Should Know About Regionalism", keynote address presented at World Bank Conference on What Policy Makers Should Know About Regionalism, Geneva, May 1998

Rivlin, Paul. *Arab Economies in the Twenty-First Century*. (Cambridge, MA: Cambridge University Press, 2009)

Roberts, Sue Lloyd. "Saudi Arabia Show of Force Stifles 'Day of Rage' Protests", BBC Newsnight (11 March 2011). http://news.bbc.co.uk/1/hi/programmes/newsnight/9422550.stm

Robinson, Glenn E. "Being Yasir Arafat: A Portrait of Palestine's President," *Foreign Affairs*, 82:6 (November-December 2003)

Robson, Peter. *The Economics of International Integration*. 3rd ed. (London: Allen and Unwin, 1987)

Roemer, Michael. *Fishing for Growth: Export-Led Development in Peru, 1950-1967*. (Cambridge, MA: Harvard University Press, 1970)

Rose, David. "The Gaza Bombshell", *Vanity Fair*, April 2008

Rosen, Barry. *Iran Since the Revolution*. (New York: Columbia University Press, 1985)

Rosman-Stollman, Elisheva. "Qatar: Liberalization as Foreign Policy," in: *Political Liberalization in the Persian Gulf*, ed., Joshua Teitelbaum, (2009)

Ross, Michael L. "Does Oil Hinder Democracy?", *World Politics*, vol. 53 (April 2001), pp. 325-361

Rubin, Barry. "The Containment Conundrum: The Right Kind of Containment", *Foreign Affairs*, vol. 89, no. 4 (July-August 2010), pp.

Rubin, Barry. "Why Israel Shouldn't Attack Iranian Nuclear Installations Unless it Has to Do So", Rubin Center for Research in International Affairs (14 July 2010). http://www.rubincenter.org/2010/07/why-israel-shouldnt-attack-iranian-nuclear-installations/

Rugh, William. *The Arab Press: News Media and Political Process in the Arab World*. (Syracuse, NY: Syracuse University Press, 1979)

Rutherford, Thomas F. and Josephina Martinez, "Welfare Effects of Regional Trade Integration of Central America and Caribbean Nations with NAFTA and MERCOSUR", *World Economy*, vol. 23 (2003), pp. 799-825

Ryan, Curtis R. "Jordanian Policy and the Arab Spring", *Middle East Policy*, vol. 21, no. 1 (Spring 2014), pp.144-153

Ryan, Curtis R. "Jordan's Unfinished Journey: Parliamentary Elections and the State of Reform", POMED, Policy Brief (March 2013)

Sachs, Jeffrey. *The End of Poverty: Economic Possibilities for Our Time*. (New York: Penguin Press, 2005)

Sadowski, Yahya. *Scuds or Butter?: The Political Economy of Arms Control in the Middle East.* (Washington, DC: Brookings Institution, 1993)

Sager, Michelle A. "Regional Trade Agreements: Their Role and the Economic Impact on Trade Flows", *The World Economy*, vol. 20 (1997), pp. 239-252

Salem, Paul. "Kuwait: Politics in a participatory Emirate" in: Marina Ottaway and Julia Choucaire-Vizoso, eds., *Beyond the Façade: Political Reform in the Arab World*, (2008)

Sampson, Anthony. *The Seven Sisters: The Great Oil Companies and the World the Shaped.* (New York: Viking Press, 1975)

Sands, Philippe. *Lawless World: America and the Making and Breaking of Global Rules from FDR's Atlantic Charter to George W. Bush's Illegal War.* (New York: Viking, 2005)

Sapir, Andre. "The European Community: A Case of Successful Integration? A comment", in: *New Dimensions in Regional Integration*, eds., Jaime De Melo and Arvind Panagarya, (1993)

Saudi Gazette, 23 August 2004

Saudi Gazette, 21 May 2008

Saudi Press Agency. "Gulf Cooperation Council Sets Up 20 bn-dollar Fund for Bahrain: Oman Projects", 11 March 2011

Sayigh, Yezid. "The Assad Regime: Winning on Points", Carnegie Endowment for International Peace (10 April 2014). http://carnegie-mec.org/2014/04/10/assad-regime-winning-on-points/ h7vJ

Schiff, Maurice and L. Alan Winters. *Regional Integration and Development*. (Washington, DC: International Bank for Reconstruction and Development/The World Bank, 2003)

Schiff, Maurice and L. Alan Winters. "Regional Integration, Security and Welfare", in: *Regionalism and Development: Report of the European Commission and World Bank Seminar, Brussels 2 June 1997.* Studies Series (European Commission); no. 1 (Luxembourg: Office for Official Publications of the European Communities; Lanham, MD: Bernan Associates [Distributor], 1998)

Schumpeter, Joseph A. *The Theory of Economic Development: An Inquiry into Profits, Capital, Credit, Interest, and the Business Cycle.* Harvard Economic Studies; vol. 46. (Cambridge; MA: Harvard University Press, 1932)

Sciolino, Elaine. "Ally's Future: US Pondering Saudi Vulnerability," *The New York Times*, 11 November 2001

Senate Armed Services Committee (SASC), *Crisis in the Persian Gulf Region: U.S. Policy Options and Implications*, Hearings 101st Congress, (Washington, D.C., U.S. Government printing Office, 1990)

Sexton, Sarah. "Trading Health Care Away? GATS, Public Service and Privatization", *South Bulletin*, vol. 15 (July 2001)

Sharansky, Natan. *Defending Identity: Its Indispensable Role in Protecting Democracy.* (New York: Public Affairs, 2008)

Shaxson, Nicholas. *Poisoned Wells: The Dirty Politics of African Oil.* (New York: Palgrave MacMillan, 2007)

Sherbiny, Naiem A. and Mark A. Tessler (eds.). *Arab Oil: Impact on the Arab Countries and Global Implications*. Praeger Special Studies in International Business, Finance, and Trade. (New York: Praeger, 1976)

Singer, David E. "Big Challenges Remain Despite Progress on Iran", *The New York Times*, 29 September 2013

Skocpol, Theda. "Bringing the State Back In: Strategies of Analysis in Current Research" in: *Bringing the State Back In*, eds., Peter Evans, Dietrich Rueschemeyer and Theda Skocpol. (Cambridge, CA: Cambridge University Press, 1985)

Stanislaw, Joseph and Daniel Yergin. "Oil: Reopening the Door", *Foreign Affairs* (September-October 1993)

Staples, Brian R. "Trade Facilitation", Draft paper prepared for the WTO 2000 Conference, Geneva, (Washington DC: World Bank, 1998)

Stauffer, T. "Income Measurement in Arab States" in: Beblawi and Liciani, eds. *The Rentier State in the Arab World*, (1987) pp. 22-48

Stepan, Alfred and Juan J. Linz, "Democratization Theory and the 'Arab Spring'", *Journal of Democracy*, vol. 24, no. 2 (April 2013), pp. 15-30

Stepan, Alfred, Juan J. Linz and Juli F. Minoves, "Democratic Parliamentary Monarchies", *Journal of Democracy*, vol. 25, no. 2 (April 2014), pp. 35-51

Stevens, Paul. "Co-operation between Producers and Consumers", in: *Handbook of Oil Politics*, ed., Robert E. Looney. (London: Routledge: Taylor and Francis Group, 2012)

Stiglitz, Joseph E. *Freefall: America, Free Markets, and the Sinking of the World Economy*. (New York: W.W. Norton, 2010)

Stiglitz, Joseph E. *Globalization and Its Discontents*. (New York: W.W. Norton and Company, 2002)

Stiglitz, Joseph E. et al., *The Stiglitz Report: Reforming the International Monetary and Financial Systems in the Wake of the Global Crisis*, (New York: New Press, 2010)

Stoakes, Frank. "Social and Political Change in the Third World: Some Peculiarities of Oil-Producing Principalities of the Persian Gulf," in: *The Arabian Peninsula: Society and Politics*, ed., Derek Hopwood. Studies on Modern Asia and Africa, no. 8, (London: Allen and Unwin, 1972)

Stockholm International Peace Research Institute (SIPRI). Military Expenditure Database

Stocking, George W. *Middle East Oil: A Study in Political and Economic Controversy*. (Knoxville, TN: Vanderbilt University Press, 1970)

Streeten, Paul. "Governance" in: *Current Issues in Economic Development: An Asian Perspective*, eds., M. G. Quibria and J. Malcolm Dowling. (Oxford: Oxford University Press, 1996)

Stucliffe, Robert B. *Industry and Underdevelopment*. (London: Addison-Wesley Publishing Company, 1971)

Sturn, Michael, et al. "The Gulf Cooperation Council Countries: Economic Structure, Recent Developments, and the Role in the Global Economy". *Occasional Paper Series*, no. 92, (European Central Bank: 2008)

Sussman, Anna Louie. "Repression in the United Arab Emirates", *The Nation*, 1 June 2011. http://www.thenation.com/article/161058/repression-united-arab-emirates

Takeyh, Ray. *Hidden Iran: Paradox and Power in the Islamic Republic*. (Washington, DC: Times Books, 2006)

Telhami, Shibley. "2006 Annual Arab Public Opinion Survey", Brookings Institute, (February 8, 2007)

Teitelbaum, Joshua (ed.). *Political Liberalization in the Persian Gulf*. New York: Columbia University Press, (2009)

Teitelbaum, Joshua. "Understanding Political Liberalization in the Gulf: An Introduction," in: *Political Liberalization in the Persian Gulf*, ed., Joshua Teitelbaum, (2009)

The National. "IMF Tells Kuwait to Cut Spending or Risk Running Out of Oil Money", (17 May 2012)

The National, 1 December 2011

The New York Times. "In Bid to End Crisis, Kuwait's Parliament Is Dissolved", 7 October 2012.

http://www.nytimes.com/2012/10/08/world/middleeast/in-bid-to-end-crisis-kuwaits-parliament-is-dissolved.html?_r=0

The New York Times, 11 May 1993

The New York Times, 9 August 1990

The New York Times, 3 April 1986

The New York Times, 10 October 1981

The Peninsula Qatar, 1 June 2003

The Peninsula Qatar, 5 October 2002

The Toronto Star. "Inside the Coddled Kingdom", 17 February 2011

The Washington Post, 27 April 2007

Time. "The Bush-Saudi Axis", 15 September 2003

Times of Oman, 3 October 2003

Todaro, Michael P. and Stephen C. Smith. *Economic Development*. (New York: Addison-Wesley, 2003)

Transparency International. *Corruption Perceptions Index 2013*. http://cpi.transparency.org/cpi2013/results

Tugwell, Franklin. *The Politics of Oil in Venezuela*. (Stanford, CA: Stanford University Press, 1975)

Tyler, Patrick E. "Saudis Plan to End US Presence", *The New York Times*, 9 February 2003

Ulrichsen, Kristian Coates. *Insecure Gulf: The End of Certainty and the Transition to the Post-Oil Era*. (New York: Columbia University Press, 2011)

Unger, Craig. *House of Bush, House of Saud: The Secret Relationship between the World's Two Most Powerful Dynasties*. (New York: Scribner, 2004)

United Nations. *Human Development Report, 2007-2008: Fighting Climate Change: Human Solidarity in a Divided World*. (New York: United Nation Development Report, 2008)

United Nations Conference on Trade and Development (UNCTAD). *World Investment Report 2004* (Geneva: UNCTAD, 2004)

United Nations Development Programme. *Arab Human Development Report 2003: Building a Knowledge Society*, (New York: United Nations Publications, 2003)

United States Senate, *The International Petroleum Cartel. Staff Report to [i.e. of] the Federal Trade Commission Submitted to the Subcommittee on Monopoly of the Select Committee on Small Business: Congress* (Washington, DC: US Govt., 1952)

United States Senate Committee on Foreign Relations, *The Gulf Security Architecture: Partnership with the Gulf Cooperation Council*, Majority Staff Report (19 June 2012)

Vandewalle, Dirk. "After Qaddafi", *Foreign Affairs*, vol. 91, no. 6 (November-December 2012), pp. 8-15

Villanger, Espen. "Arab Foreign Aid: Disbursement Patterns, Aid Policies and Motives". CMI: 2007 http://www.cmi.no/publications/publication/?2615=arab-foreign-aid-disbursement-pattern

Vitalis, Robert. *America's Kingdom: Mythmaking on the Saudi Oil Frontier*. (London: Verso, 2009)

Vogel, Ezra F. *The Four Little Dragons: The Spread of Industrialization in East Asia*. (Cambridge, MA: Cambridge University Press, 1991)

Wade, Robert. *Governing the Market: Economic Theory and the Role of Government in East Asian Industrialization* (Princeton, NJ: Princeton University Press, 1990)

Wall Street Journal, 25 June 2004

Waterbury, John. "Unthinkable: Iran, the Bomb, and American Strategy by Kenneth M. Pollack (Review)", *Foreign Affairs* (January-February 2014), p.

White, Paul J. and William S. Logan. eds. *Remaking the Middle East. Nationalism and Internationalism* (New York: Berg, 1997)

Wilson, Peter W. and Douglas F. Graham. *Saudi Arabia: The Coming Storm*. (New York: M. E. Sharpe, 1994)

Winckler, Onn. "The 'Arab Spring': Socioeconomic Aspects", *Middle Policy*, vol. 20, no. 4 (Winter 2013), pp.

Winckler, Onn. "Labor and Liberalization: The Decline of the GCC Rentier System," in: *Political Liberalization in the Persian Gulf*, ed., Joshua Teitelbaum, (2009)

Wittes, Tamara Cofman. *Freedom's Unsteady March: America's Role in Building Arab Democracy.* (Washington, DC: Brookings Institution, 2008)

Woodward, Bob. *The Commanders.* (New York: Simon and Schuster, 1991)

Woodward, Bob. *Plan of Attack.* (New York: Simon and Schuster, 2004)

Woodward, Bob. *State of Denial.* (New York: Simon and Schuster, 2006)

Woodward, Bob. *The War Within: A secret White House History.* (New York: Simon and Schuster, 2008)

World Bank. *Arab Development Assistance: Four Decades of Cooperation.* (Washington, DC: World Bank, 2010)

World Bank. *World Development Indicators 2010.* (Washington, DC: World Bank, 2010)

World Bank. *Doing Business 2013: Smarter Regulations for Small and Medium-Size Enterprises.* (Washington, DC: World Bank, 2009)

World Bank. *From Privilege to Competition: Unlocking Private-Led Growth in the Middle East and North Africa.* (Washington, DC: World Bank, 2009)

World Bank, "Hashemite Kingdom of Jordan: Resolving Jordan's Labor Market Paradox of Concurrent Economic Growth and Unemployment", World Bank Report no. 39201-JO (Washington, D.C.: World Bank, 23 December 2008) http://datatopics.worldbank.org/hnp/files/edstats/JORpub08.pdf

World Bank. *World Development Report 2003: Dynamic Development in a Sustainable World.* (New York: World Bank, 2003)

World Bank. *World Development Report 2002: Building Institutions for Markets.* (New York: World Bank, 2002)

World Bank. *Can Africa Claim the 21st Century?* (Washington, DC: World Bank, 2000)

World Bank. *Trade Blocs.* A World Bank Policy Research Report (Oxford: Oxford University Press, 2000)

World Bank. *World Development Report 1997: The State in a Changing World.* (New York: World Bank, 1997)

World Trade Organization. *International Trade Statistics 2002*, (Geneva: WTO, 2002)

Wright, Robin. *Dreams and Shadows: The Future of the Middle East.* (New York: Penguin Press, 2008)

Wright, Robin and Peter Baker. "Iraq, Jordan See Threat to Election from Iran; Leaders Warn Against Forming Religious States", *Washington Post*, August 12, 2004

Yergin, Daniel. *The Prize: Epic Quest for Oil, Money, and Power.* (New York: Simon and Schuster, 1991)

Yergin, Daniel. "Insuring Energy Security". Foreign Affairs, (March-April 2006)

Yew, Lee Kuan. *From the Third World to First.* (New York: Harber Collins Publishers, 2000)

Yom, Sean L. and F. Gregory Gause III, "Resilient Royals: How Arab Monarchies Hang On", *Journal of Democracy*, vol. 23, no. 4 (October 2012), pp. 74-88

Yom, Sean L. and Wael al-Khatib, "Jordan's New Politics of Tribal Dissent", *Foreign Policy* (7 August 2012). http://foreignpolicy.com/2012/08/07/jordans-new-politics-of-tribal-dissent/

Yousef, Tarik M. "Development, Growth and Policy Reforms in the Middle East and North Africa since 1950", Journal of Economic Perspectives, vol. 18, no. 3 (2004), pp. 91-116

Zahlan, Rosemarie Said. *The Origins of the United Arab Emirates.* (London: Macmillan Press Ltd, 1978)

Zakaria, Fareed. The Future of Freedom: Illiberal Democracy at Home and Abroad. (New York: W.W. Norton and Company, 2003)

Zarrouk, Jamal. "A Survey of Barriers to Trade and Investment in Arab Countries," in: Ahmed Galal and Bernard Hoekman, eds., Arab Economic Integration: between Hope and Reality, (2003)

Zarrouk, Jamal. "Intra-Arab Countries Trade", in: *The Determinants of Intra-Regional and Extra-Regional Trade in the Arab Countries*, ed., Said El-Naggar (Abu-Dhabi: Arab Monetary Fund, 1991)

Zogby International, Six Arab Nations Survey Report, Submitted to the World Economic Forum's Arab Business Council (November 2005)

Index